THE DISENCHANTED ISLE

Mrs. Thatcher's Capitalist

Revolution

THE
DISENCHANTED
ISLE

Mrs. Thatcher's Capitalist
Revolution

CHARLES DELLHEIM

W.W. Norton & Company
New York / London

Copyright © 1995 by Charles Dellheim, Ph.D.

All rights reserved
Printed in the United States of America
First Edition

The text of this book is composed in Janson
with the display set in Bernhard Modern
Composition and manufacturing by the Haddon Craftsmen, Inc.
Book design by Jam Design

Library of Congress Cataloging-in-Publication Data

Dellheim, Charles, 1952–
The disenchanted isle : Mrs. Thatcher's capitalist revolution / by
Charles Dellheim.
p.   cm.
Includes bibliographical references and index.
1. Capitalism—Great Britain—History—20th century.   2. Thatcher,
Margaret.   3. Great Britain—Economic policy—1945–   4. Great
Britain—Economic conditions—1945–   I. Title.
HC256.6.D448   1995
338.941′009′048—dc20   94-41712
ISBN 0-393-03812-2

W. W. Norton & Company, Inc., 500 Fifth Avenue, New York, N.Y. 10110
W. W. Norton & Company Ltd., 10 Coptic Street, London WC1A 1PU

1 2 3 4 5 6 7 8 9 0

Auden, W. H. "Musee des Beaux Arts," from W. H. Auden:
Collected Poems by W. H. Auden, edited by Edward Mendelson.
Copyright © 1940, renewed 1968 by W. H. Auden.
Reprinted by permission of Random House, Inc.

To Laura with all my love

Contents

England is a family with the wrong members in control.
—GEORGE ORWELL

Glendower: I can call spirits from the vasty deep.
Hotspur: Why so can I, or so can any man. But will they come
  when you do call for them?
—WILLIAM SHAKESPEARE,
Henry IV, Part I

Preface

SINCE I FIRST WENT TO BRITAIN AS A STUDENT IN THE AUTUMN of 1976, I have spent a good number of years and nearly every summer there doing research on various aspects of its history. Inevitably, when I returned to America, friends asked me about the condition of Britain and the fortunes of Margaret Thatcher. These questions stuck in my mind as I taught British history, but it did not occur to me to take them up in earnest until the spring of 1990, when I was visiting Harvard as Newcomen Fellow in Business History. Conversations with Peter Berger, Norman Cantor, and Asa Briggs convinced me that a study of Mrs. Thatcher's Britain was worth pursuing.

The book that follows is addressed primarily to an American audience, especially for the student of history and the general reader. It attempts to place Thatcher's Britain in broad historical perspective, focusing on the relationship between the capitalist revolution and British culture. The book is rooted in a debate about the causes of Britain's relative political and economic decline and examines how Mrs. Thatcher attempted to reverse it and to what effect. It draws on my own studies of British cultural history and corporate culture and on the work of American historian Martin Wiener, *English Culture and the Decline of the Industrial Spirit 1850–1980* (1981); and British historian Correlli Barnett, *The Audit of War* (1986). Cultural explanations of decline have been much criticized; indeed I have expressed my own reservations about such interpretations in articles in the *American Historical Review* (1987) and *Notebooks in Cultural Analysis* (1985). In any case, Wiener and Barnett provide an indispensable reference point for understanding the cultural collisions that took place in the 1980s.

The central theme is the rise and fall of Margaret Thatcher's capitalist revolution. As an historical account of culture, politics, and the economy, it focuses on domestic affairs rather than international politics. In other words, it is a study of "economic culture," the interplay between values, institutions, and behavior. This book does not purport, however, to be a comprehensive history of the Thatcher era. While I refer, too breezily perhaps, to "Britain" throughout, I do not assume that the various parts of the United Kingdom experienced the turns and twists of the 1980s in the same way or with the same spirit. The action I narrate takes place in England (above all, in London) rather than in Scotland, Wales, or Northern Ireland. My aim is to describe and disentangle certain conflicts that took place at the core of British society.

This is the story of how Mrs. Thatcher awakened Britain and how the dream she envisioned compared to the reality that resulted. This is also the story of how a once great world power in desperate need of change resisted the day of reckoning in the name of compassion and consensus. And this is a Victorian tale brimming with suitable, if controversial, moral lessons, a tale in which colorful protagonists, believers in vice and virtue, address some of the great questions that shape the fate of nations and disturb the sleep of individuals. Finally, this is a modernist narrative bringing together different voices, some heroic and triumphant, others ironic and ambiguous, and still others disheartened and depressed. It provides little in the way of closure and even less perhaps in the way of consolation.

As an historian, I am more inclined to serve as a detached witness than act as a hanging judge. I did not begin with the premise that a capitalist revolution is necessarily a time for celebration or an occasion for wailing. My main purpose, then, is neither to praise nor to bury Thatcher. But this does not mean that I refrain, at times, from lauding or criticizing the protagonists of this story, or from taking a position on its consequences. In so doing, I may well offend the partisans of the left who demonize Mrs. Thatcher and the partisans of the right who idolize her. For my own part, I have a qualified admiration for certain of Mrs. Thatcher's goals, but I am highly critical of certain means she used to attain them and have substantial doubts about how successful she ultimately was in realizing them.

Such commentary apart, though, this book tries to present a fair and balanced account of a controversial subject. The book adopts a narrative form to explore a number of questions. It begins by asking how and why Britain declined relative to other great powers and how Mrs. Thatcher proposed to restore its greatness; what cultural obstacles stood in the way of her project and what cultural resources remained at her disposal; how a relative outsider managed to come to power in the first place; how she translated her principles into practice and to what effect when she did; how the capitalist revolution she led affected the business environment; how cultural critics viewed and responded to what she wrought; and how she fell from power.

Writing contemporary history is both elating and elusive. For an historian trained in the archives, among other places, it is a pleasure to write for once about persons and events whose current relevance is obvious. But the quest to grasp the contours of our own times is also frustrating because much of what happened to Britain in the Thatcher years remains interred in confidential government documents that will not be opened for decades. Being barred from the archives may produce scholarly tristesse in those who mystify their contents (in the belief that documents not yet penetrated are superior to those already touched). But considerable grist still remains for the historian's mill. And so I have drawn on memoirs and interviews, speeches and newspapers, literature and films, architecture and photography, theology and social commentary, to tell this story.

Contemporary history, though, is a moving target. If "the past" is not as stable or fixed an entity as historians once believed, and if our interpretations are more provisional than we would like to admit, the obstacles to assessing living persons and recent events are more formidable still. No historian writing so soon after the end of an era, insofar as it is indeed over, can claim much in the way of perspective, usually part of our stock-in-trade, or borrow the judicial mantle that comes with the passage of time and the cooling of passions. This is especially true with a protagonist like Margaret Thatcher, whose fall has by no means led to her disappearance from the public scene. If anything, she seems more visible these days in the United States where she is still lionized than in Britain where she is no longer a required taste or unavoidable presence.

This is a story of what took place in little more than ten years in a once majestic island. Like any other unit of time, the decade is an artificial construct whose apparent neatness appeals to the human desire for order and closure. Yet the 1980s did, in fact, witness a break with the immediate socialist past, even though a number of major shifts in policy and attitudes began before the Tories came to power. Although my subject is a decade or so of British history, I attempt to treat both the Thatcher years and its leading figures as pivots in a much wider and more complex drama. Such a perspective is justified, in part, because the actors themselves, none more so than the Prime Minister, tended to see the age, for better or worse, as a turning point.

In the course of researching and writing this book I incurred many debts that are easier to acknowledge than to discharge. Not only did Peter Berger prove to me that there is indeed a free lunch but he provided me with a fellowship and an opportunity to spend a term in a most stimulating and hospitable intellectual atmosphere: the Institute for the Study of Economic Culture at Boston University. Norman Cantor gave me intellectual counsel and moral support as he has done since I first began to study history seriously under his direction years ago. As always, Asa Briggs provided wise counsel at the start.

I am particularly grateful to Steven Mintz, Brooks Simpson, and Norman Cantor, all of whom offered excellent criticisms of various drafts of this book. I would also like to thank Peter Berger for his comments on the final manuscript; and Gerry McCauley and Paul Miller for reading some early chapters.

As my literary agent, Gerry McCauley generously guided me through the world of trade publishing, offering honest criticism, gentle prodding, and steady encouragement. Ed Barber, my editor at W. W. Norton, reined me in when I needed it, greatly improved my writing, and gave this manuscript the kind of scrupulous attention that most writers dream of but few are lucky enough to receive these days. I thank him heartily for his superb work, and Ann Adelman for her careful copyediting.

My wife, Laura Gross, with one foot in Britain and the other in America, brought unmatched style and unlimited support to this book and its extremely fortunate author. She read each draft of this book more times than she would care to remember (or I would like to admit), edited and improved it without fail, and listened to me go on about its contents everywhere, especially in cars, planes, and on dog walks (with two Labradors, Samson and then Argos, who had their own agendas as well as English ancestry). And when this book was already in design Laura gave birth to our daughter, Alexandra, who had the discretion not to be born while her father was at work on it. Nothing I could say could begin to express my love for her or my appreciation of her efforts.

My friends Peter Petzal and Danielle Douek, as well as Sarena and Peter Alfandary, provided never-ending hospitality while I did research for this book in London. My mother-in-law, Marilyn Gross, furnished me with an ideal setting, good cheer, and local knowledge of Britain, while I wrote much of it in her house in Quogue. My parents and brothers knew enough not to ask how the project was going and supported me irrespective of its results.

I would like to thank the College of Liberal Arts and Sciences, the Women's Studies Summer Grant Program, and the Center for Atlantic Studies, at Arizona State University, for travel support; students in my modern British history courses and Thatcher's Britain seminars for their attention and comments. I am grateful to friends and colleagues at the Economic and Business Historical Society, especially Edwin Perkins and Kenneth Lipartito, for their comments on papers I delivered on Thatcher's Britain. Paul Tiffany, who organized the Competitive Strategy Executive Education Seminar at the Wharton School of Business, provided me the chance to test out my ideas several times on business audiences.

Since this book is based in part on oral history interviews, I owe a large debt to the many British politicians, managers, writers, and academics who took the time to meet with me. I am especially grateful to Hugh Parker, who arranged a number of interviews on my behalf with company chairmen. I hope that none of the persons who took the time to talk with me (often at short notice) will take umbrage at being lumped together in so long (though distinguished) a list. I would like to thank: Sir Kingsley Amis, Eugene Anderson, Lord Annan, Cathy Ashton, John Ashworth, Georges Bain, Beryl Bainbridge, Professor Sir James Ball, Graham Bann, C. B. B. Beauman, Baroness Tessa Blackstone, David Boole, Sir Adrian Cadbury, Jonathan Charkham, Julia Cliveden, Sir Ralf Dahrendorf, Michael Doyle, Sir John Egan, Richard Giordano, Sir Paul Girolami, Sir Nicholas Goodison, Bryan Gould, David Grayson, Rabbi Hugo Gryn, Sir Ralph Halpern, Lord Hanson, David Hare, Lord Harris, Sir John Harvey-Jones, Roy Hattersley, Paul Hirst, Sir Christopher Hogg, Robert Horton, Sir John Hoskyns, Lord Howe, Lord Jakobovits, the late Peter Jenkins, Simon Jenkins, Robert John, the late Lord Joseph, Peter Kellner, Simon King, Charles Knevitt, Lord Laing, Nigel Lawson, John Lloyd, Michael Love, Rev. Colin Marsh, John Moore, John Mortimer, Rabbi Julia Neuberger, Lord Owen, Sir Geoffrey Owen, Sir Peter Parker, Ben Pimlott, Lord Rees-Mogg, Lord Rothschild, Hilary Russell, David Sainsbury, Victoria Secretan, Bishop David Sheppard, Sir Alfred Sherman, the late John Smith, Limbert Spencer, Norman Stone, John Stopford, Andrew Tyrie, Sir Charles Villiers, Sir Douglas Wass, Lord Weinstock, Sir Gordon White, Craig Whitney, David Willett, Reverend Peter Winn, Hugo Young, and Lady Young.

New York City
March 1995

THE DISENCHANTED ISLE

Mrs. Thatcher's Capitalist

Revolution

Thatcher's End

I

ON WEDNESDAY, NOVEMBER 21, 1990, A HOST OF SOMBER MEN in dark suits headed, as usual, for the House of Commons just as Big Ben was about to strike six o'clock. Rising sheer above the Thames like a vast windbeaten neo-Gothic cliff, the Houses of Parliament commanded the riverfront at Westminster Bridge as Britain once ruled the waves. But who would now rule Britain?

Frantic activity was hardy unusual in the halls of Westminster, but this night was different. For a long three hours, Tory Cabinet ministers filed back and forth along a narrow corridor. Passing the Chancellor of the Exchequer's Room, they crossed a landing on the backstairs that led to the first floor of the House of Commons and one by one entered the Prime Minister's Room for audiences with Margaret Thatcher. Sitting on the end of a sofa next to the fireplace, she faced her ministers alone save for her parliamentary private secretary, Peter Morrison, who was present at all times during the interviews.

The Prime Minister herself had returned only that day from a summit in Paris. There she took part in discussions with other leaders. Among them were President Bush, Chancellor Kohl, President Mitterand, and President Gorbachev. The meeting was supposed to mark the formal beginning of an era of good feeling between East and West, a happy start to what George Bush dubbed a "new world order." Soon enough, the old ethnic hatreds and fascistic stirrings would explode this chimerical vision, but in November 1990 there was little way, and less desire, to foresee the massacres in Bosnia or the rise of Zhirinovsky in Russia. With these events in the future, the atmosphere of the Paris Summit was understandably triumphalist. And yet the prospect of the impending war in the Gulf suggested that the time for celebration was premature.

The woman first described as an "iron lady" by the Soviets for her ardent battle against communism had reason for pride. When the Prime Minister addressed the Paris Summit on Monday afternoon, she took up themes that should have surprised no one. In her speech the ever vigilant Mrs. Thatcher emphasized "the continued importance of human rights and the rule of law, pointing to their connection with economic freedom, and warning against any attempt to downgrade NATO which was 'the core of western defence.' "[1] More than willing as she usually was to share in the credit for victory, it must have been difficult for even so strong-willed a woman as the Prime Minister to focus thoroughly on the death of the "evil empire."

For Mrs. Thatcher's thoughts inevitably swayed back to the battle shaping up in the corridors of Westminster. Its result would determine whether she remained Leader of the Conservative Party and Prime Minister of the United Kingdom. Now the prospective end of her tenure loomed larger than the end of the Cold War. Would the Iron Lady's reign much outlast the Iron Curtain's lifting? Only Helmut Kohl directly broached the subject with her, expressing his complete support, a particularly generous gesture given their history of political differences on the future of Europe.[2]

The thought of stepping down from the heights of power came hard to the grocer's daughter who had become the first woman Prime Minister of Britain. Already in office for eleven and a half years, Mrs. Thatcher had outlasted any of her predecessors since Lord Liverpool in the early nineteenth century. Having won general elections in 1979, 1983, and 1987, she had ruled longer than her political hero, Winston Churchill. Even though she had never enjoyed an outright popular majority, from the first she had had a clear enough margin in the House of Commons to pass legislation with little difficulty. After so long and influential a run in office, a less driven or ambitious politician might have given up the reins out of exhaustion if not modesty. But Mrs. Thatcher had announced that she intended to stay on and on, perhaps for another two Parliaments, to ensure that the fruits of her victories were not aborted. The choice, though, was not entirely hers.

For the Prime Minister's position was now so precarious that her enemies could sense that she was ripe for the kill. Her abrasive style coupled with policy disagreements to bring two of Thatcherism's leading architects to the point of no return. In October 1989, Nigel Lawson, the Chancellor of the Exchequer, left the government in a prolonged huff because she would not fully support his economic policy, preferring instead the counsel of Alan Walters, her personal economic adviser. Then, in November 1990, Sir Geoffrey Howe, the Deputy Prime Minister, followed suit. No longer able to brook her humiliating treatment of him or her refusal to allow Britain to take full part in a new, united Europe, he resigned with a bang.

Political misjudgments further exposed her. None was more disastrous than the community charge, otherwise known as the poll tax, a flat levy on all adult residents of a given locality. The fact that rebates were available for those unable to pay was no consolation to the demonstrators whose protests turned into riots in Trafalgar Square in April 1990. Indeed, the poll tax only confirmed an already widespread view that Mrs. Thatcher was unfair and insensitive. To make matters worse, dubious commercial prospects threatened to hurt her supporters as well as her foes. If the Prime Minister could not deliver a healthy economy, what good was she? So it was unsurprising that in October 1990 opinion polls held that the Conservatives were trailing Labour by 12 percent and that Mrs. Thatcher was a liability. They fared badly in local government elections the past May except in London, and Tory MPs feared defeat at the next general election. The loss of a Conservative seat to the Liberals in the Eastbourne by-election in October only made them more anxious that their constituents would toss them out too if the Prime Minister remained in office.

Would such gloomy signs result in Thatcher's end?

On Tuesday evening, November 20, a throng of journalists, broadcasters, and politicians crowded into the broad, high passageway that extends from the Clerk of the Services Committee at the north end of the Palace of Westminster to the Lords of Appeal in Ordinary at the south end.[3] There they waited as Tory MPs prepared to cast their ballots in an unprecedented election for the leadership of the Conservative Party. Earlier that month, Margaret Thatcher's old political nemesis, Michael Heseltine, finally did what few thought he had nerve to do—mount a formal leadership challenge to a sitting Prime Minister.

Rich, attractive, and unrelentingly ambitious, Michael Heseltine was a man of calculated passions. Determined to be seen and heard, the highly visible Secretary of State for Defence came to loggerheads with the Prime Minister on a number of occasions. In January 1986, they fell out when Heseltine favored selling Westland, an ailing British helicopter firm, to a European consortium rather than to an American firm, Sikorsky, favored by the Prime Minister. Having failed to win over his colleagues in Cabinet, Heseltine refused to put up with, or be put down by, Mrs. Thatcher's ritual public scolding. She told him: "You will make no further statements or answer questions. This is the decision of the Cabinet and I must ask you to accept it." He responded: "I cannot hesitate in supporting what I have said." And then, to the astonishment of his colleagues, Heseltine closed his red ministerial folder, rose from his chair, left the room, and resigned from the Thatcher government.[4]

Hailing from a South Wales commercial family, Heseltine had earned his fortune in the publishing business, and had survived one notable failure. Wealth was not only an end in itself to him but also a means to an end—politics. His designs on eventually becoming Prime Minister went back as far as his undergraduate years at Oxford, where he read Politics, Philosophy, and Economics. A fiery orator whose manner, if not his accent, testified to his Welsh roots, he was elected president of the Oxford Union, long a stepping stone to a political career. He seemed to have an unerring ability to thrill Tory audiences, and the women in particular, with his speeches to the annual Party Conference. Indeed, an unnamed wag remarked: "Michael has the knack of finding the clitoris of the Conservative Party."[5] But the responses he inspired and the wealth he acquired provoked the jealousy of his not so charismatic, or hardworking, colleagues. They resented him also for assuming the rural regalia of landed society. For he was master of Thenford House, a Palladian home on a 400-acre farm. On the park gates, the newly minted country gentleman had the initials "MRDH" inscribed.[6]

In substance as in style, Heseltine offered his own alternative to Mrs. Thatcher. She believed passionately in market capitalism, extolled the virtue of self-help, and was determined that her Britain not be gulped down by a European Community dominated by Germany and France. By contrast, he was an exponent of "caring capitalism." Willing to temper competition with compassion, Heseltine felt that the state had a positive role to play in economic life. And, as a "good European," he was keen to see Britain look to the Continent, rather than across the Atlantic, for its main political ties and economic alliances.[7] Whatever the ideological recipe, by late November 1990, Heseltine had the confident look of a man whose day had finally come, perhaps.

I I

MARGARET THATCHER WAS NOT WILLING TO CONCEDE, however, that her day had passed. At the end of Tuesday's session in Paris, the Prime Minister had tea and then went upstairs to her room to have her hair done. Around 6:00 P.M. she retired to another room. There she awaited the results of the first ballot with a small group. It included Bernard Ingham, her press secretary, Sir Ewen Fergusson, the British Ambassador to France, and Crawfie (Miss Crawford), her dresser. The always diligent Mrs. Thatcher wore a black wool suit with a tan and black collar as she worked at a desk with her back to the room.[8] This was one occasion on which she had little choice but do what she rarely did: sit and wait.

Then came the first signal from Charles Powell, her closest adviser on foreign affairs. "Out of my sight," Mrs. Thatcher wrote, "he gave a sad thumbs down to the people in the room."[9] It fell to Peter Morrison to convey the official news, breaking the blow as best he could. Mrs. Thatcher had won 204 votes to Michael Heseltine's 152. But majority support was inadequate to fend off the challenge. The woman who had herself unseated Conservative Leader Edward Heath in 1975 instantly realized that she had not won. For under the bizarrely complicated rules invented in 1964 by Tory MP Humphrey Berkeley, a candidate had to receive both an overall majority and 15 percent more of the total number of votes cast than any other contender.[10] Had only two of the sixteen MPs who abstained from the contest thrown their support to the beleaguered Prime Minister, she would have won the battle. But they did not. Instead, a murmur of "Second ballot, second ballot," went up in Westminster. And so a leader with little tolerance for ambiguity found herself in limbo.

Margaret Thatcher paused for a short while to compose herself and then shot down the steps of the Paris Embassy so forcefully that she jostled John Sergeant of the BBC, who was trying to point her to the microphone.[11] "Good evening gentlemen." she said. "I am naturally very pleased that I got more than half the Parliamentary Party and disappointed that it is not quite enough to win on the first ballot, so I confirm it is my intention to let my name go forward for the second ballot."[12] In short, she would fight on. Returning to her room to change into evening dress, Mrs. Thatcher and Peter Morrison left the embassy at 8:00 P.M. Late for the ballet and dinner, they bolted through the cleared streets of Paris in a large black Citroën headed for Versailles. In the ornate and grandiose palace built by Louis XIV, the Sun King, a much-strained Margaret Thatcher was forced to contemplate her prospective eclipse. At the evening's end, George and Barbara Bush had the good grace to escort her out of the palace to keep her safe from the attentions of the press.[13]

At noon on Wednesday, Mrs. Thatcher returned to the simple classical facade of Number 10 Downing Street to the cheering of her staff and the sight of a thousand red roses sent by a supporter. Immediately she went upstairs to her private flat to see her husband Denis. "Don't go on, love," was his counsel. If she listened to any man since the death of her beloved father, Alfred Roberts, that honor fell to her businessman husband. On this occasion, though, Denis's counsel clashed with her instincts. "I felt in my bones that I should fight on."[14] At the behest of Tory Whip John Wakeham, she reluctantly consented to meet individually with her ministers rather than to wait until the Cabinet meeting scheduled for Thursday morning.

On the night of November 21, then, Margaret Thatcher sat in the Prime Minister's Room. The question was clear: Should she go once more into the fray or should she retreat? The answer, though, was anything but. It depended largely on whether her ministers were willing to give her the manifest support she needed to win on the next ballot. If one or more Cabinet members resigned, it would be next to impossible for her to carry on. Having had her own way for so long, Margaret Thatcher found herself at the mercy of men too many of whom she had slighted too often or taken for granted too easily.

For once, tact strangled fact. The first question Mrs. Thatcher asked each of her ministers was simply: "Do you think I should go on?" By the looks on their faces she might have known that she was finished. "Almost to a man they used the same formula," she noted in her memoirs. "This was that they themselves would back me, of course, but that regretfully they did not believe I could win."[15] Another leader might have taken so unanimous a response more innocently, as a sign that their judgment was correct or, at least, that their motives were honorable. But Margaret Thatcher construed their common stance as a conspiracy and an unjustified one at that. Reared in an old-time religion that divided the world into the children of light and the children of darkness, she believed that those who were not with her were against her. As an outsider who had come up the hard way, she was quick to suspect and slow to forgive. "Like all politicians in a quandary," she continued, "they had sorted out their 'line to take' and they would cling to it through thick and thin."[16] The woman who placed so high a value on perseverance, not least in her own person, found it turned against her.

If Mrs. Thatcher's men took much the same tack with her, some were far harsher, and more pessimistic, than others. When Kenneth Clarke, the Education Secretary, came in, she tried to hearten him for the fight ahead. But he was not so easily cheered. Indeed, he informed her that while he would personally support her happily for the next five or ten years, most of the Cabinet thought she should step down. For if she refused to do so, she would not only lose but she would "lose big."[17] Going on would be like the Charge of the Light Brigade. Clarke said: "The fight is over. The battle is lost. You should withdraw from the field."[18] Wounded by his unsparing candor, Mrs. Thatcher clawed back in her memoirs, "His manner was robust in the brutalist style he has cultivated: the candid friend."[19] Whatever his motives, Clarke remained in the House the rest of the evening, making clear to all who would listen that if Mrs. Thatcher did not step down, "I will resign as we are crashing on to great folly."[20]

All the while, the House whirred. Would Mrs. Thatcher fight on despite everything? So it seemed.

By the time Baker saw Mrs. Thatcher at 7:30 P.M., the force of what was taking place had begun to hit her. "It's a funny old world," the bemused Prime Minister told the party chairman who was trying to keep her in office.[21] When he saw her again at the end of the evening after the interviews were all over, the pattern was clear. According to Baker's calculations, between ten and twelve ministers were convinced that she could not defeat Heseltine on the second ballot. They would not, therefore, do their utmost to reverse the tide lest they be drowned in the undertow. Still, he encouraged her to go on. Pale and subdued, Mrs. Thatcher shook her head as she told him, "I am not a quitter, I am not a quitter."[22] Indeed, she was not. But intent as she was when the day began to press ahead and contest the second ballot, by day's end her resolve had faltered.

Margaret Thatcher later recalled that she was "sick at

heart. I could have resisted the opposition of opponents and potential rivals and even respected them for it; but what grieved me was the desertion of those I had always considered friends and allies and the weasel words whereby they had transmuted their betrayal into frank advice and concern for my fate."[23] Beneath the impervious public mien of the Iron Lady was a vulnerable, hurt woman suddenly confronted by the prospect of losing power and losing face.

When the Prime Minister returned to Downing Street, she looked for Denis, who consoled her before she went down to the Cabinet Room. There she began to write the resignation speech for delivery the following day during the Commons debate on a no-confidence motion. Meanwhile, Michael Portillo, Michael Forsyth, and Michael Fallon—all of them members of the aptly named and steadfastly right-wing No Turning Back Group—rushed to Downing Street to try to convince her that all was not lost and that she could win on the second ballot despite the Cabinet's betrayal. But it was too late.[24]

I I I

DREARY AND FUNEREAL WAS THE ATMOSPHERE AT NUMBER 10 the next morning as the ministers waited in the Cabinet Room for the meeting to begin.

Soon after 9:00 A.M. Mrs. Thatcher came downstairs. She wore a dark suit, looked red-eyed and distraught, but tried to compose herself for what lay ahead. Eager to avert each other's glances, and still more eager to avert the Prime Minister's, those present looked down at their blotting pads like embarrassed schoolchildren. They did not want to see one of their number punished, all the more so since they had turned on her in a weak moment.[25] During the meeting some ministers were in tears or close to them. As Margaret Thatcher began to read her prepared statement, she could not stop herself from breaking down in front of those who had deserted her. When she began to cry a second time, Cecil Parkinson turned to the Lord Chancellor and said: "For Christ's sake you read it, James." But Mrs. Thatcher replied, "I can read it myself," and proceeded to redouble her efforts.[26]

What the Prime Minister said was: "Having consulted widely among my colleagues I have concluded that the unity of the Party and the prospects of victory in a general election would be better served if I stood down to enable Cabinet colleagues to enter the ballot for the leadership."[27] Then she turned from her own troubles to the business of the day. Afterwards, she sent messages to Bush and Gorbachev, went to Buckingham Palace to inform the Queen of her decision to resign, and returned to Number 10 to work on her speech before going back to Westminster once again.

Around three o'clock on Thursday afternoon, Michael Heseltine entered the Chamber of the House of Commons. Labour MPs applauded him for finally accomplishing what they themselves had failed to do. But the day was not his. For the Tory benches exploded into cheers when Margaret Thatcher rose to speak. Having despatched her so summarily, her erstwhile colleagues gave their former leader a bumper send-off. Long a skillful parliamentary performer who gave far better than she took, the Prime Minister fended off the Opposition at Question Time. Standing in a signature bright blue suit, with all the dash and energy of a victor, she defended her government's record and hearkened back to how the world had changed in the past decade. Ever the patriot, the Prime Minister ended her speech by saying, "There is something else which one feels. That is a sense of this country's destiny: the centuries of history and experience which ensure that, when principles have to be defended, when good has to be upheld and when evil has to be overcome, Britain will take up arms."[28] Even those who disliked her policies and never cared for her person could hardly deny that on that day Margaret Thatcher had been magnificent.

At all events, the second ballot of the Conservative leadership contest took place the next week, on November 27. While the Prime Minister awaited the results with family and friends in 10 Downing Street, someone remarked that her colleagues had done an awful thing to her. "We're in politics, my dear," replied Mrs. Thatcher. When the votes were counted, John Major, the Chancellor of the Exchequer, had won 185; Michael Heseltine 131; and Douglas Hurd, the Foreign Secretary, 56. Like Mrs. Thatcher, Major had fallen two votes short of victory. But this time Heseltine conceded defeat. He had unseated, but not succeeded, the Prime Minister. When Major's victory was assured, Mrs. Thatcher discreetly entered the Chancellor's Residence through the door that connects Numbers 10 and 11 and hugged her newly anointed successor.[29]

On Wednesday, November 28, then, Margaret Thatcher left office. A Range Rover full of household belongings swept her and her husband through the tall black gates that guarded Number 10 Downing Street toward their new multi-million-pound home in Dulwich, a prosperous suburb to the south of the Thames.[30]

It was over.

I V

BUT WHAT HAD ENDED? WAS MRS. THATCHER KNIFED IN THE back by her colleagues or was she responsible for her own downfall? Did short-term difficulties catapult her from office or did she lose power because her party and the public rejected her policies? Did her resignation mean that she never had succeeded wholly in rallying the nation behind her or had she simply stayed too long? Much more than the genial Ronald Reagan, Mrs. Thatcher had offered an explicit economic vision: her mission was to destroy socialism and restore capitalism. The results included a bitter cultural civil war as proponents and opponents struggled for Britain's soul and its future.

At all events, as the former Prime Minister rode away from Downing Street, political commentators had an unequaled field day. They hauled out literary allusions and tragic echoes, turning to the Greeks and Shakespeare for inspiration. Mrs. Thatcher's fate apart, though, the critical question was what had happened to Britain during her prolonged reign. Had the deposed leader saved the nation from decline or sent it hurtling downward to darkness? Not every story has two sides, said Edward R. Murrow, but this story was certainly open to a number of contradictory interpretations. The 1980s were a far more ambiguous decade than the Prime Minister's own blinkered narrative suggested. For the record of the Thatcher government was not simply a tale of capitalism victorious any more than her downfall was merely a story of treachery within.

To be sure, Mrs. Thatcher had ample reason to be proud of her political achievements. This was all the more so had she reflected on the state of the realm when she first came to power in May 1979. The nation which had built the greatest empire of modern times was afflicted by a set of ills popularly known on both sides of the Atlantic as the "British disease." Pushed to the margins in both world politics and international business, some wondered if they had seen "the last of England." Britain faced fundamental economic problems, among them sluggish productivity, labor strife, inadequate capital investment, paltry research and development, persistent stagflation, and chronic unemployment. The nation which had led the Industrial Revolution had become an emblem of economic decay, barely able to compete with the

United States, Germany, or Japan. In once great commercial centers such as Manchester and Birmingham, inefficient or luckless factories closed, threatening to strand their workers in permanent redundancy. The nation which had prided itself on political civility was also faced with an eruption of brutal racism. In the East End of London, where Oswald Mosley's Fascist Brown Shirts had attacked Jews in the 1930s, the National Front terrorized Asian immigrants who had mistaken a Commonwealth passport for a gracious welcome. And the nation which prided itself on public order and fair play watched its reputation fall into disarray as the rise of soccer hooliganism turned sporting matches into armed camps.

By the "Winter of Discontent," the round of public service strikes of 1978–79, it seemed that Britain had indeed become "ungovernable." Addressing the nation in an election broadcast in April 1979, Mrs. Thatcher described the course of events which facilitated her historic victory:

> We have just had a devastating winter of industrial strife— perhaps the worst in living memory, certainly the worst in mine. We saw the sick refused admission to hospital. We saw people unable to bury the dead. We saw children virtually locked out of their schools. We saw the country virtually at the mercy of secondary pickets and strike committees and we saw government apparently helpless to do anything about it.[31]

The grocer's daughter who learned homilies about self-help on her father's knee was not content to preside over the "orderly management of decline." Having coming of age as Britain emerged from World War II with a moral imperative as well as a political victory, she would not give way to what she viewed as the enemy within any more than Churchill had given up to the enemy without.

Margaret Thatcher's end was to awaken Britain in order to reverse its gradual, relative economic and political decline and restore it to what she deemed to be its proper place among the world's nations. Soon after taking office, then, the new Prime Minister proclaimed: "The mission of this Government is much more than the promotion of economic progress. It is to renew the spirit and solidarity of the nation."[32] Her ability to revive the realm hinged partly on whether she could eradicate a deeply entrenched bias against industry that had corrupted the work ethic of the world's first industrial nation. And she had to save the island from the eroding tide of socialism which had worn down the Victorian virtue of self-help once so abundant on its shores. Since the advent of the Welfare State in 1945, the British had looked to government to take care of them from cradle to grave. Mrs. Thatcher's antidote called for a change of policy and a change of heart. From 1979 to 1990, her successive governments carried out an experiment designed to turn British values and institutions. To this end, she reduced taxes, tamed the trade unions, and returned publicly owned industries to private hands.

By Mrs. Thatcher's standards, the program was a great success. In little more than a decade, it had arrested economic decline. Were the British people better off now than they were a decade or so ago? The majority would have answered yes, with more or less conviction. The standard of living had risen in the course of the 1980s. More people owned their own homes and enjoyed holidays abroad than before she came to power. Nowhere were the prodigious consuming passions of the Thatcher years more strikingly apparent than in the capital, lined as it was with up market boutiques from Knightsbridge to Hampstead. The unabashed market leaders of the boom were the young merchant bankers and traders who made their fortunes in London, as in New York, during the bull market. Postponement of gratification was, for them, a thing of the bourgeois past. Their extravagant habits proved profitable for those who sold holiday homes in the country or BMWs and Porsches for the city.

Under Margaret Thatcher's direction, foreign investment rebounded as she made clear that Britain, Inc., was under new management and open for business. In her vision the country was to become an "enterprise culture" that accorded new prospects and status to the entrepreneur and promised rewards to match. Her welcome attracted the Reichmann family, the owners of Olympia & York, the Toronto-based Canadian giant. Refugees from Hitler, these self-made entrepreneurs held private control of their property development firm and were equally private about their philanthropic donations. At a reception in 1988, Paul Reichmann congratulated Mrs. Thatcher on her efforts to turn Britain around. They would not have pulled out of their British holdings in 1979, he said, if they had known how dramatic a difference her policies and philosophy were going to make. But new opportunities lured the two brothers back.

The Reichmanns did more than merely talk, though. Indeed, they invested billions in the property development scheme, Canary Wharf, which was about to open to the public in November 1990. Located about two and a half miles to the east of the City of London, Britain's Wall Street, the project brought new vitality to the Docklands, a moribund area bombed during World War II and neglected thereafter as shipping declined. Under Thatcher, it became what Sir Geoffrey Howe, the Chancellor of the Exchequer, called an "Enterprise Zone," designed to increase wealth creation and regenerate run-down inner-city areas by freeing investment of various taxes. Although Docklands was far from the center of the metropolis, its proximity to the City of London made it an attractive site for companies that needed more space than the booming one-square mile could afford.

Near the Tower of London, one sign pointed tourists in

the direction of the Roman Wall and another pointed business people in the direction of the Docklands Light Railway. A high-tech iron and glass structure in marked contrast to the ancient buildings in its vicinity, the station was painted a bright and cheerful red, white, and blue, a leitmotif repeated on the train itself as well as down the line. A signal triumph of automation, the Docklands Light Railway transported its passengers through the East End of London, the historic home of immigrants and cockneys. The train swept past dreary back-to back housing with laundry hanging outside in the damp, and then past plain, ugly modern blocks of public housing en route to an altogether different milieu. Within minutes, passengers could see the grandiose commercial palaces that sprang up from Heron Quay and West India Dock. Designed by architects such as Cesar Pelli and replete with luxurious Italian marble and decorative ornaments, the towers offered unsurpassed views of London at unsurpassed prices.

All in all, Canary Wharf seemed a perfect emblem of enterprise reborn. It was one proof among many that much had been accomplished while Margaret Thatcher was in power.

V

BUT THE OTHER SIDE TO THE STORY WAS FAR DARKER.

Were the British more prosperous in November 1990 than before the Tories had come to power? The answer depended on who you asked and where you looked. The economic boom of the mid-1980s had not spread its bounty or blessings evenly by any means. It reverberated throughout most of London and the Southeast of England, but proved more hollow than resonant in much of the industrial North and Scotland. In Thatcher's Britain, as in Reagan's America, the new economics aggravated the old inequalities, further polarizing rich and poor.[33] Most persons, especially those in the middle and upper classes, were better off than they had been under James Callaghan's Labour government. But those on the bottom were worse off on two fronts. They were forced to take the economic brunt of cuts in social spending, the fragile net woven to shield those who could not support themselves. The poor also had to endure the emotional burden of being impoverished in an age that had neither the stomach to face deprivation nor the heart to cure it.

Marks of weakness and marks of woe abounded. Had the Prime Minister wanted to investigate England's underbelly she could have taken a good look at the people of Liverpool, a once prosperous port city whose main bragging points to the world had become their soccer team and the Beatles. Even in Liverpool, there were some indications that an economic revival was not completely out of reach. Both during and after Michael Heseltine's time as Environment Secretary, he put forward a vision of regeneration. The most visible sign of renewal was the newly restored and refurbished Albert Docks, which tried to infuse a new spirit into the sepulchral remains of the shipping industry. But such public showpieces had done little as yet to change the lives, or improve the prospects, of most Liverpudlians.

Had Margaret Thatcher, the most religious of twentieth-century prime ministers, attended Anglican services in St. Michael's in the City, a slum-ridden parish in the broken center of Liverpool, she would have seen how many were left out of, if not thrown down by, her economic boom. The priest who presided over this troubled flock was a youngish cleric, the Reverend Colin Marsh. He was used to break-ins in the rectory and his car. Sharply critical of Mrs. Thatcher for disregarding the poor and unfortunate, he had nothing good to say about the ethics of the rich or the values of the enterprise culture. At least he came by his objections honestly, having seen what the decline in social services had done to his parishioners.[34]

Mrs. Thatcher also would have seen at St. Michael's in the City a middle-aged man. He came from a family of mixed African and Irish descent which had worked on the docks for generations. Out of work for many years, he lived off the dole in a ramshackle housing estate, a dark and dilapidated place riddled with crime. The virtues of the free market escaped him. He had nothing more than resentment for Mrs. Thatcher and for the policies which had made his own life and the lives of those he knew needlessly harder. Angered and embittered by perennial defeats, he declared: "If Mrs. Thatcher was lying on the floor here now, I'd stamp on her."

But the Iron Lady need not have gone to Liverpool to recognize that the trickle-down effect of supply-side economics only went so far. She might have followed the lead of William Ewart Gladstone, the great Victorian Liberal Prime Minister, who sometimes surveyed insalubrious sections of the capital at night to help him feel what wretches felt. Gladstone's mantle did not suit her, however. This was a woman more prone to lecture than to romanticize the poor. Surely London appeared far more affluent in 1990 than in 1979; but at the same time the poor seemed more numerous and miserable. In November 1990, as Mrs. Thatcher fell from power, far humbler folk had to contend with problems which she had neither caused nor cured.

Hopeless poverty fouled the display of wealth. Walking in the West End near Harrods, which lit up the Brompton Road even on dark nights, you passed a bevy of lavishly appointed and equally expensive shops. They sold Gucci, Bally, and Burberry to well-heeled natives and tourists. In the brightly lit doorway of one fashionable boutique, an older man, barely covered by makeshift blankets, slept rough in a cardboard box below a red-and-white sale sign (which itself suggested that retail sales were sluggish). This was not an isolated instance. Similar sights abounded along the Strand or in back of Waterloo Station close to the National Theatre.

Even the economic miracle that promised to deliver Britain and enrich its people seemed a mirage. Nowhere was this more visible than at Canary Wharf. Begun at the height of the boom when business confidence was at its peak and rents seemed unstoppable, it was by far the largest, and most visible, victim of the recession. The Docklands Light Railway was indeed a symbol of Thatcherism at work: an example of rationalized efficiency, it employed advanced technology but created few jobs after construction was complete. The new train system was up and running. But Canary Wharf itself seemed to be going down and out. The Reichmanns and their backers had poured money into showcase buildings that failed to please critics, who found their postmodernist flourishes pompous and lifeless. In any case, the entrepreneurs discovered, too late as it happened, that the demand for, and value of, London office space was no longer at a premium as companies cut back or went under when the boom vanished. So the expensive new edifices were only partially occupied. All the concerned parties waited for better news and more auspicious times. The owner of a de luxe Italian sandwich shop that had been open, and nearly empty, for months, remarked: "Business is terrible. . . . Maybe it'll pick up in ten years." The Reichmanns, though, had neither the time nor the money to wait so long. In 1991, they finally filed for bankruptcy, leaving unfinished towers in the cityscape. Did the fate of Canary Wharf symbolize the aborted end of the enterprise culture?

V I

A CAPITALIST REVOLUTION TOOK PLACE IN BRITAIN DURING the Thatcher years. By this, I mean the attempt to undo socialism, contain the Welfare State, domesticate the trade unions, privatize nationalized industry, institute supply-side economics, enliven the free market, and stoke the entrepreneurial spirit. Riches without embarrassment, self-help without guilt, individual responsibility without fail—these were the cornerstones of Mrs. Thatcher's plan to restore Britain's lost greatness. All told, the political, economic, and cultural reforms she sponsored constituted a revolution both in the modern sense of a break with the present and the ancient sense of a periodic turning of the spheres.[35] In short, her mission was to revive Britain by turning socialist decay into capitalist prosperity.

What happened in Mrs. Thatcher's Britain was part of an age of capitalist revolution. This age began with her accession to power in 1979, continued in 1980 with Ronald Reagan's election, and proceeded in more modest fashion with unexpected turns to the right by Socialist leaders François Mitterrand in France and Felipe Gonzalez in Spain.[36] The capitalist revolution originated in the West in democratic societies with mixed economies. But it culminated in the toppling of Communist regimes with command economies in the Soviet Union and the Eastern bloc. Yet it would be wrong to exaggerate the similarities between what took place in East and West from 1979 to 1991. The course of events during these years was not a cavalcade of world-historical forces winding their way around the globe. Even though democratic capitalism was, as Francis Fukiyama put it, a worthy "end of history," its course is still incomplete.[37]

But the capitalist revolution began in Britain and to its history we must now turn.

CHAPTER TWO

Queues or Ladders?

I

When Margaret Thatcher moved to 10 Downing Street, she hung a portrait of Winston Churchill in the antechamber of the Cabinet Room.[1] The choice was appropriate, for Churchill's leadership and resolve had made the wartime leader her political hero. When the Nazis invaded Poland in 1939, Margaret Thatcher (née Roberts) was a fourteen-year-old schoolgirl living in the small Lincolnshire town of Grantham. By the time victory in Europe was declared in 1945, she was an undergraduate studying chemistry at Somerville College, Oxford.

Four decades later, though, Mrs. Thatcher became the second British leader to address a joint session of Congress. She followed in the footsteps of the man she called by the familiar "Winston." The affinity between Churchill and Thatcher did not go unnoticed, especially in the United States, where both were unusually popular. When Thatcher received the Winston Churchill Foundation Award, the citation noted that like Churchill she was "known for courage, conviction, determination and will power."[2] The grocer's daughter and the aristocrat's son also shared common ground. Both were ardent patriots. Both were deeply attached to the "special relationship" with the United States. Both had a strong sympathy for the Jews. Both were fired by the conviction that socialist government was at odds with personal liberty. And the political fates of both leaders, and indeed the nation itself, were affected by the decisions the British people took in the general election of 1945. So it is therefore worthwhile to look at how the course of postwar British history led to Mrs. Thatcher's accession.

As the results of the general election of 1945 were about to be announced on July 26, Churchill seemed to be on the verge of a great victory. Or was it simply inconceivable to him and his supporters that he could be brought down in a moment of triumph? Smoking a cigar and clad in his blue siren suit, Churchill sat in his chair in the Map Room and awaited the results. Almost since the inception of World War II, he had been surrounded day and night, at home and abroad, by maps. They were dotted with pins plotting defeats which augured his worst fears and triumphs which stirred his best hopes. But no emblem could ever begin to capture the havoc wrought by the planes, ships, tanks, and guns which scorched so many communities and broke so many lives. As First Lord of the Admiralty during the early months of the war, Churchill lived and worked in Admiralty House, which contained the War Room and Map Room. It overlooked Whitehall on the one side and Pall Mall on the other. After the famed dinners he held on Tuesday nights for government and military officials, he would regularly invite his honored guests on a tour of the War Rooms.

In charge of the Upper War Room was Captain Richard Pim, an officer and gentleman who stayed in Churchill's service until the end of the war. It was Pim who was responsible for turning an elegant three-century-old library into the Map Room. On one wall of this sacred domain was a map of the world; on the other, regional maps. All of them could be covered by curtains to keep their contents secret, when necessary, from unauthorized viewers. Much to the chagrin of the captain, the amateur painter did not care for the strong colors of the first maps he designed. Instead, Churchill asked for pastel shades more comforting to the eyes. He slept in a bedroom one floor above the Map Room. Often he came down to inspect the charts in search of the latest reports in the middle of the night or early in the morning, appearing in a multi-colored dressing gown.

When Churchill became Prime Minister he moved into a private flat in No. 10 Annexe near St. James's Park. Pim fitted another Map Room for him. The two men saw each other most days of the war. But Pim bravely managed to sneak away so that he could be present during the evacuation of Dunkirk. Too often, Pim had the unhappy obligation to give reports of defeat and destruction to the Prime Minister. So it was fitting that he also had the honor of informing him that on May 8, 1945, all hostilities would cease. Churchill responded: "For five years you've brought me bad news, sometimes worse than others. Now you've redeemed yourself." Soon after, Pim fitted a new set of maps in the No. 10 Annexe for a very different conflict, the political battle between the Conservative and Labour parties.[3]

These were the maps which Churchill viewed as he sat in his secret sanctuary on July 26 awaiting the results of the general election. Not quite three months earlier, the Prime Minister had proudly announced victory in Europe to a grateful nation, which he thanked for never having "failed in the long, monstrous days and in the long nights black as hell." No one could doubt the enormous debt the British people owed Churchill. It was he who railed against the dangers of appeasement in the 1930s, accusing the leaders of his own party of dishonoring themselves and disgracing Britain in the name of "peace in our time." No one could deny the stature of the

man who led the National government, the "Grand Coalition" as he liked to call it, through the darkest days of the war
when Britain stood alone against Nazi tyranny as France fell
and America wavered. But neither Churchill's personal
qualities nor his wartime achievements, majestic as they
were, ensured victory. Still there seemed to be every reason
for confidence, at least in the minds of the pundits who predicted a Conservative triumph. Even Stalin took the British
premier aside in the middle of the Potsdam Conference to
assure him that his sources predicted the Tories would enjoy
an eighty-seat majority in the Commons. And yet the night
before the votes were to be announced, Churchill remarked
that he awoke with "a sharp stab in almost physical pain . . . a
subconscious conviction that we were beaten broke forth and
dominated my mind."[4]

The general election of 1945 was one contest which the
good warrior did not want to fight. Winston Churchill himself much preferred the mantle of national to party leader.
Such a role befitted a man whose aristocratic lineage seemed
to encourage maverick conduct, a man who crossed the
House of Commons not once but twice, abandoning party
loyalty when principle demanded. Reluctant as he was to go
to the country before the end of the war with Japan, he did so
at the behest of his compatriots in the National government.
Initially, Clement Attlee, the Labour Party leader, told
Churchill that he was favorably disposed to carrying on the
coalition until victory with Japan. As proof of good faith,
Churchill agreed to Attlee's stipulation to make every effort
to implement the proposals for social security and full employment contained in the White Paper before Parliament. It
soon became clear that Labour activists were not content to
merely stand and wait, though. Eager to conquer the enemy
within, the social and economic plagues that ravaged working people in the 1930s under Conservative rule, they favored
dissolution. When Attlee finally informed a shocked Church-

ill on May 21 that Labour was unwilling to remain in the National government, he opted for a quick general election, to take place on July 5. (However, the ballots would not be tallied finally until July 26 so that the Armed Forces could take part and their votes counted.) Surely voters would not turn him out after his finest hour.

II

THE GENERAL ELECTION OF 1945 WAS A WATERSHED IN BRITISH history. It was a conflict between the old and the new, a struggle for Albion's soul played out in a land wasted by war.

The Labour Party put forth its social philosophy in *Let Us Face the Future*. This appropriately entitled election manifesto detailed an immodest program for a new society. When World War I finally ended, there had also been calls, sincere summons at that, to make Britain a land fit for heroes. Such grand talk did not survive the return to business as usual in which broken promises were ignored or dismissed with the usual excuses. This must not happen again, Labour contended. The British people deserve and must be assured a happier future than faced so many of them after the last war. Facing the future meant comprehensive social insurance, a national health service, and the nationalization of certain industries. *Let Us Face the Future* marked the road away from Wigan Pier, away from the insecure, hopeless world of the industrial poor described so movingly by George Orwell. The manifesto charted the path to a promised land not so distant as to be beyond reach but not so close as to be taken for granted. It provided a map for socialist pilgrims supplemented by a gazetteer full of facts and figures to persuade the skeptic.

The socialist vision acquired a special poignancy and undeniable appeal when Britain's survival was in doubt in the early years of World War II. "The English Revolution started several years ago," wrote Orwell in *The Lion and the Unicorn* (1941). "Like all else in England, it happens in a sleepy, unwilling way, but it is happening."[5] A people threatened by conquest, hammered by bombing, and frustrated by austerity had every reason and every need to dream of a better future. National leaders invoked an idealized past whose civilized traditions would be undone by the barbarous Hun. Raising morale also depended on distinguishing between the ideals which inspired Britain and its merciless adversary. Germany was a "warfare state," a monstrous machine driven by death and destruction. Britain was to become a "welfare state," dedicated to caring and compassion. A people's war was a prelude to a people's peace.

To bring Jerusalem to England's green and pleasant land: the biblical image evoked by William Blake was a leading theme of the Labour Party. It was a pilgrimage led by enlightened intellectuals, scions of the professional classes, who were never quite at home with industry. In the early years of World War II, they conceived a vision of New Jerusalem, a just world which might redeem the failures of peacetime and the sufferings of wartime, the indignities of unemployment and the afflictions of battle. Horrified by the legacy of Victorian capitalism, they envisioned an authentic community in which high-mindedness would conquer greed. A protective network of social services would shelter the British people.[6]

The prophet of the Welfare State was the Liberal social scientist Sir William Beveridge, former Director of the London School of Economics, Master of University College, Oxford, and a senior civil servant. The son of a judge in the Indian Civil Service, he was educated at Charterhouse and Balliol College, Oxford. Like many intellectuals of his generation, he came into direct contact with the poor in mission work at Toynbee Hall in the East End of London. A detractor claimed that Beveridge wouldn't have given a penny to a blind beggar. But an admirer contended that he was the kindest man who ever lived.[7] If so, this escaped the young Harold Wilson. When he worked for Beveridge at Oxford on a study of aspects of labor demand, he found him to be an impossible person and a terrible boss. What struck Wilson was Beveridge's "arrogance and rudeness to those appointed to work with him and his total inability to delegate."[8] He was a severe taskmaster with an indefatigable appetite for a regime that he expected others to share. During the summer months they spent at Avebury, Beveridge's Wiltshire cottage, the day began with two hours' work before breakfast, followed by tennis all afternoon, and then work all night.[9]

Beveridge's views also sometimes rankled. Wilson disliked his boss's notion that unemployment was "frictional," that is, caused by the immobility of labor. His family's own bitter experience told him otherwise. In August 1938, Beveridge spent a weekend with his old Fabian friends, Sidney and Beatrice Webb, at their Hampshire home, Passfield Corner. During long walks on the Downs with Beatrice, the conversation naturally turned to questions of social research and welfare. Beveridge contended that "the only remedy for unemployment is lower wages."[10] This would have warmed the most hard-hearted of capitalists.

By the time Beveridge wrote *The Pillars of Security* (1943), he had settled on a more stirring vision for the future. "The sustained free effort required of the democracies today, to lead them to die and to kill in every quarter of the globe, until the forces of barbarism in every quarter are overcome, must be directed not by anger or fear or hate, but towards a clearly seen aim beyond the war—to the making of a world in which the common people of all nations and their children after them may live and work in security."[11] As chairman of the Committee on Social Insurance and Allied Services, his brief was an unpromising theme for prophetic exaltation. Determined to conquer the "Giants" of Want, Sickness, Squalor, Ignorance, Disease, and Idleness, he brought to his work a profound moral passion rarely found in government treatises. The Beveridge Report, as it soon became known, was published in December 1942 after the victory at El Alamein, and sold more than 800,000 copies. It sketched a universal plan of comprehensive national insurance, which would provide social services including ample housing, social security, free medical and dental care, and unemployment benefits. Beveridge also called for the abolition of the invidious means test which stigmatized the poor. On one crucial issue, the report was vague, though: how to pay for the admirable reforms it championed.

It was experience of the home front and the battlefront which changed social ideals in Britain. Those who earned ten pounds a week and those who inherited ten thousand a year had little in common, but the German Blitz united them nonetheless in bomb shelters in the London Underground. Thousands of feet beneath the streets of the capital, the leisured classes and the overworked masses met and talked in tube stations. During the long hellish nights when the bombs fell on London with little warning and no mercy, the usual chasm between the classes collapsed, bringing together those whose smooth cadences qualified them for BBC broadcasts and those whose cockney accents came from the East End. In the usual course of human events, one can choose to neglect the suffering of others, as W.H. Auden depicts in his "Musée des Beaux Arts," where

> ... everything turns away
> Quite leisurely from the disaster ...

In the midst of a war that threatened the survival of the nation, and indeed of civilization itself, it was far more difficult to admit that

the dreadful martyrdom must run its course
Anyhow in a corner. . . .

When the war was over, socialist intellectuals made every effort to ensure that the sense of community endured. In J. B. Priestley's play *Three Men in Suits* (1945), he depicted socialism as a coming of age for Britain. For Priestley, socialism was the road to true autonomy. It was not at all the path to dependency that Mrs. Thatcher denounced. Planning, sharing, and cooperation—these were to be the cornerstones of the new socialist Britain. The desired result was an egalitarian society.

As the sun set on the disbanding British Empire after World War II, the dream of New Jerusalem provided a domestic surrogate. Grand in scope, noble in purpose, and distinctive in character, the Welfare State attempted to end the inequality and exploitation that were evident both at home and abroad during the height of British power. Not only did it offer new hope for the working class, but also it gave the ruling class a new sense of mission. This was especially true for the progressive, enlightened members of the establishment, public-spirited, public school graduates like Beveridge who came from the professions, the gentry, or the aristocracy. The old paternalism that pervaded the Empire, though, also carried over to a point in the Welfare State. Indeed, what Lord Bryce once said of British India had some bearing on postwar Britain: Much was done for the people, but little by the people.

I I I

BUT THE WELFARE STATE DID NOT FIT INTO THE VISION, SUCH as it was, of the Conservative Party. In the general election of 1945, the Tories were the defenders of the old Britain. Some objected to the Welfare State out of self-interest alone. En-joying a privileged, comfortable existence themselves, they had scant desire to improve the condition of working people, much less to create New Jerusalem. Unlike the ancient He-brews, these self-satisfied souls were perfectly at home in Zion, but they were not so hospitable as to welcome new-comers who were strangers in a strange land. And yet there were also honest doubters whose voices were not so easily dismissed. Winston Churchill was preeminent among them.

His doubts did not stem from a lack of compassion, a charge often leveled against Margaret Thatcher. "The main end of modern government was the improvement of the con-dition of the British people," Churchill had announced in 1899 during his unsuccessful first bid for a seat in the House of Commons.[12] Privileged and insulated as he was, it is doubtful that he knew what the wretched felt. When he became a Member of Parliament for an industrial district in Manches-ter, though, he saw how poverty disfigured life. Determined to find a middle path between the callousness of the classes and the radicalism of the masses, the young Churchill be-came an advanced Liberal, an ardent follower and friend of Lloyd George, committed to social insurance. A fierce enemy of appeasing foreign aggressors, Churchill did believe in mollifying class bitterness, even though some suspected him of taking part in the infamous suppression of Tonypandy miners in 1910. Age did not rob Churchill of concern for the poor, but experience did make him aware that every farthing of the cost had to be paid.

Churchill liked to distinguish between facts and dreams. This was a cavalier distinction given that the facts of his life resembled the dreams of ordinary people. Born in 1874 in Blenheim Palace, where he was surrounded by portraits of his ancestors and emblems of their power, his grandfather was the seventh Duke of Marlborough and his father a one-time Chancellor of the Exchequer. An MP at age twenty-five, he became Home Secretary ten years later. Not that all the facts he faced were altogether pleasant or all the dreams he held easily realized. An enviable pedigree did not lessen the loneliness the young Churchill felt as a child at boarding school, separated from his adored parents. Family connections helped launch his political career but did not keep him out of the wilderness in the 1930s. His dream of retaining India within the British Empire was undone. And his dream of becoming Prime Minister was postponed until late in life. It was fulfilled only then because of a national emergency.

The Welfare State was not without grandeur, but the fact remained that it was impractical. As it happened, Winston Churchill was sympathetic to many of the proposals of the Beveridge Report. But his enthusiasm faded when the Conservative Chancellor, Sir Kingsley Wood, told him that Britain probably could not afford to fund so premature and impracticable a vision. "The time for declaring a dividend on the profits of the Golden Age," Wood noted sardonically, "is the time when those profits have been realised in fact, not merely in the imagination."[13] Was it feasible or wise for a debt-ridden nation with an exhausted economy and depleted treasury to make enormous capital investments in social services?

"There is still a lot to do. . . ," the Prime Minister announced in a radio broadcast soon after VE-Day; "you must be prepared for further efforts of mind and body and further sacrifices for a great cause if you are not to fall back into the rut of inertia." Churchill did not deny that "holiday rejoicing is necessary to the human spirit, yet it must add to the strength and resilience with which every man and woman turns again to the work they have to do."[14] Socialism, especially socialism now, would mean misery for all. Far better to devote the resources, and focus the resolve, of the British people on the enormous task of economic reconstruction before entertaining visions of social justice, however beguiling.

Although the Conservatives' *Declaration of Policy to the Electors*, bloodless document that it was, offered many of the social benefits promised by Labour, the perils of socialism became Churchill's campaign theme. This was a serious error. His argument was that socialism was incompatible with freedom. It constituted an attack not only on property but also on liberty. Socialism led to abject worship of the state. It would culminate in a totalitarian regime, uprooting every English virtue, destroying every English value. "No Socialist Government conducting the entire life and industry of the country," he contended in a broadcast on June 4, 1945, "could afford to allow free, sharp, or violent-worded expression of public discontent. They would have to fall back on some sort of Gestapo." This outrageous comparison suggested how out of touch Churchill was with the sentiments of ordinary people.[15]

His preoccupation with the dangers of socialism blinded him to its wartime benefits. "It did no one any harm," Sarah Churchill wrote insistently to her father the following day, "and quite a lot of people good. The children of this country have never been so well fed or healthy, what milk there was, was shared equally ... and there is no doubt that this common sharing and feeling of sacrifice was one of the strongest bonds that unified us. So why, they say, cannot this common feeling of sacrifice be made to work as effectively in peace."[16] To such arguments Churchill had no satisfactory answer.

I V

BUT HOW WOULD THE BRITISH ELECTORATE RESPOND? THAT was the question.

Waiting with Churchill in the Map Room for the results of the general election on the morning of July 26 were his daughter Sarah and his brother Jack, along with his private secretary, John Colville, and three friends, Lord Beaverbrook, Lord Margesson, and Brendan Bracken. The day had not begun well and the atmosphere was gloomy. When the first results came in at 10:00 A.M., Captain Pim went to find Churchill, who was still in the bath. He was surprised, if not shocked, to learn that Labour had already won ten seats from the Conservatives. The BBC News at 1:00 P.M. reported that Labour was about to win an astonishing victory. By the time the party sat down to lunch, it was clear this would be Churchill's last day as Prime Minister.[17]

The general election revealed that the British people preferred the uncertainties of the future to the errors of the past. Labour won 47.8 percent of the vote, the Conservatives 39.8 percent, and the Liberals a meager 9.5 percent. Labour's participation in the wartime coalition helped it obtain a 146-seat majority in the House of Commons; it also managed to outpoll the Conservatives even in their traditional county strongholds. Blamed for interwar failures, the Tories received little credit for wartime achievements. Those who endured long nights in Underground shelters would not be denied their chance of building a city on the hill. Even if the country could not afford the economic cost of New Jerusalem (and this was not certain), it was equally true that Britain could not afford the social cost of abandoning it. At the moment of victory, after so many years of hardship, years of denial, and years of sacrifice, there was little enthusiasm for further austerity. Some voted for Labour in the mistaken belief that Churchill would still remain Prime Minister. Even his immense personal popularity could not outweigh the passionate longing for a better future.

It was not the end of everything, but it was the end of an era. Odious as defeat must have been, Churchill showed uncommon grace in the face of facts that shattered his dreams. Few such compliments would accrue to Thatcher after her fall. When Lord Moran, Churchill's private physician, complained to him about the "ingratitude" of the British people, the Prime Minister would not hear of it. His generous reply was: "I wouldn't call it that. They have had a very hard time of it." Sitting in the bath at the end of the following day, Churchill looked so gray that Pim feared he would faint. Then he turned to the captain and simply said, "They are perfectly entitled to vote as they please. This is democracy. This is what we've been fighting for."[18] Later, he sat down with his private secretary, Pat Kinna. They reminisced about all their travels and travails through wartime Europe and beyond. With tears streaming down his face, Churchill said, "And now the British people don't want me any more."[19]

Much as Churchill fell from power soon after the end of World War II, Thatcher was overthrown soon after the end of the Cold War. Both leaders were undone at triumphant moments, but in different ways and for different reasons. It was Conservative MPs who ousted her in a coup. But the British people rejected him in an election whose results shaped the nation's fate.

V

THE NEW SOCIALIST ORDER CREATED BY THE ATTLEE GOVERNment (1945–51) was better designed to break a fall than fire an ascent, more likely to insulate the hapless than to inspire the ambitious. It was a world dominated by the queue rather than the ladder. As Churchill put it in 1951, "The difference between our outlook and the Socialist outlook on life is the difference between the ladder and the queue. We are for the ladder. Let all try their best to climb. They are for the queue. Let each wait in his place till his turn comes."[20]

The Labour Party pressed ahead with its pledge to face the future, but did so by drawing on the immediate past. When the Attlee government came to power, it built on the achievements of wartime social policy for the Welfare State, the most ambitious program of social reform in British history. The National Insurance Act (1946) provided unemployment benefit, retirement pension, widows' benefit, and guardians' allowance. It was far less controversial than the National Health Service Act (1946), which was opposed by doctors who resisted, among other things, becoming salaried employees of the state. But a compromise was finally reached, providing free medical, dental, and ophthalmic care, while retaining private facilities.

The National Housing Act (1947) enshrined the principle of social provision and state subsidy. But progress was slow in meeting the need for an estimated 3 million dwellings. This was true partly because the Welsh Socialist Aneurin Bevin, Minister of Health and Housing, initially preferred quality to quantity. He also left too much in the hands of local government councils and too little in the hands of private industry. By 1947, though, 200,000 houses a year were being built. These social programs afforded a measure of protection for those hitherto virtually helpless in the face of the terrible scourges of life—among them unemployment, illness, disability, and old age—even though they did not amount to the "national minimum" favored by Beveridge.

For those whose views of the Welfare State were shaped by the onslaught on it led by Margaret Thatcher and Ronald Reagan, it is too easy to overlook the grandeur of this humane enterprise. Whatever its abuses and failures, they are better than the fear, insecurity, and deprivation of working-class life in the interwar era. For the Welfare State did much to mitigate the utter vulnerability of the working poor, and still more, the long-term unemployed.

No writer described the deprivations of interwar Britain

better than George Orwell in his painfully vivid account of his journey to the industrial North, *The Road to Wigan Pier* (1937). The "endless misery" of unemployment was a fact of life for more than 2 million. Those who qualified for government relief had to undergo a humiliating means test. Even a hint of income from other sources such as casual labor on the docks or a meager contribution to household expenses by a parent living on a pension might disqualify them from the dole or reduce their allowance. The colorless bureaucratic phrase "housing shortage," which was much bandied about during the 1930s, sanitized the reality of being forced to live in homes "by any human standard not fit for human habitation . . . any hole and corner slum, any misery of bugs and rotting floors and cracking walls, any extension of skinflint landlords and blackmailing agents." Nowhere was the "gauntness of poverty" more visible than in the "physical degeneracy" of working people with stunted physiques and bad teeth, the result of malnutrition and lack of medical and dental care.[21] If the Welfare State did not wholly rid Britain of such afflictions, it made considerable progress in so doing.

But the Welfare State did more to shelter the unfortunate from the penalties of economic failure than to encourage economic success. It improved the condition of the working and non-working poor, but did not break the "culture of poverty." The poor suffered from inferior education, paltry opportunities, shabby housing, poor nutrition, and scanty health care. These were objective deprivations not easily dismissed, or overcome, by a better attitude. The result, though, of generations of deprivation was, as Bevin put it, "poverty of desire," the tendency to accept too little rather than expect too much. William Beveridge did promise cradle-to-grave security. But he envisioned a safety net for the unfortunate rather than a hammock for the demoralized.

Nevertheless, Mrs. Thatcher and the new right were wrong to argue that the Welfare State had created a "dependency culture." For the English working classes were not truly independent before the coming of socialism. Traditionally, they relied for their livelihoods first on feudal lords, then on capitalist entrepreneurs. Defeatism was a more serious problem than dependence. It was an understandable, but destructive, reaction to long oppression and unequal opportunities. In the United States a different attitude, if not always different conditions, prevailed. "Dream was the codeword for that ache for transcendence, for moving up and moving on, which had been sanctioned by the republic as a democratic right," observes the British travel writer Jonathan Raban in *Hunting Mister Heartbreak* (1990).[22] Britain did not encourage such dreams.

Socialism did nothing to undermine, and much to strengthen, jealous resentment of wealth and success. Contempt is a characteristic vice of the upper class, and envy a characteristic vice of the working class. Among the firms nationalized by the Attlee government was a family trucking concern which belonged to the father of James Hanson, who is now one of Britain's leading entrepreneurs and corporate raiders. At age twenty-seven he went to Canada to set up a new business. Hanson purchased "a beautiful new car" for himself at a time when they were still unavailable in Britain. Driving into the garage, he saw a trucker who was about to finish his shift. The man admired the car and Hanson asked whether he would like to drive it, an offer gladly accepted. When the trucker returned from his short test drive, he told his boss, "I'm going to own one of those one day." Now, in Britain, Hanson commented, the response would have been, "why should he have one of those?"[23] What he did not clarify, though, is that such attitudes were a response to an unfair class system. Was the queue so appealing because the ladder was out of reach?

The Welfare State was built on a dubious economic foundation at a time of scarce resources. Noble intentions did not alter the fact that some of the Attlee government's reforms were richer in largesse than realism. As Churchill pointed out during the general election of 1945, its proposed programs were extremely expensive. A depleted nation could not pay the bill for such generosity. The actual costs, as Kingsley Wood predicted, were far more than their proponents admitted or expected. The National Health Service, which became the centerpiece of the Welfare State, was projected to cost £53 million. Its cost almost doubled between 1949–50 and 1951–52. Faced with an apparent choice between economic growth and social justice, the Attlee government chose justice.

V I

AFTER WORLD WAR II, BRITAIN NEEDED TO BECOME A STATE dedicated to pursuing welfare and production rather than seeking one at the expense of the other.

But the political culture of the postwar socialist order neglected efficient creation of wealth in favor of its fair distribution (much as the old capitalist order had done the opposite). This was a worthy goal in the short term perhaps in view of historic inequities. In the long term, though, it was a dubious strategy. An uncertain tide threatens all ships. The divorce between social justice and economic productivity was not inevitable. Britain's leading progressive firms, notably the retailer Marks & Spencer and the consumer goods manufacturer Cadburys, saw worker welfare and business efficiency as two sides of the same problem. They did not regard decent wages, job security, educational opportunities, and medical care as charitable afterthoughts or humane frills. Rather, they were indispensable elements of commercial success.[24]

In 1945, Britain was in such desperate condition that John Maynard Keynes believed it faced an "economic Dunkirk."

During World War II Britain lost no less than one fourth of its national wealth, about £7,000 million. Britain's international trading position collapsed, as it abandoned two thirds of foreign trade in the name of the war effort. The national debt tripled. So Britain became ever more dependent upon ever less certain aid from the United States. But American largesse evaporated with President Truman's sudden cancellation of Lend-Lease. The gravity of Britain's situation was little surprise to the authors of a Board of Trade report issued in June 1944. They drew a sobering picture of Britain's postwar prospects: "One of our dangers, perhaps the main danger, is that this country will fail to see clearly and early enough the grave difficulties that lie ahead of British industry after the transition from war to peace."[25] The report took exception to the heady talk which predicted an average increase of 50 percent in exports. How could this happen unless there was a commensurate increase in competitive power and, indeed, increased prosperity in foreign markets?

No such gloom marked the public pronouncements of leading industrialists, among them Lord McGowan, chairman of Imperial Chemical Industries. "When the history of this war can be written I am sure we shall find," he said in 1944, "that every new manifestation of enemy research, whether at sea, on land or in the air, has been matched, and more than matched, by counter-discovery in this country, to say nothing of the lead we have given to the Allies in all sorts of connections not only with attack and defence, but with the health of the people."[26] How could the nation responsible for the invention of both penicillin and the jet-propelled aircraft fail to succeed in peace as in war?

In *The Audit of War* (1986), the British historian Correlli Barnett offered a controversial answer that many historians dispute. He argued that the alleged industrial miracle of World War II was largely the product of economic and technological aid from the United States and insulation from in-

ternational competition. Barnett's portrait of British industry
is almost altogether dismal. Classic industries such as coal
were still under the sway of the cult of the practical man, lads
who had come up in the works with little managerial training
or technological know-how. The achievements of the much-
heralded aeronautical industry were exaggerated. Apart from
the jet engine, major British developments in the technology
and manufacture of wartime aircraft borrowed heavily from
foreign competitors. The development of the jet engine from
drawing board to launch pad was so slow as to mock its name.
At any rate, the British aircraft industry was unable to attain
the economies of scale and scope enjoyed by its American
counterpart. The manufacture of British high-technology
equipment during the war would have been impossible without the help of the American machine-tool industry. In short,
the wartime performance of British industry was as much
myth as miracle.[27]

In 1945, Britain needed a radical program to renew a run-
down social, economic, and technological base—a grand national crusade uniting government, business, and labor. Unable or unwilling to work toward an economic miracle, the
Attlee government took refuge in an industrial wonderland.
Its central tenet was the commitment to public control of industry. Long an article of faith for the Labour Party, which
found neither romance nor justice in capitalist individualism,
it was not until World War II that strong support for a
planned economy prevailed. In Orwell's words, "The fact
that we are at war has turned Socialism from a textbook word
into a realizable policy."[28] The lessons of the war were misin-
terpreted, though. The war experience did reveal the value
of cooperation for the sake of a great national purpose. And it
did demonstrate the efficiency of large managerial enterprises which exploited economies of scale and scope. Nevertheless, there is little evidence that their success stemmed
from the intrinsic virtues, such as they were, of public owner-

ship of the means of production and distribution.

No such practical doubts impeded the ardor of those responsible for carrying out "the socialization of industry" called for in clause four of the Labour Party Constitution. So the Attlee government nationalized the Bank of England, civil aviation, cable and wireless, gas, coal, and finally iron and steel. But the run-up to nationalization betrayed few signs of thought or preparation. In 1945, Emanuel Shinwell, who had joined the Independent Labour Party in 1904 at age twenty, became Minister for Fuel and Power. He complained that though nationalization had been on the Labour agenda for over fifty years, they had done little or nothing to prepare plans for it. Wags joked that when he ransacked the archives of Transport House for guidance about the coal industry, all Shinwell could find was a pamphlet written in Welsh. The industries brought under public ownership were by no means the most profitable or healthy sectors of the economy. Some were better candidates for hospitalization, if not mercy killing, than nationalization.

The transfer from private to public ownership had remarkably little effect on the running of enterprises. Contrary to expectations, the Labour government compensated capitalists generously, perhaps too much so. It also kept managers in place with little regard for performance (welfare for the middle class). Although Prime Minister Attlee rejected the prospect of worker-controlled industry, he had high hopes for joint consultation. But nothing much came of it. Workers, he said, "had been against the boss for so long they found it difficult to start co-operating with him. And some of them didn't want to. Didn't want the responsibility or couldn't get used to the feeling of it . . . 'Us and them' problems, you know."[29] So much for the possibility that national ownership would be the launching pad for a new model of management-labor cooperation.

The Attlee government might as well have put up a large

sign saying, "Under New Ownership," then adding the reassuring words, "Business as usual."

VII

MAKING PEACE WITH THE FUTURE RATHER THAN TRYING TO resurrect the past was the best chance for the Conservative Party to return to office. So Churchill came to realize. He proved willing to do what Margaret Thatcher rarely did (or, at least, rarely admitted to doing): he compromised. He opened the general election campaign in 1951 with a warning. Although Britain had been able to withstand and surmount the shocks and strains of "this terrible twentieth century and its two awful wars," its "very existence" was endangered "if we go on consuming our strength in bitter party or class conflicts."[30] The country, then, needed a period of social peace unmarred by party dogma.

This required reaching an accommodation with organized labor. During the railway strike of 1953, Rab Butler, the Chancellor, made it clear to Churchill that he feared an inflationary wage settlement. Negotiations went on into the early hours of the morning. Churchill did not see fit to wake Butler. When he finally called him with the news that the strike was settled, the Chancellor asked, "On what terms was the strike settled, Prime Minister?" Churchill responded: "On their terms, of course, old cock."[31] This was fair enough given how poorly paid workers often were. But could the British increase productivity to keep pace with wage increases?

The search for harmony was a driving force in the new Britain. It was a reaction against the economic gulf between the idle rich and the needy poor during the interwar era. It was a reaction against the social conflicts manifest, for example, in the General Strike of 1926. Broadly speaking, it was also a reaction against the humiliating legacy of a class society obsessed by categorizing and preserving difference. In theory, the old aristocratic order prized harmony, but it was inegalitarian and hierarchical to the core. Class distinctions, of course, were not unique to Britain. Unequal incomes and opportunities were facts of life in every modern society. Yet it was no accident that it was a British sociologist who defined class as how one person treats another. The survival of a poisonous feudal mentality which held that certain persons were immutably and ineradicably better than others made the sting of class especially painful. One of many reasons that socialism was appealing was its promise of equality. Democracy might have done the trick, but the extension of the franchise did not destroy paternalistic habits of authority.

Consensus became the avowed order of the day in the 1950s and 1960s. It began in the early days of the Churchill government (1951–55), which proved far more hospitable to the Welfare State than it was in the wake of World War II. The change in attitude was more a matter of political expediency than philosophical principle. For the 1945 election taught Conservatives a lasting lesson: Churchill's open opposition to the Welfare State was political suicide. So both the Labour and Conservative parties took part in establishing new welfare programs and institutions. In the United States, the Red Scare of the late 1940s and 1950s impeded the spread of such munificence. Although Britain had more than its share of real Communist spies, it did not go through the same convulsions that wracked its ally. Rather, Britain forged ahead with the "progressive consensus" derided by Mrs. Thatcher—mixed economy, full employment, social welfare, economic planning, labor peace, and interventionist state. Corporatist bias shaped, and constrained, decision making. Government had to take into account the views of trade unions as well as management in forming policy and practice.

A convergence took place between the two major parties. Labour moved in the Conservatives' direction on foreign policy. In turn, they moved in Labour's direction on domestic affairs. *The Economist* invented the term "Butskellism" to describe the new bipartisan approach. It referred to the growing common ground that united Rab Butler, a progressive Conservative, with Hugh Gaitskell, his moderate Labour counterpart. Yet "Butskellism" masked real differences between, and indeed within, the left and the right. Nevertheless, when Mrs. Thatcher assailed the harmful impact of collectivist policies on Britain, she was fighting against a set of institutions and attitudes endorsed, if not created, by the leaders of her own party.

Conservative leaders who remembered (as Mrs. Thatcher did not) the travails faced by the British people, especially working people, during the 1920s and 1930s did not scoff at the achievements of the postwar years. The man who helped rebuild the Conservative Party along more progressive lines was Rab Butler. And it was under Butler's chancellorship that the new prosperity surfaced. But the man who took the lion's share of credit was his old rival, Harold Macmillan, who defeated him for the party leadership.[32]

A publisher's son who married a duke's daughter, Macmillan was born in 1894 at the end of the Victorian age to a comfortably off middle-class family. Growing up in London on Cadogan Place, he remembered, as Alastair Horne, his official biographer, wrote, "the clop and jingle of the horse-drawn trams, and . . . the hammer and anvil from a blacksmith's shop in the mews below."[33] His education at Eton and Balliol College, Oxford, did not prepare him for the horrors he encountered during his time in the chic Grenadier Guards during World War I. But his experience as an officer instilled in Captain Macmillan a genuine respect for, and sympathy with, the life of workingmen who he would never have gotten to know otherwise. "They have big hearts, these soldiers," he wrote to his mother.[34]

Macmillan's compassion for their plight put him in good

stead when in 1924 he became MP for Stockton, a once prosperous shipbuilding town in the Northeast. Knowing little about any businesses apart from publishing and printing, he was shocked by what took place in his new constituency in the 1920s and 1930s. One of England's most depressed industrial towns, joblessness ran about 25 to 30 percent by his estimate. "Many men, and indeed whole families, had been without work and wages for long periods, with corresponding difficulties and hardship. Their clothes were worn out; their furniture in disrepair; their savings gone; their homes dilapidated," Macmillan wrote in his memoirs. "I shall never forget those despairing faces, as these men tramped up and down the High Street in Stockton."[35] This memory haunted him for years to come. When he was elevated to the House of Lords, the title he chose was Earl of Stockton.

Macmillan was fortunate enough to witness the realization of the "middle way" between capitalism and socialism that he had called for during the 1930s. The contrast between Stockton during the Depression and Britain during the Macmillan government (1957–63) was a cause for celebration. And no one made more skillful use of the new affluence than Macmillan. On July 20, 1957, the Prime Minister gave a famous speech in which he described the country's apparent good fortune:

> Let's be frank about it; most of our people have never had it so good. Go around the country, go to the industrial towns, go to the farms, and you will see a state of prosperity such as we have never had in my lifetime—nor indeed ever in the history of this country.[36]

He was right, to a point. The long period of Conservative rule from 1951 to 1964 witnessed a dramatic rise in the standard of living. As usual, the spoils were not divided evenly. The wages of manual workers went up by about 50 percent. But the value of shares shot up by about 180 percent. After years of sacrifice in which the shadow of the ration book obscured the pursuit of happiness, who could resist pudding today and pudding tomorrow? For all the protestations that the British weren't materialistic (less so than the Americans, at any rate), they welcomed the cornucopia of consumer goods. Cars, televisions, washing machines, and the like flooded the country. None of this would later stop Margaret Thatcher from denouncing the "progressive consensus" under which such a consumer boom took place.

Yet serious problems remained. As Macmillan pointed out in his "you never had it so good" speech, Britain's prosperity was like a house of cards. Delicately built, it might be easily undone.

> What is beginning to worry some of us is "Is it too good to be true?" or perhaps I should say "Is it too good to last?" For amidst all this prosperity, there is one problem that has troubled us—in one way or another—ever since the war. It's the problem of rising prices. The great mass of the country has for the time being, at any rate, been able to contract out of the effects of rising prices. But they will not be able to contract out for ever. For, if that happens, we will be back in the old nightmare of unemployment. The older ones among you will know what this meant. I hope the younger ones will never have to learn it.[37]

The illusion of enduring affluence blinded the British, and indeed many of their leaders, to the specter of economic decline. In elegantly written private papers Macmillan voiced anxieties which he did not care to express in public pronouncements. The superficial prosperity of the moment, however enjoyable, would not survive if Britain was unable to withstand foreign competition, particularly from Germany and Japan. The British were certainly better off than they had been in the immediate aftermath of World War II. But they were no longer Europe's dominant economic power.

The expectations and realities of consensus did not jive. In theory, consensus was based on cooperation between management, labor, and government for the common good. Too often, though, it was a hasty cover-up which tried to keep the peace at all costs. The result was a negotiated decline in which everyone got something if not quite what they needed.

VIII

A PREOCCUPATION WITH DECLINE SURFACED EVEN AS LONDON became known as the fashionable capital of the "swinging sixties." Social critics such as Michael Shanks and Anthony Sampson suggested that the advent of socialism had not destroyed the British establishment; an incompetent gerontocracy who owed their positions more to connections than merit still ran the nation, one way or another. "Effortless superiority" gave way to "effortless inferiority." Gentlemanly amateurs continued to remain supreme. But Britain no longer did.

All this enraged Harold Wilson. The former Oxford economist became Labour leader in 1963. He seized upon modernization as the cure for the stagnant society.

Family background and social milieu shaped his political vision. Wilson was born in 1916 in Huddersfield, an industrial town in the West Riding of Yorkshire famous for its textiles, wools, and worsteds. During World War I, Huddersfield became a center for the production of explosives, a boom town in more than one sense. The Wilson family were good chapel going Baptists. Their political sympathies veered back and forth between the Liberals and Labour. As Wilson's biographer, Ben Pimlott, shrewdly points out, his background was closer to Margaret Thatcher's than to that of any other British Prime Minister. Both were petty bourgeois provincials with Nonconformist roots. Both had a fervor for education that took them to grammar schools and then on to Oxford. Both were earnest strivers whose ambitions translated into a passion for political office.[38]

But there were, at least, two telling differences in their backgrounds, as Pimlott makes clear. The first was that Margaret was nine and one half years younger than Harold. So he came of age during the Depression, but she did not. Her formative period coincided with World War II. The second difference was that Margaret's father, a shopkeeper, was self-employed while Harold's father was an employee. In charge of the explosives department at Leith & Company, Herbert Wilson prospered during World War I and was able to move his family to a nicer house and neighborhood. The armistice marked the end of his ascent. There was worse to come. In 1930, he lost his job. This was a blow to his pride and a disgrace to his family, who tried to hush up his shame. "Unemployment more than anything else made me politically conscious," Wilson observed.[39] For Harold, the lesson was to avoid ending up at the mercy of capitalists. For Margaret, the lesson was to stay independent at all costs. The one became a socialist, the other its scourge.

The boy who had seen his father thrown out of work by the vagaries of the market took naturally to economic planning, if not to William Beveridge himself. The son of a scientist (even if Herbert had no degree), Harold Wilson had a far more exalted vision of science's role in Britain's future than Margaret Thatcher, who was herself a chemist by training. Much as Wilson objected to the Soviet political system, as late as 1964 he was convinced that its coordinated planning was far superior to what the West had to offer.[40] Without science, though, planning was inadequate. "I believe Socialism will come through applying the scientific revolution to our country," Wilson once said. He gained a far clearer idea of how to do so by participating in meetings with eminent scientists (such as C. P. Snow, J. D. Bernal, and Jacob Bronowski) and Labour politicians at the Reform Club in the 1950s.

At the Party Conference in 1963, the newly chosen Labour leader put forth a vision that fired the national imagination. It was beautifully timed to pick up on the anti-establishment sentiment manifest in the irreverent political satire "That Was The Week That Was" and the birth of a new ethic of sexual freedom. In his great speech, Wilson attacked the privileged few and their obsolete ways. Luckily, he was not a member of the high-toned Frognal set of public school Socialists like his rival Hugh Gaitskell, who lived in Hampstead. As it happened, though, he lived up the road. But his address mattered less than his "cheeky chappie" persona and Yorkshire accent. Both helped convince the electorate that he was "one of them."

In the white heat of technological revolution, Wilson promised that a new Britain would be born. The transformation he advocated was more than a matter of providing more resources for engineers and scientists (though this certainly made him popular in these circles). The scientific revolution also depended on an educational revolution (more jobs for academics, who also were drawn to Wilson's talk about finding the "best brains"). But his vision could not "become a reality unless we are prepared to make far-reaching changes in economic and social attitudes which permeate our whole system of society." This meant scrapping the old boy network to create opportunities for ordinary people. It meant replacing incompetent amateurs with trained professionals. "To the problem of Britain's declining industries and Britain's declining areas," Wilson said, "we shall provide the enterprise and we shall decide where it goes."[41] The result would be a more fair and productive society.

Modernization through science, then, was the enthralling promise of *Labour and the Scientific Revolution* (1963) and of *The New Britain* (1964), the Labour Party Manifesto. The results were not nearly so impressive. When Harold Wilson came to power in 1964, the talk of "white heat" turned into so much hot air. On the economic front, he soon faced a sterling crisis. He said time and again that he would not devalue the pound because doing so would be a national disaster. Then he did precisely that in 1967 and acted as if it barely mattered. The Wilson government promised to forge a new Britain. In the event, it dissolved into infighting between the left and right wings of the Labour Party. The Prime Minister was understandably eager to hang on to his position and to keep the peace. But as he became increasingly assailed by his critics, he ended up spending more of his time hatching, or stopping, political schemes than enacting his scientific dreams. He guarded his back from enemies, imagined and real. He also managed to stab himself.

One of the thorniest issues Wilson faced was how to deal with the trade unions. In 1966, during the seamen's strike, he tossed off the baseless charge that it was the work of Communist agitators. This outraged both the unions and much of the Cabinet. He was on firmer ground when it came to calling for trade union reform. Wilson supported Barbara Castle's *In Place of Strife*, a valiant attempt to bring much-needed industrial peace to Britain. But he could not provide sufficient support to carry it. Indeed, the debate over the document only aggravated growing internal conflict. Brian Walden, a Labour backbencher (and future champion of Mrs. Thatcher), told the Chancellor, James Callaghan, that union reform was inevitable. Callaghan's response was: "OK, if it's so inevitable, let the *Tories* pass it. All I'm saying is that it's not *our issue.*"[42] A mistaken notion. Given the ties, political as well as emotional, between Labour and the trade unions, it certainly was their issue. And it was foolish to let the Tories capitalize on it.

Planned growth proved more chimerical than real. Again, the political interests of the Labour Party stood in the way of putting Wilson's vision into action. The Industrial Reorganization Corporation was meant to finance new investments and increase efficiency through mergers (which were also rife in the private sector in Britain and America). But it turned into a sanctuary for lame ducks and their quack supporters. Among others bailed out by the IRC were Clydeside shipbuilders who could have won awards for inefficiency. A plan to close 5,000 miles of loss-making railway tracks also went down the tubes. When Richard Marsh, a trade union MP who was Minister of Power, recommended closing the line from Shrewsbury to Cardiff, the Secretary of State for Wales objected: "But, Prime Minister, this line runs through three marginal constituencies." It remained open.[43]

Labour's preoccupation with the inequities of the past blocked the path to a better future. The politics of resentment contaminated the quest for social justice. A ludicrous tax system (top rates of 83 percent on earned income and 97 percent on unearned income during the late 1960s and early 1970s) disciplined and punished the able and ambitious. Harold Wilson enjoyed the support of a number of industrialists attracted by his vision of modernization, but his party never overcame self-righteous rage against individual wealth. When the long-repressed egalitarian spirit finally erupted in a divided society obsessed with social niceties and class boundaries, leveling was an irresistible temptation. Successful entrepreneurs who made money in their own businesses were often considered (and sometimes were) dubious figures.

The prospect of modernizing Britain was blocked by the conduct of management and labor. Both seemed more intent on exploiting rather than reforming a faulty system. Workers were often ill-paid and harshly treated. But there were also real abuses for the unions' critics to cite. Rational pursuit of self-interest could, and did, lead to irrational results. For example, take featherbedding. It was a response to the pervasive unemployment of the interwar era and the scarcity of domestic labor during the war. Workers were eager to help their mates; capitalists wanted to hoard labor. But this practice still had destructive economic consequences.

Gordon White (who later became James Hanson's partner) owned a business in London which produced a weekly magazine. This meant that he had to deal with SOGAT, the powerful printing union. One Friday afternoon, White went into the men's room. There he found six men sitting around playing cards when they should have been working. "What are you fellas doing?" he asked. "We're waiting to get paid," they answered. "Don't you work while you're waiting?" White countered. To which they responded: "No, we're on swing shift . . . we don't work." Certain that this would not do, White proceeded to modernize the factory. He installed new machinery which reduced the number of operators needed. Even though the machines could be run by three people, the union forced him to keep all six on the payroll. Convinced that doing business in Britain was futile, White emigrated to the United States. After Mrs. Thatcher came to power, he divided his time between New York and London.[44]

Unproductive activity, though, wasn't the exclusive preserve of trade unionists. Martin Sorrell (who eventually went on to become the head of WPP, a giant marketing group) returned to Britain after an MBA at Harvard and some work experience in America. He took a position as finance director of an advertising agency, Saatchi & Saatchi. Given punitive tax laws, he had to find new incentives to stimulate employees. So Sorrell devised a scheme of leasing suits (and not just gray-flannel suits) to copywriters, designers, and executives. Once the suits were worn, Sorrell depreciated them as used goods. As a result, he could sell the clothing to staff members for a pound—a bargain on anyone's balance sheet. He worked out a similar arrangement to supply carpets for their homes.[45] Clever, yes; productive, no (except for the rag trade). But this was the kind of financial shuffling the tax system inadvertently encouraged.

I X

WHILE THE LABOUR AND CONSERVATIVE PARTIES CONCEIVED plans to rebuild the British economy, some questioned whether the pursuit of productivity was itself desirable. This was largely an issue for professional people who lived in a cozy, comfortable world and could afford to harbor such concerns. They could afford to place a low priority on industrial renewal. But such attitudes did little to help those who struggled to make a living and lacked the wherewithal to enjoy Britain's pleasures. Surely there was no lack of goodwill among intellectuals who wanted working people to participate in the good life they themselves so enjoyed. How could this come about without a strong economy and a social conscience to match?

The dream of a "civilized existence" in a charming, old society drew American expatriates (among others) to Britain. There they found a welcome respite from a competitive, driven world in which it seemed that every family would soon have its own shopping mall. When I arrived in London as a student, I found it hard to resist a country in which the bus conductress called me "love." The man who sold me the morning newspaper had the sense of humor (and social nuance) to call me "Guv" when I took *The Times* or "Comrade" when I reached for the *Guardian*. My list of British virtues was unoriginal but long. Large public achievements and small private pleasures both had a place. Socialized medicine and safe public transportation, affordable theater and interesting television, small shops and fresh bread, milk delivery and cream teas—all these made British life seem eminently "civilized." On rare hot summer afternoons when the sun shone unabated in an unblemished sky, it seemed that England's endless green would endure all manner of hardship. It was too easy to forget how fragile was the engine which fueled this realm.

Its weakness came to the fore during the Heath government (1970–73). Like Harold Wilson, Edward Heath was born in 1916 and came from the lower middle class. The son of a builder, he was a grammar school boy bent on self-improvement. He spent much of his time reading in his room and showed little inclination to see family visitors when they arrived. On one occasion, when his mother worried that he was working too hard, he supposedly told her: "Mother, sometimes I don't think you *want* me to get on."[46] Brought up on the Kent coast, the man who finally brought Britain into the European Community grew up looking out across the Channel, unlike the land-locked Iron Lady.

It was Heath rather than Thatcher who broke the mold of the old-style Tory. He was the first modern leader of the party who was not a product of the upper or upper middle class and the public schools. For his efforts, he found himself lumbered with the nickname "The Grocer" (which shows how contemptuously the squires regarded Mrs. Thatcher's people). This marked his roots and his mentality as being different and inferior. In fact, though, Heath was no more vulgar than he was narrow. An organ scholar at Balliol College, he was a highly cultured man. Still he had to endure, but managed to transcend, the snobbery of those whose only cachet was high birth. What made Heath's rise more difficult was that he tended to be shy and unsociable. Kindly and devoted to his friends, he could also be prickly and abrasive. These were traits that did no politician any good.[47] He was better at getting on than fitting in.

Like Wilson, Heath believed in modernization and was something of a technocrat. Heath too had been disturbed by the unemployment of the 1930s. However, he offered a very different cure for economic torpor. He proposed a free market philosophy based on a hands-off attitude to state intervention. So he started out as the purported dragon-slayer of collectivism. But he became first its victim and then its advocate. Already by 1970, Heath was granting special exemptions from his stated principles. Far from refusing to subsidize ailing firms, he bailed out Rolls Royce through nationalization. For good measure, he restored Upper Clyde Shipbuilder's subsidies. In 1972, he retreated from other promises. Faced with deepening recession, rising unemployment, and wage inflation, he made his infamous "U-turn." Panicked about the political consequences, and indeed the human costs, of his policies, the Prime Minister made an embarrassingly fast about-face.

Heath abandoned market economics in favor of what had become business as usual in postwar Britain—centralized economic management. In short, he did almost everything he said he would not do. Far from refusing to countenance state intervention in managing supply and demand, he instituted an incomes policy. Far from disciplining recalcitrant trade unionists, he found himself at the mercy of miners. Their strikes led to power cuts and to the emergency measure of three-day work weeks that began on New Year's Day of 1974. Two million people were out of work. Streets went dark; offices stayed unlit; factories closed. "Heath's Dark Age," as Wilson cleverly called it, helped to bring down his government. When the Prime Minister asked the voters "who ruled Britain?" they answered, "Not you." So Wilson's Labour Party returned to power.

Heath's failures also led to the political ascent of Margaret Thatcher. For the new right, his U-turn was a reprehensible failure of nerve. He had come down from the mountain with the sacred tablets describing the path to the promised land of economic liberty. When the prophet saw the people worshipping the golden calf, he just joined in. Having lost three general elections, however, he was vulnerable, more so than most Tories thought, to a coup. Unmoved by traditional claims of loyalty, Mrs. Thatcher struck where more genteel folk refrained. In 1975, she took on, and brought down, Heath. On the second ballot, she won the leadership of the Conservative Party. Determined to reverse the trend of postwar British history, Mrs. Thatcher and her allies took up the battle against socialism which Churchill had lost in 1945. But the nation she resolved to rebuild was, at best, in a wobbly condition, as events that took place in the autumn of 1976 revealed.

Labour had one more chance.

The British Disease

I

On Tuesday, September 28, 1976, Britain faced a financial crisis which, if unresolved, threatened to destroy international confidence in the country's economy and bring down James Callaghan's minority Labour government. After three decades of extravagant spending and paltry earnings, Britain stood at the precipice. With characteristic restraint, the Tory tabloids announced that Britain was broke. The immediate challenge was to arrest the continuing plunge of the pound against the dollar. Its free fall was yet another dramatic blow to Britain's self-image, a symbol of how far the nation had descended in the eyes of the world. Britain's economic problems went far beyond sterling's slide. Rising inflation, mounting unemployment, continuous labor unrest, and low productivity had undermined the world's faith in Britain. For the moment, though, it was necessary to steady the testy nerves of the financial community in the City of London (and indeed beyond), which was predisposed to believe that socialism would mean ruin for them if not misery for all.[1]

The two men charged with solving the crisis were the

Right Honorable Denis Healey, Chancellor of the Exchequer, and Gordon Richardson, Governor of the Bank of England. A dark-haired man with an imperious frame and no less imperious mind, Healey was then fifty-nine years old. A lover of the arts and a skilled linguist, he was known, among other things, for his knowledge of international relations. Richardson, fair and attractive, with aristocratic looks which belied his provincial roots, was an extremely able and cultured barrister. He had come to the Bank after a ten-year stint as chairman of an eminent merchant bank, Schroeder Wagg. Both Healey and Richardson had risen from relatively modest backgrounds to positions of great distinction within the British establishment. Friendships between London bankers and Labour politicians were unusual, but the two worked well together, enjoying a relationship of "creative tension," in Healey's words.[2]

Whether the looming crisis would provoke earnest cooperation or mutual accusation was unclear. In any case, the Chancellor and the Governor had little time to reach an accord, for Healey was about to board a plane bound for Hong Kong. He was set to attend the Commonwealth Finance Ministers Conference before going on to the annual meeting of the International Monetary Fund (IMF) in Manila. Unable to agree on a package of measures to ease mounting panic, Healey and Richardson decided to continue their dissuasions en route to Heathrow Airport.

I I

IT WAS A WARM, BRIGHT AUTUMN DAY, A FITTING END TO A glorious summer that would be remembered for years thereafter by those who relished sunbathing at lunchtime in London parks, wearing light clothing usually reserved for holidays abroad, and eating outside. Familiar with the sights of the city and distracted by the predicament they faced, there was little time for Healey and Richardson to scrutinize what they saw as their official car headed for the airport. The journey was telling, nonetheless. For it furnished tangible, if unwanted, evidence of Britain's sharp decline as well as poignant reminders of past greatness. It also revealed a declining nation burdened by an image of historic grandeur out of sync with its current status; a nation with a dignified facade unmatched by internal efficiency; a nation on a long spending spree which it could not pay for; and a nation hampered by a gulf between the opulent life of the rich and the deprived world of the poor. These facts were at the heart of the crisis the two men were trying to resolve.

From their car, Healey and Richardson could have seen a Britain they knew well, a venerable world of historic grandeur. Had they departed for Heathrow from the Treasury, they would have traversed Whitehall and Westminster, the ancient citadels of British supremacy. This precinct of stone edifices with neoclassical or Baroque facades descended from Trafalgar Square down Whitehall to Westminster Abbey. The visible remains of the greatest empire of modern times endured after its colonies finally had escaped from British dominion. Dispersed throughout the Royal City of Westminster were architectural vestiges of imperial rule. The grand Admiralty Arch guards the entrance to the Mall and Nelson's Column springs up from the middle of Trafalgar Square. Darkened with soot and weathered by age, the gravitas and grace of the great public buildings seemed undiminished. Closer inspection of the ancient seat of government's elegant frontages, though, revealed signs of faded glory and frayed grandeur, unwelcome emblems of Britain's decay.

The Houses of Parliament dominated the riverfront. Massive and asymmetrical, their vaulting towers lurched above a three-floor facade. There was perhaps no more picturesque sight in London than this silhouette seen from the south bank of the Thames against a dark sky perforated by city lights. But now the new Palace of Westminster was obscured, covered with scaffolding. Teams of workmen sandblasted the stones to restore their rich original hue. No repair work on Big Ben could stop the bells which tolled for Britain. It was easier to refurbish the seats of power than to arrest the nation's undignified slide. The state opening of Parliament was due to take place in a few weeks. It would show that Britain was now better known for theatrical splendor than political supremacy. The Gentleman Usher of the Black Rod summons the Commons to listen to the Queen's speech. The mystique of archaic rites delighted foreign tourists, but to what avail? Such ceremonies, however impressive, only postponed the moment when the Chancellor would have to defend his economic policies in the House.

Yet few visitors to Whitehall and Westminster failed to be impressed by Britain's long-envied political tradition. It was difficult not to be swayed by the old myths glorifying the historic continuity of the unwritten English Constitution, the superiority of parliamentary institutions, and the administrative genius of the ruling class. The present state of the nation was not so reassuring, however. Growing pressure for devolution, meaning greater self-rule for Scotland and Wales, threatened the United Kingdom's integrity. For all the intellectual power and polish of mandarins with first-class degrees from Oxford and Cambridge, the Civil Service was under fire for inefficiency, obfuscation, and exclusiveness. Britain's much-vaunted political achievements did not jive with the fact that no government, no group, no party, and no person had discovered the means, or the will, to reverse a century of gradual, relative economic decline.

Moving from Parliament Street to Great George Street and then west along Birdcage Walk, the car would have passed Wellington Barracks on the left and on the right St. James's Park, the favorite resort of Charles II and his many dogs. Then on to the Mall, the grand boulevard that led to Buckingham Palace. There battalions of tourists flooded the gates as they awaited the Changing of the Guard. Yet the royal precincts preserved an aura of splendor more in keeping with an imperial past than an uncertain present.

III

DRIVING ALONG BUCKINGHAM PALACE ROAD, MONUMENTAL buildings dropped out of sight. The wide street still boasted nineteenth-century architecture with attractive ornaments, lion-shaped sconces, and wrought-iron balustrades. Yet arriving at Victoria Station, Britain's railway link with the Continent, was unpleasant. Tourists found themselves in a dingy quarter of souvenir shops, dirty pavements, and cracked roads which only looked sound compared to the giant potholes of bankrupt New York. The message was sad but clear: Britain had seen better days.

Nevertheless, islands of wealth and inlets of prosperity still flourished in the capital. Had Healey and Richardson paused to look out the car window as they moved through the West End, they would have seen another, and more affluent, Britain. For socialism had not ruined the rich. If their driver had taken them past the British Airways City Terminal and Victoria Bus Station, within minutes they would have been in the world of "great houses" described by H. G. Wells and C. P. Snow. The squares and terraces of aristocratic Belgravia were an august enclave of elegant residences built on the Grosvenor Estate in the mid-nineteenth century. Belgravia betrayed few signs of how ominous Britain's economic condition had become. Indeed, it reminded onlookers that inherited wealth was not confined to Victorian novels; a small cadre of powerful aristocratic families still owned much of London's choicest property.

Consider Eaton Square, the largest in London. Its residents included those like the Bellamys of *Upstairs, Downstairs* whose deaths would be recorded in *The Times*. Vulgar ostentation the British rejected, but the discreet display they perfected. Belgravia's white stucco mansions had six floors of spacious rooms and impressive facades. Decorated with balustrades and balconies, columns and cornices, pediments and porticos, these grandiose homes announced the elevated station and refined taste of their owners. A certain splendor remained. Yet outward dignity often prevailed at the cost of internal efficiency. Even hugely expensive properties sometimes lacked central heating. Instead they relied on gas fireplaces, which were more gentle and picturesque than effective.

From Belgravia, it took only a short time to drive to Knightsbridge. A number of leading department stores lined the Brompton Road. Catering to tourists and natives, they suggested that the British were better at consuming or, at least, selling, luxury goods, than at producing enough to make their way in the world. The passion for acquisition seemed undiminished even as the nation's place in the world dropped. But much had changed. Now many of the best customers were Arab sheiks, who descended on London in the mid-1970s with immense capital, masked wives, and alien manners that even the Foreign Office's would-be Lawrences of Arabia found difficult to romanticize. The undisputed top of the range was Harrods, a store which prided itself on being a national institution. An imposing building with a terracotta facade and towering dome, it was located on a huge island site on a city block that it had gradually swallowed up. Outside the store, black cabs and chauffeured Rolls-Royces and Jaguars fought for spaces while liveried Harrods "Green men" struggled to keep order.

Harrods betrayed few manifest signs of the economic crisis that the Chancellor and the Governor grappled with as they drove to Heathrow. In fact, the sterling crisis was a godsend to American tourists who came away with green and gold shopping bags. The plunging pound meant that the dollars they exchanged at Harrods' bank were worth more.

"Enter a different world," suggested Harrods, with typical modesty. Dignity was sometimes more abundant than efficiency, though. So customers found out during the hot summer of 1976, when the air conditioning failed. Even a quick tour of the ground floor suggested that if the British were not themselves materialistic, they were extraordinarily tolerant of the whims of foreigners. The famous Food Halls carried more than 15,000 lines and managed to sell 3 tons of smoked salmon, ¼ ton of caviar, 11 tons of whole and baby Stiltons, 9 tons of chocolate, and 24,000 bottles of Perrier in a single December.[3]

Further down the Brompton Road were the monuments of another Britain, the cultural world in which both Healey and Richardson moved easily. Past a number of pubs, the Prince of Wales and the Bunch of Grapes, and Gloriette, a Viennese-style café, were the glories of South Kensington. Amid the Italianate villas stood the Victoria and Albert Museum, the Science Museum, and the Natural History Museum, a Romanesque building laced with tan and blue brickwork. A cultural elite presided over these institutions. Insulated by public monies from the shocks of the marketplace, especially under Labour rule, the mandarins had little inclination to worry about the nation's productive capacities. Or so they thought.

I V

CULTURAL LANDMARKS AND TOURIST ATTRACTIONS DISAPpeared from view as the journey to Heathrow continued along the Cromwell Road. All along the route, new development was rare, the bulk of buildings Victorian or interwar. Moving beyond central London to the metropolis's outlying areas (as in many cities), the townscape became depressing, the houses dilapidated, the shopfronts tatty, and the roads unkempt.

Had Healey and Richardson looked out from the car, they would have seen a threadbare Britain whose residents had few good economic prospects. This was a world of queues rather than ladders—far removed from Whitehall's grandeur, Belgravia's luxury, and Knightsbridge's opulence. The Welfare State had taken some of the sting out of poverty, but the chasm dividing the affluent and the indigent persisted.

At the outskirts of the city en route to Heathrow were social groups who lived on the margins, able to survive but not prevail. Alongside the A4, the road passing through Hammersmith and Chiswick, there was a torrent of chimneys attached to modest terraced houses, some splashed with half-timbering, others with stucco. Whatever their aesthetic shortcomings, they stood up well against the huge tower blocks of council flats, public housing projects that flanked the road. These abominable structures were extremely unpopular with a people, many of whom hated living high off the ground. More notable for good intentions than satisfactory results, they housed working people and unemployed people. Beneficiaries of the Welfare State, they could rent, but not purchase, flats of their own. Small, dreary apartments without character or ornament, they were in no danger of being mistaken for the drawing rooms of Belgravia. In these holding tanks, it was difficult to avoid despair. The only consolation was that the commitment to social welfare survived, for the time being at least. But would Britain be able, or willing, to pay for such programs if its financial condition continued to degenerate?

Leaving the A4 brought some visual relief. Then the car moved onto the M4, the Great West Road stretching to

Wales. A fairly attractive three-lane motorway with lush green banks, it was free of the spate of billboards, gas stations, and fast-food restaurants that disfigured American highways. The M4 went through Hounslow, passing the Post House, a styleless hotel whose only virtue was the view from the top-floor bar at night. Then, finally, you followed the blue signs for Heathrow, exiting on the left. It was a relatively old air-port with three large terminals, a facility strained beyond ca-pacity and so plagued by robberies of luggage that it was nicknamed Thieves' Row. Iron and glass buildings without signature, Heathrow's terminals were vaguely modern but utterly unadventurous. They failed to capture or even reach for the romance of flight embodied in Eero Saarinen's eagle-shaped TWA terminal at Kennedy Airport.

Heathrow offered further evidence of Britain's tattered economy. The airport was the hub of BOAC (British Over-seas Airways Corporation), later reincarnated as British Air-ways. This firm epitomized the ills at the heart of Britain's decline. From its founding in 1939, BOAC was a nationalized company, "no mere capitalist business, the be-all and end-all of which is profits and dividends," as the Labour politician Herbert Morrison put it. Public corporations did not use the vulgar word "profit," preferring instead the term "surplus"— as if they were storing up nuts for winter. But unlike squirrels subject to the laws of nature, British Airways and its brethren had no great need to practice such economy. Indeed, nation-alized companies employed so many workers that they were almost untouchable politically, especially when Labour was in power.

High-minded devotion to the public good was an unobjec-tionable goal, but British Airways' service was slovenly and inefficient. No wonder that it sometimes retained a small "surplus." For the airline enjoyed a virtual monopoly in its market. BOAC got away with charging prices that ensured that most members of the great tax-paying British public could not afford to "fly the flag" they funded. So frustrating was the task of running the airline, which was subject to frequent strikes from pilots, engineers, and ground staff, that from 1945 to 1970 it had twelve chairmen. Among them was an admiral, Sir Matthew Slattery, who remarked, "I think the way it is expected to operate is bloody crazy."[4]

V

BUT WHEN HEALEY AND RICHARDSON FINALLY ARRIVED AT Heathrow, they had far more pressing matters on their minds than the quality of British Airway's service.

Moving through the crowded terminal, they headed for the relative calm and comfort of the VIP lounge to wait for Healey's flight to board. There they learned that in disastrous early morning trading the pound had fallen an additional 4.4 cents against the dollar, and showed no signs of bottoming out. Where would it end? In front of the usual crowd of major and minor notables, prosperous managers and tourists, two men rushed out of the lounge. Had they simply been ordinary victims of forgetfulness or incompetence who lost their passports or left their luggage and tickets at home, their behavior would have been unremarkable. But it was the Chancellor of the Exchequer and the Governor of the Bank of England who bolted without warning or explanation.

When Healey learned that the pound was still falling, he quickly called Prime Minister Callaghan, who was about to leave his hotel in Blackpool to deliver a speech to the Labour Party Conference, opening that day. Healey told him that the Bank was considering a substantial sale of its dollar holdings to support the tumbling pound. Callaghan argued against the plan, preferring that they sweat it out. Only fifteen minutes before his flight for Hong Kong was due to take off, Healey had a sudden change of heart. He abruptly switched his plans and decided to return to London immediately. Healey justified his behavior by explaining that if he took the plane, he would be cut off from all contact with London for seventeen hours.[5] But he knew this before he arrived at Heathrow. And he also knew that the Bank of England had predicted the pound would fall to $1.50. For onlookers, his turnabout amounted to something little short of public panic. So extraordinary was Healey's conduct that when news of his canceled trip reached the already nervous City of London, it went into a hysterical frenzy which lasted for two days. However ill-advised his decision, it took courage to return to London. Now he had to face the music, and it was bound to be dissonant Schoenberg rather than mellifluous Mozart, performed with a halfhearted orchestra for an audience who had come for something completely different.

Disheartened and depressed, the usually ebullient Healey was in the midst of the worst period of his political life. Doubling back from Heathrow Airport, he and Gordon Richardson headed for London. The journey's end promised no easy solution, though. For if Healey failed to restore confidence in the economy, everything he had devoted his political career to would be under siege. Bon vivant and man of the world that Healey was, he did not return to London to safeguard the privileges of the rich. Longtime Member of Parliament and Cabinet minister, he did not return hoping to revive the fine anachronisms of a dead Empire.

The world he tried to save was the world of the Welfare State. Denis Healey was a representative man of the postwar era, one of the best and brightest of the Labour movement. Collectivist politics aside, he was by temperament an individualist. On childhood jaunts in the Yorkshire Moors he walked paces ahead of his family, a habit which hardly faded in later life. Comradeship and cooperation were lessons Captain Healey learned from his wartime experience: "I am only one of the hundreds of young men, now in the forces, who long for the opportunity to realise their political ideals by actively fighting an election for the Labour Party. These men in their turn represent millions of soldiers, sailors and airmen who want socialism and who have been fighting magnificently to save a world in which socialism is possible." Only a more glorious future could make up for the annihilation of the past Healey had witnessed.[6] Winning a seat in the Commons in 1952 for a constituency in industrial Leeds provided his opportunity.

For Healey, the quest for social justice was a personal crusade rather than an abstract enthusiasm. He was not, by birth, one of the great and good intent on helping the unfortunate. The Chancellor of the Exchequer came from far humbler roots. As a child he lived in London, but not the London of Belgravia mansions attended by family servants. Until he was five, the family home was a wooden hut lit with candles, located in a makeshift neighborhood built as temporary housing for armament workers in World War I in Woolwich, a nondescript South London suburb. Unlike Karl Marx, he did not have to go to the Reading Room of the British Museum to study the impact of the Industrial Revolution on the working class.[7]

The grandson of an Irish tailor, and son of an engineer, Healey grew up in Keighley, a gray stone town in the West Riding of Yorkshire where his father served as principal of the Technical School. It was a region of wool and worsted factories that rose to prominence early in the nineteenth century, but was long past its heyday during his youth. The decline of the industrial North did not impede the progress of all its children, though. Healey's path to the top came through education. Like others with more talent than status, and more determination than money, he did not attend one of the great public schools that cultivated the British establishment. His ascent began with a scholarship to Bradford Grammar School, a distinguished and competitive institution ruled by merit and aspiration. As an exhibitioner at Balliol College, Oxford, Healey read "Mods and Greats," a mixture of classical literature, ancient history, and philosophy.

It was at Balliol, a college with long-standing links to government, that Healey cultivated his passion for politics. Left-wing politics was the natural choice for an enlightened intellectual from a generation that tended to construe right-wing views as a sign of stupidity, if not downright wickedness. A political radical, Healey joined the Communist Party, but age tempered his youthful ardor. Idealistic but skeptical, he was not a true believer lost on the road to Utopia. Aligned with the right wing of the Labour Party, Healey became a social democrat devoted to piecemeal progress and incremental change. "Socialism emphasizes the community rather than the individual, consensus rather than confrontation; public welfare rather than private gain; it puts the quality of life before the quantity of goods."[8] It was this vision of Britain which the sterling crisis could destroy. An intellectual in politics, Healey happily followed the logic of argument to its inconvenient conclusions; the only cheeks he turned belonged to his unfortunate opponents. Not a man to trifle with, his ability to gore his adversaries would be useful in the debates of the coming months.

But Healey now needed a plan. Returning with Richardson to the Treasury, an early Victorian building graced with marble staircases and decorated with busts and paintings of honored predecessors, he could turn for advice to senior civil servants. Distinguished by a collegiate atmosphere not far removed from the whiff of Oxbridge common rooms and high tables, the Treasury was an informal world whose residents were known for devotion to classical music and vigorous argument. The Treasury prided itself on being an aristocracy of talent rather than birth, composed of highly educated meritocrats who were the pick of the Civil Service entrants. Its Permanent Secretary was the formidable Sir

Douglas Wass. A grammar school boy who had been at Nottingham High School with Gordon Richardson, then a Cambridge wrangler who became involved in weapons research during the war, Wass set great store by diplomacy and tact.[9] Resented inside and outside Whitehall for its power and arrogance, the Treasury became a favorite scapegoat in the mid-1970s for national decline. Critics from all shades of the political spectrum assailed its princes for amateur management, consensus policies, and a bias against production. All the same, Healey could count on Wass and his staff to set forth the available options without "enthusiasm" but with "energy."[10]

But the final decision rested with Healey. For the moment, he may as well have been alone. And, indeed, he was virtually alone; James Callaghan and his Cabinet colleagues were in Blackpool. Besides, Healey's bullying style had made him enemies on both sides of the House of Commons who would be certain to enjoy the prospect of seeing him falter at Question Time when Parliament opened. A blunder now could destroy his political career, ending any hopes he had of moving next door from the Chancellor's residence to 10 Downing Street. If he failed to stop the panic in the City, there would be little talk of the collective responsibility discussed in the handbooks on Cabinet government. The consequences would be grave, nevertheless, because there was no assurance that the minority Labour government could command the votes necessary to survive a motion of no confidence. It would be futile for Healey to complain that the markets were hysterical, the newspapers prejudiced, and the Tories implicated in the sterling crisis. This was a game of perceptions, but a game he could ill afford to concede. Nothing short of a dramatic gesture would restore international confidence in Britain. Three hours after his return from Heathrow, Healey finalized his plan.

The following morning he called a press conference. He

announced that the Labour government planned to apply to the International Monetary Fund (IMF) for an immense loan, $3.9 billion, by far the largest in the organization's history. Healey's move succeeded at once in steadying the frenzied markets. This was not the end of the matter, for there was no doubt that it would be difficult to negotiate an agreement all the concerned parties could live with. Certainly the IMF would demand huge cuts in public spending, just as certain to upset Labour politicians and trade union leaders whose support was by no means certain. It promised a field day for the fledgling, and not yet very impressive, Tory leader Margaret Thatcher, who hoped to capitalize on Labour's misfortune.

Going to the IMF for a bail-out was a far more serious matter than an earnest chat with an exceptionally well positioned bank manager. Founded with the assistance of John Maynard Keynes, this organization was supposed to be a federation of governments rather than a cabal of bankers. Its purpose was not to make the world safe for plutocracy. World economic stability and growth were its goals. When the IMF was founded in 1945, Britain was still one of the three "Great Powers" which decided the fate of nations. In 1976, however, Britain found itself in a far less enviable position. Like a proud gentleman from a distinguished family fallen on hard times, the Callaghan government was forced to curry the favor of wealthy relatives. By any measure, it was humiliating for Britain to be seen as a beggar nation. Who would have thought that it would be counted with the likes of Mexico, Portugal, and Italy, all of which were in the midst of IMF rescue operations? Fiscal embarrassment and mismanagement might be expected from former colonies, but what justification could Britain offer for its embarrassing plight? The disaster at Suez had revealed that without its Empire, Britain was no longer a major power except in the minds of its leaders. The IMF loan application suggested that the pio-

neer of the Industrial Revolution had become a charity case,
or, at least, an also-ran in an economic race which it had not
run nearly hard enough.

VI

THE IMF CRISIS, AS IT CAME TO BE KNOWN, BEGAN WITH A SE-
ries of miscalculations.

In February 1976, the Bank of England and the Treasury
had concluded that sterling was overvalued. Unless the currency was nudged down, it would hamper the economy by
making British export prices artificially high. When foreign
exchange dealers became convinced, however, that the Bank
favored devaluation, they sold sterling. A gentle descent
turned into a violent fall. Sterling plummeted below $2.00 for
the first time in early March and hovered around $1.80 by
mid-April.

The measures taken to relieve the crisis succeeded only in
worsening it. Fearful of the consequences of a run on the
pound, the Bank spent substantial reserves to strengthen it.
The unassailable civil servants of the Treasury overesti-
mated the deficit by £2 billion. To be sure, a forecasting error
was hardly an original sin in a science that sometimes seemed
closer to astrology than astronomy. But this was a gigantic
blunder. It gave credence to critics who questioned the nu-
meracy of the highly touted, finely educated, and well-paid
individuals who thought of themselves as the pinnacle of
Whitehall. More to the point, the blunder led Healey to believe that the condition of Britain was worse than it actually
was and to plan accordingly. No wonder that he promised to
do for economic forecasters what the Boston Strangler had
done for traveling salesmen.[11]

In the meantime, the Chancellor had to soothe the manic
mood of the markets. In June 1976, Healey obtained a $5.3 bil-

lion credit from the Group of Ten industrial nations. It was, he reassured the House of Commons, a loan without strings. What he failed to note was that it contained enough rope to force Britain into the hands of foreign bankers if it failed to repay the loan within six months. To do so, Healey had to convince the Cabinet (which he did with difficulty) to assent to £1 billion in spending cuts. During the long, hot, and dry summer of 1976, the Bank of England used a considerable portion of the credit to shore up sterling. When it stopped intervening in the markets in early September, sterling flagged once more.

The day of reckoning had arrived. The Callaghan government could have paid off the balance-of-payments deficit, £3 billion, and the projected budget deficit, £10.5 billion, only by dropping even further into debt. But this would have further weakened international confidence in Britain. As government officials were quick to point out, the crisis was not Labour's sole responsibility. Healey's Conservative predecessor, Anthony Barber, had overheated the economy in search of quick growth. So Healey inherited a fragile position. The sterling crisis also stemmed partly from the fact that the pound was still an international reserve currency second only to the dollar. Its high status was another mark of continuing delusions of grandeur, for it rested on the historic strength of the City of London rather than the current position of the British economy. This vestige of better days had become a dubious honor because it made sterling especially vulnerable to economic vicissitudes. In the eyes of the public, the fine points of economic policy and the useful arts of political maneuvering changed nothing. In popular perceptions the sterling crisis augured national ruin.

VII

JUST AS THE PERIOD FROM 1910 TO 1914 WITNESSED THE "strange death of Liberal England," the brief but hardly shining moment from 1976 to 1979 witnessed the unexpected demise of Socialist England. The unraveling of the socialist dream was not really apparent at the time. It had its amusing moments, but it was, in essence, a tragic drama rather than a comic scenario. The leaders of the Labour government were generally honorable, intelligent persons moved by a vision of social justice as well as by a desire to hold on to political power. Trapped in historical circumstances difficult to predict, much less master, they did not fall because of malevolence or stupidity.

Rather, Labour was undone by its own noble ideals. In classical fashion, it had the weaknesses of their strengths. Authentic champion of the working class, determined to help the weak and disadvantaged, Labour's economic and spiritual foundation was the trade union movement. But cooperation with the unions constrained the choices open to the Labour Party. With their unqualified support, it might have sponsored painful changes that went against the grain of socialist principles and short-term economic self-interest. This was not to be, however. The Callaghan government also failed to shift resources to new industries for fear of offending their working-class partners. For all the talk about industrial regeneration, it protected declining industries in the North and the Midlands, its political heartland.

Good intentions were not everything. In 1974, Tony Benn, Secretary of State for Industry, pushed the Wilson government to invest in a workers' motorcycle co-operative in Meriden, a Midlands town near Coventry. Formerly part of Norton–Villiers–Triumph, it was singled out for closure, but workers kept it open. Civil servants argued that Meriden was not a viable enterprise. Nevertheless, Benn managed to win support for the plan despite opposition. To be fair, there were some reasons for optimism. The world motorcycle market was strong and export prospects to the United States seemed especially attractive. For Benn himself, Meriden was an opportunity to see the realization of his new passion for workers' control. As a result, the government invested some £5 million in the co-op in the form of grants and loans.

In August 1974, Benn and his American-born wife Caroline (they had met at Oxford) paid a visit to the co-op. In his diary, he noted: "It was a fantastic spectacle. There was the freshly painted factory with an old picket tent and brazier on the gate and a couple of bikes out front." Going around the works and talking with the workers, Benn concluded enthusiastically that it "was just like going round a Chinese factory—they were speaking with such confidence about their own skill and their work and how they wouldn't need as many supervisors and so on." Over tea in the canteen, Benn made a speech explaining the government's (more likely his own) industrial policy. He was touched when the men sang "For He's a Jolly Good Fellow."[12]

But the Meriden co-operative failed. Far more than £5 million was needed to make the factory efficient. Workers' control may have reduced alienation, but it did not compensate for a lack of managerial skill or business expertise. In May 1981, Mrs. Thatcher used Meriden as an example of the ills of British industry. While the co-op produced more than the Norton plant to which it was once connected (this was an achievement), it could not begin to approach the productivity that a Japanese competitor, Yamaha, reached through robotics. Finally, Sir Keith Joseph wrote off the co-op's debts.[13]

About the failings of socialism, free market right-wingers were often wrong and always hyperbolic. On one point, though, they were right: A nation cannot distribute what it does not produce. Britain's economic growth was respectable enough in absolute terms. Indeed, it was higher at many times during the postwar period than it had been before advent of socialism. The economy was not strong enough, however, to fuel extensive social spending. Britain lagged behind competitors crippled by war but resurgent in peace. The caring society enshrined in the Welfare State improved the lot of the unfortunate and neglected, but it did so at a cost. Kind to a fault, British socialism was unable to withstand mounting pressures, ultimately failing its dependents.

In the autumn of 1976, Britain suffered from a severe case of economic woes apparent throughout the Western world. Unemployment was at 5.6 percent, an unacceptably high figure for a Labour government committed to full employment. Then there was the puzzling problem of how to overcome stagflation. Inflation had been cut in half, but was still running at more than 12 percent and threatened to spiral up again if strikes led to high-priced wage settlements. Britain's economic growth was substantially below its European competitors, if only marginally lower than the United States. Even Italy, a nation better known in Britain for comic opera than business acumen, was bypassing its standard of living. According to Treasury calculations, public spending devoured about 60 percent of gross domestic product. This estimate also proved incorrect (by about 10 percent).

Adversarial industrial relations were at the heart of Britain's economic problems. Both management and labor protected their own interests with predictably disastrous results, amounting to more 2.3 million lost days from 1964 to 1967, and 6.8 million in 1969 alone. It was especially difficult to solve disputes because of the fragmentation of the trade union movement. There were 117 separate bargaining units in Britain as opposed to 15 German counterparts. The intransigence of organized labor received more than its fair share of media attention. To be sure, industrial strife made a more colorful story than technological backwardness. The problems, however, were hardly imaginary. It was an ironic sign of the times that the term "industrial action" referred to strikes, work stoppages, slow-downs. In 1972, Harold Wilson had forged a "Social Contract" with the trade unions. They exchanged voluntary wage restraint for hospitable policies and government access. But this proved to be a worthless deal in the end. Wages rose by 26.4 percent in 1974, booting up inflation to intolerable levels. This trend alarmed Jack Jones, the left-wing secretary of the powerful Transport Workers' Union. He won approval in September 1975 from the Trade Union Congress for a new agreement, also voluntary, a universal flat-rate increase of six pounds a week or less. By the autumn of 1976, however, the relative industrial peace of the past two years seemed to be over. There was trouble yet again at British Leyland, the nationalized automobile manufacturer; an all-out national strike threatened by the National Seamen's Union; and a strike declared at Ford on the same day Healey announced the IMF loan application.

The sterling crisis became an emblem of Britain's decline. It was extraordinarily difficult for Healey to restore confidence in the British economy because since the early sixties commentators had presented Britain as a society on the verge of a breakdown. The nation was afflicted with a set of ills popularly known as the "British disease," a term used by *The Times* in 1971 and echoed throughout the higher journalism. "Hardly anyone needs to be told now," wrote Vermont Royster in 1975 in the *Wall Street Journal,* "that Britain is the sick man of Europe."[14] Critical voices were not confined to the right. Anthony Howard, editor of the left-wing *New Statesman,* depicted a Britain "without any bearings, let alone a sense of direction," its "economic policy in ruins," and its "leaders playing an increasingly ludicrous game of blind-man's bluff."[15]

Political commitments shaped views of what went wrong and how to set it right. The household gods the various parties worshipped determined the devils they condemned. The Tories attributed Britain's economic decline primarily to two culprits. One was the Welfare State: it undercut individual initiative, innovation, and enterprise by diminishing the profit motive. The other was the trade unions: their crime was ruthlessly using strikes to serve their interests at the expense of the nation's. Not so, replied Labour. It cited a variety of factors for Britain's weak economic performance, among them the inefficiency of British management; the proclivity of City bankers to invest in foreign rather than domestic markets; and an unjust, rigid system dedicated to the pursuit of inequality from the royal family to the "deferential worker."[16]

VIII

THE WAY FORWARD FOR BRITAIN, AND THE OBSTACLES IMPEDING it: this was James Callaghan's theme in the address he gave to the Labour Party Conference as Healey and Richardson rushed back to the Treasury from Heathrow. The site was Blackpool, a seaside resort built in the nineteenth century when the textile towns of Lancashire were still prosperous. Long favored by working-class holiday makers before they could afford package tours to the Costa del Sol, Blackpool had a lengthy pier and pebble beaches redolent with the smell of fish, chips, and vinegar.

Jim Callaghan had waited thirty years to stand before the Labour Party Conference as Prime Minister. By then, he was an exceptionally experienced politician, sixty-two years of age. He had already held three great offices of state: Home Secretary, Foreign Secretary, and Chancellor of the Exchequer. This was particularly impressive given his roots. The grandson of a ship's captain, and the son of a chief petty officer, he had little formal education but succeeded, nevertheless, in passing the Civil Service exam. A strong union man, he believed that the purpose of government was to improve the lot of the poor and the underprivileged. What he came to realize by the autumn of 1976 was that Labour had to find a new means to preserve, and extend, the achievements of the Welfare State.

Britain was living on borrowed time, and time had run out. "For too long this country—all of us, yes this Conference too," Callaghan told the would-be faithful, "has been ready to settle for borrowing money abroad to maintain our standards of life, instead of grappling with the fundamental problem of British industry." No longer was it possible to apply the old Keynesian magic. For spending your way out of a recession only exacerbated the twin evils of unemployment and inflation. These plagues fell most heavily on those least able to stand them, and these were the people that Callaghan wanted to protect at all costs. Salvaging the socialist dream that he had fought for all his life demanded new methods. His proposed antidote was to balance the creation of wealth with its fair distribution, rebuild industry by reducing labor costs and renewing technologies, and bring down public spending. All of these measures depended on the cooperation of the trade unions. This "grim and courageous" speech, as *The Times* called it, won the approval of Western leaders. Among them was President Gerald Ford, who telephoned Callaghan to congratulate him.[17]

The Prime Minister's monetarist message received a far more tepid response from the Labour Party Conference. Its poor reception dramatized the internal conflicts which made it all the more difficult to find a solution to the IMF crisis, much less to turn around the economy. For all the ritual chanting of "Jerusalem" (the Labour Party's hymn to progress through solidarity), the proceedings of the conference prefigured the socialist war of all against all. Never a slave to economic reality, Tony Benn, the Secretary of State for Energy, was blind to the facts of life. He called for more socialist measures and public ownership when the country could barely meet its current obligations. Far better to turn to a siege economy based on import controls than to make the major spending cuts which the IMF would demand. Such talk led Healey to accuse left-wingers on occasion of being "out of their tiny Chinese minds."[18] Their approach was ludicrous. And yet more sensible politicians were concerned that acceding to IMF limits on public expenditure would jeopardize social welfare.

It was, therefore, no small matter to convince the Cabinet to expose British policy to the scrutiny, let alone the control, of the IMF. Among the constraints which the leadership faced was the distorting power of memory. In 1931, there had also been a run on the pound. Labour legend had it that the fall of Ramsay Macdonald's Labour government and the formation of a National government in its stead was the result of a "banker's ramp" caused by the City of London. Kenneth Morgan, a leading historian of Labour, interpreted it very differently. In his view, the crisis was a result of "the total bankruptcy of the Labour Party in trying to produce a viable or intelligible programme to remedy unemployment or industrial stagnation."[19]

Would the IMF affair be a repeat performance?

I X

DETERMINED TO AVOID THE DIVISIONS THAT AFFLICTED Labour in 1931, James Callaghan held no fewer than twenty-six meetings of his increasingly fractious Cabinet to forge a consensus on the IMF loan.

Keeping peace in the parish had embarrassing consequences. It created a public impression (correct) of a divided, indecisive government. As the Labour champion of the IMF loan, Healey was an embattled man with little support. He had to face the opposition of the left, for whom the IMF was doubly damned because it was seen as a financial arm of the American government, Mammon's men in Washington. Even his centrist colleagues kicked at the prospect of reducing social spending in the name of fiscal stability.

The Prime Minister himself would not show his hand.[20] Surely the situation reminded James Callaghan of his travails as Chancellor. During the sterling crisis of 1967, Harold Wilson had refused to support his pleas for devaluation. Instead, he preferred to indict the "Sell England Short Brigade" in the City, before caving in. Without a majority in the House of Commons, Callaghan feared that any precipitous action would provoke ministerial resignations which might bring down the government. Not until the late autumn did he declare his support for the IMF loan.[21]

Dissent from within and ridicule from without was the daily fare of the Callaghan government during the autumn of 1976. Quarrels in the Cabinet and questions in the Commons faced Healey. He found himself on the firing line defending an uncertain position on an issue not yet agreed on by his colleagues. The Tory Opposition's aim was to use the IMF loan application as a lever to bring down the government, or at least to discredit its economic policies. This came to the fore in a debate in the Commons on November 11. Sir Geoffrey Howe, the Shadow Chancellor, argued that the British people did not want to go on borrowing to maintain their standard of living. They would rather "face the realities of economic life" and make deeper cuts in expenditure than Healey contemplated. The Chancellor responded: "I have always noticed in my political career that those who foul their own nest at some stage in the game dislike the smell; and I know that is the experience of hon. Members opposite."[22] But his retort obscured the fact that both parties had deluded themselves, and the country, into believing an accounting fantasy in which the outflow of cash could exceed its intake without eventually paying a huge penalty.

The Callaghan government was, at best, profoundly ambivalent about the IMF loan application. The promise of political relief was appealing. Yet the political stigma of the begging bowl and the social costs of spending cuts were anything but. The results of such ambiguous sentiments were mighty, but ultimately ineffective, efforts to save face, proudly spurning and then hesitantly courting the IMF. In November 1976, an IMF team arrived in London for negotiations. Its leader was an Englishman, Alan Whittome, a former official of the Bank of England. Checking into their hotel, the team used assumed names as if they were on an espionage mission. Far from being attacked by the natives, they were simply ignored. The Prime Minister refused to allow Healey's Treasury officials to meet with the IMF. He preferred that they cool their heels for a few weeks.

Stalling was partly a rational maneuver on Callaghan's part to get the best deal by not appearing to want any deal. Keeping the IMF waiting, out of indecision or spite, however, was a brilliant example of the politics of passive aggression, providing a minor victory at best. The Callaghan government was not in the position of a high-born Victorian lady who could afford to stall eager suitors with great expectations and meager prospects; or of a wealthy, prudent banker carefully weighing up the collateral of a prospective borrower. This was hardly the time to exercise the old imperial pride. But the handling of the IMF affair threw into high relief habits of denial which were at the core of national decline: the refusal to recognize the dangers of spending more than you earn and the insistence on maintaining a dignified facade in spite of the cost.

The absurdity of the situation attracted the media. Television cameras transmitted to the world the embarrassing spectacle of the IMF team comfortably encamped at Brown's

Hotel off Piccadilly. There they awaited the pleasure of Her Majesty's Dithering Government. In the meantime, though, Whittome's team was not lonely. They received far more attention than they wanted from American government officials. Arthur Burns of the Federal Reserve Board and Ed Yeo of the U.S. Treasury both were determined to force Britain into deep spending cuts. Those who would not save themselves would be saved in spite of themselves.

Still more comical machinations were required to protect wounded national pride. At the end of November, William Simon, the American Secretary of the Treasury, traveled to London to expedite negotiations. He was not a man to be deterred by the fact that he belonged to a lame-duck Ford administration which was soon to be replaced by President-elect Jimmy Carter and his appointees. Nor was he deterred by having to carry out his mission in secret meetings. Hounded by the press, he devised "something rather devious" to avoid surveillance. The venue Simon chose was an unusual but strangely fitting place to fashion an economic policy to suit a once genteel nation that could not pay its bills. He selected Wells of Mayfair, a bespoke tailor catering to those to the manner born and those with the cash handy. This was a ludicrously ironic choice, but it conformed to a certain idea of England common among upper-crust American tourists—a charming but archaic country, once expensive but now on sale. "We met the Treasury people," Simon recalled, "and there was generally a small parade of folks in and out of this tailor and I ended up buying three suits I didn't need; but nonetheless we pretty well set the parameters."[23] This amusing, if outrageous, scene was not part of a Restoration comedy packed with fast exits and sudden concealments. Rather, it was a sad and poignant commentary on the condition of a nation that settled its affairs in so bizarre a manner. No doubt Simon left London a more elegantly dressed man, but he was still unsure whether the British Cabinet would approve the IMF loan.

The day of decision came on Thursday, December 2. At Cabinet, the Prime Minister asked his colleagues one by one for their votes on the IMF loan. He added one proviso, instructing them to agree only if they were willing to support painful cuts. A majority endorsed Healey's position, agreeing to reduce spending by £1 billion the first year and to raise an additional £500 million in revenue by selling British Petroleum (BP) shares.

X

THE IMF AFFAIR ENDED RELATIVELY WELL. THE STERLING CRIsis was resolved and confidence restored. For the moment, Britain stayed on the right edge of the precipice. Tory tabloids indicted the "Chicken Chancellor" for his refusal to make deeper cuts, but in the event Denis Healey drew only half of the IMF loan. Indeed, the government could have repaid it early. His personal stock also recovered. By 1978, he was in a position to succeed Johannes Witeveen as managing director of the IMF.

There was still enormous fall-out, though. No single event provided more dramatic proof of the extent and consequences of the eclipse of British power than the IMF loan. It would be unfair to blame the sterling crisis only on Labour. The Conservatives were also responsible for overspending, and by the time the IMF moved in, spending cuts were already under way. But the fact that Labour was left holding the bag, and little else, delighted Tory critics. They took up the opportunity to question their opponents' managerial ability and economic policies.

The short-term crisis was the product of long-term causes

that remained unresolved. It augured the end of the socialist era that began in 1945 when a victorious but exhausted Britain committed itself to creating a Welfare State. The popular challenge to the dream of equality and justice did not come initially from a philosophical revaluation. Nor did it come from a change of heart, much less a change to heartlessness, on the part of the British people. By the end of 1976 it was unclear, however, whether government could, or should, continue to fund a wide range of social services.

The year 1976 was a turning point which promised, but never quite delivered, a new approach to old social goals. Following the lead of Harold Wilson, Healey moved toward a peaceful accommodation with capitalism. He was the first monetarist Chancellor, and he pioneered privatization with the sale of BP stock. But the capitalist revolution Healey launched was a project Labour was unable or unwilling to complete. It scraped against the grain of socialist philosophy, the perceived interests of the trade unions, and the increasingly militant left-wing radicalism of grass-roots activists. The result was a split in the Labour Party that made it virtually unelectable. In their hearts, Labour leaders had little liking for capitalism and failed to see that it might create enough wealth to provide the basis for a decent life for everyone. In 1976, the Labour right turned the corner, but they kept looking back fondly and sentimentally to the old socialist world, until they finally ran into an iron wall. Margaret Thatcher was one woman with no compunction about the costs of capitalist enterprise and no affection for the socialist order she hoped to dismantle. And so Labour lost a great opportunity: not the chance to worship the free market, as Mrs. Thatcher did, but rather to tame it for the greater good of the country, above all for the people at the bottom.

The chill in the air that overtook Britain in the autumn of 1976 turned into a deep frost during the "Winter of Discontent," the public services strikes of 1978–79. In an epidemic of foolishness, union leaders helped bring down the Labour government as surely as if they had campaigned for Margaret Thatcher. In the end, Callaghan found out the hard way that he should have gone along with trade union reform. "Labour isn't working"—this was the verdict baldly announced in posters designed by Saatchi & Saatchi for the Tories. Even those who disagreed had reason to wonder whether it would ever be "glad, confident morning again."

Spiritless Capitalism

I

DURING THE RUN-UP TO THE GENERAL ELECTION OF 1983, MARgaret Thatcher described the virtues she learned in her father's house:

> We were taught to work jolly hard. We were taught to prove yourself; we were taught self-reliance; we were taught to live within your income. You were taught that cleanliness is next to godliness. You were taught self-respect. You were taught always to give a hand to your neighbour. You were taught tremendous pride in your country.[1]

In an interview with the Prime Minister, Brian Walden, the former Labour MP who was one of her first journalistic champions, called these homely ideals "Victorian values." The phrase stuck with the Prime Minister. It also stuck in the throats of her critics. The left-wing *New Statesman* had a good time poking fun at her. It depicted Mrs. Thatcher on its cover clothed as Maggie Regina, Queen Victoria, tight-lipped, forbidding, and unamused. In a special section of the magazine, socialist historians hammered home how unrealistic Mrs. Thatcher's view of the Victorian age was. And they made clear how undesirable it would be to try to restore so confining a culture. For Britain's power, they insisted, came at the expense of the exploitation of the working class and the oppression of women.[2]

The Victorian legacy was indeed more troublesome an inheritance than Margaret Thatcher imagined. For the Prime Minister's project involved turning back the course of a century of gradual, relative economic decline that had robbed Britain of its role as industrial leader and threatened to undercut its remaining prosperity. What stood in the way of rebuilding the economic base was not simply obsolescent plants, incompetent managers, and hostile workers. There was also a hostility to industrialism rooted in the national past. The spiritlessness of capitalism antagonized intellectuals, but its unspirited performance disturbed businessmen. The split between Britain's business culture and its intellectual culture was at least as deep and dangerous as the schism between the arts and sciences that C. P. Snow decried in his famous Reith Lectures in 1957.

Although Ralf Dahrendorf, Director of the London School of Economics, was no Thatcherite, he still believed that reviving Britain's economic fortunes was, on one level, a cultural battle.[3] Mrs. Thatcher's capitalist revolution was an attempt to transform a destructive economic culture that did more to impede than to enhance national competitiveness. For *Homo economicus* is far more than a hermetic figure unmoved by what economists complacently refer to as "externalities." He is also a cultural animal who seeks profits, makes rational calculations, and explores markets in social worlds that shape his consciousness and constrain his actions. No single cause can explain why one nation, industry, or enterprise rises and others decay, why some flourish or others falter.[4]

But culture counts. As Michael Porter of Harvard Business School, the leading authority on competitive strategy, contended:

> A nation's success largely depends on the types of education its talented people choose, where they choose to work, and their commitment and effort. The goals a nation's institutions and values set for individuals and companies, and the prestige it attaches to certain industries, guide the flow of capital and human resources—which, in turn, directly affects the competitive performance of certain industries. Nations tend to be competitive in activities that people admire or depend on— the activities from which the nation's heroes emerge.[5]

Comparative advantage—and disadvantage—are partly cultural affairs, as evidenced by the legacy Margaret Thatcher inherited.

The economic culture of the world's first industrial society contained an entrepreneurial tradition which Mrs. Thatcher wanted to revive and an animus against capitalism which she wanted to squelch. "At the end of the day," predicted Martin Wiener in 1981 in his highly influential study, *English Culture and the Decline of the Industrial Spirit 1850–1980*, "it may be that Margaret Thatcher will find her most fundamental challenge not in holding down the money supply or inhibiting government spending, or even in fighting the shop stewards, but in changing this frame of mind. English history in the eighties may turn less on traditional political struggles than on a cultural contest between the two faces of the middle class."[6]

The cultural tensions Mrs. Thatcher had to contend with also manifested themselves in terms of regional conflicts. Nineteenth-century England was not as divided a society as the United States, but geographical and class struggles still rent both nations. These conflicts culminated in civil wars, one peaceful, the other violent, which shaped their future characters. It is possible to imagine the course of modern English history as a battle between North and South. Although the dividing line between these regions was long marked by the River Trent, it was the rise of industry that gave the North-South antithesis its peculiar slant. These regions represented states of mind as well as stretches of land, as Mrs. Gaskell's novel *North and South* made clear. According to popular stereotypes, the North gave England grit and the South gave it class. The northern character was independent, practical, rough, calculating, and enterprising. Energy, ingenuity, and adventurousness were its archetypal virtues; materialism, Philistinism, and selfishness its archetypal vices. The southern character was romantic, aristocratic, graceful, genteel, and traditional. Rooted in ancient custom, devoted to the land, respectful of social hierarchy, the southerner was stable and secure, but also soft and snobbish. When taken literally, though, the North-South antithesis breaks down. Not only does it more or less ignore the Midlands, it also overlooks the internal differences within both North and South. Nevertheless, these ideal types do embody different faces of English culture.[7]

The fate of Mrs. Thatcher's experiment rested partly on her ability to reverse the result of the Victorian civil war which the South won. Understanding what she was fighting for and against requires a journey into the past.

I I

THE ENTREPRENEURIAL TRADITION TO WHICH MRS. THATCHER belonged and which she intended to rejuvenate stemmed from the Industrial Revolution when England seized an economic initiative it later squandered.

The advent of industry did not begin in London, political, cultural, and financial capital that it was. The spirit of enterprise caught fire in the social periphery, in small villages and towns far from the choking grasp of ancient municipal regulations and near waterways offering sources of fuel and transportation. The Industrial Revolution transformed the regional balance of power. It brought new status and prominence to booming provincial cities in the North and Midlands like Birmingham, Manchester, and Leeds. The inventors, engineers, and entrepreneurs who created the new industrial world came from the middling ranks of society. No religious group was more heavily represented among them than the Nonconformist Protestant sects—Quakers and Baptists, Methodists and Congregationalists. Their emphasis on hard work, individual effort, self-denial, and Spartan living spurred business success. This was the religious tradition in which Margaret Thatcher was reared in the Finkin Street Methodist Church in Grantham.

The majestic power of technology touched the popular imagination at the beginning of the Industrial Revolution. Nowhere was its grandeur more striking than in the world's first cast-iron bridge. It was built by the Darbys, a Quaker dynasty of ironmasters, in 1779–80 in the village of Coalbrookdale, Shropshire, one of England's most scenic counties. The Iron Bridge spanned the River Severn with a single arch supported by five iron ribs. Depicted in poems and paintings, tokens and engravings, it was, as Viscount Torrington noted in his diary in 1784, "one of the wonders of the world." In an engraving done two years earlier, Michael Angelo Rooker had captured the harmonious union of nature and technology in the Iron Bridge. He represented an unsullied blue river flowing between the abutments of a graceful bridge. Horses and wagons crossed between the lush green banks. The lesson of this tranquil, welcoming rural scene was as clear as the image: There was nothing to fear from, and much to admire in, industry.

Far from representing the new world of technology as

prosaic, dull, or exploitative, contemporaries accented the "romance of industry," meaning its heroic and sublime aspect. Labor-saving machinery was a boon, for it liberated humankind from dependence upon nature, rendering superfluous the "tedious toil of needless hands." The men who invented and operated the new mechanical marvels became heroes spawning prosperity which would benefit the entire society, or so it seemed.[8]

The Industrial Revolution altered cultural values as it changed the means of production and distribution. Upstart towns and cities grew without mandate or direction. New entrepreneurs challenged the preeminence of the landed gentleman. Unlike parasitic landowners living off the labor of others, the capitalist was the linchpin of society and the fount of its wealth. The essence of the gentleman was to be, but the mission of the entrepreneur was to become. The gentleman's arrival was announced by birth and perpetuated by reputation. The entrepreneur's success came from effort and was ratified by wealth. Yet there was an affinity between them. For the gentleman possessed an entrepreneurial legacy and the entrepreneur harbored gentlemanly ambitions.

By the Great Exhibition of 1851, the triumph of the entrepreneurial spirit seemed complete. This early version of the World's Fair was housed in London's Hyde Park. The vast conservatory (1,848 feet long, 408 feet wide, and 66 feet high) was a symbol of the age, erected in only seventeen weeks thanks largely to prefabrication.[9] A dazzling iron and glass structure that shimmered like an industrial fairyland, it was dubbed the Crystal Palace. Fittingly, the architect was a self-made man of the new industrial age, Joseph Paxton, whose humble origins did not prevent him from becoming a successful engineer, railway director, and promoter of newspapers and magazines. He adapted the design for the Crystal Palace from Lily House at Chatsworth, the Duke of Devonshire's preserve where he had served as superintendent of gardens. The organizers, preeminent among them Prince Albert and Henry Cole, used the Great Exhibition to advertise Britain's commercial supremacy and technological superiority. Within the Crystal Palace were models of steam engines, locomotives, bridges, and tunnels. More than 6 million visitors came to the exhibition to watch a world aglow with improvement.

The Great Exhibition also affirmed middle-class values. Free trade, self-help, hard work, and entrepreneurial flair were the path to prosperity. There was little doubt in mercantile and manufacturing circles as to who was the backbone of the nation and the fount of its wealth. The great reformer Richard Cobden struck the keynote: "Commerce is the grand panacea, which, like a beneficent medical discovery will serve to inoculate with the healthy and saving taste for civilization all the nations of the world."[10]

Although British visitors to the Crystal Palace had reason for pride, the moment for complacency had not yet arrived. Writing to Friedrich Engels in October 1851, Karl Marx commented, "The English admit that the Americans carried off the prize in everything."[11] If this was true, what would the future bring?

As it happened, the work ethic faded in established firms and families in classic industries. Pride in industry, fascination with technology, and the gospel of work were left largely to new blood. Had Margaret Thatcher sought turn-of-the-century entrepreneurial heroes, she could have found them among the upwardly striving and their new methods. Consider Jesse Boot, founder of Boots the Chemist. Even today his firm is the largest high-street pharmaceutical chain in Britain. His rise would have made a good chapter in Smiles's *Self-Help* or *Industrial Biography*. Raised in a pious Nonconformist working-class family in Nottingham, Boot worked sixteen hours every day until his health failed him. He broke the monopoly of private pharmacists by virtue of low profit margins and high turnovers, and by manufacturing many of his own lines of pharmaceutical articles. He also captured public attention by extensive advertising campaigns and by building shops as attractive in appearance as they were convenient in layout.[12]

For all the efforts of inventive entrepreneurs, a midlife crisis took hold of industrial Britain at the turn of the century. The confident mood which pervaded the world of the Crystal Palace gave way to waning energy, mounting self-doubt, and intimations of mortality. The economic boom that began in 1851 ended in 1873 with the crash of the Stock Exchange and the failure of major banks. The Great Depression, the fall in profits and prices which ensued, ended in 1896 with the rise of consumer spending. Even then problems lay unresolved. Britain remained "an ancient and still powerful state," as Arthur Balfour told a Cambridge audience in 1908; but, he continued, "there spreads a mood of deep discouragement when the reaction against recurring ills grow feebler."[13]

The man who took up the battle to resuscitate the nation was Joseph Chamberlain. He was the first, and certainly the most colorful, of the long line of politicians (extending to Margaret Thatcher) who were determined to turn back the tide of relative economic decline. A successful entrepreneur, he made his fortune as a screw manufacturer in Birmingham, a nuts-and-bolts trade in a nuts-and-bolts town. A rarity among British statesmen, he was capable of discussing trade and industry with the confidence and credibility of an insider. A man of parts known for solid business habits, incessant cigar-smoking, and constant talk of politics, Chamberlain was not averse to attracting attention. Any man, indeed any true Englishman, who would appear in public in a seal-skin topcoat was surely a man of destiny, a Caesar or Napoleon, commented a local writer.[14]

In 1869, Chamberlain won a seat on the Birmingham Town Council in 1869. There he earned the reputation as a "modern dictator" which he never quite shook. When he became mayor in 1873, he implemented a "civic gospel" that gave Birmingham the reputation of being the "best-governed city in the world." Elected Liberal MP for Birmingham in 1876, Chamberlain vowed to secure for the nation what he achieved in his own city. However, formidable obstacles stood in "Radical Joe's" way. For if Birmingham was a second-class city trying to make up for lost time, Britain was a world leader trying to retain its threatened position. Even in his late sixties, Chamberlain was an energetic giant, buoyed by public approval. His many admirers greeted him with cries of "Well done, Joe." They attended his speeches en masse and waved flags and banners as his train swept behind their homes. Britain could not match his vigor. It had become, in Chamberlain's famous phrase, a "weary titan."

How could Britain, Chamberlain asked, avoid the fate of Venice, the beautiful city of the Adriatic that had failed to sustain its great commercial supremacy?[15] For how long could British power endure?

It was not the absolute position of Britain that troubled Chamberlain. The country was richer than ever before. The total volume of trade rose from £1.317 billion in 1870 to £2.084 in 1900, with a commensurate rise in per capita income. The relative decline of Britain haunted him, though. "Sugar has gone, silk has gone; iron is threatened; wool is threatened; cotton will go! How long are you going to stand it?" he cried.[16] The United States and Germany had overtaken Britain in critical industries and Britain's share of international trade fell from 25 percent in 1880 to 21 percent in 1900. What Chamberlain might have sensed was that the overall growth of the new industrial competitors also exceeded Britain's. One estimate held that from 1870 to 1913 Britain grew at only 1.6 percent per annum, while the United States grew by 5 percent and Germany by 4.7 percent.

For Chamberlain, the root of Britain's economic difficulties was the unfair trade practices of its rivals. The United States and Germany enjoyed easy access to the British market thanks to its continuing commitment to free trade, but guarded their home markets with restrictive tariffs. Nowhere was the outcry about such inequities more vituperative than in E. E. Williams's *Made in Germany*. This best-selling tract denounced the Germans for their trade policies and for working too hard. Retaliation against the enemy was well justified, Chamberlain believed. Tariffs on foreign goods were a start, and an important one at that, but such measures were not enough. His solution was to create an imperial economic union, a common market uniting Britain and its colonies. He offered an added incentive: the economic advantages that accrued to the nation would be used partly to fuel social reforms to improve the condition of the working class.

This flamboyant bearer of bad tidings aroused great hostility. He angered both the Liberal Party which he had deserted and sections of his own Tory-Unionist Party. His critics denied that Britain's economic condition was as gloomy as Chamberlain suggested. They pointed out that the volume of exports had risen, as indeed it had. The fate of companies that failed and industries that faltered was the result of inefficient methods rather than the lack of protective tariffs. The fault was in themselves, not their enemies. Following Chamberlain's prescription, argued Herbert Asquith, was to accept an invitation to "commit industrial suicide in a fit of hypochondria." The young Winston Churchill, who had himself recently joined the Liberal Party, happily predicted that Balfour and Chamberlain "will cut their own throats and bring their party to utter destruction between them."[17] He was right. In the general election of 1906, the Liberals were returned to power with an enormous majority, partly because of the unpopularity of Chamberlain's program.

The decline of British industry was precipitated from without, but it was executed from within. Of course a small island not particularly rich in natural resources would have struggled in any case to keep pace with larger nations. Inevitably, the British would lose some ground to newcomers who adopted and improved their methods and techniques. No iron law of economics dictated, however, that Britain had to surrender its lead with so halfhearted a fight. But the country's industrial priority proved disadvantageous by the late nineteenth century. Heavy investment in textiles, coal, iron, and railroads discouraged serious commitment and quick adaptation to technological innovations, some of which were developed by British inventors. As long as businessmen could make a profit using existing technologies, there was little incentive to inject huge capital investments in new processes. The failure to do so, though, meant that Britain's infrastructure and technologies gradually became archaic.

For all the entrepreneurial tradition's glories, it had severe weaknesses which undercut Britain's international competitiveness. Conservative resistance to new methods of organization and production contributed to technological shortcomings. The cult of the practical man, the ingenious tinkerer who made dramatic advances through trial and error, was a legacy of the heroic age of the Industrial Revolution. All too often, however, capitalists failed to recognize the dangers of blindly following formulae for past success. They preferred the "lad who had been through the works" to the university-trained scientist or engineer. And so they resisted adopting new scientifically based industrial processes, as did the workers who feared displacement.

There were some notable exceptions in Britain. Often, they were the work of foreign entrepreneurs. For example, there was Brunner, Mond, founded in 1870 by John Brunner, a Swiss Protestant businessman, and Ludwig Mond, a German Jewish chemist. In the alkali works they built in Cheshire, in northwest England, the partners followed German rather than British practice. The firm became a pioneer in research and development. Mond recruited and rewarded scientists who would have otherwise kept well away from commerce. Brunner, Mond joined German scientific professionalism with a gentlemanly style that was quintessentially English. The living symbol and social center that embodied this unique ethic was Winnington Hall. A gentleman's house which had been fortuitously preserved on the chemical works, it became a suitably exclusive management club. The "college-like atmosphere" attracted professional men who aspired to enjoy the grace of a gentlemanly life while performing scientific or managerial tasks.[18]

But the majority of British firms did not follow Brunner, Mond's example. Their failure to do so proved particularly disadvantageous during the second industrial revolution. For it was precisely in the key new industries (chemicals, heavy machinery, and electrical equipment) that the Germans and Americans beat the British (with some exceptions), first in international markets and then on home ground. The stubborn attachment to traditional organizational structures only aggravated technological deficiencies.

In Germany and the United States, managerial capitalism replaced personal capitalism at the turn of the century. Pioneering companies hired teams of professional salaried managers. They built managerial hierarchies to administer functional areas, production, marketing, and distribution among them. While founding families and their heirs often retained the power to make important decisions, they tended to distance themselves from the increasingly complex daily operations of individual operating units. Leading firms were able to exploit the advantages of scale and scope by investing in management, manufacturing, and distribution. In so doing, they became first movers in the second industrial revolution.

In Britain, though, the ongoing dominance of family firms blocked the development of large-scale managerial enterprise. Owners were largely unwilling to share power with outsiders. This was partly because of the low "radius of trust" that prevailed in their riven class society. In light industry and retailing where there was relatively little foreign competition, it was easier to establish new forms of organization. This was not the case, though, in new science-based industries, where British firms were deprived of the cost advantages or market power of their competitors.[19]

In 1867, Karl Marx had seemed wholly justified in arguing that the classic ground of capitalism was England. By 1900, economic decline belied this reading. The complacent belief that the wealth of nations was a Brisish prerogative rather than a Scottish treatise blinded politicians and businessmen alike to the reality of their condition. The costly delusion that national setbacks were aberrations and foreign advances flukes made it all the more difficult for the British to come to terms with the facts that their markets were embattled and their technologies worn. And even when they did awake from their torpor, there was more talk than action—fine, stirring talk about fair trade, technical education, and industrial renewal, to be sure. But the grand plans amounted to little or nothing.

The entrepreneurial tradition survived, however battered, into the twentieth century. But it also fell victim to an onslaught from those who lived far from the workaday world of once great factories.

I I I

THE FORCES THAT CONTAINED THE CULTURE OF INDUSTRIAL Britain in the course of the nineteenth century were similar to the forces that Margaret Thatcher tried to squash in her quest to create an "enterprise culture."

Britain was the world's first industrial nation, but the rise of industry did not transform it as completely as it changed the United States.[20] Before the Industrial Revolution, Britain was a status society, a hierarchy based on land in which status followed birth. Everyone knew who owed him deference and to whom he had to defer. The old society survived partly because of the progressive stance taken by much of the aristocracy and gentry. Eager for profits, they took part in, rather than take exception to, modernization. This meant that key changes proceeded under their aegis rather than over their heads. Enterprising gentlemen such as the Duke of Bridgewater laid the groundwork for industrialism. They enclosed common lands, built roads and canals, and sponsored urban housing estates.[21]

Britain's path to modernity was relatively smooth and peaceful. The paradoxical result of this was that certain old ideals and institutions persisted well into the new industrial age. Canny enough to share power with the middle class, the landed elite was able to retain control of the seats of power. As the "age of equipoise" began at midcentury, the conflicts between the aristocracy and the middle class largely subsided.[22] The result was a peaceful compromise. This was one source of England's much-envied stability, but it did nothing to fuel the industrial spirit.

The cultural power of the aristocracy survived because of the wide appeal of the gentlemanly ideal. A gentleman was distinguished by birth, but elegant appearance, graceful bearing, polished passions, and easy manner also set him apart. A life of privilege brought obligations such as public service and aiding the poor. Such good works also had more practical uses. They allowed the old elite to provide patronage, which cemented the loyalty of their grateful social inferiors. The entrepreneurial drives and material acquisitiveness that had resulted in the great landed fortunes figured little in Victorian images of the gentlemen. Yet their alleged distaste for trade was easy to exaggerate and to misinterpret. Those who lived off rents from their estates and interest from their capital could well afford to be nonchalant about moneymaking, and indeed much else. But this was little more than rank hypocrisy.

Whatever the faults of individual gentlemen, the finest examples of the nobility were impressive. "Gone, one of Britain's noblest gentlemen," ran a poem in the *Manchester Guardian* describing the passing of the Duke of Westminster in 1899. An extremely wealthy man, whose inherited income from his town and country properties was about £150,000 a year (and rose to £250,000 thanks to his own efforts and luck), the duke was also a philanthropist. He saw himself as "not so much a private millionaire as the head of a great public institution or trust." On his Eaton Hall estate he built 48 farmhouses, 360 cottages, and eight schools. A sportsman, he had been master of the Cheshire Hunt in his youth. In later life, he won the Derby five times. And he was a redoubtable hunter and fisherman. The duke also enjoyed his domestic life. When he returned to Eaton Hall, his ancestral seat, the bells of the great clocktower duly played "Home, Sweet Home."[23]

The gentlemanly ethic that the Duke of Westminster embodied did not appeal to everyone. Thorstein Veblen, a dour critic repelled by grand display, thought the essence of gentility to be a life of conspicuous wastefulness:

> Sport, on the scale, and with the circumstance attending its cultivation in the United Kingdom, cannot be incorporated in the workday scheme of life except at the cost of long and persistent training of the popular taste.... It is quite beyond the reach of imagination that any adult male citizen would of his own motion go in for the futility of British shooting, or horse racing ... or for such a *tour de force* of inanity as polo, or mountain climbing or expeditions after big game.[24]

The habit of conspicuous consumption provided a dubious model for those of humbler origins.

However foolish the conduct of the leisure class, its impact on Britain's economic culture might have been relatively slight without the complicity of the middle class. Marx and Engels had predicted that bourgeois capitalism would sweep away the "ancient venerable prejudices" of the old order. But this did not happen. The middle class failed to drive the landed aristocracy from the seats of power. Cast to play a "most revolutionary part" in modern history, the middle class refused to cooperate. Instead, its various members opted for a number of different roles. The idealization of the landed gentleman spurred the sons, or the grandsons, of many successful businessmen to discard their devotion to self-help, enterprise, and practicality. They fell in love with the aristocratic way of life Marx supposed they would supplant. So the scions of the middle class were more eager to assimilate into, than to destroy, landed society. The path to gentility was difficult but well marked. It involved purchasing a country estate, sending one's sons to public schools, marrying off one's daughters to one's betters, and, perhaps, acquiring a coat of arms or a title (as did Simon Stoke in Thomas Hardy's *Tess of the D'Urbervilles*). A man does not burn down the house he intends to occupy, observed R. H. Tawney. Even those who were unable to emulate the grand aristocratic style could still look forward to weekend invitations.

The appeal of the gentlemanly ideal tampered with the indiscreet ambitions of the middle class. The "pursuit of Ease" did little to enhance, and much to dampen, the entrepreneurial tradition. Certain business dynasties did indeed disintegrate as later generations found the pleasures of country life more enticing than the rigors of the business world. For example, the Marshalls of Leeds used the wealth they earned in textile manufacturing to win social status and acceptance. As the Marshalls blended into landed society, they gradually severed their ties to the old family firm.

Testifying before a parliamentary commission in 1903, the

economist Alfred Marshall (who was not kin to the slackers from Leeds) explained the delusions sparked by England's early industrial and technological lead. It encouraged many to believe, quite wrongly, "that an Englishman could expect to obtain a much larger real income and to live more luxuriously than anybody else, at all events in an old country; and that if he chose to shorten his hours of work and take things easily, he could afford to so." This encouraged certain sons of successful businessmen to "follow mechanically the lead given by their fathers. They worked shorter hours, and they exerted themselves less to obtain new practical ideas than their fathers had done; and thus a part of England's leadership was destroyed rapidly."[25]

Samuel Courtauld IV was the heir of an old industrial dynasty that bore his family name. A notable collector of Impressionist paintings, he founded the Courtauld Institute in London where he displayed his acquisitions. From 1921 to 1946, Courtauld served as chairman of the world's leading rayon-producing firm. This position did not stop him from pointing out the evils of materialism. In 1942, he told the Engineers' Club in Manchester that "the worship of material values is the fatal disease from which our age is suffering."[26] The United States, predictably, was his favorite whipping boy; "Americanization" his greatest fear. He admired Americans' technical achievement, but loathed their way of life.[27] Such talk cost Courtauld little. Already a rich man, he could afford lordly contempt. Indeed, it did him some good because it helped prove that he was a gentleman. Yet it is dangerous to take him at face value. For it would have been unacceptably vulgar for him to have descanted on the virtues of profitability. The fact that Courtauld affected indifference to material gain reveals as much about his public image as his private motives.

Whatever the ambiguities of the gentlemanly ethic, artists and writers shaped an anti-industrial frame of mind that impeded Margaret Thatcher's capitalist revolution. Long before Karl Marx, Romantic poets such as William Wordsworth had declared war against the new industrial civilization. Born in 1770, Wordsworth spent his earliest years in the finest house in Cockermouth, a small town on the northern border of the Lake District. The region he celebrated in his poetry witnessed the incursions of industry even in his childhood. On Windermere there were freight carriers used to ship coal to the ironworks in the South. On the Tilberthwaite and Coniston Fells there were mines and quarries. The poet's father, John Wordsworth, was indirectly involved in the advent of industry in the Northwest. He served as lawyer and agent for an enterprising, if unloved, local magnate, Lord Lowther, who had interests in iron ore, coal mining, shipping, and real estate.

Pride, prejudice, and principle all conspired to turn William Wordsworth against industrialism. At stake was the sense of belonging, loyalty, and roots the orphaned poet craved and cherished. The economic distress that erupted in the form of food riots and frame-breaking during the Napoleonic Wars shocked and dismayed him. In the English aristocracy he found a moral mortar holding together a society under siege. He also found patrons who promised to be more reliable than the vagaries of the market. Wordsworth had little, if any, direct experience of industry or extensive acquaintance with manufacturers. But scanty knowledge did not stop him from framing weighty opinions.

Wordsworth attributed a host of social evils to the coming of industry. The "spreading of manufacturers through every part of the country" and the rise of "Houses of Industry" were sometimes "deemed great discoveries and blessings to humanity," but the poet found far more to bemoan than to praise. The factory system and child labor had led to a rapid decay in the domestic affections of the lower orders. Having lost both his mother and father when he was only a child,

Wordsworth was particularly sensitive to any disruption of family life. So he decried all the more what he saw taking place in factories. "Parents are separated from their children, and children from their parents; the wife no longer prepares with her own hands a meal for her husband, the produce of his labour; there is little doing in his house in which his affections can be interested; and but little left in which he can love."[28] For all his fear of the viciousness of the mob, Wordsworth had compassion for the poor. Those who could not support themselves had a justified claim upon the care of the nation. So he opposed the new conception of poverty, which held that the laborer alone was responsible for his fate.

Threats to the rural landscape he worshipped also troubled Wordsworth. The author of "Tintern Abbey" found in the English countryside the natural seat of rooted affections and tranquil pleasures unavailable elsewhere. When, in 1844, there was a proposal to cut a railway line into the Lakes as far as Lawn Wood, stopping just short of Ambleside, the poet objected. A railway line would destroy the beauty which delighted the residents of the Lake District and the tourists drawn to it. For him it was necessary, at all costs, to preserve the hedgerows and copses of his youth. But Wordsworth paid little heed to the need to build decent factories which might provide a basis for a decent life for the great mass of humanity.[29]

Matthew Arnold echoed and elaborated the intellectual animus against industry that contributed to Britain's economic decline. Born in 1822, he too spent his childhood in the Lake District. He sailed on Windermere and roamed Rydal Vale like Wordsworth before him. The son of Rugby headmaster Dr. Thomas Arnold, who nicknamed him "Crab" as a boy, the young Arnold rebelled against the earnestness and piety of his father's household. At Oxford he sought and won a reputation as a dandy who sported extravagant waistcoats. He called his friends "my love" and "my darling."[30] The poet and critic made his living as a civil servant, serving as a school inspector. Touring England, and indeed the Continent, on Her Majesty's affairs, he had the opportunity to observe worlds far removed from Rugby and Oxford.

Why did such an intelligent, cultivated individual as Arnold turn away so vehemently from the industrial world? Unlike Wordsworth, he knew something of the world he criticized. But familiarity did not breed affection or even respect. It could hardly have been easy or satisfying for a man who had grown up in learned circles and had devoted himself to the life of the mind and the quest for beauty to spend much of his time with businessmen who hardly shared such concerns. In famous essays such as *Culture and Anarchy* (1869) Arnold had his revenge.

The tragic flaw of the new industrial civilization and its liberal masters was the lack of cultural commitment and social conscience. Arnold bemoaned an imbalance between the "Hebraic" spirit of right conduct and the "Hellenic" spirit of personal cultivation. The cause was the harsh spirit of Nonconformist faith. An Anglican himself, he considered it narrow, semi-literate, and puritanical in the extreme. He found middle-class "Philistinism" insupportable. His surveys of Continental education convinced him that only the centralized state could foster an excellent system of national learning. But manufacturers, among others, stood in the way. They so treasured their individual liberty and so distrusted the state (long the creature of the aristocracy) that they refused to give up a measure of power to make monuments to imperishable beauty. Drugged by business, they lived a severely workful life given up to Mammon. "Would any amount of wealth be worth having," Arnold asked, "with the condition that one was to become just like these people by having it?"[31]

The voices of Wordsworth and Arnold might have had limited impact on shaping attitudes to industry had they not reverberated in the public schools. These ancient religious foundations were clearly and purposefully out of step with the new industrial order. This was not surprising given that their purpose was to prepare boys for Oxford and Cambridge. As meeting grounds and playing grounds for the sons of the aristocratic and middle-class elites, their mission was to turn out graduates fit to govern the realm. "It is not necessary that this should be a school for three hundred, or even one hundred men, but it *is* necessary that it should be a school for Christian gentlemen," declared Thomas Arnold of Rugby.[32]

The classical curriculum of the reformed public schools all but ignored subjects like applied science or political economy. They promoted indifference, if not downright hostility, to the world of practical affairs. Rugby, Eton, Harrow, and Winchester all directed their boys away from commercial, much less from technological pursuits. Rather, they encouraged them to seek prestigious careers in the domestic and foreign Civil Service and the established professions. As the "chief nurseries of our statesmen," in the words of the Clarendon Commission, the public schools geared their pupils for government rather than business. They equipped boys to administer a vast Empire rather than build a great company. Their immense cultural standing made business seem inferior, at best second-rate. In the name of national greatness, the public schools contributed inadvertently to national decline.

"The spirit of our highest culture," noted Thomas Hughes, the radical author of *Tom Brown's Schooldays* (1858), "and the spirit of our trade do not agree together. The ideas and habits which those who have most profited by them bring away from our public schools do not fit them to become successful traders."[33] A Rugby graduate, he tried to remedy this schism by creating a pioneer community in Tennessee of all places. In 1880, Hughes traveled to the Cumberland Plateau to visit the colony of Englishmen he helped found and named Rugby. The small delegation of public school graduates who greeted him took part in a co-operative enterprise. They all worked with their hands and led a manly outdoor life in an atmosphere modeled after an old-fashioned village. But the experiment fell apart. Rugby, Tennessee, is now just a minor tourist attraction.

The reformed public schools helped shape a new professional ideal hostile to industrial values.[34] Professional men rejected businessmen's acquisitive struggle, preferring the mantle of public service to the stigma of private profit. In short, they were uneasy with business. Take the experience of Burroughs Wellcome, a pharmaceutical firm founded in 1880 by two American expatriates. Henry Wellcome made a great effort to attract physicians and scientists to take the lead in research and development. He offered higher salaries and better benefits than were available elsewhere. Even so, he found that "first-class men" were uneasy about working for a commercial concern. As a result, he established private research institutes and kept them physically and legally separate from the firm so that researchers could keep up appearances. Still, it took a good deal of cajoling to convince Henry Dale, a young Cambridge-trained physiologist (and later a Nobel laureate) to accept a position at the Wellcome Physiological Research Laboratory.

As Britain's industrial mastery eroded, and then finally evaporated, at the turn of the century, the world of the factory became associated with decline as well as exploitation. Failure exposed a multitude of sins obscured by success. Even if the hostility of writers and artists toward industry did not directly contribute to relative economic decline, challenges to England's industrial supremacy only heightened the appeal of a conception of Englishness that made the business world seem marginal. In the cultural civil war, the South and its aristocratic traditions defeated the North and its entrepreneurial ways.[35] At heart, if not in fact, England was a garden rather than a workshop.

Antagonism to industry pervaded the educated classes in the late nineteenth century. But it was not unique to Britain any more than criticism of capitalism began in the modern age. Why, then, did the anti-industrial frame of mind promoted by writers and artists and transmitted by the public schools and Oxbridge prove so harmful to Britain's economic prospects? Contempt for trade and aversion to technology, after all, did not prevent Germany from becoming Europe's leading industrial nation. Unflattering literary stereotypes that pictured the man of business as a greedy, unscrupulous Philistine were conventional in Europe and, for that matter, in the United States.

Anti-modern reaction in Germany was, by any measure, far more vicious than its British counterpart.[36] Agrarian romantics like Paul de Lagarde uttered a primal cry of "Blood and Soil" that foreshadowed Nazi barbarism. By contrast, the gentle pastoral idylls of Richard Jefferies did little more than celebrate rural England's fading way of life. For German reactionaries, fanatical hatred of the Jews, who were sometimes condemned as capitalist scoundrels, sometimes as socialist revolutionaries, proved useful. Demonizing the Jews allowed them to enjoy the bounty of an increasingly potent industrial machine while preserving the myth of Aryan spirituality. Anti-Semites condemned Jews as evil capitalists and praised Germans as chivalrous businessmen. This is a case of what psychoanalysts call a process of "splitting," ascribing wicked intentions to one group to exonerate another.

The British expressed their ambivalence about industrialism differently. Anti-Semitism was hardly unknown; for example, the portrayal of Fagin in *Oliver Twist*. Generally, though, they did not vent their anxieties about capitalism on the backs of the Jews. Why not? First, there were relatively few Jews in Britain until the 1880s and 1890s. Second, Britain was, whatever its faults, a liberal society with a profound sense of decency. Finally, the British were able to vent their racist sentiments on the colonial peoples of the Empire. In any case, they focused their fears of industrial capitalism largely on each other. Grasping northerners were the offenders, or failing that, greedy Americans.

There was another reason that anti-industrial biases did more economic damage in Britain than in Germany. Indictments of the industrial world did not go unanswered in Britain. But the country did not possess a powerful network of educational or religious institutions to temper such hostile attitudes. Like the public school, the German "Gymnasium" fostered classical learning and humanistic ideals with little regard to their practical uses. Far from ignoring such concerns, though, Germany also boasted an unrivaled national system of scientific, technical, and craft instruction. Britain did not even begin to match it. The Protestant ethic remained undiminished in Germany, as Max Weber made clear in his classic treatise, fueling the march of capitalism. This was not true in Britain. There the "discovery of poverty" by social investigators such as Edward Cadbury and Charles Booth touched the religious conscience. It also inspired a social gospel which discouraged the pursuit of profit in favor of a life of service.

The British Empire was a far grander enterprise than its modest German counterpart. And it enjoyed a nearly universal popularity until the Boer War. The public schoolboys who read the stories of Rudyard Kipling and John Buchan saw in the colonies the prospect of a romantic and thrilling life no longer to be found in the decadent world at home. Idealistic officials, courageous soldiers, and colorful adventurers were their heroes. The industrialist, the inventor, and the engineer were all but ignored.

I V

LONG BEFORE THE ADVENT OF THE WELFARE STATE, THE BAT-
tlelines were drawn. Had Margaret Thatcher sought one
book to epitomize the collision between entrepreneurial
drive and intellectual resistance, she could hardly have done
better than choose E. M. Forster's *Howards End* (1910).

The plot hinges on the relations between two English families at the turn of the century, the literary Schlegels and the
commercial Wilcoxes. The novel, Lionel Trilling observed,
dramatized a war within the middle class over who would inherit England.[37] (For all the virtues of the Merchant and
Ivory film version of *Howards End*, it fails to capture the nature, or extent, of the cultural and class conflicts depicted in
the novel.) "Does she belong to those who have moulded her
and made her feared by other lands, or to those who have
added nothing to her power, but have somehow seen her,
seen the whole island at once, lying as a jewel in a silver sea,
sailing as a ship of souls, with all the brave world's fleet ac-
companying her towards eternity?" The prize is Howards
End, "old and little, and altogether delightful," a house in
once rural Hertfordshire. It is in danger of being swallowed
up by London suburbia and fouled by the smell of petrol
along the North Road which led prosperous businessmen out
beyond their offices in the metropolis. The "genius loci" is
Mrs. Wilcox, a steady, unselfish woman who instinctively
venerates the past and worships nature, a descendant of the
yeoman class that Forster idealized.

"Only connect"—the famous epigraph of the novel—is no
easy task. A gulf separates the party of business, the Wilcoxes, and the party of culture, the Schlegels. For Henry
Wilcox is a person of far different mettle than his wife. A successful entrepreneur whose motto is "Concentrate," he
knows what's what and who's who. Unafflicted by doubt, the

commanding chairman of Imperial and West African Rubber lives behind "a wall of newspapers and motorcars and golf-clubs." Riveted by the "outer life of telegrams and anger," he is corrupted by "the inner darkness in high places that comes with a commercial age." Philistine and unimaginative, Henry Wilcox is also gritty and masculine. His masterful qualities attract Margaret Schlegel. After his wife's death, Henry and Margaret marry, much to the consternation of the outraged Helen Schlegel.

It is difficult not to like the sisters Schlegel. Effervescent and articulate, they have all the graceful charm so lacking in the Wilcox children. In their "female house" they lead a "life of cultured but not ignoble ease." Dedicated to art, ideas, and friendship, the sisters are certain, more or less, that books are the real world, as Helen puts it. Believers in temperance, tolerance, and social equality, theirs is a vaguely socialist life founded on an inherited income, £600 per annum. Aesthete and rentier that Margaret Schlegel is, she becomes increasingly loathe to "draw my income and sneer at those who guarantee it."

The connection between the Wilcoxes and the Schlegels explodes over the question of who is responsible for the lower orders. The sisters take up a "little clerk" living on the edge of gentility. Leonard Bast gazes at books of the galaxy at work but is too poor to sustain the loss of an umbrella. Touched by his cultural aspirations, they provide him with a taste of a life he craves but can ill afford. This does not suit Henry Wilcox. He believes that "one sound man of business does more good to the world than a dozen of your social reformers." Wilcox accuses the sisters of holding a romantic view of a man who does not deserve it. Bast finally falls into the "abyss of poverty," partly because of Wilcox's glib and misleading counsel. But the rich industrialist refuses to help Bast (whose wife Jackie was once Wilcox's mistress). More comfortable with the pat statement than the generous gesture, Henry's attitude is simple and self-righteous. The poor are poor; one feels sorry for them, but there it is. The final issue of Helen's "perverted sense of philanthropy" is an illegitimate child fathered by the aptly named Leonard Bast.

Confronting her seducer with a crime against womanhood, Charles Wilcox, Henry's elder son, accidentally kills the clerk. Bast dies buried under a mountain of books. At the end of the novel, it is Margaret, the rightful heir designated by the late Mrs. Wilcox, who inherits Howards End. In the last scene, Helen and her son look out at the cut field and the big meadow promising "such a crop of hay as never!" After all, England is the country and it is the country which heals.

Howards End dramatizes a host of conflicts which came to the fore again during the Thatcher years. The novel raised questions not easily answered or resolved: whether the guardians of culture or the captains of commerce contributed more to the public good; whether capitalism was inevitably a soulless engine which ploughed down the poor; whether the poor were the architects of their own misfortunes who had to overcome dependency or victims of long exploitation and neglect who deserved state benefits; whether *bienpensant* intellectuals truly understood the needs of the downtrodden or whether they simply idealized them from afar; whether the good life rested on material plenty or spiritual riches or on both; whether it was possible, or desirable, to reconcile the demands of business and the requirements of culture; whether Britain was to be a workshop or a garden and whether they were mutually exclusive or symbiotic. A reader of *Howards End* would predict that the authors of the capitalist revolution would have as little time for its intellectual critics as vice versa; that threats to the safety net which protected latter-day Basts would raise the ire of latter-day Schlegels; and that whatever victories were won would come at a great cost.

Such complexities aside, there is no doubt where Margaret

Thatcher stood in the clash between the Wilcoxes and the Schlegels. For liberal intellectuals devoted to social welfare and aesthetic cultivation, she had little patience. For energetic businessmen devoted to moneymaking and self-help, she had great admiration. For those who could not fend for themselves, she showed little pity, at least publicly. At the end of the day, the question remained: who would inherit Britain and what would be its fate?

A Different Voice

I

On a snowy day in January 1980, Margaret Thatcher went to the Carlton Club.

Located in the heart of St. James's, the Carlton is in the vicinity of a number of royal London residences. Close to both Clarence House, a home of the Queen Mother, and to St. James's Palace, a home of the Duke and Duchess of Kent, it is also within walking distance of Buckingham Palace itself. For those whose social circle is not quite so exalted, though, the Carlton has the virtue of being near Savile Row and Jermyn Street, where a gentleman can have shirts made at Turnbull & Asser and enjoy a hot shave with a straight razor at Trumpers. The Carlton is also a short shot from a bevy of other exclusive gentleman's clubs that flourished in the bad old days and have stumbled along in more enlightened times. Among them are Boodle's, White's, Union, East India and Sport, and the Devonshire.

None of these estimable institutions, though, could equal the Carlton's role in Britain's political history. Founded by the Duke of Wellington in 1832 around the time of the Great

Reform Bill that he had chosen to oppose, the Carlton soon became a mainstay of Tory power, a center for socializing and strategizing. And so it remained, more or less, as amply demonstrated by the names of the Disraeli Room (which contains the famous round table he once kept in his Dover Street flat), the Churchill Room, and the Macmillan Room. Damaged by German bombing in 1940 while members such as Harold Macmillan, Quintin Hogg, and Rab Butler happened to be in the club (and managed to escape unharmed), the Carlton moved to a site that hitherto had been the home of Arthur's Club.

Margaret Thatcher was at the Carlton Club for the unveiling of a sculpture of her head by Oscar Nemon. Among those present was Harold Macmillan, who had become chairman of the Carlton (his grandson Alexander was secretary of the Political Committee) when he was eighty-three. The old fox had taken great pleasure in her election as party leader in 1975. In an otherwise gloomy letter he wrote: "However there is one delightful feature which has relieved us all: the breakthrough of women's lib into the Conservative party from which men have been deposed and a gracious lady has taken the leadership in her stride amid universal acclaim." He continued: "She is the product of her own strong character and good sense and of the pent-up animosity against the regime which in ten years has destroyed the Conservative party."[1]

So Macmillan had good reason to be pleased when the Carlton honored Mrs. Thatcher in 1980. Indeed, he gave a speech for the occasion. His biographer, Alastair Horne, furnishes a vivid account of this poignant scene: "Macmillan at his courtliest, gazed around the room at portraits of Tory statesmen, and speculated, 'I wonder what they would make of the performance? I know one who would have welcomed it—Disraeli, who disliked the company of men and liked the company of women.' "[2] For his part, Macmillan added his best wishes: "I wish you well with all my heart, mam. God bless you."[3] Afterwards, they chatted for an hour or so. Macmillan sat in an armchair with Mrs. Thatcher at his feet.

Being honored by the Carlton Club must have been particularly gratifying for Margaret Thatcher because of how far she had come. As party leader and Prime Minister she was an honorary member of the Carlton, as indeed all of her predecessors had been since 1832. But it was still a gentleman's club. And members of such clubs had led the movement that opposed women's suffrage in the late nineteenth century. Clubmen feared that giving political rights to women represented yet another unwanted incursion into man's sphere. Those who came to St. James's to escape their wives or mistresses also feared that women would use the vote to enforce an intolerably strict morality. "Votes for women, chastity for men," a favorite slogan of the first family of feminism, the Pankhursts, was enough to put off those who had no wish to change the Victorian double standard.[4] In any case, it was almost unbelievable that anyone whose father happened to be a grocer would be proposed for membership at so discriminating a club as the Carlton, much less escape the blackball at the moment of truth.

Almost as soon as Margaret Thatcher became Prime Minister, her critics accused her, with good cause, of being dogmatic and intolerant. Indeed, she became notorious for asking: "Is he one of us?" Construed by Hugo Young, the *Guardian* columnist who was her preeminent biographer, as the "emblematic question of the Thatcher years ... it defined the test which politicians and other public officials aspiring to her favour were required to pass. It epitomised in a single phrase how she saw her mission."[5] This is true, but it also misses the point. For the question, "Is he one of us?" was hardly unique to Margaret Thatcher. Indeed, the overwhelming need to place, and keep, individuals in specific social categories was commonplace in Britain, a society that had perfected particularly odious forms of snobbery. Gentleman's clubs were unmarked because the cognoscenti knew what and where they were. Cliques preserved their power by blackballing undesirables. The graduates of public schools wore old school ties for personal advantage as well as sentimental reasons. "Foreign" was often a pejorative rather than exotic term. London postal codes provided a wonderful guide as to who had a good address and who did not, who was "U" (upper class) and who was "non-U." So when Margaret Thatcher purposefully asked, "Is he one of us?" she was following in the ways in which she had been raised, and managed to raise herself.

I I

REGION AND CLASS, GENDER AND UPBRINGING, RELIGION AND history all played a part in making Margaret Thatcher a capitalist revolutionary.

Born in Grantham, Lincolnshire, on October 13, 1925, Margaret Hilda Roberts was an English provincial. She grew up in the heart of middle England. The town of Grantham is an hour and twenty minutes north of London on the fast train from King's Cross. En route from the metropolis, the landscape is green and lush, but not exceptional. From the windows of the inter-city train, one sees little evidence of the changes wrought by the Industrial Revolution. There are few signs of manufacturing. Both the northern and southern approaches to Grantham are steep and hilly. The railway station is unassuming. A plain structure in a town of no great importance, it minds its own business far more discreetly than the great railway stations of the metropolis such as the neo-Gothic St. Pancras on the Euston Road.

Grantham's town center is only a few minutes walk from the railway. Its most prominent feature is a marketplace that pleases the eye by virtue of its irregularity. Sometimes there is an open-air market where small-time merchants sell inexpensive goods. Cloth coats are visible everywhere. The sight and smell of fish and chips are unavoidable. There are the requisite number of shops, but none of them have been smartened up in a spare, modernistic style. And, of course, there are pubs. Among them is the Blue Bull, a Whitbread pub in which the regulars look up as newcomers enter. Never a major industrial town, Grantham did contain Richard Hornsby's ironworks. Under its auspices, the town was lumbered with the usual depressing back-to-back red brick houses built in the nineteenth century for the working class. All in all, Grantham seems to be a modest, undistinguished provincial community without great character and charm. Surely it does not have the beauty of neighboring Lincoln, a medieval town with a stunning cathedral. Nevertheless, some connoisseurs of English parish churches list Grantham in their top dozen.[6]

The approach to Margaret Thatcher's childhood home, Number 1 North Parade, is on a street called Watergate. North Parade itself contains mostly early nineteenth-century terraced houses. Built by speculative builders driven more by money than art, it was an appropriate venue for the future paragon of "Victorian values." While she grew up above her father's grocery store (which also served as a local sub post office), her surroundings were pleasant if by no means elaborate. One of her critics, Jonathan Raban, describes the Roberts store and residence as "Solidly, Georgianly genteel with its golden-section windows and moulded porticos. It is sturdy, tidy, tall, unimpeachably mercantile and middle class."[7] The smallish brick dwelling is now the Premier Restaurant. Decorated with a floral carpet, the Premier makes a point of serving champagne—as well as Budweiser brewed in Czechoslovakia. It is owned and operated, ironically enough, by Europeans rather than the good English stock much favored by Mrs. Thatcher.

Growing up in Grantham meant that Margaret spent her childhood and youth in a milieu that remained far more "Victorian" in character and texture than London. For the English provinces changed far more slowly than the metropolis. Somnambulant and dull, Grantham was more notable for what it was not than for what it was. Located in the North Midlands, it was a market town and railway center that linked London and the North. But Grantham displayed few of modern industrial civilization's problems or achievements. It was, therefore, not likely to evoke a powerful reaction against the evils of capitalism. So Margaret wasn't exposed to the worst excesses of the factory system or the plight of its victims.

Few Americans know, or care, what Ronald Reagan's father did for a living. But who in Britain does not know, and care one way or the other, that Margaret Thatcher is the daughter of a Grantham grocer? This is true partly because she made adroit political use of her modest family background. She was careful to project an image of a woman who intuitively understood the concerns of ordinary people. And yet her husband's money enabled her to live a very comfortable life in Chelsea, well insulated from those whose interests and ideals she claimed to defend. As she noted in a telling interview with *The New Yorker:* "The passionately interesting thing to me, is that the things I learned in a small town, in a very modest home, are just the things that I believe have won the elections."[8] Correct or incorrect as this assertion may be, the interest in her social origins is also a symptom of the inveterate snobbism which came too easily to the landed gentry. Such habits also infected obsequious Tory poseurs who enjoyed making speeches about "One Nation" as long as they did not have to dine with those they patronized in generous rhetoric. For that matter, it also touched, in a different way, the upper-middle-class socialists who were more comfortable loving the people from afar than mixing with them.

Snobbism aside, however, Margaret Thatcher's lower-middle-class roots were important in shaping her consciousness as well as her opportunities; had she come from another social group, her outlook would have been markedly different. The shopkeeper's daughter had no natural tie, much less allegiance, to the soil, or to the pre-industrial world of birth, land, deference, and hierarchy. Unlike Tories of the old school, or their *nouveaux riches* imitators, Margaret was not predisposed to becoming a modern representative of traditional upper-class virtues. *Noblesse oblige* meant little to a woman whose ancestors were more likely to have been the objects of aristocratic patronage than its munificent dispensers. The commitment to paternal responsibility was not part of her class legacy. Taking care of one's own was a far more realistic goal.

The lower middle class in which the grocer's daughter was raised had a distinct cultural psychology. It was largely shaped by a social and economic position that was both ambiguous and tenuous. For Marx and Engels, the lower middle class was a transitional group, "tossed about between the hopes of entering the ranks of the wealthy class and the fear of being reduced to the status of proletarians or even paupers." It acted as, in George Orwell's words, the "shock absorbers of the bourgeoisie," a role for which its members received little thanks or compensation. Belittled by intellectuals, among them those like H. G. Wells who came from their number and fled their company, the lower middle class was both unloved and scorned. Not high enough like the aristocracy to command admiration or low enough like the working class to elicit sympathy, the lower middle class lived in fear of falling and hope of rising. Fear of falling stemmed from the threats posed by the machine and the department store. Hope of rising stemmed from the opportunities open to those who embraced the classic bourgeois virtues—work, thrift, perseverance, and self-help.

Determined to improve their lot, the lower middle class was a strongly individualistic group dedicated to social mobility and private property. Its members maintained a distinct class-consciousness that hinged on a sense of superiority to those below them, in particular to manual workers who were an "indispensable negative reference point," shoring up their self-esteem.[9] Given that the lower middle class could not always count on earning a significantly higher income than skilled workers—sometimes quite the opposite held true—it was their militant respectability and unflinching restraint that set them apart from rougher fellows less willing to postpone gratification and moderate appetites for the sake of future prospects. Good conduct mattered as much as comfortable living.

Margaret Thatcher's family background was classic petit bourgeois. Her mother, née Beatrice Stephenson, was the daughter of a railway cloakroom attendant. Her father, Alfred Roberts, was the son of a Northamptonshire shoemaker. He hailed from an artisan tradition deeply affected by Samuel Smiles's philosophy of self-help. It was an ideal that served Roberts well. Growing up with few advantages, he had to make his own way in the world. And he succeeded in doing so despite the fact that he had little formal education. After working for a grocer, he opened his own shop and then another across town. The main store, above which the family lived, was, as Margaret later recollected, "quite a big shop. It had a grocery section and provisions section, with all the mahogany fitments that I now see in antique shops, and beautiful canisters of different sorts of tea, coffee and spices."[10]

The fact that Alfred Roberts was a grocer affected his daughter's economic views. So she freely admitted in her memoirs:

My father was both a practical man and a man of theory. He liked to connect the progress of our corner shop with the

great complex romance of international trade which recruited people all over the world to ensure that a family in
Grantham could have on its table rice from India, coffee from
Kenya, sugar from the West Indies and spices from five conti-
nents.[11]

He filled Margaret with a sense of the "romance of trade," a
popular Victorian notion, long before she read any of the liberal economists.

National and international forces had an effect on Roberts's store. But as a shopkeeper in a small provincial town he
was a far more important local figure than he would have
been in London or than he would have been now in the age
of supermarkets. Although Roberts could take pride in his independence, he could not rely on private capital or public
benevolence to rescue him or his family if he failed. Doing
business in the provinces, he was not as pressed by large
stores as his metropolitan counterparts. Still, he faced growing competition from the Co-operatives. Never truly affluent, much less wealthy, the Roberts family was reasonably
well off even during the trying days of the Depression. Yet
Alfred Roberts dutifully practiced, and duly imposed, a strict
regime of domestic economy that amounted to extreme parsimony. Perhaps his tight-fisted regime stemmed from memories of scarcity in his own childhood. In any case, it was unsurprising that for all the attention he devoted to Margaret,
hers was not a childhood marked by material indulgence.

From the rudiments of Margaret Thatcher's early life, she
fashioned a personal saga of dramatic individual ascent. "You
can forget all that nonsense about 'defence of privilege,'"
Mrs. Thatcher insisted in 1974. "I had precious little 'privilege' in my early years."[12] A middle-class evangelist for capitalism, the politician presented a picture of a childhood that
seemed harsher in her narrative than it was in fact. The Roberts family home did have an outhouse rather than indoor

plumbing for many years, but this was out of moral choice rather than economic necessity. Her father was very frugal, but he was not poor. Exaggerating her own deprivations was emotionally satisfying because it made her success appear all the more remarkable. And such fanciful revision was also politically useful. By insisting on her humble roots, the future Prime Minister distanced herself from the well-born and well-heeled. In so doing, she also made herself more attractive for less prosperous voters. Her rise, however exceptional, was no rags to riches story.

I I I

THE SO-CALLED VICTORIAN VALUES OF THE ROBERTS FAMILY shaped Margaret's ideals and conduct.

Responsibility, work, frugality, cleanliness, religion, and patriotism were the cornerstones of life, according to Alfred Roberts. These were the moral values that colored how the grocer raised his daughter. Margaret Thatcher's parents were, as she recollected, "neat, tidy, always as well dressed as they could afford, the kind of people who even if they had only one shirt or blouse would get up a few minutes earlier in the morning to put an iron over it."[13] It was, however, a rare occasion when she spoke publicly of both Alfred and Beatrice. For, as their daughter put it in a triumphant moment following the Conservative victory in the general election of 1979, "Well, of course, I just owe almost everything to my father. He brought me up to believe all the things I do believe."[14]

As her father's daughter, it is possible to read Margaret Thatcher's life, on one level, as the story of Electra of Grantham. In photographs, Alfred Roberts appears to be an early twentieth-century version of a Victorian worthy. Tall and slender, rigidly held and tightly controlled, with a shock of white hair, he seemed somber and dignified, the proud pater-familias surrounded in a conventional pose by his unsmiling family. A school friend of Margaret's described him as "a very courteous, straightforward, honest sort of man, much respected in Grantham, in fact perhaps at one time the most respected Grantham citizen."[15] His wife was a far less arresting figure. "I loved my mother dearly," Mrs. Thatcher said in an interview in the *Observer* in 1988, "but after I was fifteen we had nothing more to say to each other. . . . It was not her fault. She was always weighed down by the home. Always being in the home."[16]

Alfred Roberts's younger daughter was privy to a male world denied her mother and her elder sister Muriel. There is no way to tell whether Alfred hoped that his second child would be a boy. But it is clear that the role conferred upon Margaret was that of an honorary son. At least, she was an heir apparent who shared his interests in learning and public affairs. Happy or unhappy as Alfred and Beatrice Roberts were together, theirs was a marriage more marked by practicality than passion. They always took separate holidays so that one of them could mind the store. It seems likely that Muriel was closer to her mother, Margaret to their father. In any event, the two sisters had markedly different dispositions. Muriel went on to work as a physiotherapist with the handicapped; Margaret showed little interest in the disabled and dependent.

The longing for male power and the fear of female dependency was a lifelong pattern rooted in Margaret's own family romance. Profoundly attached to her father and barely tied to her mother and sister, she learned to depend on men rather than women. She sought the company and counsel of those she admired or those who could help her career. It was her unapologetic lack of interest in other women that made her fairly unpopular among feminists. Her ability to navigate in a male world hostile or indifferent to women stemmed, though, from the unsentimental education she received in her father's house. Like her mother and sister, Margaret worked in the family grocery business, but it was she who became her father's helper and companion in other matters. Margaret regularly borrowed books of history, political biography, and current affairs from the public library for her father. This self-taught man and prolific reader regarded the library as his university.[17]

Also it was Margaret who took part in the political career of Alderman Roberts. She watched her father perform at the Town Council, the Magistrates Court, and the Rotary Club. He was, in the words of Hugo Young, "a paragon among political parents," who prepared his daughter for a political career as assiduously as any highborn Tory politician, imparting a deep sense of public duty.[18] More or less a Lloyd George Liberal in his youth, Roberts was elected as an Independent to the Grantham Town Council, a group that usually voted with the Conservatives. Considered sympathetic to the Labour Party, he never joined it, presumably because of its ties to the Co-operative movement, which threatened the position of independent shopkeepers. A patriotic politician, he favored thrift in public affairs and in private life. In 1945, Roberts became mayor of Grantham. During his tenure he proved himself to be a municipal activist, committed to government action. Finally deposed by Labour in 1952, his defeat aggravated his daughter's antagonism toward the left, adding personal grievance to ideological antipathy.

Margaret, with or without her father's prompting, blurred conventional gender lines in her private and public life. "You decide what to do yourself," he insisted, "and if necessary you lead the crowd, but you never follow"—an exhortation made by many parents but by few more earnestly or effectively.[19]

In other words, Margaret Thatcher came to speak in a different voice, but it was not the different voice described and valorized by developmental psychologist Carol Gilligan.[20] Unlike certain feminist theorists of the 1960s who were so taken with androgyny that they actually believed that there were no fundamental differences between men and women, Gilligan's studies of the moral growth of adolescent girls suggested that they were, in fact, more caring, giving, sensitive, and compassionate than their male counterparts. Although Mrs. Thatcher's critics and champions disagreed on her dominant characteristics, she is often described as being pushy, aggressive, strident, and unyielding—qualities rarely acceptable in women. One can, of course, argue with Gilligan's typology, as a number of feminist historians, sociologists, and psychoanalysts have done.

In Mrs. Thatcher's political statements and public policies, though, "feminine" values such as conciliation, association, and nurturing hardly figure at all, while "masculine" values such as struggle, independence, and competitiveness are unmistakable. The irony is that it fell to a woman, and one who was both wife and mother, to challenge the leading assumptions of the Welfare State, preaching self-reliance rather than solidarity and productivity rather than redistribution. Her example did little for the theory that societies would be more caring and supportive were they run by women rather than men.

The most infamous, and misunderstood, example of the woman politician undermining conventional expectations of feminine instinct took place while Mrs. Thatcher was Secretary for Education under Edward Heath. When she carried through a plan conceived by her late predecessor to discontinue free milk for young schoolchildren, she found herself dubbed "Thatcher, Thatcher, milk snatcher." She never quite shook this hurtful and misleading label, despite the fact that Labour governments had already stopped funding similar programs for older students. What made the image of the "milk snatcher" particularly potent, and indeed poisonous, was that far from representing Mrs. Thatcher as the nurturing mother breast-feeding a dependent infant, it depicted her as a woman depriving needy children of nourishment. Faced with the necessity of cutting spending in her department, she had to choose between eliminating milk subsidies or constraining educational instruction. Characteristically, she chose to favor education because doing so would, in the long run, bolster individual choice and economic opportunity.

Mrs. Thatcher's negotiation of gender roles was more complex than it initially appears. Shy and unsophisticated, enjoying neither social prestige nor economic advantages for all her natural ability and gritty application, her early vulnerability is a key to understanding her later behavior. As an ambitious woman eager to rise in the clubby world of British politics, and as a member of a political party hardly known as the avant-garde of feminism, she was in a much more difficult position than her male counterparts even when she was often clearly more able and energetic.

Her personal compromise was to assume what the psychoanalyst Wilhelm Reich called a "character armor." Its purpose was to provide a sense of internal safety and security by disguising feelings of weakness and exposure. This was particularly important for a woman who feared that appearing to be soft would make her more likely to be trodden upon or merely ignored by powerful or aspiring men who were her social superiors and on whom she depended for professional advancement. The need for a character armor was especially strong because Margaret Thatcher was an obsessive type, a personality formed on the assumption that the world is a dangerous place in which continual vigilance is necessary for survival. Driven to compulsive rituals such as constant work in order to deaden anxiety, the obsessive tends to create strong defenses in order to appear invulnerable to potential adversaries. Few sobriquets could, therefore, have brought her more psychic satisfaction than that of the Iron Lady: it embodied the desire to be impenetrable and therefore impervious to harm, but also to be a lady worthy of respect if not admiration.

Margaret Thatcher's desire to be, as well as to appear to be, a strong woman led her, consciously or unconsciously, to eschew certain feminine stereotypes that seemed unbecoming in a political leader. No one could accuse her of being the stereotypical woman once derided by Herbert Asquith as hopelessly ignorant of politics, credulous to the last degree, and flickering with gusts of sentiments like candles in the wind. Better suited to Mrs. Thatcher's robust mettle was the phrase, "The lady's not for turning." Over and over again she used it to justify her refusal to change economic policies that seemed as ill advised as they were unpopular during her first government.

Convinced that it was particularly dangerous for a female politician to appear irresolute or uncertain, Margaret Thatcher took excessive pride in her own rigidity. She refused to apologize for mistakes. Likewise she resisted even the appearance of changing her mind. As Sir William Pile, Permanent Secretary at the Department of Education during her time there, recalled in a puzzled tone: "She is the only person I know who I don't think I've ever heard say 'I wonder whether.' Most of us, at moments of uncertainty or when faced with a lot of conflicting circumstances and confusion of objectives will say, 'Well, what's it all about? What should we do?' " Not so Mrs. Thatcher. Sir William ascribed her refusal to express doubt to "always having ready the answer in herself springing from her character."[21] This may be so, but it is equally possible that her resolve was an attempt to counter the stereotype of the indecisive female.

On occasion, Mrs. Thatcher temporarily abandoned her character armor, allowing herself to appear as the soft, caring woman, eager to heal the nation. When she became Prime

Minister in 1979 she invoked St. Francis of Assisi, whose feeling for nature, compassion for the unfortunate, and repudiation of wealth made him a less than obvious soulmate for the Tory champion of Enterprise. "Where there is discord, may we bring harmony," proved to be, at best, an ironic wish, for she succeeded in doing the opposite and expressed few regrets about the conflicts she provoked. More typical of Mrs. Thatcher's public persona was her attempt to combine feminine power and martial strength, figuring herself as defender of the nation and guardian of its virtue. As a politician, she was more comfortable in the role of warrior queen than nurturing mother. The image she liked to project, Marina Warner observes, was "womanly, combining Britannia's resoluteness, Boadicea's courage with a proper housewifely demeanour."[22]

In personal relations, Mrs. Thatcher was much gentler than her public image suggested. For all her public duties and personal ambitions, the politician never wholly abandoned the traditional female role of wife and mother. Even as her career prospered, she continued to care for her husband Denis, and deferred to him in certain matters. Again, Sir William Pile is a good witness. He recalled her unusual conduct in 1970 in the middle of an important budget discussion. As he was briefing Mrs. Thatcher on a Wednesday before the next day's Cabinet meeting, she suddenly interrupted him.

> She said, "Oh, I must go and get some bacon." And I said, "What do you mean?" She said, "I must get Denis some bacon." And I said, "Well, the girls in the office outside can get it for you." "No," she said, "they won't know what kind of bacon he likes." So she got up and she went down, she put her hat on, she put her coat on, I remember she put her gloves on because it was, after all, November, and she walked down to Clarges Street, across the road into Shepherd Market, bought apparently a pound of streaky bacon, came back into the of-

fice, took her gloves off, took her coat off, put the bacon down, sat down on the chair and said, "Now where were we?"[23]

Although the incident can be interpreted as a minister putting a civil servant in his place, it also suggests that she really was comfortable with her domestic role.

Unnerving or undesirable as it was to expose her vulnerabilities in public, Mrs. Thatcher recognized that it was politically useful to advertise traditional feminine behavior. Gordon Reece, her media adviser during the 1979 general election, reinforced this lesson. The grocer's daughter was canny enough to recognize that the good housekeeping ethic which derived from Victorian conceptions of sound domestic management was a potent metaphor. The figure of the thrifty, meticulous housewife made economic theory more readily accessible to ordinary people. But as critics pointed out, it oversimplified complex matters. In any event, Mrs. Thatcher was careful to orchestrate the public display of conventional femininity. So she allowed photographs or films of her washing dishes, stacking the larder, hanging wallpaper, and cooking for her government ministers. Such images displayed a certain homeliness in her character that made her less threatening and more palatable to those who would have preferred that the term "woman politician" remain an oxymoron.

Brought up to control herself and to harness her emotions, Mrs. Thatcher found it difficult to express feelings in public. "This doesn't mean," she explained, "that you aren't compassionate in the face of *other people's* failures and disappointments; it means you don't indulge in self pity, and that you don't encourage anyone else to."[24] The woman who refused to express sympathy with the plight of the long-term unemployed or single parents was a far more considerate and caring friend than her public image suggested. This was a point often made by her loyal defenders. Ian Gow, who was both a personal friend and political confidant of the Prime Minister, noted: "Her capacity to feel affection for people in distress, her capacity to feel affection for her friends was something which they understood and which I understood but which the world doesn't seem yet to understand."[25] When Gow was assassinated in 1990 by the IRA, Mrs. Thatcher rushed down to Eastbourne to comfort his wife Jane. And when her own driver died, she made time to attend his funeral.

I V

ONE WOULD EXPECT NOTHING LESS OF A GOOD CHRISTIAN whose character was shaped by her father's religious faith.[26]

Methodism was, as the political commentator Peter Jenkins put it, the petty bourgeoisie at song; even if the song did not much appeal to those with more posh ears.[27] Alfred Roberts was a well-known lay preacher. The atmosphere of his home was severe, moralistic, and workful, not much given to frivolity. He insisted on a Sabbatarian regime, ensuring that his family observe a traditional English Sunday with few of its pleasures. Two or three times a day on Sunday, Alfred (and sometimes Margaret) walked to the Finkin Street Chapel, an early Victorian classical building that could accommodate a congregation of one thousand. As Prime Minister, Mrs. Thatcher delighted in asking members of her Cabinet to identify passages from Scripture even when they were more likely to know passages from Pliny or Horace. "We are Methodists, and Methodist means method," remarked the politician, who retained the commitment to a systematic and orderly existence even after she joined the Church of England.

But Methodism also meant much else to her. As a member of a Nonconformist sect in a country where the elite was solidly Anglican if not profoundly pious, her Methodist roots reinforced the sense of marginality that came also from her geographical origins and class position. This only strengthened Margaret Thatcher's feeling of being embattled. Born to an evangelical tradition preoccupied by the stain of sin and hope of redemption, it was natural for her to become a "conviction politician," a righteous leader who loathed compromise. Her Methodist faith confirmed that life was a struggle, indeed a Manichaean struggle between the children of light and the children of darkness. In the industrial regions of Wales, Lancashire, and the West Riding of Yorkshire in the nineteenth and twentieth centuries, Methodism often had radical social implications. It helped fire an egalitarian ethic that contributed mightily to the Labour movement, offering the prospect of closing the gap between the kingdom of God and the kingdom of man. And so chapels were sometimes the bedrock of working-class socialism.

The Methodist milieu in which Margaret was raised, however, was much closer to the "Hebraism" described and derided by Matthew Arnold in *Culture and Anarchy*. There was little room for, or even awareness of, the contemplative life celebrated in Arnold's beloved "Hellenism." Oversimplified as his unsympathetic portrait of English Nonconformity is, the faults Arnold ascribed to Margaret Thatcher's nineteenth-century precursors apply equally well to her: excessive individualism, insensitivity to the plight of the poor, and a distrust of the state. The "Hebraic" character of the Methodist ethic helps explains her remarkable elective affinity with Jews and Judaism.

Indeed, the conservative columnist Peregrine Worsthorne announced in the *Daily Telegraph* that Judaism was the new creed of Thatcherite Britain, a claim that was not entirely welcomed by all Gentiles or Jews.[28] Her identification with the Jews stemmed partly from the deep Methodist concern with the meaning of the Old as well as the New Testament. As an ambitious, aggrieved outsider in search of acceptance and success, it was natural for her to see Jews as kindred spirits. For it was natural for her to admire those who triumphed over adversity through intelligence and determination, as she herself did. Her Protestant ethic also accorded well with certain Jewish values: reverence for education, dedication to hard work, belief in self-reliance, and admiration for achievement. Although Jewish tradition was not universally hospitable to the pursuit of wealth, generally it took a far more positive view of business than the genteel, anti-industrial ethic.

"I have enormous admiration for the Jewish people, inside or outside Israel," wrote Margaret Thatcher in her memoirs. Her philo-Semitism was not unheard of among British statesmen and politicians. Oliver Cromwell, Winston Churchill, and Harold Wilson were all known for a certain sympathy for the Jews. But anti-Semitism was commonplace (while Jews were not) in the old Tory squirearchy and indeed in the world of small provincial towns in which Margaret grew up.

Finchley, the only parliamentary constituency Mrs. Thatcher ever represented, had a high proportion of Jewish residents. So she had both the opportunity and the motivation to get to know Jews individually. Always a hardworking constituency MP, she would occasionally attend services in a Northwest London synagogue. She particularly admired the fact that Jews took care of each other in her district and elsewhere. "In the thirty-three years I represented it, I never had a Jew come in poverty and desperation to one of my constituency surgeries. They had always been looked after by their own community," she noted.[29]

It was also no accident that the Prime Minister's favorite clergyman was the Chief Rabbi of the British Empire, Sir Immanuel Jakobovits. An Orthodox German Jew whose father was a rabbi, he came to Britain as a child when his family fled from the Nazis. Sir Immanuel's old-fashioned commitment to self-help and individual responsibility delighted Mrs. Thatcher. In her memoirs, she observed: "I often wished that

Christian leaders would take a leaf" out of his teaching.[30] For her part, she borrowed his phrases and drew on his philosophy. Lest her message, or his achievement, go unheeded, she also rewarded him with a life peerage.

Mrs. Thatcher's admiration for Jews was not confined to the chief rabbi. "There have always been Jewish members of my staff and indeed my Cabinet. In fact, I just wanted a Cabinet of clever, energetic people—and frequently that turned out to be the same thing."[31] Whatever the cause, there was a remarkably large number of Jews in the various Thatcher governments. At one time or another, they included Sir Keith Joseph, Nigel Lawson, David Young, Leon Brittan, Malcolm Rifkind, and Michael Howard. One reason Mrs. Thatcher opted for so many Jewish Cabinet ministers was that they provided a welcome counterweight to the paternalistic Tories of the old school.[32] Hugo Gryn, an Auschwitz survivor, charismatic Reform rabbi, and well-known broadcaster, offered a more personal explanation of Mrs. Thatcher's kinship with the Jews: Her ideal man was the good Jewish husband and father, a reliable, hardworking type like Alfred Roberts.[33]

V

FOR MARGARET THATCHER, AS FOR MANY AMBITIOUS GENTILES and Jews, education figured prominently in the story of her success.

Her means of ascent began with a county scholarship to a grammar school, a fee-paying institution that offered an excellent education to those who were intellectually curious or upwardly mobile. As a grammar school girl, she came from a different caste from the former public school boys who ruled the Conservative Party and who were also influential in the Labour Party. Alfred Roberts was a governor and then chairman of the Kesteven and Grantham School for Girls. Both

Margaret and her sister attended this school, which was built in 1911. When the former Prime Minister became Lady Thatcher, the newly created baroness eschewed Grantham in her title just as she had abandoned it in her youth. Instead, she referred to Kesteven, invoking the section of Lincolnshire in which she grew up and, perhaps, her old school as well.

Dutiful, hardworking, and able, Margaret was sometimes called "Snobby Roberts" by schoolmates. This was a testimonial to her manner rather than her origins. A childhood friend, Dreda Chomacki, who was brought up near the Roberts shop, recalled what Margaret was like during their days together in primary school. She was a serious girl, but not so serious as to forego playing games like hide-and-seek. "I always remember her bulging satchel; it could never close, and mine never seemed to have anything in it." Another school friend, Margaret Wickstead, remembered that when an author came to school to talk about spies, Margaret Roberts asked him questions using quasi-parliamentary language. She asked, "Does the speaker think so and so?" as if she was getting ready for Question Time in the House of Commons.[34] Prematurely haughty she may have been, but Margaret was nonetheless successful. She gained a place at Somerville College, Oxford, even though it was offered at the last minute.

Oxford was the royal road to entry into the British elite. As the university that educated more prime ministers than any other, it offered potential access to the highest reaches of government. Wartime Oxford, though, was far different from the extravagant milieu of Evelyn Waugh's *Brideshead Revisited*. Margaret's Oxford was not divided between cultivated aesthetes and athletic carousers. Nevertheless, the ancient university with its elaborate traditions and social rites must have been overwhelming to a grocer's daughter from Grantham who was neither wealthy nor intellectual.

Rather than study Classics, Modern Languages, Modern

History, Law, or PPE (Philosophy, Politics, and Economics), Margaret had earlier opted for Chemistry. This choice set her apart not only from most other female students but also from male politicians who tended to study arts subjects. Had she received a more traditional humanistic education she would have been better equipped to assimilate into the British elite, where it was smarter to refer to Cicero than to Lavoisier at cocktail parties. The fact that Edward Heath had studied at Balliol and was a devoted organist helped compensate for his own modest lower-middle-class origins.

Although British education in the 1930s and 1940s was not as severely specialized as it is today, the rift between the "two cultures" was still very much in evidence. As the only British Prime Minister trained in the hard sciences, Margaret Thatcher was later able to understand technical matters with a professionalism unavailable to those who had studied "Classical Greats." However, there is little evidence that she was an enthusiastic research scientist eager to uncover nature's laws. She decided to study Chemistry because she believed that it would be easier to obtain a place at Oxford in the sciences rather than the arts. Besides, she did not have the financial means to be an amateur. She needed a profession that would allow her to support herself if need be. Great talent as a chemist she did not possess, but she was as always able and diligent, taking a second-class degree. One of her teachers, Professor Dorothy Hodgkin, later a Nobel Prize laureate in Chemistry, "came to rate her as good. One could always rely on her producing a sensible, well-read essay."[35]

Far more condescending was the view put forth by Janet Vaughan, who became Principal of Somerville in 1945. "She was a perfectly adequate chemist. I mean nobody thought anything of her"—a sniffy statement which reveals more about the eye of the beholder than the talent of the beheld.[36] At all events, the study of chemistry strengthened a preeminently practical frame of mind. It contributed to Margaret

Roberts's tendency to conceive the world in terms of problems and solutions with little nuance or ambiguity. Chemical experiments did not encourage the philosophical penchant of quantum physicists for exploring the meaning of Einstein's theory of relativity, or later, Heisenberg's uncertainty principle.

Although Margaret Thatcher's entry into politics began at Oxford, world events rather than academic theory shaped her public consciousness. Even if she was not untouched by the economic traumas of the Great Depression she witnessed in childhood, it was the experience of World War II that moved her most deeply. Before the outbreak of hostilities she recognized the impact of Nazi tyranny through the testimony of her sister's pen pal, Edith, an Austrian Jew, who lived for a time with the Roberts family after she emigrated. Edith's experience deepened Margaret's sympathy with the plight of Jews. Coming of age during a national crisis that threatened Britain's survival, the most telling lessons of Margaret's painful political education were the dangers of appeasement and the value of combativeness.

As a young girl growing up in an absolutist moral universe, Margaret Roberts came to see the shameful and near-disastrous results of Neville Chamberlain's unsuccessful attempt to pacify Hitler. The lesson learned on her father's knee and reinforced by chapel preaching—there could be no compromise with evil—was solidified by the war. She was, therefore, bound to admire Winston Churchill's great wartime speeches in which he affirmed again and again, "We shall never surrender." The martial spirit in the service of morality would inspire her politics long after VE-Day.

Outsider that Margaret was, her path to a political career was impeccably traditional: Oxford, the Bar, and Parliament. At Oxford, she joined the Conservative Party. This was a relatively unusual, but by no means unheard of, affiliation for a member of a generation that came to maturity under the glow of Utopian dreams. But unlike so many of those who lived through the trials of World War II, it hardly made her a socialist. Excluded as a woman from participation in the Oxford Union, a stepping stone to political office in the wider world, Margaret took another route. She joined the Conservative Association at Oxford and eventually became its president. Unremarkable in her political orientation, she was among many young Conservatives who sided with party reformers. They realized after, if not before, the general election of 1945 that it was necessary to change their approach to avoid annihilation by Labour.

After coming down from Oxford, Margaret had to postpone her dream of a political career while she earned a living as a research chemist, first at British Xylonite Plastics in Essex and then at J. Lyons in London, where she tested the quality of cake and of ice cream. The fact that she was the youngest woman to stand in the general election of 1950 did not help her win a virtually unwinnable Dartford seat. As she sought political office, however, she studied for the Bar. This was an excellent place for a future politician, especially a Conservative, to make contacts. But Margaret had difficulty finding chambers that would take her on, because she was a woman. However much she may have resented, or simply accepted, such discrimination is an open question. What is clear, though, is that her legal training afforded her an entree into an upscale social milieu and a good look at some classic fuddy-duddy establishment types. Again, we do not know if she was impressed or depressed by what she saw at the ancient Inns of Court. In any case, she specialized in tax law, an uncommon choice for a woman but one which suited her technical bent and financial interests.

The economic independence the grocer's daughter needed came, however, from a more traditional source. At the end of 1951, she made a "good marriage" to Denis Thatcher. A Tory stalwart, he was managing director of the

Atlas Preservative Company, a family firm that began making weedkiller and sheepdip and later diversified into paint and chemicals. His personal fortune provided Margaret the financial freedom she needed to study at the Bar and then to pursue a political career. Denis also helped her understand the workings of business. As John Hoskyns, himself an able businessman as well as onetime director of the Policy Unit at Downing Street, commented: "She is married to someone who has been in business all his life, does understand balance sheets, does understand how people tick, does understand the imperatives of business. I've very often heard her say on topics that have cropped up in nationalised industries and so on, 'Well, Denis looked at the balance sheet and said, "you know, there seems to be an awful lot of debt there which ought to be capitalised." ' "37

Margaret Thatcher's first moment of political victory came in the general election of 1959. She entered the Commons as MP from Finchley, a seat she won by 16,260 votes, handily increasing the already comfortable majority of 12,000 enjoyed by the Conservatives. When she first represented Finchley, her constituency still included Hampstead Garden Suburb and Totteridge, wealthy suburbs with strong Conservative followings. These areas apart, Finchley was preeminently middle class. It was, therefore, a comfortable seat for Margaret Thatcher, who would not have done so well in a county constituency where she would have had to contend with ladies with very large hats and gentlemen with very old pedigrees. Finchley, with a high proportion of owner-occupied houses and a substantial number of Jews, was better suited to her, and vice versa.

This was all the more so because the Jewish community in Finchley (as in most sections of Northwest London) tended to be conservative in politics and traditionalist in religion. At any rate, its members were further to the right and closer to the strait and narrow than their more intellectual or assimilated brethren. Moreover, Finchley Jews tended to be upwardly mobile. Many were small businessmen or accountants one generation out of the East End. (The Asian community that later settled in Finchley had some of the same ideals and traits.) Their values were broadly similar to, or at least compatible with, the Methodist ethic upheld by Alfred Roberts's younger daughter.[38] From the first, she was philo-Semitic. This endeared her to her constituents, who resented the fact that in the late 1950s, the Finchley Golf Club (like many of its ilk) was "officered by prominent Conservatives" who excluded Jews from membership.[39]

Finchley is thirty minutes or so from central London by Underground if the Northern Line runs on time. Thanks to the expansion of the railway, Finchley grew rapidly at the turn of the century. Like many of the villages on the outskirts of London, it was duly gobbled up by the metropolis. Reasonably close as it is to the Hertfordshire countryside, Finchley is not rural. And it is too far removed from the West End to have an urban face or feel. While Finchley is near to Hampstead and Highgate (as well as to Hampstead Garden Suburb), it does not stand up well to comparison with any of them. As suburbs go, Finchley is a poor relation (in both visual character and property values). Both Highgate and Hampstead are hilly, picturesque districts with interesting architecture and good views. They have the added advantage of being close to Hampstead Heath, North London's most beautiful open space. In sensibility and townscape, Finchley bears little resemblance to these pockets of the intelligentsia.

To be fair, though, Finchley is a pleasant, if ordinary, suburb. Main streets such as Ballards Lane and Regent's Park Road contain some attractive Victorian buildings. Some have Flemish gables, others ornamental friezes, and still others proudly display in fine lettering the year they were built. Finchley has its share of standard order red brick terraced or semi-detached houses of turn-of-the-century vintage. And it has a number of boring, but probably harmless, low-rise blocks of flats, some built in the 1960s, others in the 1980s. On Hendon Lane, a longish and windy road, there are some very large new houses which have Tudor-style half-timbering or three-car garages (a rarity in Britain). Finchley also has at least one delightful place. This is the area called the Villages, a group of cottages in the vague but charming "olde England" style commonplace at the turn of the century. They are set asymmetrically on an inviting village green, which at one time was presumably the site of local cricket matches. Now their main use is dog walking.

Although suburban Finchley has no industry, it does have plenty of retail stores. Most are dowdy; few are trendy. Still, there is the usual mixture found on most English high streets. Finchley has building societies like the Abbey National where you can save in hope of buying a house (a prospect improved during the Thatcher years). It has a job center (for those who were inspired or fired during the economic ups-and-downs of the 1980s). Small grocery shops (usually run by enterprising Indian or Pakistani families) stay open in the evening. There is also a plain, large building that contains Tesco's, a supermarket chain founded by the Cohen family, admirers of Mrs. Thatcher. Whether or not Finchley is a land of opportunity is hard to say. What is clear, though, is that it is a land of take-away. Not only are there a number of Indian and Chinese restaurants, but also an abundance of American-style fast-food places like Domino's Pizza, Pizza Hut, and Kentucky Fried Chicken. For Jewish families who left the East End but refused to depart from ancient ways, Finchley offers kosher bakeries such as the Parkway Patisserie. And for those aspiring folk who want to equip their old or renovated homes with an instant touch of the past (or, at least, facsimiles thereof) there is a store that sells Doric arches, fake Greek sculpture, marble fireplaces, as well as the odd frieze or molding.

Finchley was Mrs. Thatcher's constituency, but her own style was very different. In short, she lived a far more privileged and wealthy (though not ostentatious) existence than the run of the mill middle-class Finchley family. Until 1969, the Thatchers and their twins, Mark and Carol, lived in Kent, in a general area sometimes called the stockbroker belt and among a class of people sometimes called the gin-and tonic set. They had a sizable house with a swimming pool (not much good in an average English summer) plus three acres of land. Then they moved to Chelsea. This was a step up in the world. Not only was Chelsea far smarter than Kent, but also it was close to Parliament and within easy reach of Mrs. Thatcher's constituency. Kingsley Amis describes the Thatchers' house, No. 19 Flood Street, as "one of those neat little joints between the King's Road and the Chelsea Embankment, comfortable but ungrand and decorated in a boldly unadventurous style."[40] Like many Chelsea houses, it is smallish, cozy, and discreet. It is also expensive.

Chelsea is one of the loveliest, and most satisfying, parts of London. A onetime riverside village that spread out from the north bank of the Thames, most of Chelsea's mansions yielded to smaller brick houses and terraces during the eighteenth century. In the 1870s and 1880s, the "Queen Anne" style (also known as Pont Street Dutch) flooded the area around Cadogan Square. Around the same time, a host of imaginative, playful houses sprang up around Cheyne Walk. It was, above all, Norman Shaw who colored Chelsea's new face. Rich in bohemian undertones, Chelsea attracted a host of artists. But the fact that its aesthetic appeal was kept intact was largely the work of the Cadogan Estate. The aristocratic landowners and their agents who owned much of the area enforced regulations on exterior architectural design and kept developers at bay or at heel. The agreeable milieu in which Mrs. Thatcher and her family lived, then, might have been very different if the free market she so admired had run its course in her neighborhood. Brimming with establishment types from aristocratic or gentry backgrounds, Chelsea was an ideal place to live a quiet, understated life.

In the 1960s, real estate prices were still low enough to permit some writers to live there. So when the Thatchers moved to Chelsea, it was full of artists with floppy hats (as well as colonels with tweedy coats, brogues, and walking sticks). Also it had artists' supply stores like Green & Stone at the end of King's Road near World's End (so named for a landmark pub there). As a hub of the "swinging sixties," Chelsea became a mecca for the young and trendy, with or without artistic aspirations or talent. The King's Road contained hip shops like Mary Quant's, beneath which was a popular restaurant called Alexanders. The Rolling Stones hung out at The Drug Store. All this attracted a flock of American expatriates, most of whom were involved in film or media. In Chelsea they found an intriguing mixture of the old and the new. The Americans brought brash manners, central heating, ice makers, and strong showers to houses and persons used to none of this. In the course of the late 1960s, though, the face of Chelsea changed somewhat as large stores like Safeway replaced small boutiques; The Drug Store eventually gave way to McDonald's.

While England was swinging and Chelsea grooving, the Thatchers were barely moving. Or, at least, Mrs. Thatcher was moving backwards in an effort to recapture the enterprising spirit of the Victorians. Her sympathy was for the free market rather than free love. If nothing else, she could content herself with the fact that Chelsea was a solid Tory seat, whatever decadent nonsense may have taken place there. At any rate, it was in Chelsea that she conceived the capitalist revolution. But her vision hearkened back to what she had learned on her father's knee, and it was more in keeping with Finchley's values than Chelsea's style. The irony was that her revolution left little room for the gentry, and little honor for the artists, who peopled Chelsea. With the cash register in mind and the balance sheet in hand, Maggie went to the barricades.

VI

YET MARGARET THATCHER'S POLITICAL ASCENT AND ECO-nomic philosophy would have been unthinkable without the rise of a conservative counter-establishment. Not an intellectual herself, she turned to others for a source of ideas and a base for power. "In the beginning was the mood," quipped conservative intellectual Alfred Sherman, and the mood was Margaret Thatcher's.[41] Although there are few traces in her early political career of the capitalist revolutionary she later became, the ideology she came to espouse accorded well with her own deepest instincts. As an undergraduate at Oxford she read Friedrich von Hayek's *The Road to Serfdom* (1944), in which he argued that Socialist planning, no less than the Fascist state, would lead to totalitarianism.

During her first unsuccessful bid for a parliamentary seat, Mrs. Thatcher denounced Labour as the party of natural envy and class hatred. The Welfare State produced people who resembled a caged bird that lacked the freedom to fly out and live its own life. Even though some of the elements of her later thinking are apparent in her early career, a coherent ideology was necessary to turn Thatcher's mood into an effective movement. She was, in this regard as in many others, far luckier than Heath. Her predecessor "did not have what Margaret Thatcher had—the backing of an intellectual revolution," as Lord Blake, historian of the Conservative Party, observed.[42]

The leading figures who influenced Margaret Thatcher were rebels. They rejected the social democratic consensus that had prevailed in postwar Britain. Preeminent among the

Conservative politicians who sought an alternative to prevailing orthodoxies was Sir Keith Joseph, the philosopher of the new right. "Passionately English and passionately Jewish," Sir Keith was born in a beautiful home with an Adam interior in Portland Place in the West End, far from the slums and markets of East End immigrants. His social milieu resembled the privileged, serene, Anglo-Jewish world that C. P. Snow captured so well in his novel *The Conscience of the Rich.* Little, if anything, from Sir Keith's childhood smacked of the exuberant, striving world of East European Jews.

The son of a Lord Mayor of London who founded Bovis, a successful building concern, Sir Keith attended Harrow and took a first at Magdalen College, Oxford, in Jurisprudence. He served courageously during World War II and was elected a Fellow of All Souls, Oxford. Like Charles March in *The Conscience of the Rich,* Sir Keith read for the Bar and had a strong social conscience. It led him to social work in the East End and, finally, to a political career. Unlike March, however, he did not become a socialist.

An English gentleman by virtue of birth and education, Joseph was far more intense and uneasy than his Gentile compatriots. Sometimes characterized as a "mad monk," he did the done thing but agonized over nearly everything else. His preoccupation with social issues led him to the Ministry of Housing. There he became involved in clearing slums and building better homes for the people. A moderate Tory in tune with "the middle way" between capitalism and socialism espoused by Harold Macmillan, Sir Keith fit in reasonably well with Edward Heath and Company. But in April 1974, he underwent a conversion experience. Unlike St. Paul, whose epiphany on the road to Tarsus taught him that man is totally dependent on God, Sir Keith was struck down by a panoply of free market angels. They sang a chorus of "Thou shalt not intervene." And they preached that man must depend on himself rather than the state. "I was converted to

Conservatism. I had thought that I was a Conservative but I now see that I was not one at all."[43]

The newly enlightened Sir Keith Joseph sought the counsel and support of political outsiders. Along with Margaret Thatcher, he was responsible for setting up a rival to the Conservative Party Research Department, the Centre for Policy Studies (CPS). This right-wing think tank initially received the blessing of Edward Heath. But he would have been better off slaughtering the goose whose golden egg ended up on his face. However influential CPS became, it was the Institute for Economic Affairs (IEA), founded in 1957, that first advocated free market economics and criticized the Welfare State. Funded by Anthony Fisher, who made his money in the chicken business, and headed by the economist Ralph Harris, its mission was to revive and adapt classical liberal economics. Rather than focus exclusively on the "Stupid Party," as John Stuart Mill once described the Tories, the IEA was intent on changing the thinking of all the political parties.[44]

In search of new ideas, Mrs. Thatcher and Sir Keith Joseph turned to an assortment of relative outsiders to form a conservative counter-establishment. Of these the most important was Alfred Sherman, who became director of CPS. The son of a Labour councillor, Sherman was an East End Jew known for being fiery rather than genteel. A born-again capitalist, he was once a true believing Communist, who served as a machine gunner during the Spanish Civil War. Impatient with the Conservative hierarchy, he acted as an economics tutor of sorts to both Joseph and Thatcher. A number of businessmen joined the fold. They included David Wolfson of Great Universal Stores, Norman Strauss of Unilever, both of whom were Jewish, and John Hoskyns. A Winchester graduate who went into the Army, Hoskyns joined IBM and then began a highly successful computer software business which he eventually sold in 1975. Straightforward and clearheaded, Hoskyns had been a Labour supporter in the sixties before he had the business experience to realize "what a disaster socialism was."[45] Along with Wolfson and Strauss, Hoskyns brought to the counter-establishment perspectives from the business culture that were foreign to more conventional Tories with little experience of, or taste for, systems theory and business strategy.[46]

The counter-establishment shared common views on what went wrong with Britain and how to set it right. They started from the assumption that in 1945 Britain still stood high in the world, a powerful and righteous nation that had defeated the Nazi menace. In their narrative, the history of postwar Britain was a tale of decline. In an IEA pamphlet, for example, Robert Allen bemoaned the economic consequences of the disdain for trade, the failure of the public schools and Oxbridge to educate future business leaders, the cult of the amateur, and the complacency of businessmen's heirs.

The "British disease" was a symptom of profound national decay. "Unless we change our way and direction," Mrs. Thatcher said in an unusually purple passage, "our greatness as a nation will soon be a footnote in the history books, a distant memory of an offshore island, lost in the mists of time, like Camelot, remembered kindly for its noble past."[47] Socialism was the demon undoing Britain. Mrs. Thatcher did not deny the need for the Welfare State or suggest a return to laissez-faire. But she did attack the "progressive consensus" which held that the state was responsible for promoting equality, providing social welfare, and redistributing wealth and income.

Socialist practice was even more flawed than Socialist theory. Britain had too few producers and too many consumers, as Oxford economists Walter Ellis and Robert Bacon argued. The great obstacle to British recovery was the trade union. The unions' historic link with the Labour Party "institutionalised a romantic, outmoded and economically illiterate socialism," argued Sir Keith Joseph.[48] The unions were selfish and irresponsible. They demanded pay hikes that caused an inflationary spiral which had to be stopped. "Inflation is threatening to destroy our society," wrote Joseph.[49]

If socialism was the cause of the British disease, capitalism was surely the cure. Socialism was unfair. It concentrated power in the hands of government officials and deprived the individual of basic economic freedoms. Economic inequality was the result of different levels of effort and achievement. Capitalism was morally superior to socialism. The founders of classical and modern liberal thought provided a philosophical foundation for this conviction. Adam Smith taught that capitalism was the "natural system of liberty" and, moreover, that the rule of law and competition were its twin cornerstones. Friedrich von Hayek taught that political and economic freedom were inseparable. Milton Friedman taught that the Keynesian commitment to government intervention in economic life crippled the market.

At the core of Margaret Thatcher's vision, then, was a call to return to the free economy. This meant "A man's right to work as he will, to spend what he earns, to own property, to have the State as servant and not as master."[50] But it did not mean, at least in her speeches during the mid-1970s, that government spending on social welfare was illegitimate. Rather, Mrs. Thatcher maintained that profit was a social good. For it was "wealth creation" that provided the resources which ensured job security for workers and social services for the community.

The counter-establishment took some pains to argue that their economic thinking was in line with Tory tradition. At very least, Mrs. Thatcher and Sir Keith could claim that their project was consistent with the free market emphasis of Peter Thorneycroft when he was Chancellor in the late 1950s and Edward Heath before his U-turn.[51] Nevertheless, the new right's cure for the British disease seemed to owe little if anything to the shades of Tory sages Edmund Burke or Benjamin Disraeli. Traditional Tory concepts such as hierarchy, service, obligation, and compassion were all but forgotten in monetarist economics. And yet the free market ideology of the counter-establishment was not simply the bastard child of Victorian liberalism and political opportunism. For all the talk of freedom, Margaret Thatcher and Sir Keith Joseph believed that inequality was inevitable and denied that it was undesirable.

It was Heath's miscalculations and misfortunes that provided Margaret Thatcher's opportunity to gain power. After losing two general elections in 1974, Heath's leadership came into question among Conservative backbenchers who regarded him as an electoral liability. Misreading the mood of the party, he failed to resign and was forced to stand for election to remain Leader of the Opposition. Only when Heath's likely right-wing opponents, Edward du Cann, chairman of the influential 1922 Committee of backbenchers, and Sir Keith Joseph, refused to stand did Margaret Thatcher decided to oppose him. Even then, she was a dark horse. She had not held a major ministerial position, and she did not belong to the inner circle of the party. Her prospects would have been negligible were it not for the fact that the Tories had made a conscious choice in the mid-1960s to shed some of their patrician, oligarchical past. After the election of Lord Home, they scrapped the old system of informal consultation from which the leader "emerged" and replaced it with a democratic system whereby MPs elected the leader.

The new rules under which Heath was elected ultimately jeopardized his power. Backed by senior party figures, peers, and constituency workers, his support among Tory MPs was far weaker than his managers suggested. On February 4, 1975, he lost the first ballot to Mrs. Thatcher by 130 votes to 119. So Heath resigned immediately, making way for mainstream candidates more to his liking, notably William Whitelaw. But

Whitelaw suffered from his ties to Heath and his reluctance to stand in the first round. By the second ballot, it was too late.

Thatcher's election was a "peasant's revolt," as the Conservative MP Julian Critchley put it. In other words, it was a backbench rebellion led by a woman whose ascent, like Heath's, marked the triumph of a meritocratic strain within a party whose front benches were still largely controlled by upper-middle-class products of the public schools and Oxbridge. Once installed as party leader, however, the leader of the peasants was quick to make peace with the aristocrats. Margaret Thatcher was, as she liked to announce, a "conviction politician," who believed that British politics was, at heart, a battle of ideas. It was necessary, as Sir Keith Joseph argued, to move from the "middle ground" of the political spectrum to find "common ground" among ordinary people.

Nevertheless, Margaret Thatcher proved less radical in practice than in theory. Perhaps the grocer's daughter retained a certain deferential attitude to the high and mighty in spite of herself. Perhaps she simply recognized that her support was too thin to allow her to consolidate power quickly. Whatever the reason, she made few changes in the Shadow Cabinet. Most of Heath's people stayed on even though he remained unreconciled to his conqueror. Mrs. Thatcher also reached out to influential moderates such as William Whitelaw and Sir Geoffrey Howe, both of whom became key figures. And she was, for all her commitment to free market economics, cautious in tactics and policy.

Careful to make amends with the Tory establishment, the new Leader of the Opposition tried her utmost to discredit and undermine James Callaghan's minority Labour government. Without great success, though, judging by opinion polls. The genial Prime Minister proved more popular, trustworthy, and competent in the voters' eyes than his opponent. But he did not take her quite seriously enough. For all the problems that beset Labour around the time of the IMF crisis, the Callaghan government had made a creditable recovery, denting both unemployment and inflation. It was the supposed friends of Labour who proved its undoing in the strikes and slow-downs during the "Winter of Discontent." These included a "day of action" by 1 million local government workers, the largest single stoppage since the General Strike of 1926. Ineffective as the Callaghan government was, it did not go to the country until it lost a vote of confidence debate on March 28, 1979, and then by a margin of one.

The beneficiary of labor strife was Mrs. Thatcher. Tim Bell of Saatchi & Saatchi advised her to emphasize freedom, choice, and minimal government intervention. The economic issues stressed in *The Conservative Manifesto, 1979* were the need to control inflation and trade union power on the one hand and to restore incentives on the other hand. Whatever anxieties the voters had about Mrs. Thatcher proved less telling in the end than the frustrations that fueled their desire for change. And it was Margaret Thatcher who promised radical change to the voters, while James Callaghan defended the status quo in the name of fairness and cooperation. The Conservative lead in the opinion polls slipped in the course of the campaign from 11 percent to 5 percent. On May 3, the day of reckoning, though, they gained an overall majority of 43 seats in the Commons. They won the election with 43.9 percent of the vote, compared to Labour's 37 percent and the Liberals' 13.8 percent. Although they enjoyed only a plurality of the popular vote, the 5.1 percent swing to the Conservatives was the largest in the postwar era. It was most pronounced in the southernmost regions of England and in Wales and among skilled workers who deserted the Labour Party.

When Margaret Thatcher returned from her audience with the Queen at Buckingham Palace and entered 10 Downing Street, the capitalist revolution was under way. But what did it mean? Although there was popular support for greater economic efficiency, this did not imply a rejection of social welfare. Tax reduction appealed to voters, but not if it meant a reduction in government services.

Even Mrs. Thatcher's supporters had their doubts. *The Economist* described her as a "leader uncertain under pressure . . . [who had] yet to demonstrate an ability to inspire great confidence or affection among the uncommitted voters, let alone among those who voted against her."[52] Peregrine Worsthorne predicted that "There will be neither revolution nor counter-revolution."[53] Margaret Thatcher did not share his skepticism. She had asked the British people for a "last chance" to reverse the nation's decline. Now, how would she use it? As she often said to her advisers, with a belligerent confidence that belied her need for counsel: "Don't tell me *what*. I know *what*. Tell me *how*."

While Britain Awoke

I

Shortly before Sir Geoffrey Howe, the Chancellor of the Exchequer, was about to present the first budget of the Thatcher government, Peter Jenkins, a leading columnist for the *Guardian,* telephoned Sir Ian Gilmour, the Lord Privy Seal. The commentator asked whether it was true that value-added tax (VAT), the indirect national sales tax levied on most goods, was about to be virtually doubled. Ever cool and civilized, Sir Ian responded that he had "no idea of the contents of the budget." There had been "no question of any kind of cabinet consultation," yet it was "surely inconceivable that anything so silly could even be contemplated."[1] So radical a change seemed unthinkable to Sir Ian, even though he hardly entertained a high opinion of the monetarists responsible for economic policy. A Tory political theorist of wit and distinction who valued experience and loathed dogma, Sir Ian believed that these were men "possessed by ideology and delusion."[2]

There was all the more reason for intense public interest in the budget because the new Prime Minister had promised a "change of direction." For all the intemperate rhetoric which shook her more conventional and consensual colleagues, however, Margaret Thatcher was wary of telling the voters what, if any, detailed plans she had. Hardly known for reticence, she held back partly because she did not know how deep her support was within her own party, partly because she did not know how much change the country would stand, and partly because she did not know what the results of her economic experiment would be.[3] Yet she was still intent on dispelling the comfortable illusions that accompanied decline and on hammering home the notion that Britain had to earn its place in the world.

Unlike Ronald Reagan, who later announced that it was "morning in America," the woman who became his closest ally offered little comfort to her audience. Like an unrelenting alarm clock without a snooze button, ringing in an unheated house on a cold, dark, and wet morning, Margaret Thatcher scolded the English for having overslept—for more than a century by some estimates. It was now high noon, as a character in one of Ronald Reagan's beloved Westerns might have put it.

In office for little more than a month, the Prime Minister and the Chancellor seized the opportunity to make sweeping changes by presenting a budget immediately rather than holding off until the coming year. Long before the Tories returned to office in May 1979, though, preparations had begun for what amounted to an economic search-and-destroy mission. Yet Howe was shocked by the gloomy economic news contained in the blue plastic folder he received upon taking office. The legacy of the outgoing Labour government was even worse than the Chancellor had feared: inflation was climbing, unemployment rising, and oil prices shooting up. Precisely how he intended to respond to these conditions was a closely guarded secret, for unlike other decisions made by the government, "taxation must not be put into commission," as an old Treasury saying put it.[4] In other words, the budget was the exclusive preserve of the Chancellor rather than the collective responsibility of the Cabinet.

By the time Howe became Chancellor of the Exchequer, he was known as a safe pair of hands. Often characterized as the archetype of the caring country lawyer, he was, in fact, an accomplished barrister. Howe was born in 1926 in Port Talbot in South Wales, a predominantly working-class community whose economy was based on coal and tinplate. Although he came from an industrial town, he had little to do with the gritty world of factories and forges around him. Indeed, Howe's maternal grandfather, a highly successful grocer with a chain of stores, supposedly had Manny Shinwell horse-whipped from Cardiff docks for trying to initiate a strike. The closest the young Geoffrey Howe came to the realities of unemployment was the sight of the Labour Exchange which was not far from his Aunt Lil's house. "The dole queue," he recalled, "was a very real feature of my young life, but mercifully in the background rather than in the fabric of my existence."[5] The son of a successful solicitor, Howe hailed from a well-to-do professional family and went to Winchester and Cambridge.

Experienced and respected politician though Howe was, many were surprised when Margaret Thatcher selected him as her Shadow Chancellor. In the early 1950s he had been an influential member of the Bow Group, an organization of socially progressive young Tories, and he had edited its magazine, *Crossbow*. Although Howe's early pamphlets did call for greater economic freedom, they also suggested that the state could create a fairer society by enlarging welfare and improving opportunities—hardly the foundations of the house Mrs. Thatcher wanted to build. Knighted by Heath, he was likely to be damned by Thatcher. For Howe had been in the thick of the 1970–74 Conservative government. As Solicitor General, he was the author of industrial relations legislation which failed to stop the miners' strike. And as Minister for Trade and Consumer Affairs, he went to great lengths in the name of incomes policy. Fighting the good fight against inflation sometimes led to encounters that were unusual for a member of Her Majesty's Government. Once Howe was obliged to telephone a Cambridgeshire vicar to ask him not to increase the charge he made for burials.[6] Such loyal service did little to help Howe when he opposed Mrs. Thatcher, to little effect, on the second ballot of the leadership election.

At least Mrs. Thatcher did not have to fear that Howe would upstage her. Even friends pronounced him best suited to small gatherings. Charming in private, he appeared colorless in public, a poor parliamentary performer for all his experience at the Bar. As Denis Healey put it, in an endlessly repeated jibe, having an argument with Howe was "like being gored by a dead sheep." Like Margaret Thatcher, the Chancellor flourished on great detail and little sleep, but these traits did not endear him to all her acolytes. Among them was Nicholas Ridley, the old Etonian who was Financial Secretary of the Treasury under Howe from 1981 to 1983, a post his great-grandfather had held in the 1890s. "Delegation was not a word he understood."[7]

Whatever common ground Howe and Thatcher shared on policy, a chasm divided their styles. Despite an interconnecting door between Numbers 10 and 11 Downing Street, it is doubtful that the Prime Minister's visits were altogether friendly or welcome. The righteous missionary who detested compromise had little sympathy for her chancellor. Latin tags came more easily to Howe than Victorian homilies. Not one to see visions, hear voices, or burn heretics, "for him politics is about being reasonable, and persuasion a matter of patient education," as his successor Nigel Lawson observed.[8] Howe himself had little taste for Mrs. Thatcher's style. "I am not at all sure about Margaret," he confessed to free-marketer Arthur Seldon in 1969. "Many of her economic prejudices are certainly sound. But she is inclined to be rather too dogmatic for my liking."⁹ On occasion, Howe's reticence angered Mrs. Thatcher, who could live with a Shadow Chancellor but not with an invisible man. Exasperated by his silence during a campaign appearance, she once told him, "For God's sake, say something, Geoffrey." For her part, Mrs. Thatcher said far too much to him. Mistaking his quiet discretion for weakness, she humiliated him in Cabinet, to the consternation of colleagues. Loyal out of principle or ambition, Howe seemed to do little to defend himself from her onslaughts.

All that mattered on June 12, 1979, though, was the reception of Sir Geoffrey's economic plan for national recovery. By any measure, budget day was an extraordinary occasion in the parliamentary calendar, so much so that some MPs still dressed up for the annual rite in the years before it was televised. Budget day ordinarily took place on a Tuesday, according to an ancient custom meant to enable those from the hinterlands to reach London in time for the proceedings. The budget statement itself was usually the longest speech of the year. William Gladstone, the greatest Chancellor of modern times, took four hours to present his famous 1860 budget, during which he fortified himself with draughts of a mixture of egg and wine prepared by his wife.¹⁰

Trailed by cameras and journalists, around 3:00 P.M. Howe set out for Parliament, a short trip from his residence at 11 Downing Street. Dressed in an unsurprisingly traditional pinstripe suit, Howe proudly carried in his arms the fabled red dispatch box that contained the budget for the coming year. Originally made for Gladstone in 1860, it was used by all his successors save James Callaghan, who eschewed it in favor of a modern blue surrogate in 1965, perhaps in the vain hope of signaling the future that never was. By the time Howe was entitled to hold the battered red Gladstone box, it was as faded and frayed as Britain's fortunes. Inscribed in gold on the dispatch box was a barely legible royal seal with the letters ER (standing for Elizabeth Regina), and below the words "CHANCELLOR OF THE EXCHEQUER." Housed for safe-keeping in the Treasury within another box custom-made for this purpose, the Gladstone box was displayed only on budget day.

As Howe looked out at the House of Commons, he could see the likely foes and friends of the plan he was about to detail. He could take for granted that Labour would oppose him at nearly every turn; but with a solid parliamentary majority there was little reason to take their protests too much to heart. Far more troubling than the predictable dissent of the right honorable members on the other side of the Commons was the uncertain reaction of the members of his own party who sat behind him, in particular those on the front benches such as Sir Ian Gilmour, the intellectual leader of the Tory left. For Howe was not about to recite the usual affirmations of social responsibility that came easily to Tory gentlemen proud of their aristocratic finesse and paternalist sentiments. In the seventy-five-minute speech that followed, the Chancellor spoke about the need for economic freedom rather than the right to social equality. Indeed, he was careful to begin with a caveat that "there is a definite limit to our capacity, as politicians, to influence these things for the better." And he ended the budget statement with the assertion that "It is people and not Governments who create prosperity."

Nevertheless, Sir Geoffrey's theme was what government could do to check the relative economic decline that threatened to become absolute. His diagnosis of the British disease held that the root of the malady was "a growing series of failures on the supply side of the economy." The Keynesian approach which advocated managing demand, increasing public spending, and fine-tuning the economy had "been tried almost to destruction." Clear principles guided Howe's antidote: Strengthen incentives by allowing people to keep more of what they earn; reduce the role of the state in order to enlarge individual freedom of choice; lighten the burden of financing the public sector in order to stimulate the private sector; and convince managers and trade unionists that the only real basis for an increase in wages and salary was to raise productivity. The budget was, in short, based on a version of supply-side economics. It assumed that encouraging the able and ambitious to create wealth would ultimately benefit the entire society.

But what would Howe suggest to turn theory into practice—this was what those inside and outside the Commons needed to know. What he proposed was a set of dramatic measures that affected tax structure, exchange controls, monetary policy, and public expenditure. However, none of the reforms would prove effective unless "inflation was squeezed out of the system" and sound money restored. To this end, the Chancellor announced that he would seek a progressive reduction in the growth of the money supply from its current annual rate of 13 percent to a target range of 7–11 percent and would raise interest rates from 2 to 14 percent. In addition, Howe intended to reduce the public sector borrowing requirement, otherwise known as the deficit, from 9.25 percent (5.25 percent of gross domestic product) to 8.25 percent (4.5 percent of gross domestic product) in 1979–80. This required huge spending cuts in the amount of £1,400 million. They came from a number of areas, ranging from reducing subsidies to the insatiable nationalized industries and to certain social welfare programs such as National Health Service prescriptions.

Most momentous of Howe's plans were calls for profound changes in tax structure and exchange controls. From the first, though, those who were already comfortably off would benefit most directly from the reforms. The rest of the country was supposed to wait for the gold to trickle down to their humbler level. Determined to restore incentives, buoy entrepreneurship, and reward businessmen for supporting the Tories, Howe slashed the highest rate of income tax from 83 percent to 60 percent, a move that signaled the end of the "leveling down" happily executed by Labour governments. But even if the tax reduction was a bonanza for the affluent, it spurred entrepreneurs' and managers' financial motivations. What was less than fair, however, was the fact that no such largesse was possible for the ordinary wage earner. Howe cut the basic rate of income tax from 33 percent to 30 percent, but this political gesture did little to relieve what was still a heavy burden.

Such generosity on the Chancellor's part had its price. It cost the Treasury approximately £4 billion in revenue, some of which he tried to recapture by shifting from direct to indirect taxation. So, as Peter Jenkins had surmised, he did indeed announce a rise in VAT from 8 percent to 15 percent—a proposal that initially made the Prime Minister very nervous. Determined to liberate the market economy, Howe announced that he intended to ease out exchange controls. Instituted as a temporary measure after the outbreak of World War II, exchange controls were never abandoned, despite the fact that they were more severe than elsewhere in the industrial world. Not only did they inconvenience tourists who could take only paltry sums on their foreign holidays, but they also crippled overseas investment. Anxious about a run on the pound, however, Howe advocated a cautious schedule of reforms beginning, for instance, by authorizing a £5 million overseas investment per project per year.[11]

This was an opportunity budget, not a give-away, the Chancellor maintained as he finished his statement to the House. "It is designed to give the British people a greater opportunity than they have had for years to win a higher standard of living—for their country and for their families as well as for themselves." At least Tory MPs responded to the opportunity to cheer Howe's speech with enthusiastic applause.

Not so Her Majesty's Loyal Opposition, led by James Callaghan; in his response to Howe, he called the plan a "colossal gamble."[12] The following day, Healey, the Shadow Chancellor, argued that the budget rewarded the rich and punished the poor in typical Conservative fashion. And he warned that it would "produce a massive increase in both prices and unemployment."[13]

But perhaps the most telling reactions to Howe's budget came from one of his Cabinet colleagues. Jim Prior, the Employment Secretary, recalled in his memoirs: "It was really an enormous shock to me that the budget . . . was so extreme." Prior simply did not believe that the economy would expand in response to newly liberated market forces if a better balance was achieved between the public sector and the private. What shook him all the more was the recognition that "Margaret, Geoffrey and Keith really had got the bit between their teeth and were not going to pay attention to the rest of us at all if they could possibly help it." Where would this leave Prior, the only economic minister who was not a monetarist? Thanks to her treatment by Ted Heath, Mrs. Thatcher knew what it was like to be cold-shouldered in the Cabinet. Would she do the same to those who did not agree with her?[14]

To criticisms of the budget from within and without, John Biffen, the Chief Secretary of the Treasury, candidly responded: "I do not deny that this is a severe package. The severity is made necessary by the situation we inherited."[15] After years of denial, shock treatment was in order to revive a stubborn patient. But would it awaken or bury England?

I I

WHETHER THE ECONOMIC POLICIES OF THE THATCHER GOVernment provided a basis for prosperity or an invitation to catastrophe, they were part of a larger program designed to reverse decline by making socialist Britain an "enterprise culture."

Monetarism was not enough, as Sir Keith Joseph had argued in his 1976 Stockton Lecture. The remedy for the British disease had two main elements: the implementation of economic policies that provided a healthy basis for enterprise, and the fostering of cultural changes that made it respectable and rewarding. In a passage of Nigel Lawson's illuminating memoirs, *The View from No. 11* (1992), he describes the philosophical underpinnings of the economic policies he was so influential in designing: "we were not seeking simply to remove various controls and impositions, but by so doing to change the entire culture of a nation from anti-profits, anti-business, government-dependent lassitude and defeatism, to a pro-profit, pro-business, robustly independent vigour and optimism."[16] Or, as Margaret Thatcher herself put it in 1984: "I came to office with one deliberate intent. To change Britain from a dependent to a self-reliant society—from a give-it-to-me to a do-it-yourself nation; to a get-up-and-go instead of a sit-back-and-wait-for-it Britain."[17]

Shifting policies without altering attitudes would not work, however, because Lawson believed that "a necessary precondition of economic success is a fundamental business optimism based on self-belief and the will to succeed."[18] But more than self-belief was required to overturn an animus against business that dated back to the Victorian age and a penchant for defeatism that stemmed from decades of decline. Plotting and executing a genuine transformation of Britain's economic culture was not simply a question of monetary discipline or tax cuts.[19] The ultimate success of Mrs. Thatcher's capitalist revolution hinged on her ability to reform policies, attitudes, and institutions whose champions would not give way without a fight. To capture the hearts and minds of the British people, Mrs. Thatcher needed to legitimize capitalism, proving in other words that it was fair as well as profitable.

However prosaic the Prime Minister's vision, her capitalist revolution provoked a bitter civil war. It was a conflict that began on the home front. Much as Reagan delighted in branding Washington bureaucrats, his compatriot crossed herself at the very mention of the Civil Service. Margaret Thatcher's distrust of the urbane skeptics who ruled Whitehall dated back to her early days as a junior minister. Afraid of being patronized, she had been quick to execute preemptive strikes not soon forgotten by her targets. Within ten minutes of arriving at the Department of Education and Science in 1970, the new Secretary of State handed a rather shocked permanent secretary, Sir William Pile, a page from an exercise book with eighteen things she wanted done that day.[20]

Particularly nefarious was the Treasury, the "praetorian guard," as one of their own number, Sir Leo Pliatzky, called it. The great fear of men like Sir John Hoskyns, the Prime Minister's chief adviser in her first years in office, was that senior civil servants would block the advent of the monetarist dispensation.

The fear proved groundless, for the Treasury was by no means as eager to impede the forward march of Thatcherism as acolytes believed. The atmosphere of "carbolic and parsimony" that prevailed in its hallways was hospitable for a government determined to reduce public spending.[21] There were, moreover, some officials who were receptive to economic alternatives partly because they were eager to regain the prestige the Treasury had lost during the mid-1970s. Nevertheless, Mrs. Thatcher made sure to bring in her own men as soon as she could. When, at the end of 1979, Fred Atkinson was due to retire to as Chief Economic Adviser to the Treasury, the Prime Minister appointed in his place Terry Burns. Lawson vetted this monetarist economist, the thirty-six-year-old director of the Centre for Economic Forecasting at the London Business School, over lunch at the Garrick Club (always a good test, it seems) and duly recommended him.[22] And when Sir Douglas Wass—whose integrity and judgment finally won the Prime Minister's respect—retired in 1982, his successor was Peter Middleton, one of the Treasury's first known monetarist sympathizers.

A photograph of the Thatcher Cabinet taken when it first came into office captures an apparently conventional group untouched by radical dreams. The only evidence of something extraordinary was the fact that a woman was at the center of this entourage. Otherwise, the Cabinet contained an unsurprising assortment of Tories educated largely at the public schools and Oxbridge. But it boasted few true believers in Mrs. Thatcher's new dispensation. What made this all the more surprising was the fact that before taking office she had announced in a well-publicized interview that "As Prime Minister I couldn't waste time having any internal arguments.... It must be a 'conviction' Government."[23]

A decade later, Mrs. Thatcher elaborated on her philosophy. When the novelist Mario Vargas Llosa decided to run for the presidency of Peru, he met with the British Prime Minister. She told him: "The question that decides everything is: 'Do you hold back or do you press on?' But if you hold back it's almost impossible to pick up where you left off until later on: the reforms will be lost. But if you continue you will have to endure a great deal of loneliness." So she advised Llosa to surround himself with a group of like-minded people. Her watchword: "surround yourself with Thatcherites."[24]

Had Mrs. Thatcher followed her own counsel? The man most responsible for shaping the Cabinet was Willie Whitelaw, who himself became Home Secretary. A Tory of the old school, the rich landowner trounced by Mrs. Thatcher in the battle for the Conservative leadership subsequently become loyal to her and she increasingly reliant on his counsel. Large and gregarious, he looked every inch the Victorian squire.

At Whitelaw's behest Mrs. Thatcher appointed mostly moderate and traditional men (who had been in the Shadow Cabinet), members in good standing of the establishment that had presided over Britain's long decline. The Prime Minister sent Lord Carrington to the Foreign Office, Francis Pym to Defence, Jim Prior to Employment, Peter Walker to Agriculture, Michael Heseltine to Environment, and Mark Carlisle to Education—none of them monetarists. Equally skeptical of the economic experiment were the Cabinet ministers without portfolio: Sir Ian Gilmour, Lord Privy Seal; Christopher Soames, Leader of the Lords; Lord Hailsham, the Lord Chancellor; and Norman St. John Stevas, Leader of the Commons. The grocer's daughter harbored a "soft spot for the aristocracy" and appointed to the Cabinet a number of grandees, including Peter Carrington, a courtly hereditary peer and old Etonian, who was able to both charm and stand up to the Prime Minister.[25] The same could not be said of Jim Prior or Peter Walker. Both possessed agribusiness interests and a paternalistic outlook that clashed with Thatcherism. Michael Heseltine was also a man to watch and Margaret Thatcher watched him with mounting suspicion.

The Prime Minister was unable to have a Cabinet that reflected her own views because they seemed so extreme, but she did ensure that economic policy was largely in the hands of the faithful. She could trust the Chancellor and Sir Keith Joseph, her closest ally, who took over the Industry portfolio and so became the supreme ruler of the state-owned corporations that he condemned. Mrs. Thatcher also appointed to the Cabinet two monetarists of recent vintage: David Howell, an economist who became Energy Secretary; and John Nott, a merchant banker who became Minister for Trade. Veteran politician Angus Maude, who had won his spurs as a critic of the economic policies of Macmillan and then of Heath, became Paymaster General. John Biffen became the Chief Secretary of the Treasury. A trained economist and an early disciple of the market capitalism espoused by Enoch Powell, he was "just the man to put the intellectual stuffing into Geoffrey," as one colleague put it.[26] The son of a Somerset farmer, Biffen was a grammar school boy who won a scholarship to Cambridge but never lost his West country burr. The Prime Minister took to him all the more because he was a man with an untainted economic past who had opposed Heath's incomes policy and industrial strategy.

Equally formidable was Nigel Lawson, the Financial Secretary of the Treasury. The son of a successful tea merchant, Lawson grew up in Hampstead, attended Westminster School, and was a scholar at Christ Church College, Oxford, where he joined the Chatham, a somewhat decadent High Tory dining club famous for the consumption of claret. But this did not stop him from earning a first-class degree in PPE, a rigorous course favored by future politicos.[27] He later abandoned the economics he had learned from Keynes's pupil and biographer, Roy Harrod. But Lawson's training in linguistic philosophy proved helpful because it sharpened his ability "to think clearly and identify nonsense, however dressed up," a useful if hardly abundant skill among politicians. A financial journalist and editor of the *Spectator,* Lawson could not contain his cleverness—much to the annoyance of old-line Tories. As an MP, he had a habit of suddenly starting to roar with laughter in the middle of a speech in the Commons, anticipating a joke he was about to make—far ahead of his audience.[28]

Ideology apart, the Thatcher Cabinet Room did not impress all observers. At a meeting of the Conservative Philosophy Group, Harold Macmillan described it as containing "a brilliant tyrant surrounded by mediocrities."[29]

I I I

WHATEVER THE CHARACTER OR QUALITY OF THE THATCHER government, the woman who led the capitalist revolution came to office without a detailed master plan. Strong on vision Margaret Thatcher may have been, but she was weak on planning. Like Jimmy Carter, she did not know when to pry herself away from work that might have been done by others. In the autumn of 1981 when her popularity was at its nadir, David Howell expressed his concern about the "strategic direction of the government . . . and how on earth we were going to be in shape to win the next election." The Prime Minister's replies to such ministrations tended to be, "Don't bother me with strategy. I have to be up all night rewriting press releases and getting speeches straight as it is."[30] But even so, Mrs. Thatcher and her inner circle had an attack plan that focused on three key targets: banishing inflation; conquering the trade unions; and reforming the nationalized industries one by one.

The battle for Britain began with a declaration of war against the leading macroeconomic problem that monetarists believed government could and should address. "Our prime and overriding objective is to unwind the inflation coils which have gripped out economy," argued the uneasy alliance of left- and right-wing Tories who put together *The Right Approach to the Economy.* The preoccupation with curing inflation rather than abolishing unemployment marked a radical shift in economic ethics, for full employment only became a sacrosanct commitment with the advent of the Welfare State in 1945. It was not until the postwar era, especially under the leadership of Harold Macmillan, that the Conservatives had tried to shake off the reputation they had earned in the 1930s as the "party of unemployment." Although Macmillan did not ignore inflation entirely, he never quite understood its dangers even when it became dangerously high in the 1970s. "People quite like inflation really. The poor like it because they've more pound notes in their pocket, the rich like it because they can always sell a picture or something. It's only retired colonels who don't like it," Macmillan said in his grand Edwardian manner.[31]

Mrs. Thatcher's Treasury team, which included no retired colonels, did not share his tolerant view. Such sloppy attitudes were one thing for a millionaire publisher, but they would not do for a grocer's daughter weaned on sound money and good housekeeping. Besides, Mrs. Thatcher and Sir Keith Joseph believed that the original sin that eventually led to Heath's electoral defeat was his abandonment of the drive against inflation. With this example in mind, they vowed to continue the holy war despite the pressures of infidels. And they also vowed not to haul out once more the rusty machinery that supposedly regulated incomes. Such a faulty physic would not remedy inflation, despite the promises of Keynesians who were forever fine-tuning a defunct device. Yet another round of incomes policy would succeed only in sustaining the bargaining power of trade union leaders and ensuring continued entree to Number 10, a result to be avoided at all costs. For Margaret Thatcher harbored no secret wish to be Harold Wilson. The woman who was happy to fry eggs and bacon for members of her Cabinet had no intention of offering union leaders "tea and sympathy" in place of Wilson's famous "beer and sandwiches." The Prime Minister could afford to suggest that the unions try self-service, for a change, because monetarist theory held that she did not have to rely on the kindness of their leaders to hold down inflation.

Lawson explained the founding assumption of the monetarist theory the Thatcher government tried to put into practice:

Rapid and continuous inflation is not due to excessive pay settlements, world commodity price movements or disappointing productivity trends. All these things may precipitate an initial upward movement of prices and pay; and they may increase the unemployment cost of curbing inflation. But prices and wages cannot carry on chasing each other ever upwards unless a sufficiently easy money policy accommodates the process.[32]

If this was indeed the case, then the antidote for inflation was stringent control of the money supply. But if few things in life are as tangible as money, or especially the lack thereof, monetarist theory offered no clear answer as to which financial instrument should be used to regulate its circulation. The Thatcher government, therefore, followed the lead of its Labour predecessor and the Bank of England, which had used the formula known as M£3 (cash plus bank deposits) to measure monetary targets since the IMF crisis of 1976.

However impeccable monetarist logic seemed to the already converted, Treasury skeptics took a different view of the probable impact of Howe's first budget. Trouble broke out almost immediately when the Prime Minister concluded that the Treasury was stonewalling her demand for substantial spending cuts in public expenditure. The *Observer* reported how Hurricane Margaret changed their minds and taught them a lesson:

During the pre-budget discussions, Mrs. Thatcher became enraged with what she considered the dilatoriness of the Treasury in coming up with the required public expenditure cuts. It couldn't be done, said the mandarins. She promptly summoned all five Treasury ministers and all five Treasury knights to Downing Street. They came out shaking from what was an unprecedented dressing down. A week later the Treasury came up with £1,400 million in cuts.[33]

Thus Mrs. Thatcher won the battle of authority, proving who held the reins. But it did not follow that she would also win her crusade against inflation.

In the pre-budget discussions, Wass maintained that the effect of the budget would be to drive rather than to reduce inflation. In July 1979, he warned the Chancellor of the dangers of a backlash against economic policies that were "relatively strange to a British audience."[34] Wass's point was well taken, for whatever the intrinsic weaknesses of monetarist economics, the Thatcher government was largely ineffective in explaining its workings or goals to the public. But Sir Douglas's cautionary notes did little to impede monetarist pilgrims intent on riding a tight money supply to the promised land of economic renewal. Given ideological differences, it was easy enough to dismiss Treasury counsel as the misleading advice of yesterday's men.

The relationship between the Treasury team and the Bank of England began on a more harmonious note. Gordon Richardson, the Governor of the Bank of England, managed to get on reasonably well with the Prime Minister, even though he believed that "she was canine and he feline." Metaphors aside, he had the great advantage of not being afraid of Mrs. Thatcher, which was more than many could say. After a year of unexpected peace, though, conflict broke out between the Iron Lady and the master of the Old Lady of Threadneedle Street (as the Bank of England was sometimes called). A grammar school boy from Nottingham who had taken to the hierarchical world of the Bank where the Governor's word counted, Richardson found himself assailed by a woman who did not like his patrician airs any more than his economic views.

Richardson, for his part, could not bear a style of government that verged on assault and battery. "I'm not sure which Gordon found more distasteful," a Bank official opined, "having his word questioned by that woman, or being forced by her to eat a cream bun at the end of one of her attacks."[35]

The Thatcher government and the Bank clashed over the issue of the "corset," a charming term that referred to the existing 12.5 percent ratio between bank assets and reserve. In Sir Geoffrey Howe's second budget of March 1980, he announced his intention to abolish the corset in June. What was uncertain, though, was the effect abolition would have on the all-important money supply. Bank officials guessed that it might expand by about 3 percent, but they refused to be pinned down. By the time the corset was about to be released in June, however, Richardson warned the Prime Minister that the effect might be an explosion of monetary growth. He was right: in July alone, M£3 grew by 5 percent, and then by an additional 3 percent in August. When Mrs. Thatcher met with Bank officials in Number 10 at the end of the summer holiday, she began by asking what on earth had happened to the monetary figures while she had been away.[36]

There was ample reason for concern. Within a year of her taking office, a shadow had fallen between theory and practice. The initial consequences of the Thatcher government's new economic turn were largely as unfortunate as they were unforeseen. Far from conquering inflation, it could hardly have escalated further if the new regime had consciously set out to do so. When Mrs. Thatcher came to power in May 1979, inflation was running at an annual rate of 10.3 percent; by the following May it was 16.5 percent, and by September of 1980 it had run away to 21.9 percent. Economic ministers could, and quickly did, plead extenuating circumstances. The inflationary spiral had, after all, already begun during the last months of the Labour government when Healey relaxed the financial austerity of the post-IMF budgets in the name of winning votes. And it was also true that the prospects for economic recovery were dampened by a sluggish world economy. Even the bonanza promised by North Sea oil production proved a mixed blessing when oil prices exploded after the mullahs deposed the Shah of Iran. If government "cannot find a way of living with North Sea oil, then I say: leave the bloody stuff in the ground," complained Michael Edwardes, the chairman of British Leyland, who had more reason than most to worry about the price of oil.[37]

But if external forces beyond Mrs. Thatcher's control helped push the economy into the ground, monetarist policies did little more than expedite the burial. The first warning signals came from the failure to meet the projected targets for the growth of the money supply: the £M3 target for 1980 was 9 percent, but it grew at 8 percent in July and August alone. What had made the money supply all the more difficult to control was the end of the banking "corset" in July 1980 and the abolition of exchange controls in October 1979; the unintended consequence of both of these decisions was to expose sterling interest rates to international pressures. Now that British businesses were free to deposit and borrow in the United States or the Continent as need be, they could circumvent domestic restrictions on credit.[38] The near doubling of VAT and the relaxation of price controls on the nationalized industries together added about 6 percentage points to the retail price index, the gauge of inflation used in wage negotiations. At the same time, an inflationary time bomb set by Mrs. Thatcher herself exploded. Eager to win the 1979 election at all costs, she hastily had promised to match Labour's pledge to honor the findings of the Clegg Commission, which was then reevaluating public sector salaries in light of private sector pay. Despite the warnings of Howe and Lawson, she refused to renege on an unaffordable promise certain to fire inflation. The result was that the bill for public sector salaries went up by about 25 percent just as the Thatcher government wanted to make further cuts in public spending. Such huge pay hikes, in turn, whetted the appetites of private sector employees who responded to large price increases by demanding proportionate increase in wages.

The initial result of "sado-monetarism," as Healey called it, was a serious recession that set in around 1980. Chief among its effects and most dangerous politically was the savage eruption of unemployment, which increased more sharply than at any time since the Great Depression. That it was already on the upswing when Mrs. Thatcher came to power was small consolation to workers who lost their jobs or to Tory MPs who feared losing theirs as a result. Unemployment rose from 5.5 percent in 1979 to 13.3 percent by January 1983. It more than doubled in the course of a single year, 1980–81; by mid-1982, 3 million were out of work. In manufacturing alone, 14 percent of total employment disappeared as more than 2 million jobs were lost.

Was the disastrous rise in unemployment a conspiracy to humble the working class or a miscalculation? Certainly, more than a few members of Margaret Thatcher's economic team were of the "let's knock some sense into those bloody workers" school. And it was also true that Sir Geoffrey Howe's budget statement underscored a line that became a favorite refrain: If trade union leaders insisted on seeking pay increases out of joint with productivity, they would price their members out of jobs. Nevertheless, there is little evidence that Mrs. Thatcher and company either expected or wanted unemployment to rise to a point that it threatened their political survival. It is one thing to be caught with a smoking gun, quite another to hold it to one's own head. Lawson, among others, was quick to point out that the high level of unemployment was the price to be paid for ending decades of overmanning. True as this probably was, such language conveniently screened out the fact that members of the working class were forced to pay the bill for a national imperative. Even if a shake-out was a necessary prelude to increasing productivity, this is no excuse for the fact that it was carried out willy-nilly and with little regard for the fate of those who were pushed out of work.

It was, unsurprisingly, in classic industrial towns and cities that the loss of manufacturing jobs was most glaring and severe. The Conservative strongholds in southern England, especially London and the Home Counties, were relatively untouched by the shock waves that swept through the traditional citadels of the Industrial Revolution. Even though Margaret Thatcher's version of Victorian values had a distinctly northern flavor—energy, practicality, respectability, and self-help being its cornerstones—her policies brought pain in the short run to those who lived north of the River Trent. And yet the economic decline of the North long predated the advent of the Thatcher government. Once great centers of Victorian commerce such as Liverpool were already all too familiar with the facts of industrial decay. Technological change, adversarial industrial relations, and radical politics all played a part in the downfall of the city chiefly known since the sixties as the birthplace of the Beatles.

But Liverpool's condition degenerated further as the capitalist revolution with its emphasis on enterprise at all costs took hold. A new language was used to rationalize the loss of jobs; phrases such as "slimming down," "lame duck," "shake-out," and "making Britain competitive in the marketplace" obscured the human misery which came with unemployment. Established firms that had operated with great difficulty in the Merseyside area largely because of radical trade unions found it easier to close their plants in the new atmosphere sanctioned by the Prime Minister. In the course of the 1980s, United Biscuits, Tate & Lyle, and British & American Tobacco, all of them companies with long histories in Merseyside, closed plants.

David Sheppard, the bishop of Liverpool, and Derek Warlock, its Roman Catholic archbishop, described the growing pace of "redundancies" that they witnessed and fought against in the 1980s:

It was then that the saga of "black Fridays" took hold. By making the announcement of closure at midday on Friday, the management were able to ensure minimal treatment by the press the following day. Sports coverage would fill the pages of the newspapers and there could be a natural weekend period of cooling off for those likely to be involved.[39]

Often, workers first learned they would lose their jobs from articles in the newspapers. Management by walking away rather than management by walking around seemed to be the order of the day.

Although there was never any real equality of sacrifice (and indeed there were few gestures in that direction), workers were not the only victims of sado-monetarism. The businessmen and industrialists who slouched toward Conservative Party headquarters in Smith Square in the hope of a Tory election victory soon discovered the meaning of the adage, "Be careful what you wish for—you may get it." Of course, there were certain consolations. Those at the top had reason to be grateful for Sir Geoffrey Howe's tax cuts, whether they stirred their entrepreneurial juices or simply stoked their already comfortable lives. Few expected, though, that freeing the invisible hand of the market would end up giving them a slap in the face. By early 1980, however, British business and industry was caught in a triple squeeze play. Short-term interest rates, which were running at 17 percent by July, made it all but impossible for firms to make major capital investments to increase productivity. Rising costs squeezed the profits of healthy firms and threatened to squeeze the life out of the unhealthy, who could not afford to pay back the bank loans that, for a time, kept them out of bankruptcy.

Most ominous of all was sterling's rapid ascent. It rose 20 percent from May 1979 to January 1981, running at an average of about $2.40 in the latter half of 1980. Certainly this marked a change from the days of the IMF crisis when sterling seemed to be in a free fall. Pleasurable as a bulging pound was to those who were addicted to monetary machismo, in this case it was not a sign of renewed British power. Its strength fueled the consuming passions of tourists who could get better prices at the Christmas sales at Bloomingdales than at Harrods. But it was a plague upon manufacturers, whose exports shot up in price as the pound climbed. The rate of exchange undermined British firms involved in international trade.

Given such results, it was no wonder that the infatuation of the business community (to use an overly general label) with the Iron Lady turned into one of the least romantic mornings after of recent history. In October 1980, Maurice Hodgson, chairman of Imperial Chemical Industries (ICI), paid a visit to the Prime Minister. Although he approved of her resolve to make British industry lean, the purpose of his visit was not to thank her for efforts to reverse Britain's decline. Rather, Hodgson told Mrs. Thatcher that ICI was about to report its first third-quarter loss in history. Apparently, this meant little to some of her advisers, who were quick to write off a loss they did not have to pay for. They supposedly commented that ICI was as bureaucratic as the Civil Service. Irrespective of their opinion, Hodgson's news touched Mrs. Thatcher.

A far worse blow took place the following month. The Confederation of British Industries (CBI) passed a motion at its annual conference criticizing government policy on interest rates, exchange rates, and public expenditure. Such talk was mild compared to the speech delivered by Terence Beckett of Ford, CBI's newly installed director general. He announced: "We have got to take the gloves off and have a bare knuckle fight with the Government because we have to have an effective and prosperous industry." His challenge hit the headlines and offended at least five of CBI's member companies, who resigned in protest. Two days later, Beckett emerged from a meeting with the Prime Minister at Number 10, with his knuckles unblemished and his posture transformed, insisting, "She's a lovely lady."

Unfortunately, Mrs. Thatcher could not sort out the economic problems she faced by summoning critics to her office for a little chat. In fact, the Prime Minister had scant room for maneuver largely because she was shackled by manacles of her own making. Driven by monetarist dogma, she was both unable and unwilling to spend her way out of the recession as a faithful Keynesian might have done. Determined to stick to her guns whether or not she was hitting the wrong targets, much less firing blanks, she ruled out an economic U-turn for fear of losing face, and losing power, as did Heath before her. Rather, the Iron Lady made obstinacy a virtue. When her critics requested or demanded a change of course, calling for increased public spending to finance jobs, Mrs. Thatcher delighted in replying: "There is no alternative." The tag line became her constant refrain (and was soon abbreviated into the acronym TINA).[40]

Whether the contention "There is no alternative" was a statement of fact or a proof of blindness, it was idle to claim that the results of the recession were painless. And yet Mrs. Thatcher did claim that her cure would be lasting. Although she was hardly known for a comforting bedside manner, she turned to medical metaphors to justify her direction: "After almost any major operation," she commented, "you feel worse before you convalesce. But you do not refuse the operation when you know that, without it, you will not survive."[41] Such reasoning seemed logical enough; but was the procedure wise and the surgeon skillful?

In the course of the financial year 1980–81, Mrs. Thatcher's economic team came to the unhappy conclusion that the public sector borrowing requirement was running far higher than the projected £6 billion; indeed, it seemed as if it would be at least £11.5 billion, a gap not easily bridged at the best of times, much less in a serious recession. Much of the overrun came from the rapid rise in unemployment and the consequent need for higher expenditure. But greater needs did not ensure the appearance of higher resources to meet them. When the Cabinet balked at Howe's plans for a drastic reduction of public spending in 1981–82, higher taxes began to seem unavoidable to the Chancellor and his Treasury ministers. A major tax increase during a recession was certainly a political risk for the Prime Minister, who told her advisers that she had not been elected to put up taxes. Nevertheless, she finally agreed. The Chancellor's 1981 budget raised about £4.5 billion in revenue. It proved that there was no free lunch and surely no free dessert: the British people had to foot the bill for public expenditure.

Courageous as the 1981 budget was, its reception was extremely hostile within and without Tory ranks. The most articulate, and vehement, response came in the form of a letter signed by 364 academic economists, five of them former chief economic advisers. Published on March 30, 1981, in *The Times*, it held that

> There is no basis in economic theory or supporting evidence for the Government's belief that by deflating demand they will bring inflation permanently under control and thereby introduce an automatic recovery in output and unemployment;
> Present policies will deepen the depression, erode the industrial base of our economy and threaten its social and political stability;
> There are alternative policies;
> The time has come to reject monetarist policies and consider which alternative offers the best hope of sustained recovery.[42]

Even so, Mrs. Thatcher was carrying the day. En route to her second general election in 1983, she could claim that she had won the battle against inflation as well as the Falklands War. For the moment, the grim predictions of the 364 academic economists seemed exaggerated, if not groundless. "Their timing was exquisite," Lawson wrote in a proudly triumphant passage in his memoirs. "The economy embarked on a prolonged phase of vigorous growth almost from the moment the letter was published. So far from launching the economy on a self-perpetuating downward spiral, the Budget was a prelude to eight years of uninterrupted growth and left our economic critics bewildered and discredited."[43]

After a very rough start, the capitalist revolutionaries seemed to have won the day. But what were the costs of the victory and who were its casualties?

A Fine and Private Place

I

"BRITAIN IS GREAT AT THE PAST, BUT WHAT ABOUT THE FU-
ture?'" So quipped NBC anchor Tom Brokaw to an entranced
American audience who had woken in the very early hours of
the morning to watch the royal wedding of Prince Charles
and Lady Diana Spencer in the summer of 1981. For those
British subjects who had remained loyal to the Crown as well
as to foreign tourists visiting on holiday, the royal wedding
topped a London season of sport and sociability—tennis at
Queen's and Wimbledon, boat racing at Henley, horse racing
at Ascot, and opera at Glyndebourne. All of these events
were accompanied by the requisite abundance of strawber-
ries and champagne presented for the pleasure of gentlemen
in morning suits and ladies in summer dresses.

The royal wedding itself was indeed the quintessence of
monarchical theater. But if few observers could deny that
Britain was, for better or worse, "great at the past," were such
majestic distractions any more than ephemeral interruptions
in a dark time? The prince had good reason to be disturbed
about the state of the realm he hoped to rule one day.

The summer of 1981 also witnessed a barrage of riots, the worst of the century, disturbing the sleep of a nation that had long prided itself on being peaceful and law-abiding. "Civil disturbances" was the peculiarly sanitary phrase used to describe the riots that broke out in slums which did not figure in the list of tourist attractions. The disturbances began in Liverpool 8, otherwise known as Toxteth, and spread soon after to South London's Brixton, where the first major riots had taken place in April, and then on to Manchester's Moss Side. The flash point in Liverpool came on Friday night, July 3, when police chased a young black man who fell off a motorcycle that he had allegedly stolen. When the young man cried out for help, about forty other black youths came to his rescue and he quickly disappeared into the crowd.

For the next few nights, chaos swept through the old commercial city. Rioters cried out, "Stone the bastards," and hurled a barrage of gas bombs, bricks, and even spiked iron railings at Merseyside policemen. Armed with helmets and riot shields and added by reinforcements from neighboring areas, the police attempted to quell the disturbances. But even though they used CS gas for the first time in mainland Britain, the police were forced to abandon parts of Liverpool to a screaming mob. "Scenes like this can never have been seen in a British city under the rule of law this century," observed David Alton, Liberal MP for Liverpool, Edge Hill. A festival of looting took place as a rainbow coalition of opportunists sacked supermarkets, shops, and small stores. In Lodge Lane, a local councillor saw children as young as four and five "running up and down the road with wire shopping trollies full of groceries." Equally peculiar though far less poignant was the sight of people who actually queued outside Liverpool shops to take their turn at collecting booty, which ranged from necessities to luxuries. A thick pall of smoke hung over Upper Parliament Street as rioters torched the city. On one street alone, twenty buildings were set ablaze in the course of the riots; some collapsed from the flames, while others were damaged so badly that they had to be razed.[1] All in all, it took about six weeks before the disorders came to an end.

The causes of the urban riots were complex. So argued Lord Scarman, the eminent Liberal jurist in the report he submitted in the autumn of 1982. Both Brixton and Toxteth were multi-racial areas marked by histories of tensions between police and black residents who believed that their treatment was far from even-handed. And both districts were bedeviled by unusually high unemployment; one estimate held that as many as 60 percent of Liverpudlian blacks were out of work. This was all the more galling because many members of the black community in Liverpool, which was of West African and West Indian origin, were third- or fourth-generation citizens of the city.

Some offered simplistic explanations of the riots. Among them were the chief constable of Merseyside, Kenneth Oxford; well known for his conservative views, he blamed the riots on parents who could not control their children. But others took a wider view. Given that the riots took place at a time of recession when the Thatcher government was at its lowest popularity in the polls, they were quickly taken up by critics as a sign of social disintegration. Cabinet was in session during the Toxteth disturbances and Mrs. Thatcher read aloud the periodic reports from the chief constable. Told of the widespread looting, she exclaimed, "Oh those poor shopkeepers." This was fair enough as far as it went, for the owners of small businesses did indeed suffer greatly at the hands of the rioters. But her comment (which had no trace of irony) also revealed the class boundaries of her heart. She could sympathize with shopkeepers' losses, but was inexpressive when it came to the plight of alienated men and women who had been trampled on, or simply left aside, by market forces.[2] Roy Hattersley, Labour's spokesman on Home Affairs, put the question: "Will the Government now accept its obligation to the inner cities to improve their housing, increase their prospects of employment and end the despair and disillusionment which was a major cause of this week's chaos?"[3]

One answer came from Michael Heseltine, the Environment Secretary, who went to Merseyside with a team of observers immediately after the Toxteth riots began and remained there for the next three weeks. The results of their findings included what became a famous minute, "It took a riot," in which he called for a major allocation of public resources to create jobs, and a fundamental reorientation of regional, training, and urban policies. For his enemies, however, Heseltine's conduct was yet another instance of grandstanding. The state of the inner cities gave him a stick to beat the Prime Minister and to further his own ambitions. But this did not make him any less committed to urban policy or to "caring capitalism," as he called it. Motives aside, the report Heseltine filed was certain to further antagonize Mrs. Thatcher. It included pointed observations such as: "the conditions and prospects in the cities are not compatible with the traditions of social justice and national evenhandedness on which our Party prides itself." Heseltine's arguments did not carry much weight with Mrs. Thatcher or, for that matter, with Sir Geoffrey Howe. The Chancellor argued that the option of "managed decline" should not be ruled out; "given limited resources why try to make water flow uphill?"[4] The final result was that Heseltine's ambitious plans were scotched, although he came away from Number 10 with a modest increase in funding for urban programs.

For the critics of Mrs. Thatcher's capitalist revolution, however, the disturbances that marred the summer of the royal wedding were, on one level, a revolt against the selfish greed encouraged by an economic system that was more mean than lean. The Prime Minister's attitude to the social problems exposed by the riots seemed only to confirm the new Toryism's heartlessness. In a *Times* piece which placed the Liverpool riots in historical perspective, Philip Weller of Merton College, Oxford, observed: "the rioters have something to say, and that is about the intolerable circumstances which they have been condemned to endure."[5] Whether the riots of 1981 were actually a response to policies of the Thatcher government, they were an ominous sign of growing conflict between "two nations" coming ever closer to each other's throats.

Mrs. Thatcher wanted to turn Britain into "a fine and private place," as Andrew Marvell put it in "To His Coy Mistress." In so doing, did she also make it "a grave in which none dare embrace"?

I I

AT THE END OF MARCH 1980, SIR IAN GILMOUR GAVE A SPEECH celebrating Rab Butler's thirty years as president of the Cambridge University Conservative Association. The invitation was an opportunity not to be passed up because in praising Butler, the archetype of progressive Toryism, Sir Ian could condemn Mrs. Thatcher, even if he did so in code. All the better was the timing, for the speech took place only four days after Sir Geoffrey Howe's second budget statement. Howe had argued that "It is an illusion to suppose that we have any real choice between defeating inflation and some other course. . . . So long as it persists, economic stability and prosperity will continue to elude us. So long as it persists, social coherence will also elude us."[6] Inflation was a greater threat to the harmony of "One Nation" than unemployment. Prosperity was the true foundation of social unity.

The Chancellor's argument did not move Gilmour. In response, he presented monetarism as a passing but dangerous fad, out of line with the true Tory tradition, whose keynotes were social responsibility, coherence, and order. The economic liberalism of von Hayek was a threat to political freedom because it failed to create a sense of community. The cult of the market undercut the foundations of social cohesion. For loyalty to the state was based partly on the protections it provided to the people, especially to the weak and needy, who were worried about personal survival rather than economic theory. If Britain continued to become increasingly divided between a fortunate skilled majority in work and an unfortunate unskilled minority out of work, the result might be an alienated, "Clockwork Orange" society.[7] This pointed speech only aggravated the already testy relationship between Sir Ian and the Prime Minister. At a party at Number 10 soon after, Mrs. Thatcher asked Gilmour why he didn't make any speeches supporting the government. Jim Prior congratulated Sir Ian "at full volume" for describing Mrs. Thatcher's policy as "the economics of the madhouse" (a phrase which was, in fact, probably coined by fellow dissident Peter Walker).

Mrs. Thatcher's capitalist revolution faced internal resistance, for her Cabinet was a house divided against itself. Joined together more by the euphoria of power than agreement on how to use it, personal and ideological conflicts soon threatened its unity. When Margaret Thatcher came to office she had reason to fear that the Cabinet might not accept her authority. She had to contend with the prejudices of a group of middle-aged men more at ease with taking flowers and chocolates to a lady than taking orders from a forceful woman. As Prior summed up his colleagues' sentiments: "Traditionally, politics has been a male preserve, and I think we did all find it difficult coming to terms with a woman leader."[8] What made this all the worse was a hectoring style which was particularly noxious to those who grew up in genteel circles. After one Cabinet meeting during which Christopher Soames received the standard tongue-lashing by the

Prime Minister, he turned to Howe and said: "You know, Geoffrey, the trouble with this government is that it isn't fun any more. I don't know why we do it."⁹ Whatever her strengths, Mrs. Thatcher was all the more vulnerable because she had not held one of the great offices of state; her stint as Education Secretary hardly made her a political powerhouse. This only added to the resentment of well-established and well-connected men, some of whom fancied themselves far more worthy of being Prime Minister than the relatively inexperienced Grantham grocer's daughter. Anxious that she would lose a fight on economic policy if it came to debate in the full Cabinet, Mrs. Thatcher sought control by withholding information from her potential opponents. She made sure that economic affairs were placed in the hands of the "E" (for Economic) committee, where the only likely dissenter, Prior, was outnumbered by her supporters, Howe, Joseph, and Lawson among them. But this only further aggrieved those men who felt unjustly relegated to the cold.

Mrs. Thatcher's critics became known as "wets." (The term seems to have been used first when she was Leader of the Opposition.) By contrast, "dry" was rarely used. This language became popular thanks to the media, which appreciated having a vivid image to symbolize policy differences. Nicholas Ridley, a true Thatcherite "dry" to the point of dehydration despite his aristocratic origins, explained the origins of the nickname. "Wet was a schoolboy word to describe some wretched boy who doesn't dare do something either athletic or naughty. The zenith of wetness is when somebody is described as 'so wet you could shoot snipe off him.' "¹⁰

The opening skirmishes between Mrs. Thatcher and her critics began in small but telling ways. If God is in the details, the Devil may be also. Given as she was to hectoring Cabinet ministers in a schoolmistress manner, some responded in kind, as schoolboys are wont to do, by passing notes during the meeting. Such conduct was not unique to the Thatcher Cabinet, but it seems to have been particularly rife and pointed. Prior testified: "In the early days of Margaret's Cabinet, Ministers often used to pass notes to one another during Cabinet. There were those which were meant to be amusing, or some private notes; there were those which were very private, which said: 'Wasn't he simply terrible?' or, 'She's got it all wrong.' "[11] Passing notes was, at most, a mild form of passive aggression; but another favorite Cabinet sport was far more damaging. Resentful of the Prime Minister's retentive style of government, ministers spawned a flood of press leaks and rumors.

The conflict between wets and dries was, at heart, a clash of opposing economic ethics: traditional Tory paternalism versus classic market capitalism. The authors of Tory paternalism required a measure of social responsibility on the part of the upper classes, who were expected to take care of their dependents in exchange for a certain deference; in so doing, they ensured that England was, in Disraeli's famous phrase, "One Nation." The price of power was obligation; the price of protection dependency. Both figures were too high for the proponents of market capitalism, who rejected the notion that one group was responsible for the welfare of another. It was preferable to offer members of the working class the opportunity to make their own way in the world rather than administer alms if they failed to do so. For Prior and his fellows, "What began to stick in the gullet was the growing belief that the only thing that really mattered was control of the money supply and that Professor Milton Friedman and Hayek, as the high priests of monetarism, stood above all others as prophets and gurus."[12]

During the summer of 1981 the cold war between the defenders and the critics of the capitalist revolution came to a head. Shortly before the summer recess was due to begin, the Cabinet held its final meeting on July 23. Howe announced a preliminary demand to cut next year's public spending by £5,000 million—an extraordinary announcement in view of the austerity of the past two years. What made it especially remarkable, however, was that it came at the time of the Toxteth riots. Heseltine balked at the plan, which he believed would lead to urban despair and electoral disaster; in its stead, he suggested a pay freeze, an unthinkable notion for a Prime Minister who had eschewed all talk of incomes policy. Lord Hailsham reminded the Cabinet that in Germany unemployment had given rise to Nazism and that in the United States Herbert Hoover's policies had destroyed the Republican Party for thirty years. Even John Biffen, one of the architects of Thatcher economic policy, was disenchanted by Howe's latest plans. Further cuts to public spending for the sake of future tax reductions would be profoundly destructive. Enough was enough.[13] However devastated Mrs. Thatcher was by what was said, she held firm, threatening that her government would be finished if Howe's plans were rejected.

Faced with an onslaught of critics, Mrs. Thatcher could have moderated her policies or changed her Cabinet. The lady chose burning over turning: she dismissed Gilmour, Carlisle, and Soames (having already dismissed St. John Stevas in January) and moved Prior from Employment to the Northern Ireland office, a kind of Siberia. At the same time, the Prime Minister rewarded the faithful: Nigel Lawson became Energy Secretary, Norman Tebbit became Employment Secretary, and Cecil Parkinson, then a junior Trade minister, replaced Lord Thorneycroft as chairman of the Conservative Party. Mrs. Thatcher's natural selection was for the survival of the driest.

Why did the critics fail to change a course of action that did not enjoy the full support of the government? In part, they underestimated the Prime Minister's resolve. Whether she was principled or inflexible, she was more single-minded than her opponents. A hedgehog possessed by one idea (to use Sir Isaiah Berlin's terms), Mrs. Thatcher was able to overwhelm critics who tended to be foxes attracted by many ideas. It was simply untrue that there was no alternative. But the critics' statements of general aims did not translate into a strong or coherent policy. Moreover, it was easy enough for Mrs. Thatcher to respond that incomes policy, industrial intervention, and the like had all been tried with little success in one form or another by Conservatives and Labour alike. Given her stranglehold on the machinery of economic policy, it would have been difficult for the critics to gain a real hearing in Cabinet for their views. Even had they been able to do so, however, they would have been sitting ducks ill at ease in technical discussions of the minutiae of economic policy. "All able and honourable men," Sir Ian admitted, "none of them counted economics as his strongest suit." Finally, the critics feared the accusation that they were a cabal. Plotting against the Prime Minister would have justified their dismissal.

Nevertheless, the critics could have resigned. Had a number of the weightier wets done so en masse, they would probably have made more of a splash than they thought. At an official dinner the night before the 1981 budget, Gilmour ran into Rupert Murdoch, the right-wing press proprietor, not among his usual circle of friends. Murdoch kindly informed Gilmour that nobody cared about unemployment any more; inflation was all that mattered. After his exchange with Murdoch, Sir Ian had a drink with Jim Prior, who briefed him about the budget, which both expected would only aggravate unemployment. The next day, the two men had breakfast with fellow dissenter Peter Walker. Although there was talk of leaving the government, they decided it would serve no good purpose, so they stayed in Cabinet, a decision Prior and Gilmour later came to regret.[14]

Even if the wets were able to do little to change government policy on unemployment, however, they did moderate the approach to the second target of the capitalist revolution: the trade unions.

I I I

When Jim Prior was a student at Pembroke, Cambridge, he spent one of his vacations at Dagenham taking a course offered by Ford on tractor maintenance and repair. To be sure, this was unusual training for a future Tory minister.

Prior had grown up in the genteel world of the professional middle class in rural Norfolk, far from the sites of the Industrial Revolution. The youngest of four children, he was the son of a country lawyer, a "delightful man, lazy but quite successful," more interested in sport than politics, but a Conservative nonetheless. His mother, who would have been happier as a Liberal, was an unusually active woman who expressed her social conscience through good works, visiting the local hospital, the Norfolk and Norwich, every Sunday afternoon for fifty years. Soon after the outbreak of World War II, the family duly sent young Prior to Charterhouse, a bleak-looking public school whose austere regime was strengthened by rationing. Aside from the usual schoolboy games and studies, Prior had his first taste of farming at Charterhouse, raising pigs—an activity encouraged by the government to increase food production during the war. He made a more direct contribution through National Service in the Army, after which he went up to Cambridge. When his father informed him that he would need a professional qualification since the family could not provide further financial assistance, Prior decided to study estates management to prepare for a career in farming. His decision disappointed Prior Senior, who hoped that his son would follow him into the law.

So much for Prior's road to Ford of Dagenham. The course he took on tractors did not compensate for his lack of mechanical aptitude. But he did come away with a feel for the realities of the shop floor and the concerns of working people that put him in good stead when he later became Employment Secretary under Mrs. Thatcher. He liked to see himself as the type of Tory who had an instinctive grasp of workers' concerns. This was due in large part to the family he lived with during his stay in Dagenham, in a flat near the gate of the Ford factory where two family members had worked ever since the plant opened. Skilled workers loyal to Ford, they were concerned that in producing too much they could work themselves out of their jobs. The young Cambridge student argued "the toss about productivity" with them, taking the tack that the best way to guard their jobs was, in fact, to produce more in order to lower costs and raise sales. But the most valuable lesson that he drew from his experience was that the views of working people, right or wrong, had to be reckoned with rather than dismissed. "These were the weeks when that much mocked character 'Pussyfoot Prior' began to form a judgment of how best to handle relationships on the production line," he later observed in his memoirs.[15]

Handling Mrs. Thatcher was another question. Within a day of Prior's appointment as Employment Secretary, she announced her intention of appointing "someone with backbone" as his junior minister, a comment which made it clear where he stood with her.[16] But the Prime Minister's estimate of the strength of his vertebrae surely came as little surprise to Prior, who had entered Parliament with her in 1959, or, for that matter, to anyone else who knew the both of them. In case there was any doubt about her feelings, she enshrined them forever in her memoirs, branding him as "the false squire." Such types, she wrote, "have all the outward show of a John Bull—ruddy face, white hair, bluff manner—but inwardly they are political calculators who see the task of Conservatives as one of retreating gracefully before the Left's inevitable advance. Retreat as a tactic is sometimes necessary; retreat as a settled policy eats at the soul."[17]

Still, political expediency guided Mrs. Thatcher's decision to keep Prior on as the Tory spokesman on Employment. At least one of Prior's confidants said that initially Prior was unhappy with her decision. The Prime Minister was convinced that he was irremediably soft on labor, a born compromiser who could not be trusted to take a hard line with the unions. In the late 1970s, the Tory right branded Prior a "Quisling" and an "appeaser," who would not stand up to the trade unions. When pressed about such extreme language, Mrs. Thatcher's faithful bulldog, Norman Tebbit, gruffly admitted to the Conservative Party Conference that "Jim is a dove but he's no chicken."[18]

When the Prime Minister came to power, her advisers felt sure that a confrontation with the trade unions was inevitable sooner or later. For in the gospel according to the free marketers of the Centre for Policy Studies and the Institute for Economic Affairs, unions were a leading cause of the British disease. Far from being authentic champions of the working class, they caused higher unemployment. It was the trade unions who priced their members out of jobs by demanding pay hikes out of line with productivity. Moreover, trade union barons were able to hold British governments hostage by the apparently ceaseless round of strikes, slow-downs, and work stoppages which were so common in the 1970s. And unions robbed British managers of "the right to manage" by providing enormous influence, direct and indirect, to their officials, ranging from shop stewards to national leaders. Proposals for greater industrial democracy, like those offered by the Bullock Report, were anathema to Thatcherites, who believed that managers possessed an inalienable right to manage in the name of the pursuit of profit, but denied that workers had a right to participate either in the name of efficiency or dignity.

Shortly before the Tories won the general election of 1979, Sir Geoffrey Howe gave a major speech setting out a harsh view of the trade unions that nearly drove Prior to despair. Howe openly criticized those who imagined

> a better future without having to do anything different or difficult about it; a dream world where we can have more public spending without higher taxes, higher interest rates or greater inflation; a dream world in which all this can be delivered by an economy whose manufacturing output is below the level of six years ago. It is a dream world in which there is no such thing as cause and effect . . . in which people can be paid more without producing more; where earnings always go up in good times but never down in bad; where profits can be reduced but investment and living standards increased. Trade unions are not God-given. They are given by society, by the law, by the elected government. If they are used to do economic damage and inflict human suffering it is legitimate to question their scope.[19]

Yet Margaret Thatcher faced great obstacles in taking on the trade unions. In the course of the postwar era, they had weakened three British governments: Attlee's in 1951, Wilson's in 1970, and Heath's in 1974. This was one historic cavalcade in which the first female Prime Minister hoped to escape mention. By the mid-1970s, British trade union membership had grown to nearly half of the industrial workforce. They seemed so impregnable a force that commentators questioned whether Britain was even "governable" without their consent. Although Mrs. Thatcher was forceful in her rhetoric about the trade unions while Leader of the Opposition, would she have any choice but to mollify them when she became Prime Minister? Or, as some asked rather more crudely, did she "have the balls" to take on the trade unions?

The Tories badly needed to garner the votes of a portion of the working class. And their best shot was with skilled workers, classic swing voters whose loyalties might change from electoral contest to contest. The trick was to appeal to the ambitions of the upwardly mobile without wounding their pride in their origins. Bashing the trade unions was, therefore, a risky business since strong talk might come across as the latest shot in an old class war.

From the first, the Thatcher government was divided on what to do to tame the trade unions and how quickly to do it—strategy and timing were both at issue. It was unsurprising that Howe found a gradual, piecemeal approach to reform unacceptable. As the author of the Industrial Relations Act of 1972, a sweeping package of reforms that was soon swept aside after it proved unworkable, he was determined to have one more try at employing the law to make the unions behave reasonably and responsibly—or else. But Prior did not share the Chancellor's penchant for a dramatic policy that would be hard to enforce.

Convinced that Howe's legislation had failed for lack of public support, Prior favored building a consensus on union reform so that legal changes would be socially acceptable and therefore effective. He advocated a cautious step-by-step approach rather than an all-out, immediate assault. "I wanted to hold some shots in my locker," Prior later wrote, "so that the unions would know that if they continued to abuse their power tougher measures would follow."[20] Howe may have wanted to "do or die," but Prior wanted to explain "the reason why." Unless the British people grasped and accepted the rationale behind union reform, it stood little chance of succeeding in his view. An immediate initiative, designed to obliterate all the trade unions' abuses of power, would only fortify militants eager to find excuses to disrupt the economy and undermine moderates willing to accept a measure of reform. And a moderate approach would reduce the trade unions' chance of whipping up an effective campaign of opposition to reform because the individual measures introduced hardly seemed draconian.[21] Sensible as these assumptions were, Prior did not grasp the fact that public attitudes to the unions were far less sympathetic in the wake of the "Winter of Discontent" than they had been under Heath. It was all well and good to talk about the need for consensus, but in fact it had already broken down.

Moving from theory to practice, the Thatcher government's labor strategy combined aspects of the hard line represented by the Prime Minister and the Chancellor and the soft line advocated by the Employment Secretary. Mrs. Thatcher and Sir Geoffrey Howe won out on the abolition of incomes policy. In so doing they ensured that trade union leaders would have to watch events at Number 10 on television with everyone else rather than take part in important political decisions. But Jim Prior prevailed when it came to the timing of the reforms by winning support for his step-by-step approach. His cautious pace, though, continued to cause friction with right-wing politicians and businessmen who tried to pressure him into an immediate and thoroughgoing crackdown on the trade unions. They wanted to abolish rather than reform the closed shop and to curb picketing. Particularly forceful were the opinions of tabloid newspapers which depicted the Secretary of State for Employment as "Pussyfoot Prior," tiptoeing fearfully around union bosses. At times, though, even Prior's political allies found his "softly softly" manner too timorous for their liking. Sir Ian Gilmour, for one, thought Prior could have been a bit bolder in his program of reform, even though Gilmour later concluded that the strategy had been correct.

The cornerstone was the Employment Act of 1980. Its avowed purpose was to bring about "a fairer balance of power" between the rights and duties of the trade unions and employers. The principal provisions of the bill were to provide government funding for union elections, strike calls, and secret ballots; limit picketing to a person's own place of work; change the operations of closed shops so as to provide greater protections for those who were not union members; and stop the coercive recruiting tactics of the unions. All of these measures contributed to the broad goal of controlling trade union activity through legal means. Whatever the merits of the bill, it did not prevent Mrs. Thatcher from exiling Prior to the Northern Ireland office, a position that made industrial relations seem like a summer holiday in the South of France.

The man Mrs. Thatcher appointed in Jim Prior's place as Employment Secretary was Norman Tebbit, a new Tory much more to her liking. Described by Labour leader Michael Foot as a "semi-trained polecat," Tebbit enjoyed presenting himself as the hardest of the hard and driest of the dry, the politician with the grit of a street fighter and the finesse of a rattlesnake. "Most of my opponents still thought of me as no more than a thick-headed, sharp-tongued brawler," Tebbit admitted, with little or no hint of embarrassment.[22] Not posh by any stretch of the imagination, he became the embodiment of "Essex Man," a decidedly outré area to the east of London best known as the home of taxi drivers who had come from the East End with a host of spicy opinions. His memoirs, *Upwardly Mobile,* were full of comments about money matters which Jim Prior would not have discussed, at least in print. Tebbit came by his combative stance honestly. He proved to be the worthy heir of a grandfather who once led an effort to run a group of local atheists out of town; free markets were one thing, free thinking another.

Born in 1931, Tebbit was a child of the Depression. His early life was far more trying than that of Jim Prior or Margaret Thatcher. The Tebbit family lost their home and possessions in a series of moves, always going down market, living in a variety of houses. One house was owned by a man who made tennis rackets; it was pervaded by the smell of glue boiling on cans on gas stoves. Tebbit's father went from job to job—trainee jeweler, pawnbroking shop manager, publican, house painter, and abattoir worker. Never put off by adversity, Tebbit Senior continued to look for work on his bicycle. This practice was the origin of Norman Tebbit's notorious advice to the unemployed to get "on your bike"—one of the Thatcher era's few classic phrases. Confronted with a childhood world of darkened streets, drab houses, and ration books, Tebbit was intent on rising.

The man whose first job was delivering newspapers eventually became an airline pilot for BOAC. Much as Tebbit enjoyed travel that took him to the United States, where he learned to like baseball and football, his experience only confirmed his visceral dislike for state industry. So when he entered politics, it was no surprise that he opted for "Freedom not Equality, Opportunity not Welfare. Help for the needy not handouts for the Greedy." And he was hardly able to disguise his contempt for affluent Tories with fine cadences and appropriate tailors.

For all Tebbit's bluster about the trade unions he proved more delicate in practice. Like Prior, he was careful to avoid enacting legislation that would be difficult to enforce. "I was determined first to form public opinion and then to be always just a little behind rather than ahead of it as I legislated," he explained. It was this relatively restrained strategy that earned him the name of "Timid, Tiptoe Tebbit" from tabloids that expected a holy crusade if not an inquisition against the unions. Whatever their misgivings about Tebbit, however, his Employment Act of 1982 greatly helped to tame the trade unions.

Convinced that trade union power rested largely on legal immunity from prosecution for the damages they caused by unlawful actions, Tebbit's bill made the unions legally responsible for their conduct. If they committed unlawful acts except in "pursuit or furtherance" of a "trades dispute," they were liable. In effect, this removed trade unions' immunity for damages incurred by unlawful secondary picketing and the like. Tebbit was equally eager to reform the closed shop. He saw it as a "form of conscription," which furnished unions with the "power to put people out of work with no possibility of redress if they refused to obey orders." Given that a ban on the closed shop simply would not have worked in his view, Tebbit attempted to undermine union power by a sharp increase in compensation for those dismissed as a result of a closed shop and by enabling such workers to seek compensation from both their former employer and the trade union in question. Finally, the bill tightened the definition of a "trades dispute" to narrow the scope wholly or mainly to issues of industrial relations, thus removing immunity for "political strikes."[23]

But trade union leaders did not simply cave in. The first major clash with the Thatcher government began in January 1980 when a strike was called at British Steel, a nationalized behemoth. From the outset, the dispute was seen as a test case of the Prime Minister's mettle. She in turn was determined to stay the course despite the cost in order to obtain a "demonstration effect."[24]

The strike was, on one level, sparked by the steel maker's brutal if justified policy (which had begun quietly under the Callaghan government's aegis) of closing inefficient plants. Determined to raise productivity for the sake of international competitiveness, British Steel management offered the unions a 2 percent pay raise. Sensible as this offer was, given the dreary financial results of the firm, it could hardly have been less appealing. The steelworkers had watched the miners receive a 20 percent increase and engineers about 15 percent. Why settle for less? There followed a costly thirteen-week dispute, which soon spread to private steel makers who could only watch as their works were picketed and their supplies blacked. It was Tory sympathy for their predicament, as well as embarrassment at being hardly more successful than Labour in stopping strikes, that turned up pressure on Jim Prior to toughen what became the Employment Act of 1980 by narrowing union immunities and speeding up restrictions on secondary picketing.

Unhappy with the inflexible stance of British Steel management, Prior expressed his dissatisfaction in a private meeting with journalists which resulted in one of the many damaging leaks of the Thatcher government. During a BBC television interview, the Prime Minister publicly criticized the Secretary of State for Employment but rejected the interviewer's suggestion of firing him. "You do not sack a man for a single error," was her maternal verdict; "we all make mistakes. I think it was a mistake, and Jim Prior was very, very sorry indeed." This was the sort of remark a stern but forgiving mother might make to another parent or teacher on behalf of a naughty child. The finale of the steel strike was a 16 percent pay rise that marked government defeat. But Sir Keith Joseph, the minister responsible for the nationalized industries, did succeed in holding to a rigid line that he and his colleagues returned to again and again: Managers must have the right to manage; and therefore, government must not directly intervene in negotiations. This was a fiction, and a transparent fiction at that. But it proved most useful when it came to the coal miners.

I V

WHEN MARGARET THATCHER APPOINTED NIGEL LAWSON Environment Secretary in September 1981, she told him: "Nigel, we mustn't have a coal strike."[25]

No other industry so moved the national imagination. The legions of black-faced men who spent their lives working below the surface of the earth were objects of pity and sym-

bols of courage. These manly fellows braved physical hardship and capitalist exploitation. "All of us really owe the
comparative decency of our lives to poor drudges underground, blackened to the eyes with their throats full of coal
dust, driving their shovels forward with arms and belly mus-
cles of steel," George Orwell wrote.[26] Often located in isolated areas, mining villages and towns tended to revolve
around the coal industry. Generations of miners were
weaned on a well-founded mythology of capitalist exploitation. Yet sons still followed their fathers down into the mines.
In this macho world of physical labor, coming of age and
being a man meant going down the mine, where hazards
broke bodies and spirits. But for all the dangers and disadvan-
tages they faced, coal miners enjoyed far greater independence than factory workers. In the crust of the earth, detailed
supervision was next to impossible. At the guts of the coal
miners' culture was a deep paradox: They knew full well that
theirs was a demanding, unhealthy way of life, marred by
work accidents and occupational disease. Yet for all its tragic
aspects, they wanted to preserve it from extinction at all
costs.

But it was the political force of the miners rather than their
cultural situation that preoccupied Margaret Thatcher. As a
member of the Heath government which the miners helped
bring down in 1974, she had every reason to fear their power.
Their national strikes had always taken place when the Tories were in power. Miners had been in the front lines of the
labor movement since the inception of the "new unionism"
that organized semi-skilled and unskilled workers in the
1880s and 1890s. The first workingmen elected to Parliament
under the "Lib-Lab pact," the alliance between Liberals and
Labour, were coal miners. And it was the son of a Scottish
coal miner, Keir Hardie, who founded the Independent Labour Party. By the interwar era, the miners' clout was so
great that Conservative Prime Minister Stanley Baldwin

quipped that a wise man would never take on the Pope or the National Union of Mineworkers.

When the coal mines were nationalized by the Attlee government in 1947, the industry became a "symbol of a new consensus, a post war bargain between labour and the establishment." It was intended primarily to serve social ends by securing "the safety, health and welfare of persons in their employment." Far from exploiting the miners, the born-again coal industry would make use of "the practical knowledge and experience of such persons." Economic ends came last. The coal industry had to break even, but it did not have to make a profit.[27] By the early 1960s, the National Coal Board's Hobart House headquarters had become a favorite emblem of socialist bureaucracy and mismanagement.

However powerful the miners were, they still suffered from major disruptions to their world in the postwar era. Whereas there were 700,000 working miners in 1947, only 287,000 remained by 1970. The miners' strike of 1972, though, was primarily a dispute about wages. Its outcome was to catapult the miners from seventeenth to first place in the pay league of industrial workers. The unions' indisputable political might, however, did not stave off a wave of redundancies and pit closures. Nor did the unions stop the pit transfers that took miners from one section of the country to another. This disruption further radicalized the miners, an immobile lot who tended to be deeply rooted in communities where many of their families had lived for generations.

The collapse in the market for coal took place soon after the Thatcher government came to power. But the general approach to the coal industry dated back to a 1978 group policy report chaired by Nicholas Ridley, which proposed disciplining nationalized firms by setting financial targets for them. Once in office, it did not take long for David Howell, the Environment Secretary, to conclude that the only way to reverse the tide of massive losses piled up by the National

Coal Board was to close unprofitable pits. Howell hoped to make this strategy more palatable to the miners by investing £600 million a year in new fields and by "social" grants. But as the recession worsened, demand for coal slackened even further.

The National Coal Board (NCB), however, kept up output with blithe disregard to the small matter of finding buyers for its wares. By the autumn of 1980, Derek Ezra, chairman of the NCB, warned Howell that without an additional infusion of public money into the ailing industry, it would be necessary to close more pits. After a meeting between the Coal Board and the mining unions on February 10, 1981, a "hit list" of plans to close twenty to fifty pits was leaked. The miners responded with unofficial strikes in South Wales and Kent, likely targets for closure. Some members of the government were eager to stick to their guns and fight the miners in the event of a strike. But the Prime Minister was not ready to face off with the union. She quickly backed down, much to her own embarrassment and indeed to that of Department of Energy ministers and officials. On this occasion, the Iron Lady behaved like a rubber maiden. She largely caved in to demands put forth by Arthur Scargill, the radical president of the National Union of Mineworkers (NUM). Unprofitable pits were kept open despite the cost. The nationalized electricity and steel industries were compelled to rely exclusively on British coal and to forego buying cheaper imported materials.

This was a clear victory for the miners over the market. Before Nigel Lawson succeeded Howell as Environment Secretary, he summed up the predicament in a minute to Sir Geoffrey Howe: "Our original aim was to build a successful, profitable coal industry independent of government subsidies; to demonopolise it and ultimately open it to private enterprise . . . we will make no progress towards our aim until we deal with the problem of monopoly union power."[28]

But who would have the mettle to take on the miners? Lawson recalled the advice given to him by Frank Chapple, the cockney union leader who detested Arthur Scargill, about who would succeed Ezra as chairman of the National Coal Board. Over dinner at Lawson's home, Chapple suggested: "Get someone who's not afraid of Scargill. Most businessmen will tell you they're not, but in their hearts they are."[29] The person chosen was Ian MacGregor. Then chairman of British Steel, he was not a gentleman industrialist of the old school who professed little interest in profits and the like. But even the self-made Scot had obtained his position partly through the good offices of the old boy network. David Prior, who was MacGregor's assistant at the investment banking firm of Lazard Frères in New York, had brought his boss to the attention of his father, Jim Prior, who, in turn, recommended MacGregor to Sir Keith Joseph. And it was Joseph, the right-wing intellectual who scorned all that he surveyed at the Department of Industry, who recruited MacGregor to turn around British Steel.

Here was an archetypal representative of the Prime Minister's capitalist revolution. Ian MacGregor was a true believer in the virtues of management, moneymaking, and markets. An outsider to postwar British culture and society, he had spent most of his adult life in America. This fact did nothing to improve his public image in Britain. But his roots were Scottish. He was the son of an accountant who had railed against the fact that a few union leaders had been able to hold the country to ransom during the General Strike of 1926. Growing up within sight and sound of the British Aluminium works on a fjord between Argyle and Inverness, the practical arts came naturally to him.[30] Educated at George Watson's Edinburgh grammar school, MacGregor took a first-class degree in metallurgy at Glasgow University. Soon after, a position as works manager at the Beardmore Parkhead Forge in Glasgow gave him a first-hand look at Britain's industrial decline. He arrived to find rusty sheets hanging off the building and banging in the wind and rail tracks inside the property overgrown with weeds.[31]

After serving in the United States during World War II, he decided to remain. What attracted him, above all, to America was an attitude he found wanting in Britain: optimism about making a fortune and generosity toward those who did so. In his memoirs, MacGregor describes his idealized version of the American dream: "Everyone expects the light will shine in on him and he'll be the big winner. And if it doesn't happen for him, he works damned hard to make sure his children have a chance of it happening to them. The millionaire is not a figure of envy; people don't knock the man who makes a fortune—they admire and want to be like him."[32]

MacGregor's first labor dispute taught him a lesson that never left him: "Management has to maintain its resolve, preserve its right to manage and not to have this right abridged."[33] When he became general manager of MM & M, a New England metals concern, he found the union virtually running the place. MacGregor quickly set about proving who was in charge. He refused to back down even after a strike began. When a state mediator came to his home to warn him that the union was thinking of having their friends in the Mafia take out a contract on him, MacGregor did not relent." 'What's that supposed to do for me?' I asked. 'Well,' I said, 'you go back to them and tell them that any such action would probably solve all my problems—but it would only be the start of theirs.' "[34]

It was this tough-minded persona (John Wayne with a Scottish brogue and a pinstripe suit), backed up a long string of commercial successes, that earned MacGregor the respect of Margaret Thatcher. She reportedly considered him to be "the only man who is my equal." MacGregor returned the compliment, after a fashion. In his memoirs, he noted: "In some ways she was like my mother—who always had a clear idea of what she wanted to do."³⁵

Endlessly competitive and proudly mid-Atlantic, Mac-Gregor was prone to turn anything into a contest. At one dinner party, he spent the night vying with another guest to see who had flown more miles, attended more meetings, and touched ground in more places. Nicknamed "Mac the Knife" at British Steel, where he cut the workforce in half, he was feared rather than loved—much as Machiavelli suggested a prince should be. Whatever MacGregor's faults, though, his reputation as an industrial butcher who relished eliminating jobs was unwarranted. He was not one of the capitalist horde of the 1980s who reveled in buying, stripping, and selling companies. By nature, he was a builder.

Ian MacGregor found his perfect antithesis in Arthur Scargill, the union leader who spearheaded the resistance to the capitalist revolution. The scion of a Yorkshire mining family, Scargill was not one of the happy few born with a silver spoon in his mouth. He saw no reason why those who had riches should be allowed to keep them, or why those who had not should be allowed to earn them. Intellectually able and politically passionate, Scargill was well schooled in revolutionary theory by the Young Communist League, who taught him the value of discipline. Ambivalent, at best, about parliamentary democracy, he remained a member of the Communist Party long after revelation of Stalinist atrocities and the repression of Hungary had disillusioned many of his more sensitive comrades. Even when he finally left the Party in the early 1960s, his commitment to the class struggle did not fade. He came to prominence during the miners' strike of 1972, when he rallied "flying pickets" who turned back the police at Saltey Gate in the Midlands.

An extremely industrious man who worked long hours for his cause and his men, Scargill was no dreary revolutionary ascetic. He drove a Jaguar and had a flat in the Barbican, one of London's luxurious modern blocks of flats near the City of the type Prince Charles lambasted as "carbuncles."

The collision between the Thatcher government and the coal miners symbolized basic conflicts in economic ethics which were brought to a head by the capitalist revolution. Within a month of Margaret Thatcher's 1983 election victory, a coal strike seemed inevitable. Scargill described her triumph as "the worst national disaster" for a hundred years. This was a ludicrously shortsighted remark. Once again the issue of "uneconomic pits" precipitated strike talk. When MacGregor took over at the National Coal Board, Peter Walker, the Energy Secretary, handed him a sheet of paper which outlined the party line in typically pale bureaucratic language. Coal was an important national resource, but the purpose of coal production was to earn a satisfactory return on capital by competing in the marketplace.[36] In other words, the coal industry would have to live by the market or die by the market. MacGregor's brief, therefore, was to bring genuine business management to an industry that had been run largely by engineers. The hands-on, heads-off Scottish-American executive had to cut operating costs and capacity to make the coal industry competitive. This meant establishing, once and for all, that managers had the right to manage without being held hostage by trade unionists.

Such thinking flew in the face of all that Scargill believed. In the face of an "enterprise culture" that challenged workers to become bourgeois entrepreneurs, self-made men driven by self-interest, he preached worker solidarity and class struggle. Other men might worship profit, productivity, and efficiency; the Marxist union leader held to the old faith. For all his revolutionary rhetoric, Scargill's political ideology hearkened back to the "moral economy" of the pre-industrial age. He idealized the social needs of laboring communities rather than the economic demands of the free market. His premise was that coal was a precious national asset whether or not it could be produced or sold at "economic" rates. "Where there are resources of coal . . . even if there is a loss on the production of that coal, then the coal should be produced."[37] Scargill's priority, then, was "to protect the coal industry from the ravages of the market mechanism. . . . If we do not save our pits from closure, then all our struggles become meaningless."[38] If salvaging jobs and communities was of paramount importance, it simply did not matter whether specific pits made money or not. What the market could not bear, the state should subsidize.

Why would a capitalist government pay tribute to Scargill? It seemed that his overriding aim was to bring down Mrs. Thatcher and to foment a revolution. He would have to be broken.

When the National Coal Board announced in March 1984 that it would close the Cottonwood colliery in South Yorkshire, Scargill called a national strike. But he also made two fatal errors. The first was his failure to obtain rank-and-file approval for the strike by holding an election as mandated by law. So the strike began under a cloud of suspicion, if not outright dissent, because he did not enjoy the full support of the miners. This exposed Scargill to the charge that he was more a Marxist despot than a people's herald. But the decision was neither an oversight nor an accident. For this was one union leader who had little use for democratic procedures or the rule of law. And he would probably have lost a strike ballot.

Scargill's second error was to call the strike in the spring. This meant that by the advent of winter, when the need for fuel would have been at its height, the striking miners would have been without wages for six months. So their ability to soldier on was much reduced. What made his blunder all the more damaging was that this time the Thatcher government was not caught napping. It had prepared for a strike by stockpiling enough coal to enable it to outlast the miners.

During the year-long action, the Thatcher government tried to create the illusion that it was not directly involved in the "coal strike." The term was chosen deliberately to highlight what the nation was losing as a result of the dispute and to avoid antagonizing those who were sympathetic to the plight of the miners. In fact, "Misc 101," a powerful Cabinet committee set up by Mrs. Thatcher, met every week to discuss strategy. When it came to the necessity of beating Scargill and breaking the miners, the Thatcher government was united. The man in charge of the operation was Peter Walker. The last survivor of the wets, he was a skillful manipulator of the media, whose smooth demeanor was especially useful because MaGregor was inept in public relations. On one occasion, when journalists tracked him down in a hotel, MacGregor fled down the backstairs, covering his face with a newspaper.[39]

Although Mrs. Thatcher was careful to leave negotiations in Walker's hands in order to limit potential political damage to herself, she nonetheless indicted the strikers. Her most famous (or notorious) remarks came in a speech on July 19, 1984, to the 1922 Committee of Conservative MPs. She lashed out at the violence perpetrated by the striking miners: "We had to fight an enemy without in the Falklands. We always have to be aware of the enemy within, which is more difficult to fight and more dangerous to liberty."[40] This outrageous formulation blocked out the fact that for the most part the miners were trying to preserve their jobs and homes rather than destroy democracy. Whatever the strike was about, it had nothing to do with making the Falklands safe for sheep. And even if the suffering of the striking miners and their families was partly self-inflicted, the Prime Minister never saw fit to express compassion for the hardships they courageously endured.

The Thatcher government was intent on pulverizing "the enemy within." Initially, though, the Prime Minister decided not to use new union legislation to prosecute the strikers. The task of keeping the pits open and protecting working miners fell to the police. Carrying out this mission led to violent encounters that sullied the reputations of all concerned. If the miners' strike was a class struggle, one of the key battles was fought within workers' own ranks. Conflicts between striking and working miners rent friendships, families, and communities. It would have been difficult to defeat Scargill had the Midlands miners (who had broken away from the National Union of Mineworkers) not remained at work.

In March 1985, the strike was finally settled. A face-saving agreement kept open the five front-line collieries that Scargill had made his stand over. These pits aside, it was resolved that collieries facing severe geological difficulties and those that were exhausted would be closed by joint agreement. But the settlement also signaled a broader victory for the capitalist revolution. The Thatcher government had demonstrated that the demands of the market and the results of the balance sheet were the main criteria to judge any business, public or private. As Lawson argued in the Commons on July 31, 1984, the elimination of uneconomic its was "even in narrow financial terms . . . a worthwhile investment for the nation."[41] It was a costly lesson: The National Coal Board announced a loss of £2,200 million in summer of 1985.

An additional political bonus partly made up for the financial damage. Arthur Scargill's radical excesses aggravated ideological divisions within the Labour Party. Its newly elected leader, Neil Kinnock, was damned whether he criticized or defended the miners. The one would have made him a class traitor. The other would have reinforced the soft left image he was trying to shed as he began to thrust himself and his party toward the political center.

The decline in union militancy in the 1980s had several causes. It was a product of careful legislation which was usually backed up by the political resolve of the Thatcher government. But it was also a product of the long recession. As businesses failed and work became harder to find, workers were understandably shaken and insecure and became increasingly loath to strike for fear of losing their jobs and being unable to find others. In September 1982, Sir John Hoskyns argued in *The Times:* "Today, union prestige and authority have declined beyond recognition. They are more disliked, less feared, less respected. The rift between members and leaders grows, as does that between unions in the public and private sectors. Union leaders no longer claim to speak for 'the working people of this country' because the public no longer pays attention."[42] To a point, this was wishful thinking. By the time the coal miners returned to work, however, Margaret Thatcher had pushed back the pendulum to favor management rather than labor.

V

ON NOVEMBER 8, 1985, A FRAIL BUT STILL SPIRITED HAROLD Macmillan, Lord Stockton, gave a dinner address to the Tory Reform Club in London. Privatization was his subject. In his speech he described the lamentable process by which the assets of nationalized firms and industries were transferred from the state to the private sector. The report in *The Times* the following day quoted his remarks:

> "First of all the Georgian silver goes, and then all that nice furniture that used to be in the saloon. Then the Canalettos go." Cable and Wireless, "a tasty morsel," had been sold off. Profitable parts of the railways and steel industry along with the telephone system had also been sold. "They were like the two Rembrandts still left. . . . Now we are promised the further sale of anything else that can be scraped up."[43]

Macmillan's potent image of Britain "selling the family silver" to pay the bills was both charming, vivid, and misleading. For the nationalized industries that he was so keen to keep in the common weal were not exactly great assets, much less masterpieces, especially when it came to serving the kind of people who didn't own Canalettos or Rembrandts.

As any American expatriate in London soon learned, British Telecom made AT&T (before or even after its break-up) seem the model of an efficient utility. The familiar appeal of the lovely old red phone boxes did not make up for the fact that it was difficult to find one that worked. Too often they simply flashed "emergency service only" without a trace of irony. Calling for information from central London directory enquiries was easy enough; the hard thing was avoiding the constant busy signal. All in all, British Telecom was more a forgery than a crown jewel.

What made the company attractive was the process of readying the somnambulant giant for privatization. Its stock market flotation was hugely oversubscribed. About 2 million people bought shares. So did 96 percent of the eligible workforce. This may have made little sense to Macmillan, a wealthy man without financial cares. But the prospect of profiting from shares that were sold at bargain prices aroused the appetites of ordinary people for whom the stock market had been a foreign world.

Whatever the virtues of selling the family silver, Mrs. Thatcher clearly intended to do something to tackle the nationalized industries when she came to power. They were an integral part of the socialist leviathan she wanted to dismantle. When, in 1945, the Attlee government began its ambitious program of nationalization, it cited a number of justifications for buying private firms and industries. Labour expected that it would improve industrial relations, raise productivity, foster full employment, and lead to efficient regulation of monopolies. National goals would take precedence over private profit. But the socialist dream and economic reality soon proved to be at odds. The performance of the nationalized firms varied and it was not by any means as uniformly weak as their Tory critics maintained. Both public and private enterprises in postwar Britain suffered, to a point, from some of the same managerial weaknesses and technological shortcomings. Even if state-owned corporations are not necessarily less productive or profitable than their private counterparts, however, they had fewer incentives and more protections than Adam Smith would have advocated. "What public ownership does is to eliminate the threat of takeover and ultimately of bankruptcy," Lawson argued in a speech at Oxford.[44]

Insulated from the shock waves of the marketplace and buttressed by public monies, the nationalized industries had too little motivation to attain, much less sustain, innovation and productivity. Even though they were not the root cause of the British disease, they were more a part of the problem than the solution. The Treasury Select Committee found that the aggregate return on capital had fallen from 0 percent in 1970 to 2 percent in 1979. Now it was also true that the social goals served by the railways and the like partly compensated for miserable financial results. Had the great national enterprises, such as they were, been forced to face the vagaries of the marketplaces without the largesse of the state, the family silver would have quickly been turned into family souvenirs.

Irredeemably opposed as Mrs. Thatcher was to the nationalized industries, what was to be done about them? Some assumptions were clear. The state is not responsible for the economic health of the country and intervention succeeds only in making matters worse. Profits are the basis of a free enterprise economy. There was an imbalance between the private and public sectors. The pendulum had to be pushed back to strengthen the market and constrain the state. Nationalized industries were inefficient and unproductive drags on the public purse. Apart from these premises, official statements of party policy offered little hint of things to come.

The philosophical underpinnings of privatization came largely from the Centre for Policy Studies, whose basic conclusion was that "when the state owns, nobody owns; and when nobody owns, nobody cares." John Moore, Financial Secretary to the Treasury, the minister charged with putting the privatization program into practice from 1983 to 1986, came from a working-class background. Most of his relatives were East Enders "in the print." His people were familiar with the "never never world" of loans, where buying a suit of clothes meant paying interest rates that were sometimes as high as 100 or 200 percent.

Moore found a different world in Chicago, where he stayed for five years and came to appreciate how deep the human instinct for ownership was, and how British society frustrated it, especially for the working class. In a pamphlet entitled *The Value of Ownership* (1986), Moore articulated what he saw as the spirit of privatization: "Possession means power, the kind of power that matters to ordinary people— power to make choices, power to control their own lives. Our aim is to extend this power to as many people as we can. We are doing it by extending ownership as widely as possible."

Actually, in the early years of the Thatcher government the rhetorical attack on the nationalized industries did not amount to much. Intent as ministers such as Sir Keith Joseph, the Industry Secretary, said they were about training, or chaining, state-owned corporations, when it came to it all they could muster seemed like a loud bark, no bite, lots of biscuits and plenty of walks. For all Sir Keith's talk about markets, competition, and self-help, he was a tender-hearted gentleman and had little choice but to agree to industrial aid when faced with requests for cash that came from the needy chairmen of nationalized companies.

Economic theory, in short, collided with political reality.

However profound Joseph's philosophic commitment to the free market principles of von Hayek and Friedman, the nationalized industries were large employers. Cutting off their funds amidst a recession of the early 1980s would have killed a lot of manufacturing jobs and spawned high political fallout. Joseph changed course. The Thatcher government pumped huge amounts of public capital into Britain's largest socialist drain. In 1981, Joseph authorized a £900 million infusion into British Leyland. This bail-out was a trifle, though, compared to the £6.6 billion which went into the rescue plan for British Steel. Dubious as these "investments" seemed at the time, they did pay off because they helped turn these companies around. So they became suitable candidates for stock market flotation rather than burial at sea.

A number of motives inspired the drive for privatization. The prospective sale of large publicly owned firms promised a possible bonanza for the Treasury. The government looked forward to eliminating the high cost of investing in, or bailing out, flagging firms. Privatization might improve industrial relations by giving employees a direct stake in firm's profits.[45] It became the hinge that Mrs. Thatcher hoped would turn socialist Britain into a "property-owning" democracy. And it offered a material basis for "popular capitalism," as the Prime Minister came to call it. In her vision, a nation of shareholders would commit themselves to the creation of wealth. In other words, privatization was the cornerstone of a British version of the American dream. As Lawson explained in 1985, "It gives the citizen a vital sense of identification with the society of which he is a part. It gives him a stake in the future."[46] There was also an appealing political payoff. New shareholders would be loath to support a Labour Party which had announced its intention of renationalizing privatized firms.

Dealing with a class of people who had never owned

shares, however, did not please everyone in the bastions of the City of London. As the head of one investment house said to Moore during the run-up to the sale of British Gas: "But John, we don't want all those kind of people owning shares, do we?"[47]

Translating the ideal of privatization into practice was neither quick nor easy. After the 1979 election, Mrs. Thatcher established a subcommittee to explore suitable candidates for privatization; it was called E(DL); "E" stood for Economic, "DL" for Disposal. What made the process of unloading the family silver particularly complex was that it was unprecedented. With no prior experience to draw on, was it preferable to sell the assets of nationalized firms to their managers and workers or to sell them on the stock market or just to give away shares to all citizens? In any case, the proponents of privatization had to clear a number of difficult hurdles. The nationalized industries had formidable political clout, given the fact that they accounted for about one tenth of national output, one seventh of national investment, and employed 1.75 million people.[48] So it was unsurprising that the Labour Party and the trade unions opposed privatization. And the Liberal–Social Democratic Alliance, the centrist group formed in 1981 to provide a political alternative to both the left and the right, also resisted it.

The Thatcher government had another hurdle to jump. Given the nationalized industries' record, who would line up to buy shares in them? It was the preparation for privatization rather than the actual transfer to private hands that provided the impetus to improve performance. But the run-up to market freedom was sometimes rocky. For instance, the erratic financial results of British Airways (as well as turbulence in the airline industry) delayed its sell-off.

In the event, the Thatcher government opted to privatize nationalized firms by stock market flotations. The details of the deals varied somewhat. But the state generally kept a "golden share" of the stock for a set period in order to prevent hostile takeovers. The privatization program began modestly enough in 1980 with the sale of two subsidiaries of the British Technology Group. The next year, British Aerospace and Cable & Wireless went on the block. They were followed in 1982 by Amersham International, in 1983 by National Freight, and in 1984 by one of the great names of the automotive industry, Jaguar Cars, which managed to escape from British Leyland. The turning point came in November 1984, when the sale of British Telecom raised nearly £4 billion in proceeds for the Treasury. Then came major issues of British Gas, British Airways, Rolls-Royce, and British Airports Authority.

By far the most popular of the privatization schemes involved the sale of homes. The decision to sell state-owned and subsidized "council houses," the rough equivalent of American "projects," was a stroke of political genius. It was all the more popular because tenants could purchase the flats or houses they lived in at a fraction of market value. In addition to reducing public spending, this measure allowed people who otherwise would have had little chance to own their own home to do so. It also gave them the option of selling off their new property, often at a large profit, or eventually passing it on to their children.

Privatization was, to the mind of Sir John Harvey-Jones, chairman of Imperial Chemical Industries, a great British invention.[49] It was adopted in various forms in the United States and Europe and finally in the Eastern bloc and the former Soviet Union.

But if privatization's results were impressive, they were not universally admired. Privatization raised about £29 billion in much-needed revenue for the Exchequer; the sale of council houses added another £17 billion to the public coffers; and the newly privatized firms increased their productivity in the course of the Thatcher years; rewards for both managers and workers also went up. In their private incarnations, though, they were vulnerable to both bankruptcy and to hostile takeovers. Both were rife in Britain as in America during the 1980s. Moreover, critics argued that privatization amounted to the largest fire sale of modern times. They pointed out that nationalized industries were sold to investors at well below their market value. For instance, British Gas was sold for £6 billion, but was worth £16 billion, according to John Edmonds of the Boilermakers and Associated Trades Union. Equally objectionable was the fact that once public utilities raised their prices and inflated their profits at the expense of their former owners. Britain may have made some progress toward becoming a "property-owning democracy," but the increase in the total number of shareholders did not cancel out the fact that their holdings were slim. It was the large investors who profited most out of the sales of the nationalized industries.

For the capitalist revolution's opponents, privatization symbolized the hateful materialism and commercialism that they saw overtaking the country, or, at very least, its Tory leadership. The sales of two giant public utilities, gas and water, were particularly unpopular. They seemed to be "natural monopolies" in need of strict regulation for the sake of both the consumer and the environment. The prospect of Rover Cars, a division of British Leyland, being sold to General Motors caused a great furor. The possibility that the Land Rover, a hardy jeep that was Rover's best product, could fall into foreign hands was not exactly a national tragedy. Nevertheless, there was something to the question raised in the Commons by John Smith, the Glasgow lawyer who was then the Labour Party's Shadow Chancellor: Was everything for sale?

For Mrs. Thatcher and her allies, though, Britain had become (or was at least becoming) a fine and private place. In

March 1988, Nigel Lawson, the Chancellor, told the House of Commons that "the country is now experiencing an economic miracle comparable in significance to that previously enjoyed by West Germany and still enjoyed by Japan."[50] There was indeed an economic boom in the mid-1980s. And the standard of living of most people did improve. These were significant accomplishments.

Was this "fine and private place" also a grave in which none dared embrace? Certainly Britain was fragmenting. As one critic put it, the United Kingdom was turning into a country composed of three nations: the haves, the have-nots, and the have-lots.[51] Mike Leigh dramatized the social divisions in his film *High Hopes,* contrasting the fortunes of a homeless man and a *nouveau riche* couple. In *Beyond Caring,* the London-based photographer Paul Graham captured the indignity and humiliation experienced by unfortunate persons staring into space while they queued for hours in Department of Health and Social Services waiting rooms with lemon green walls, orange Formica benches, and flickering neon lights.[52]

There was ample evidence to back up the suggestion that if the Thatcher years were the best of times for some, they were the worst of times for many others. According to one report (disputed by the government), the real income of the bottom tenth of British society fell by 9.6 percent from 1979 to 1985. During this period, the number of people at or below the poverty line increased by 55 percent. The situation of women and ethnic minorities was especially difficult because they were among those hardest hit by the rise of unemployment. While some towns in the North of England and in Scotland prospered (Glasgow was a case in point) and others in the South of England struggled, for the most part it was the South and East that benefited from the Thatcher boom. For much of the rest of the country, it may as well have been a bust.[53]

CHAPTER

EIGHT

Leaner and Meaner

I

SHORTLY BEFORE MRS. THATCHER CAME TO POWER, HUGH
Parker conducted a two-day seminar at Eton for the sons of
the rich and powerful. Parker, educated on both sides of the
Atlantic, was a fine guide, having opened the London offices
of McKinsey & Co., the top-flight management consulting
firm.

Close to London, Eton College is located in the royal reserve below Windsor Castle. Founded in 1440 by Henry VI
to provide suitable minions to staff the offices of church and
state, it offered the prospect of an education under the King's
eye. Even today, confident young boys dress in white ties,
tails, and striped trousers at Eton, reserving their boaters and
straw hats only for certain occasions. They study and live in
beautiful old stone Gothic buildings and attend Anglican services in a late medieval chapel with wall paintings of historic
figures and stained-glass panels that depict the Crucifixion.
Better known for links to government than trade, this most
exclusive of boarding schools could claim that no less than
one fifth of all twentieth-century Cabinet ministers were old

Etonians. "The Tory party is run by about five people," said Lord Poole in 1961, "who treat all their followers with disdain. They're mostly Etonians, and Eton is good for disdain."[1]

Contrary to myth, however, many old Etonians did go into business. Lord Poole himself served as chairman of Lazard Frères, whose French Jewish origins had become invisible in a merchant bank that was thoroughly Gentile and English during his tenure. When asked after the property crash of 1974 how he had avoided the immense losses that sank other concerns, he supposedly responded, tongue in cheek one hopes: "Quite simple, I only lent money to those who had been at Eton." A more enlightened ethic drove other old Etonians. Among them were Sir Adrian Cadbury, the scion of the great Quaker cocoa and chocolate family; and Henry Vincent Yorke, who managed the family engineering firm in Birmingham, and wrote novels (as Henry Green).

Hugh Parker's reception at Eton was lukewarm. Laughing about the rather perfunctory introduction extended to him by the headmaster, he recalled that the man was curiously unenthusiastic, without being openly rude of course. What he said, more or less, was: "Well, here's Mr. Parker who's going to tell us something about industry. Not particularly valuable, really, but we have to have it so let's get it over with." And so on. The point was perfectly plain. But it was not simply the headmaster who gave the topic short shrift. The boys themselves asked hostile questions. This was no great surprise to Parker, who remembered that none of his fellows at Felstead, a minor public school he had attended on an exchange scholarship, had expressed any interest in a business career.[2]

The gentlemanly disdain for industry was not confined to Eton. Nearly every year from 1806 to 1962, crowds gathered at Lord's Cricket Ground in London to watch the Gentlemen v. Players match, the gentlemen being amateurs who played for love of the game and the players professionals who were paid

for their efforts. In a classic article, Professor D. C. Coleman
has construed this great sporting ritual as a metaphor sym-
bolizing the social divide between the elite and the common-
ers and the tension in the business world between educated
amateurs and practical men.[3]

Nowhere was the old gentlemanly ethic more visible than
in the financial world of the City of London. In 1946, Siegmund Warburg, the scion of an exceptional German Jewish
banking family from Hamburg, opened a merchant bank in
the cliquish and clubby little world of the City. If English
gentlemen were nice to each other, this did not mean that
they were nice in general. Convinced that "establishment
people" were usually wrong, Warburg still had to contend
with the fact that they were up in arms against him. As he
later explained: "First of all, I was a newcomer in the City.
Secondly, I was not an English newcomer—a Jewish newcomer, a fellow who has not been educated in British schools,
a fellow who speaks with a foreign accent, all that sort of
thing." Warburg's work ethic also caused outrage: "I remember some people in very good houses talked very nastily behind my back: 'Do you know this fellow Siegmund Warburg?
He starts in the office at *eight o'clock* in the morning.' That was
considered contemptible. Most of them came to the office at
ten o'clock in the morning. I was awful. They looked down
upon me with utmost snobbism. But that didn't worry me."[4]

Strict social hierarchies also existed in manufacturing industry, as Richard Giardano discovered when he became a
director of British Oxygen in the 1970s. The son of Italian immigrants, he grew up in New York and was educated at Harvard College and Columbia Law School, so he had little
preparation for a board loaded with peers. Presumably chosen for genteel birth rather than professional worth, their role
was to put on a good show to the City of London.[5]

The relative insulation of postwar Britain helped support
this gentlemanly business ethic. Starved of consumer goods

during World War II, and in many cases for years thereafter, Britain became a classic sellers' market in which companies dictated what they would "allocate" to would-be customers. Sir Adrian Cadbury (whose family firm was reorganized by a McKinsey team led by Hugh Parker) recalled that salesmen were able to give orders as well as to take them, informing stores how much they would be able to sell to a candy-obsessed British public. With only limited competition, Britain became an insulated economic fortress.[6]

However, foreign competition and domestic politics forced British business and industry to become meaner and leaner. During the Thatcher years, Parker saw signs of a new spirit at work in his adopted country. The gentlemanly style was largely pushed aside by an entrepreneurial ethic that valued competition, profit, and growth. A different business climate, which exerted greater pressures and offered higher rewards, began to take hold. Most managers he worked with believed, as he did, that Margaret Thatcher had released enormous drive and ambition, and inspired those who wanted to make money and were willing to take risks to do so. As a new generation came to the fore, professional credentials like MBAs became more important than social background. For that matter, by 1990 grammar school boys had become more numerous than the owners of old school ties at top public companies.

The enterprise culture, with its emphasis on small business, even touched Parker personally. When he retired from McKinsey, he founded his own firm, Corporate Renewal Associates. Although he believed that on balance the pursuit of private profit had done the country more good than harm, the decline in the quality of public services disturbed him. The London Underground that thrilled him when he first arrived in England in 1936 had changed for the worse. Less than half a mile from his elegant offices in Fitzroy Square, his local tube stop at Warren Street was sitting proof: it took more than two years to modernize the escalator.

How did the capitalist revolution change Britain's business culture and to what extent did changes take place because of or despite the hard work and stern message of the Iron Lady? These are questions best answered by examining what happened to particular firms.

I I

AT NO. 9 MILLBANK STANDS IMPERIAL CHEMICAL HOUSE, grandly facing out onto the Thames and its bridges. Begun almost immediately after four chemical companies (including England's Brunner, Mond and Sweden's Nobel Industries) merged to form Imperial Chemical Industries in 1926, the nine floors of the edifice accommodated the one thousand five hundred employees the new entity brought together. August, bureaucratic, and imperial in manner as well as name, the gray granite edifice designed for ICI by Sir Frank Baines in the classical style is composed of horizontal lines that gracefully follow the sweep of the River Thames. Close enough to the Tate Gallery to permit easy cultural excursions to one of the greatest museums of British art, ICI was much closer in style and spirit to the Houses of Parliament, a mile or so upstream. Like Whitehall mandarins, ICI managers were regarded as an elite not least by themselves. They were known for a species of Civil Service mentality which came naturally to those who worked for great national institutions.

If the Palace of Westminster was a monument to English history and art, then Imperial Chemical House was a testimonial to progress through science. Stone portrait busts surrounded it, representing the founding fathers of the firm and its subsequent leaders, as well as eminent scientists such as Dalton and Cavendish, Lavoisier and Priestley. Guarding the entrance were a huge pair of bronze doors twenty feet high, whose elaborate floral decoration recalled the Baptistery in Florence, but which required electricity to open their two-and-a-half-ton weight.

The fate of Imperial Chemical House was in doubt, however. Soon after John Harvey-Jones became chairman of ICI in April 1982, he proposed selling the building—an extraordinary suggestion, which scandalized the faithful. Not an ordinary realtor by any stretch of the imagination, Harvey-Jones had both practical and symbolic motives for putting the building on the block. Determined to have a smaller board and staff, he considered the headquarters superfluous and hoped that its sale would raise considerable capital. Having decided that "nothing was sacred," and that the ailing industrial giant had to change, what better way to symbolize the depth of this intention to make ICI leaner and meaner than to hock the family silver, as it were. But as the recession forced other enterprises to slim, ICI House proved unsellable. So the chairman contented himself with leasing two thirds of the building and converting the remainder for new purposes—a symbolic solution of sorts, if not an overwhelmingly dramatic one.

The condition of ICI was more than a matter of local interest, for it represented the best in British business. An industrial titan, whose ups and downs were carefully watched, ICI was regarded as an economic bellwether for the London Stock Exchange, occupying much the same place in Britain as General Motors did, for better or worse, in America. Consistently among the top five or six chemical firms in the world, its competitors all came from the top drawer. Among them were DuPont in the United States, and Bayer, BASF, and Hoechst in Germany. As its name announced, ICI was an imperial concern. The dominant player at home, it also had strong market shares in the outposts of the British Empire—Australia, Canada, New Zealand, and South Africa.

Although ICI was one of the few world-class British firms in the 1970s, it was also a "slumbering giant," as Anthony Sampson had pointed out in his *Anatomy of Britain* (1962). An investigative article in the *Sunday Times* a decade later concluded: "if ICI is to snatch and exploit the opportunities of the future, it needs to be flexible and quick reacting, enterprising and risk taking, on a scale beyond anything it has yet reached. . . . The catalyst to release ICI's great potential has still to be found."[7]

But a powerful corporate culture stood in the way. For all its strengths, ICI was not an entrepreneurial firm. Scientific ability and technical skill were the path to the top, almost irrespective of organizational capacity. Being "bloody good technically" was the point. "Things were produced and chaps were told to sell them. You didn't really closely follow the market," one exasperated manager observed. Long success had bred complacency. As a result, many of the issues raised, and solutions proposed, by Sir Paul Chambers, who was chairman from 1960 to 1968, were still on the table, if not under it, when Harvey-Jones came to the fore in the mid-1970s. Making changes was especially hard because Millbank headquarters had become so bureaucratic, cumbersome, and top-heavy that it was nicknamed "Millstone House." But overmanning did not stop at the top of the firm: ICI was an equal opportunity employer. So much so that one joke (which could have applied to many firms) recounted a conversation between the chairman of British Rail, who bragged to his ICI counterpart that his firm had more employees, to which the ICI man replied: "Yes, but we have more passengers."[8]

ICI's traditional union of scientific professionalism with a gentlemanly style was no longer a spur to commercial success. When a flock of consultants, led by an American industrial psychologist, Douglas MacGregor, descended on ICI in the early 1960s and 1970s, the familiar boundary between gentleman and players still prevailed. And it was much resented by those on the wrong side of the team. One man recalled: "Alkali Division were always the gentlemen of ICI. They wined and dined at Winnington Hall club. They did a little work but normally arranged for others to do work for them. Works managers used to shoot quail over the lime bed in the afternoon. They would keep their dogs panting under their desks, and then take the dog for a walk around the works."[9]

Although the need for radical change was clearly recognized in certain quarters at ICI, the missing catalyst came from without. Both before and after Mrs. Thatcher took power, she made no secret of her belief that England had become stagnant, its businesses grown soft from reliance on the state, and its place in the world going downward. Sir Maurice Hodgson, who was chairman of ICI when Mrs. Thatcher ascended to office, agreed with her diagnosis and was much relieved by the Conservative victory. A chemist by training, he had little use for the hocus-pocus of t-groups and other touchy-feely revelations that organizational development consultants had foisted on the firm. Elected chairman partly to help strengthen ICI's finances, his attitude was far simpler: "let's get on with the business and make some money"—a stance the new Prime Minister would probably have applauded.[10]

For his part, Sir Maurice was optimistic about Mrs. Thatcher's economic approach. "There has been the removal of a great deal of threat and harassment, as regards the prices and incomes policy, for example," he told *Director* in an interview in March 1980. The chairman added: "There has been a tremendous liberation of energy. . . . The changes in tax rates means that there is more incentive for better management."[11] High interest rates, a tight money supply, and a hard currency was an economic formula with which he agreed. Yet the downturn in the business cycle was still worrying. "I'm afraid some companies are so sick that the dose may be too strong. Some of our own customers are being damaged this way. And so we have to keep an anxious eye on the patient"—homely talk with a Thatcheresque tone.[12]

There was also good reason to keep an eye, anxious or not, on ICI itself. When inflation rocketed in the course of 1980, ICI proved vulnerable. The good news was that its profits from North Sea oil fields amounted to £79 million in 1979; and a steady flow of oil provided ICI a raw material advantage. The bad news included almost everything else. ICI's need for working capital grew by 23 percent in 1979; its cash reserves were reduced by £256 million; and its debt climbed to £273 million. Return on assets fell from 15.2 percent to 4.6 percent. The results of some divisions were particularly lame: the organic division, which produced dyestuffs, managed profits of only £7 million on sales of £519 million. The strengthening pound exposed ICI to mounting foreign competition, in particular a major increase in American fiber exports to Europe. So, in 1980, the firm that invented polyester lost about £80 million in synthetic fibers. Then came the axman and the layoffs that reduced the number of fiber workers from about 24,000 in 1975 to 7,500 five years later.[13] To make matters worse, American imports were also beginning to damage ICI's position both in petrochemicals, whose volume was cut in half in the first nine months of 1980, and in plastics.[14]

But the epochal event which came to be part of ICI lore was the financial loss that ICI sustained in the third quarter of 1980—news that Sir Maurice elected to break to Mrs. Thatcher in person. Nothing she could have said about the need for a capitalist revolution could have had as traumatic effect on ICI as experiencing the first loss in its long history. Although the loss was not trivial, it did not jeopardize the giant company's survival. Nevertheless, the loss symbolized a threat to ICI's long-term prospects and, still more, to its collective self-image. If ICI was indeed a bellwether for Britain, it was time to ask for whom the bell tolled and to get a quick response.

The side effects of Mrs. Thatcher's course of shock treatment slapped the slumbering giant in the face. The downturn was particularly damaging to ICI because the firm was heavily concentrated in a home market under assault. To be sure, Hodgson and his colleagues had not simply stood still in the middle of economic turmoil. But it was not until the threats to ICI mounted that the champions of change had the leverage they needed to carry out what they had long advocated. Their long-term strategy was to move ICI into higher-profit businesses and to make the firm more international than imperial by investing outside of Britain. Their short-term aim was to cut operating costs, partly by reducing the workforce, whose numbers fell from 89,400 in 1979 to 73,000 in 1981. After years of inertia came the revolution that resulted in more changes from 1980 to 1983 than in the past twenty years.[15] Sir Maurice Hodgson was the man who began the revolution, but it was John Harvey-Jones who completed it.

Unless ICI had as it were, "fallen off a cliff" in the third quarter of 1980, it would have been highly unlikely at best that Harvey-Jones would have become its chairman. He bore scant resemblance to the ideal ICI manager, who was described by one insider as a neatly dressed man with shortish hair, intellectual ability, technical competence, unemotional demeanor, and conservative temperament.[16]

For all Harvey-Jones's virtues, he ran counter to ICI type. His intellectual ability was clear enough despite his lack of a university degree to testify to it. But his understanding of chemistry was modest; what he knew about the subject, he cheerfully admitted, came from reading one Penguin paperback. If Harvey-Jones was deferential, he kept it well hidden. When, in August 1974, his secretary had made the mistake of distributing a confidential consulting report to the entire board, he refused to cower before the chairman, Sir Jack Callard, who ordered Harvey-Jones to fire the offender. He replied: "no way, poor devil, I've asked him to do this. If you don't like it fire me." In the event, no one was fired; rather, in good corporate fashion, the chairman issued a pointed memorandum.[17]

Harvey-Jones's temperament and persona were nothing if not colorful. In a dull corporate environment this was a man who wore pink ties, pink pocket handkerchiefs, and pale mauve shirts. He let his hair grow well over his collar and sported a drooping mustache. A dynamic and plainspoken naval man whose salty language included liberal doses of the word "bloody," his nature was not pacific.

By virtue of birth and education, however, Harvey-Jones belonged to the gentlemen rather than the players, as his double-barreled name discreetly showed. His family were, by his own description, "the cannon-fodder of empire," faithful servants of Queen and Country to be sure, if not successful enough to rise to any great eminence on land or sea. But they were still determined that he follow a traditional and suitable path for a man of his class. So a career in industry was out of the question.[18] The young Harvey-Jones chose the Navy and therefore attended the Royal Naval College, Dartmouth, where he specialized in arts subjects—History, Languages, and English—before going on to work in Russian intelligence. As a naval officer from 1937 to 1956, he gained practical experience in what leaders can do to inspire commitment. His time on a submarine taught him a good deal about the problems of leading compact teams who must sink or be sunk.

Harvey-Jones was forced to seek another career after his daughter contracted polio and he wanted to be closer to home. As it happened, his brother-in-law and two former colleagues in naval intelligence were working for ICI and liked the company. He applied for, and took, a job as work study officer. In so doing, he rejected the chance to become

Assistant Serjeant at Arms at the Houses of Parliament. This outraged his family, who would have much preferred that he accept a prestigious position that afforded him an honorable career in public service (and the chance to sport a morning suit and black silk stockings as his daily garb). Starting out from a modest position at ICI, Harvey-Jones rose the ranks with remarkable speed. By 1970, he was chairman of the Petrochemicals Division, and then a director of the main board of ICI three years later.

What made Harvey-Jones's ascent all the more impressive was that this was a man with a different voice. A skillful politician who navigated through a notorious corporate bureaucracy, he was also courageous enough to advocate new approaches even when they were likely to be controversial. Rather than just "frig around with bits of the company," he wanted to "really concentrate on getting some major changes in the board."[19] He set up a room on the directors' floor at Millbank where anybody could put up a chart to get the board's attention without jeopardizing their career prospects.[20]

For that matter, Harvey-Jones had his own prospects to consider. White smoke did not pour out of ICI's riverfront palace on Millbank onto the banks of the Thames when the ICI board elected a new chairman, but the process still had a certain air of ritual mystery and, of course, political intrigue. As one of the three deputy chairmen, Harvey-Jones certainly had a shot at the top job because the chairman was, by custom, chosen from their number by secret ballot. "The dance for the chairman's job," *The Economist* observed in October 1981, "is really about ICI's ability to compete in a tougher, less buoyant world market."[21] If Harvey-Jones was, by most accounts, the first choice of ICI's demoralized managers, lost battalions in search of a leader, the fact that "his outspoken personality grates in the gentlemanly board room" damaged his chances.[22] Had the crisis of 1980–81 not left many an ICI director sitting white-knuckled around the boardroom, he almost certainly would have been passed over in favor one of the other deputy chairmen, both of whom were considerably less controversial. But the fact that Harvey-Jones had been banging on for years about the need for change suddenly became an advantage when business as usual was no longer viable. And so in November 1981 the ICI board elected him chairman as of the following April.

Harvey-Jones's mission was to save ICI. But "the Admiral," as he was soon dubbed, was also a wise enough leader to recognize that "Change, or the prospect of change, will frighten everybody."[23] So he began to change the company from the top down rather than blame line managers and workers for the problems and then force a harsh remedy down their virtueless throats. Eager to turn the board into the industrial equivalent of Nelson's "band of brothers," he eschewed the formal, imposing boardroom and held the first board meeting in what had been his own office.

Telling as such symbolic moves were in setting the tone for change, Harvey-Jones was also intent on transforming the structure of the organization. Willing as he was to delegate responsibility, he also made sure that he had more clout than his predecessors and more scope to change the organization. So he became the first chairman of ICI to serve as well as principal executive officer, a new position which signaled that the Admiral intended to stay on deck rather than in his cabin. Also he began to streamline ICI, stripping away layers of hierarchy so that individuals would have to take personal responsibility for decisions. In the name of making ICI a truly global firm with an international outlook, he appointed a German, a Japanese, and an American to the board. Finally, he stepped up the efforts to widen ICI's geographical spread while emphasizing specialty products.

But if Harvey-Jones was careful to begin his revolution at the top of ICI, he did not end there. A leading member of the new Social Democratic Party (SDP), he practiced what he preached. He tried to improve communication between Millbank and the divisions in order to help make ICI more responsive to market shifts. Moreover, he reorganized the giant firm into thirty-five business units, giving them greater authority to act while expecting greater accountability for performance. This was more than rhetoric. Each year their chief executives and financial officers had to undergo a "hell fortnight." On this occasion, the whip and the lash were on hand, and if need be, in hand, to encourage managers to bring in budgets and plans that would meet corporate strategy. Harvey-Jones also rewarded those who had done well with public recognition of their efforts and achievements. A pat on the back was sweetened by an unexpected bonus, monetary or otherwise. He made a habit of sending cases of wine along with a personal note to the homes of those who had done something particularly meritorious.[24]

The process of change was not always so pleasant, however. The transformation of ICI inevitably demanded rationalization, restructuring, and retrenchment, three "R's" that became catch phrases on both sides of the Atlantic during the 1980s. ICI closed uneconomic factories, combined business divisions, and made major staff reductions in the name of becoming more productive and profitable.

The results of Harvey-Jones's leadership were undeniably impressive. In 1984, ICI achieved the target he had set of £1 billion in profits. By the time he retired three years later, the vestiges of the gentlemen's club milieu were gone. Although ICI changed substantially during the 1980s, the tenor of the changes was not Thatcherite. Harvey-Jones's management philosophy was in keeping with the politics of the Social Democratic Party to which he contributed greatly. Like Mrs. Thatcher, Sir John was a strong leader who did not flinch from taking tough decisions.[25] Unlike the Iron Lady, however, he wanted to share power rather than hog it. Great believer in personal enterprise that he was, he was not a market mystic who believed that those who fell on the wayside should simply be left there to read Milton Friedman.

Looking beyond the triumphant turnaround of ICI, however, Sir John bemoaned the impact of Thatcher policies on British manufacturing industry. No amount of rhetoric about the need for Britain to earn its way in the world, true as it was, made up for the fact that high inflation, high interest rates, and an overvalued pound buried companies that might well have lived along with those that were already dead. A salutary shock to industry might have been necessary, but the problem was that the recession, and the Thatcher government's halfhearted response to it, further crippled certain firms and industries. Once players lost their market position, it was rarely recovered. One reason why Mrs. Thatcher allowed manufacturing firms to go to the wall during the recession was the conviction that Britain could prosper as a post-industrial economy based on service businesses. But Sir John rejected the notion that hamburger flippers and computer salesmen held the key to reversing the decline of the world's first industrial nation. The neglect of manufacturing was at the heart of Mrs. Thatcher's economic miscalculations.

Others took a far more favorable view. Sir Christopher Hogg had also succeeded in rebuilding a distinguished but ailing industrial concern—Courtaulds, the textile manufacturer that had invented rayon. Unlike Sir John, though, he did not feel at all neglected by Mrs. Thatcher. Quite the opposite: he was grateful for how much she had done for his own firm and indeed for the textiles industry as a whole, providing moral aid and practical encouragement by attending trade conferences and so forth.[26]

Neither of these two knights of industry could testify, though, to the effect of the capitalist revolution on the sector of the economy most directly affected by government: the nationalized industries which Mrs. Thatcher dismantled.

III

"IT WAS JUST TERRIBLE—REALLY A TERRIBLE PRODUCT," COM-
plained Hugh J. Weidinger, a car dealer in Hempstead, New
York. Some people wouldn't even make it home with their
new purchase still running. The object of his complaints was
not a lemon of the American automobile industry; not the
Corvair indicted by Ralph Nader for being unsafe at any
speed; not the Pinto, which had a nasty habit of setting itself
on fire; nor the early versions of the Cavalier, whose name
revealed more about its quality than its styling. The car he
lamented was far more revered and far more expensive: the
Jaguar.[27] Owners needed two Jaguars and a Volkswagen running behind them, according to one joke.

Humiliating as it was for Jaguar to be the object of sarcasm
and humor, the firm had more immediate worries. The 1979
model was delivered a year late to the United States, the
world's largest luxury car market. By the following summer,
Jaguar was losing £2–£3 million a month and its workers
were on strike. Had Jaguar been a private company account-
able to the vagaries of the marketplace rather than a nationalized company, it would have gone to the wall.

Jaguar Cars was largely the creation of one man: William
Lyons. Born in 1901 in the seaside town of Blackpool in the
North of England, this son of an Irish musician was a player
rather than a gentleman. Jaguar was known originally as the
Swallow Sidecar Company, but later dropped the "SS" prefix
because of its Nazi associations. Although located in Coventry in the heart of car country, it was not destroyed by German bombing during the Blitz. A brilliant designer whose
aesthetic flair quickly won public attention and admiration,
Lyons was also an unabashed and unrepentant autocrat who
ruled by fear and intimidation. Jack Randle, lifelong Jaguar
man who began as Lyons's tea boy and ended as a plant man-

ager, could recall only one occasion when he saw someone disagree with Lyons. The boss ordered the employee to leave the factory within fifteen minutes.[28]

Hampered by limited capital, Lyons built a highly successful firm on a shoestring. He was not one to go in for the latest gadgets. One of his favorite stories concerned a requisition for a wheelbarrow. Lyons sent it back with a question: "What is wrong with the two buckets you have got?" Production lines at Jaguar's famous Brown's Lane factory consisted of trestles that were pulled along by chains as late as 1959.[29] This was no way to compete with Daimler Benz, BMW, or Porsche.

Whatever Lyons's limitations, the structural weaknesses of Jaguar Cars did not really emerge until he withdrew from the business. In 1966, Jaguar merged with British Motor Corporation to form British Motor Holdings, largely because Lyons believed that Britain needed a unified car industry to meet growing foreign competition. Two years later the new entity merged with Leyland to form the British Leyland Motor Corporation. It proved impossible, though, to exploit potential advantages of scale and scope because the individual companies, which included the great names of the British motor industry—Triumph, Rover, Austin, Morris, Leyland, and Jaguar—all wanted to retain a measure of independence. The final result of its increasingly grave condition was to nationalize the ailing firm, which was renamed British Leyland. The mere fact of government ownership need not have been disastrous; what made it so was the ill-conceived strategy of centralizing the various auto makers despite huge differences in their product lines.

As part of British Leyland, Jaguar was afflicted by a particularly virulent strain of the British disease. Poor quality, bad labor relations, low productivity, and too much manpower— this was the diagnosis of the British motor industry put forth in a government report in 1975.[30] However, Jaguar faced the added problem of how to replace its colorful and autocratic leader when Sir William finally retired in 1972. It was left largely in the hands of men who had never been allowed to make any major decisions for themselves. To make matters worse, Jaguar had a new chief executive every year or so until 1980.[31] Whatever their strengths and weaknesses, they had only limited opportunity to rejuvenate Jaguar because British Leyland had taken over crucial functions, including purchasing, sales, marketing, and accounting.

This was all the more galling because the alignment between Jaguar and British Leyland was absurdly out of joint. The one was a low-volume specialist in high-performance luxury cars, and the other a huge conglomerate based on high-volume mass production. As Jack Randle put it, they were forced to report to "strangers who didn't understand Jag."[32] One reason that Jaguar was so slow to respond to its fall from grace was the stunning fact that managers, much less workers, did not even know how much money they were losing because they had no separate accounting figures.

The subjugation of Jaguar also increased the workforce's alienation. Traditionally, Jaguar workers saw themselves as an elite group of craftsmen making a fine product. As the best paid workers in Coventry, they were a cut above their fellows, and it was therefore no surprise that the children of Jaguar workers followed their parents "into the Jag" when they left school. In the course of the 1970s, however, the workforce suffered a series of shocks, including the shift from piecework to day wages and the end of old job responsibilities. But the cruelest blow was that Jaguar workers lost ground in the name of parity with their British Leyland counterparts, who made less than they did. Paying Jaguar workers the same wages as those who made the "Mini" was the British equivalent of comparing a Cadillac to a Chevrolet.

Managers and workers also had to stand by as British Leyland tried to rob them of their identity. As John Egan, who became managing director of Jaguar in 1980, recalled:

> At one stage a Jaguar flag at the entrance to the factory was torn down. Only Leyland flags were allowed to be flown on the premises and telephonists were threatened with disciplinary action if they answered with "Good morning, Jaguar Cars." Instead they were supposed to say "Good morning, Leyland Cars," and if any further address was needed, "Large assembly plant number one." Worse still, the then two constituent factories of Jaguar were put into two quite separate organisational units within Leyland—the Power and Transmission Division and the Body and Assembly Division— hardly an appropriate fate for one of the most famous marques in the world motoring industry.[33]

Such conduct enraged Jaguar workers. One line supervisor angrily recalled: "They tore our Jaguar off the gates"—"our" being the telling word.

The catalyst for change came from without; and, for that matter, it came without Margaret Thatcher. In late 1977, James Callaghan's Labour government recruited Michael Edwardes, a South African industrialist, to take over at British Leyland. When the newly appointed chairman first met the Prime Minister he confessed: "I must be frank, I don't believe in state ownership of industry, but I will do my very best to bring about BL's recovery, regardless of who owns it."[34] Widely viewed as an industrial relations disaster, British Leyland had quickly become a Tory target. "British Leyland," wrote Bernard Levin in his *Times* column in 1978, "is infected with the corrupting knowledge that others will make good its own deficiencies, and as long as that remains true, the deficiencies will not abate, but on the contrary will increase."[35]

Michael Edwardes was both willing and able to shake up British Leyland. If Callaghan must have been uneasy often about Edwardes's actions, he was still courageous enough to give Edwardes the strong backing he needed to make him a credible leader. Convinced that managers and supervisors had lost authority after years of vacillation and backpedaling, Edwardes attempted to restore their right to manage. What stood in the way was the daunting power of trade unions. Peppered as they were with Trotskyites eager to rescue their comrades from the prospect of weeks of uninterrupted labor, the radicals were never as numerous in fact as they were in Tory nightmares. But Edwardes was determined to control the unions and purge the militants; on both counts he proved far more successful than anyone thought he would be. One cartoon pictured him cleaning house, as it were: Dressed in a shirt and tie and wearing an apron, he forged ahead with a vacuum cleaner as bemused workers in cloth caps surveyed the scene and asked: "IS HE TRYING TO TELL US SOMETHING?"[36]

Edwardes was a confrontational manager, but he recognized that he could change BL only by changing workers' attitudes. He needed to convince them that their job security hinged on high productivity. He reinstated the authority of old marques such as Jaguar in the belief that by restoring identity he would raise incentives.

The capitalist revolution Edwardes inaugurated at British Leyland began under the uneasy auspices of the Labour government, but its twists and turns were shaped partly by Mrs. Thatcher's arrival in Downing Street. They met in early 1979 when Thatcher, along with Sir Geoffrey Howe, Sir Keith Joseph, and James Prior, had lunch with the BL board at the elegant Stafford Hotel in the genteel surroundings of London's St. James's. "In my innocence," Edwardes later recounted, "I thought that we would need to entice Margaret Thatcher to enter into a robust debate about the future of BL, so I placed her not on my right, but immediately opposite me—a technique that often gets a debate going. I need hardly have bothered. She had scarcely taken her seat before she fired the first salvo. 'Well Michael Edwardes, and why should we pour further funds into British Leyland?' " Her comment halted the board in its collective tracks as she proceeded to dominate the rest of the meeting.[37]

Listening to what seemed to be a harangue from a remarkable woman was an uncommon occurrence for captains of industry, but it was easier than dealing with the results of Mrs. Thatcher's economic policies. Looking forward to a period of stability after the 1979 election, Edwardes found nothing of the sort in store. It was, above all, the Thatcher government's handling of exchange rates that "brought us to our knees," as Edwardes put it. But he frankly admitted that the takeoff of the pound skewered British Leyland (BL) because it was already weak, "and any major obstacle would have had the same effect."[38] In other words, the recession peeled away BL's fragile defenses. The result was a series of major layoffs. A leaner and meaner workforce was more receptive to Edwardes's message of change and renewal than they might have been in good times. However damaging the recession was to BL's competitive position, at least it had side benefits. Even though Margaret Thatcher and Sir Keith Joseph had little love for nationalized industry, they honored Labor's pledge for BL funding in 1979. Two years later, they sanctioned another £300 million infusion despite the protests of right-wing backbenchers.

The Jaguar variant of the capitalist revolution began after Edwardes took over the helm at BL and Mrs. Thatcher was installed in Downing Street. In the summer of 1980, John Egan became managing director of Jaguar. Edwardes gave him a mandate that helped concentrate the mind: Fix it or close it. An intense, focused man, with a sense of humor and a passion for fitness, Egan was a brilliant salesman and communicator. A player by origin, his gentlemanly polish did not dull his drive or ambition. Like Mrs. Thatcher, he was a grammar school product who came from the lower middle class. The son of a Rootes (Chrysler) dealer, he studied engineering at the Imperial College of Science and Technology, University of London. After a short stint as a petroleum engineer in Saudi Arabia, Egan earned an MBA at the London Business School, which was a far rarer degree in Britain than America. He left the Unipart Division of British Leyland soon after nationalization, convinced that its results would be catastrophic. Then he headed for private business, taking over as managing director of Massey Ferguson, the tractor manufacturer.

Egan fit in perfectly with the aims and ideals of the capitalist revolution. In politics, he was a Thatcherite who hated the fact that Britain had gone from being the workshop of the world to an industrial joke. He attributed the nation's decline to a lack of training and research and, above all, to the trade unions. Shortly before the 1987 election, he wrote a piece in the *Sun* praising Margaret Thatcher, particularly for her contribution in taming the trade unions. "Labour's promise to repeal all Tory Trade Union legislation," Egan warned, "would spell a return to the industrial relations jungle of the 'seventies. None of us should forget the chaos that existed then, the intimidating mass meetings and the violent secondary picketing."[39] Too many workers were unwilling to do a decent day's work. Jaguar itself was the "sickest part of a sick industry . . . about to become another tombstone in the national industrial graveyard."[40]

The "Fix it or close it" mandate Egan brought with him to Jaguar seemed all the more genuine a threat thanks to Edwardes's reputation for brinkmanship and Thatcher's for heartlessness. But if Egan wielded a big stick when he came to Jaguar, he also had an appealing carrot: the prospect of freeing Jaguar from the subjugation of British Leyland. For Egan, Jaguar's renaissance depended on making dramatic improvements in product quality and reliability. As he told *The Times:* "Jaguar must be not as good as the Germans and Japanese, but better."[41] This hinged on the ability of managers to manage and the willingness of workers to work. As a well-trained and experienced MBA, Egan systematically devised his plan for Jaguar by carefully studying its problems, identifying viable solutions, and then acting quickly. With the prospect of closure hanging over the firm, this was no time for lengthy meditation.[42]

If the methods Egan applied at Jaguar came partly from the turnaround techniques of business schools, a Japanese tinge also colored what he and his management team did in the early 1980s. It was during these years that the fascination with Japanese management surged in the United States and Europe as established firms and industries saw their competitive edge and technological lead eroded by Japan, Inc. Popular works such as *Theory Z* and *The Art of Japanese Management* became best-sellers as Western managers sought alternate answers to a classic problem: how to motivate employees. Egan dispatched a team of Jaguar observers to Japan to see what Coventry could learn from Kyoto. They concluded that it was possible to import certain Japanese methods as long as they adapted them to Jaguar style. The working group concept encouraged fresh ideas and an entrepreneurial outlook through quality circles. They also found ideas and methods to improve quality control and product timing and how to use robotics. And they discovered how the "family concept" could improve communication with, and strengthen the commitment of, a demoralized workforce.

For Egan, unless quality became job one (as a Ford slogan put it), warranty work would be job two, and closure the final task. A study showed that Jaguar quality was far inferior to its German competitors. As the former head of Unipart, Egan was sensitive to how parts could undo the whole. Another study revealed that about two thirds of defects came from faulty components made by its suppliers, among them Lucas, whose on-again off-again electrical products were notorious. Egan's solution was to work with suppliers to improve products, or, failing that, to drop them, as he did in at least six cases. But Jaguar's shortcomings were also homemade. Egan got rid of the product inspectors who constituted 12 percent of the workforce but could only blow the whistle when it was too late. In so doing, he signaled that product quality had to be everyone's business or there would be no business to employ anyone.

However, there was considerable resistance to overcome, as one might imagine. An alienated and angry workforce was ill-disposed to working hard on the latest plan from a new management they had no reason to trust. The workers were far more likely disposed to turn to shop stewards for information than to front-line supervisors. What made Egan's project all the harder was the fact that most workers did not believe that product quality was a problem. The legend of racetrack victories and engineering excellence persisted long after the time that Jaguars, which were always temperamental creatures, had become problem-ridden embarrassments.

In the age of MTV, Egan used videos to communicate directly with Jaguar workers, going over the antagonistic heads of union officials and avoiding their spins on his plans. Jaguar's first homemade video, *The Price of Quality*, was an extended exercise in disillusionment; it compared Jaguars with Mercedes and BMWs and showed them wanting. Driving the point home, the video turned to Appleyards, a major Jaguar dealership in Leeds, where salesmen, mechanics, and customers bitterly complained about the cars. The purpose of the video was to highlight the gravity of the situation to the disbelieving workers as well as to appeal to their sense of pride. The moral of the story was that if you cared about keeping your job, you'll care about quality. This was the first in a long line of videos shown to some two to three hundred workers per screening.

Egan introduced quality circles to make actual improvements in Jaguars. When these were first instituted, they incurred the wrath of union officials who saw collaboration as collusion. Initially, the officials tried to ensure that the participants were limited to shop stewards whose loyalties were not in question—a prospect quickly rejected by management, who hoped to weaken union power rather than give it additional support. Front-line supervisors were also threatened by quality circles largely because their power and credibility had been eroded in the 1970s until it was invisible. So they were reticent to share what little authority they had left.

The experiment began uneasily. The first quality circle was much rowdier than its Japanese antecedents. Line managers were forced to listen to more complaints than suggestion, including the unanswerable question—"When will we get a chance to own one?"—referring to cars they built but would never be able to buy.[43] After this fiasco, however, quality circles garnered support and gathered interest. Even though shop stewards sometimes pulled their men from the working groups, by 1984 there were sixty quality circles with about a dozen members each. They were indispensable in getting rid of "car kickers."[44]

Quality circles were only part of a broader program to raise employee involvement. This was all the more difficult because Egan had to contend with a morale that hit rock bottom as Jaguar downsized its workforce from about 10,000 in 1980 to 6,500 in 1983. Criticized for such savage cuts, Egan stated the remaining jobs were secure. The mixture of rationalization within Jaguar and recession in the West Midlands produced a sense of crisis that helped focus the minds of workers, who came to realize that the whole company could go down the tubes. The fact that Mrs. Thatcher was in power only made the prospect of closure seem more plausible.

But Egan used more than fear to gain the support of the Jaguar workforce. A highly effective, charismatic leader, he turned the crisis to good effect with his own version of "blood, sweat, toil, and tears." With their backs to the wall, Jaguar workers had little to lose by giving his plans a chance. Fundamental to his success was his ability to convince managers and workers that a comeback really was possible. Although he had his critics, he was also lauded as a genuine Jaguar leader. "Egan is the man I would have chosen myself to do the job. He's running it just as I would have managed it. He's carrying on where I left off," said Sir William Lyons.[45]

In fact, Egan's approach was far different in many respects from Lyons's, but he was still regarded by many as a worthy successor. Quick to seize on slogans and symbols that would help sell his program to the workforce, he used campaigns such as "In Pursuit of Perfection" and "Building the Legend" to rekindle product identification and company pride. He restored Jaguar's colors and logo everywhere and displayed Jaguar cars, past and present, in the factories to remind everyone of both historic achievements and current challenges. And he returned Jaguar to the international racing circuit, a particularly popular move.

The program designed to win over the workforce came to be known as "Hearts and Minds," a name which Egan used despite its allusion to the Vietnam War.[46] The unifying concept was to present Jaguar as a family. The main event was "Family Nights," which included a film about Jaguar and display of its products. Managers served a meal to workers and their families (a symbolic role reversal), and the evening ended with a cabaret and then music and dancing. At first, the union opposed the plan on the grounds that it was meant to coopt workers, which of course it was. But the initial call for a boycott did not prevent thousands of employees and family members from attending. The purpose of such shows of goodwill was to encourage workers to see management in a better light and to recruit their families as allies in this cause.

By 1984, it was clear that the turnaround at Jaguar was a success. Having been in danger of drowning in red ink with estimated losses of £47 million in 1980 and £32 million in 1981, by 1982 it posted a modest pre-tax profit of £9 million in 1982 and of £50 million in 1983. Unit sales went up from 13,933 in 1981 to 28,467 in 1983, much of it thanks to increased exports in the United States. Average output per employee increased from 1.4 cars per person in 1980 to 3.4 cars per person in 1983. Most important for the future was the fact that the first new model in a decade was in the final stages of testing. All of these improvements took place while Jaguar was still under government ownership.

Both the Thatcher government and Jaguar management were eager to take advantage of the turnaround; but how? Egan and his fellows strongly preferred a management buy-out, which would have given them full control of the firm and a chance for far greater wealth, but the BL board demurred. There were also other interested buyers, notably General Motors, but selling a famous British marque, newly refurbished, to a foreign company would have entailed political fall-out that was both unnecessary and unwanted. So the Thatcher government finally decided to privatize Jaguar Cars by a stock market flotation. It guarded against a take-over by limiting any one buyer from obtaining more than 15 percent of the shares and by retaining a sufficient holding in Jaguar, the "golden share," until 1990.

The prospective sale brought enormous publicity both to Jaguar and to the Thatcher government, which seized upon it as proof of its economic success. Yet there was also something faintly comical about a country auctioning off a company. A *BusinessWeek* cartoon depicted a wildly smiling Mrs. Thatcher perched on a Jaguar in an open-air car lot complete with flags, pointing to a large "FOR SALE" sign in the front window.[47] She had good reason to be enthusiastic, and indeed somewhat anxious about Jaguar's fate, since financing lame ducks came hard to a woman who had wanted to float part of BL, if not sink the rest. Ideology aside, however, the flotation was all the more important politically coming as it did on the back of the botched sale of Enterprise Oil and a few months before the crucial offering for British Telecom.

In the event, the flotation of Jaguar in August 1984 was a great success. There were eight times as many applications for shares as there were shares available. Those able to buy made a quick profit because the results of early trading suggested that Jaguar had been undervalued by about £25 million.

Indeed, Jaguar Cars seemed a fitting fable of the capitalist revolution, an unalloyed triumph for the Thatcher government. Extremely successful in the wake of privatization, its pre-tax profits rose to £91.5 million in 1984 and £121.3 in 1985 and its share price increased likewise. The XJ-6, the new model which had been delayed for two years, was finally launched.

Then Jaguar's fortunes suddenly turned. The effects of the stock market crash in October 1987 curbed many customers' appetites for luxury cars. The fall of the dollar reduced the value of Jaguar's sales in its largest market, the United States. Jaguar also faced new competitors as Honda, Nissan, and Toyota entered the luxury car market and promised technologically sophisticated cars that cost thousands less than Jaguar's least expensive model. Profits declined severely in 1989 and 1990. What made this all the more serious was the fact that Jaguar was in desperate need of funds for plant modernization and product design. Despite its recent success, strained engineering resources put Jaguar at a great competitive disadvantage. "Can we get away with this scam much longer?"—that was the question.[48]

Certainly Jaguar Cars was a vulnerable takeover target. However eager management (and presumably labor) were to stay independent, they had few defenses against a multinational with deep pockets and a long reach. The British government's golden share was due to expire in 1990 and with it Jaguar's last line of defense. By early 1989, Egan and his colleagues had hesitantly concluded that they would probably not be able to go it alone even though they feared losing the autonomy they had regained so recently. Two suitors, both American, began to court and pressure Jaguar into marriages of one sort or another. General Motors, long a Jaguar supplier, was willing to respect its independence by bidding for only 30 percent of its shares. Ford insisted on total ownership. Although this was a fate which Sir John Egan (knighted in 1986) wanted to avoid, he and his fellows gradually came round. Ford's offer seemed much better conceived than GM's and it was willing to pay a very high price. So, in 1990, Ford purchased Jaguar Cars for $2.5 billion.

Jaguar's takeover may not have been a corporate tragedy, much less a national disaster, but the fate of the recently privatized firm was one of the ironies of the capitalist revolution. If nothing else, it gave new meaning to the American advertising campaign that asked consumers: "Have you driven a Ford lately?"

I V

RISING ABOVE THE DENSE, NARROW STREETS AND TIGHT MEDIEval grid of the ancient City of London near Leadenhall Market stands the archetypal emblem of the Thatcher years' financial boom: the Lloyd's Building. Yet Richard Rogers, the architect whose firm designed the £163 million structure (and who hitherto was best known for the Pompidou Center in

Paris, which he designed with Renzo Piano), was himself a critic of the greedy materialism that the Prime Minister's capitalist revolution promoted. Difficult as it is to imagine a more modernistic design than Lloyd's new headquarters, nothing of the sort was true of the insurance underwriters housed in the famous private marketplace. A bastion of the British establishment, its brokers and "names" (the wealthy backers who put their personal fortunes on the line to guarantee policies) were not known for avant-garde ways—quite the opposite. And while the "kind of architecture found in Lloyd's is about honesty, frankness, visibility, and control," these were not the hallmarks of the institution itself, which was riddled by scandal during the Thatcher years.[49]

Variously described as an oil rig, a supermarket, a multi-story parking garage, a Tinker-Toy set gone wild, and a coffee percolator (a good fit, given Lloyd's coffeehouse origins), high-rise towers surround this remarkable metal, glass, and concrete structure. Indeed, Rogers's Lloyd's Building is arguably the City's most important, and arresting, building since Christopher Wren's St. Paul's Cathedral. Given that Lloyd's had already outgrown its housing three times in the twentieth century, Rogers's brief was to allow room for commercial expansion and technological change. To this end, he employed a prefabricated kit of parts to take Lloyd's into the twenty-first century. The result is a relentlessly high-tech structure replete with sophisticated gadgetry. Yet it makes some attempt to blend the old and the new, evoking the traditional aristocratic grace of Lloyd's clubby confederation. Rogers's building therefore includes the original Robert Adam–designed boardroom and requisite period furniture. But such flourishes as Doric arches and quilted doors in the interior should not disguise the fact that the Lloyd's Building is a profit-making machine. While the building bears little relation to the historic styles of the City, the enormous barrel vault in its center evokes the Crystal Palace that Joseph Paxton designed for the Great Exhibition of 1851. In so doing, Lloyd's recalls the brief moment when Britain was the world leader in both industry and design.

Even dramatic changes in the City of London's physical face symbolized larger alterations in international finance and business practices. Reagan's America and Thatcher's Britain both witnessed an unprecedented bonanza. "Greed is all right . . . ," Ivan Boesky declared to a Berkeley audience in 1985; "you shouldn't feel guilty." The following year he took a somewhat higher road: "I urge you as a part of your mission—to seek wealth." But, he added, "Give back to the system with humility—and don't take yourself too seriously."[50] However apposite or ironic Boesky's advice, there is no doubt that the opportunities for making a fortune expanded enormously (as did the incomes of those at the top) during the 1980s.

Corporate mergers and acquisitions came of age. An enormous wave of takeovers, hostile or friendly, spilled over into the American heartland, along with an array of financial devices, including leveraged buy-outs, high-yield (junk) bonds, arbitrage, white knights, poison pills, green mail, and the like. For all the shady dealings that landed financiers in Hamptons beach houses or in light-security jail cells, the takeovers had a certain moral justification. Or so their proponents liked to argue. Corporate raiders maintained that it was morally right and financially beneficial to gain control of inefficient, bloated behemoths and throw out their retrograde managers. The Reagan White House made the hunt easier by deregulating finance and persuading the once vigilant Securities and Exchange Commission (SEC) to let the market rule. Whether dishonesty rose by the by, the rewards for insider dealing, parking securities, and the like shot up beyond expectation. In a single year Michael Milken, the ascetic financial wizard and philanthropist who ran Drexel, Burnham, & Lambert's Los Angeles office, made $550 million, one way or the other.

The takeover wave also washed over Britain during the Thatcher years. Financial services, always a strength of the modern British economy, boomed. Merchant banking, traditionally a preserve of the well-born and well-connected, became an unusually popular and lucrative career. Even those who did not have double-barreled names had a shot at success. As the rules of the game shifted in London as in New York, so the opportunities for moneymaking and wrongdoing also shot up.

When Dennis Levine was arrested at age thirty-three in May 1986, he was earning a million dollars a year, had an apartment on Park Avenue, a summer house on Long Island, and a red Ferrari.[51] A British counterpart, Geoffrey Collier, had also done well, though not nearly as well, before he went down for insider dealing at the year's end. In his first fifteen months at Morgan Grenfell, Collier earned £125,000 while building a promising new securities business from scratch. To boot, he owned a red Porsche, two other cars, and a house outside of London, Oldbury Place, for which he paid £525,000 and which he eventually sold for £900,000—a testimonial to the property boom of the Thatcher years. Even the rewards for white-collar crime were higher in America, where everything really did seem bigger. Levine grabbed $12.6 million from his alleged fifty-four trades, while Collier, a relative neophyte, culled only £15,000 for one insider deal. This was barely enough to pay for his wine cellar and a few well-chosen bottles to stock it.

Although financial deregulation was certainly not the sole cause of the scandals of the 1980s, it was a mighty catalyst in Britain as in America. Indeed, the legal and regulatory changes inaugurated by the Thatcher government seemed so great that they became known as "Big Bang." Agreed upon by the government and the Stock Exchange in July 1983, the City felt the effects from the start even though the changes did not take place until October 1986.

"Big Bang" was a response to concerns that London was falling behind its international competitors in financial services; its information technology was not up to par. Open competition was limited thanks to the cozy relationships between a network of institutions who benefited from backslapping and price fixing. Before "Big Bang," the City suffered (but also profited) from a version of the closed shop syndrome that Mrs. Thatcher denounced in the unions. Determined to ensure that London remain an international financial hub, deregulation seemed the best spur to competition.[52]

The advent of "Big Bang" demolished the traditional boundaries fencing off the activities of various City institutions. For the first time, then, merchant bankers, insurance companies, stockbrokers, stockjobbers, and the rest could merge or form joint ventures if they so chose. The conventional wisdom was that only the strong would survive and that strength depended on size. In other words, "big was beautiful." So as the day of reckoning approached, small firms combined with the great in an effort to maximize profits, to enter new businesses, and to fend off foreign competition, in particular from American and Japanese firms. The immediate effect of their descent was to blow the ceiling off salaries. In search of native guides to the well-trod terrain dominated by personal connections, they raided British firms, offering higher compensation. The new no-nonsense "let's get rich" attitude appealed to the young and upwardly mobile.

In the mid-1980s, the mythical City gent with pinstripe suit, black bowler hat, and tightly furled umbrella had to contend with the "thundering horde," the term which came to denote the invasion of American, Japanese, and Swiss firms. By custom, even the British monarch had to stop at the border of the City of Westminster to ask the freemen of the City of London for permission to enter. But no such inhibitions held back the enthusiastic legions of foreign bankers and brokers who failed to pause at the stone lions that guarded the entrance to the City. The American way of doing business came as an unwanted shock to those used to a more "civilized" atmosphere: the newcomers had breakfast meetings; drank Perrier rather than St. Emilion at lunch; expected everyone to work long hours to finish deals; and jogged to stay leaner and meaner than the competition.

Although "Big Bang" strengthened and accelerated changes that were already under way in the City, it did little to inhibit insider dealing or outright dishonesty. Consider the Guinness Affair. What became the greatest financial scandal of the 1980s began innocently enough at the end of November 1985 when Roger Seelig and Ernest Saunders lunched together at 23 Great Winchester Street, the London headquarters of Morgan Grenfell.

A bulwark of the financial establishment, Morgan Grenfell was a blue-blooded merchant bank whose reigning spirit had been the ghost of the American tycoon John Pierpont Morgan. Even in the postwar era, a genteel atmosphere akin to a country house library suffused the firm. Directors worked together in the intimate world of the Partners' Room, where a traditional code of honor was supposed to prevail and dishonesty was out of the question.[53] But the old regime was exclusive and bigoted. So it was unsurprising that Morgan Grenfell was part of the anti-Semitic gang that opposed Siegmund Warburg's takeover of British Aluminum. The gentlemanly ethic faded in the 1960s and 1970s, thanks to a spate of hostile takeovers and the ascent of new men. Preeminent among them was Christopher Reeves, a hard-driving public school graduate who served in the rifle brigade in Kenya and Malaya. He became the bank's chief executive in December 1979, soon after Mrs. Thatcher came to power. Morgan Grenfell became the province of "tough smoothies," British versions of the "masters of the universe" Tom Wolfe satirized in *Bonfire of the Vanities.*[54]

"Big Bang" facilitated changes that were already under way at the firm. Enormous growth largely effaced Morgan Grenfell's traditional character. From 1979 to 1986, staff quadrupled and profits rose from £5 million to £54 million. Its strategy was to become a Wall Street–style integrated bank. So Morgan Grenfell reorganized its entire structure, separated banking, investments, and securities, purchased a securities firm, and became a public company. Under Christopher Reeves's direction, Morgan Grenfell turned into an aggressive, entrepreneurial operation—the Drexel, Burnham, & Lambert of Britain. By 1986, it was at the top of the league table in corporate finance (known in America as mergers and acquisitions), advising 163 clients on transactions worth £11.6 billion that year alone. En route, it became notorious for sharp practice. "Some say we go round the rules. I think we innovated," said Reeves. "Clients want to deal with people with original ideas, so new rules have to be created."[55] But the very "originality" that helped make Morgan Grenfell the market leader in the takeover mania of the mid-1980s also made it the market leader in white-collar crime.

By the time Roger Seelig, one of Morgan Grenfell's most original members, lunched with Ernest Saunders in November 1985, he was the most successful takeover artist in London. A graduate of Dulwich College and the London School of Economics, Seelig's pedigree was not as high-toned as many of his fellows. But this did not impede his making a fortune in banking or mimicking the gentry's style of life. He rode to hounds in the Beaufort Hunt and spent weekends with his mother in a stone country manor in the Cotswold town of Tetbury. Unlike the more sedate princes of the City whose clubs lined Pall Mall, Seelig's favorite haunt was Annabel's in Berkeley Square, London's poshest nightspot. There he was seen with mobile phone and mobile clients, making contacts and making deals.[56]

But this attitude did not seem to worry his lunch companion. Like Seelig, Ernest Saunders was an extremely successful outsider in a business full of bluebloods. He was one of the new breed of management heroes who flourished in Mrs. Thatcher's enterprise culture. Tall and handsome, with the patrician bearing of a Roman senator, Saunders was not the native Englishman he pretended to be. In fact, he was the son of an Austrian Jewish physician father and a Gentile mother who had him baptized. In 1938, the family fled to England after the *Anschluss*. They changed their name from Schleyer to Saunders; Ernst became Ernest. However jolting the refugee experience, the family was prosperous enough to send their son to a top London public school, St. Paul's, and then on to Cambridge where he studied law. Yet Saunders managed to distance himself from his family roots; in his *Who's Who* entry, he simply omitted his parents. This made him a self-made man in more than the usual sense.

Saunders went into marketing and became a top international brand manager at Nestlé. In 1981, he became chairman of Guinness, a family firm whose famous black stout was poorly served by management more distinguished by aristocratic titles than commercial expertise. Armed with a band of highly paid number crunchers from Bain & Co., an unusually secretive Boston-based management consultancy, Saunders sold or closed over 140 Guinness companies. In only three years he built a £1 billion international business with a host of brands and increased after-tax profits by 240 percent. But apparently this still did not put him on an equal footing with his aristocratic masters. When the man who thought himself to be an "adopted Guinness" went to a family wedding, he quickly discovered where he really stood when he found himself seated with the family retainers, old and new, including their tax adviser and estate manager.

The target Seelig and Saunders hit upon was Distillers—a striking takeover candidate. A venerable whiskey maker weighed down by weak brand management and marketing to match, its share of the Scotch market had tumbled from about 75 percent in the early 1960s to 15.5 percent by 1984. This whetted the appetite of James Gulliver, an entrepreneur who had an uncertain reputation in the City despite the fact that he had built Argylls, a £300 million food business. On December 2, 1985, Gulliver struck, filing a bid for a company three times Argyll's size, offering £1.87 billion for Distillers. He also insisted on the unprecedented step of relating underwriting fees to success, offering institutions 2.5 percent if Argyll won the bid but only 0.125 percent if they failed.

Before the long Christmas break, Saunders made his first approach to John Connell, Distillers' chairman. As a Distillers manager later recounted: "He was a bit naughty, perhaps this was part of his technique, that in the middle of the worst bit with Gulliver" he rang Connell and asked "was there anything he could do to help. Those were evil words."[57] Perhaps, but Saunders was more pleasant, and wily, than Gulliver, who had questioned the competence of Distillers' management.

So determined was Distillers to break out of Gulliver's net that the board hesitantly accepted a most unconventional proposal. Saunders stipulated that the firm pay the costs for its rescue, indemnifying Guinness against losses incurred in the takeover battle to come. Although he played the role of a White Knight, "Deadly Ernest" was more like a bounty hunter. It was as if Galahad had brought a calculator on his quest for the Holy Grail. For Distillers, a merger with Guinness—a great name in the drinks business—seemed preferable to being saddled, if not quartered, by Argylls, a food company with a down market image. A Distillers director later explained: "We still thought this was meant to be an equal merger. We were in no doubt that the initiative would lie with Saunders—he was in fact a better businessman and had a better track record—but we did think, foolishly as it now seems, that this was indisputably a benevolent meeting of two like-minded companies. We were certain that this was a better future than Gulliver."[58]

By late January 1986, Seelig had set up a deal whereby Guinness would top up Gulliver's £1.89 billion offer by an additional £350 million. What Morgan Grenfell and its client did not count on was trouble from the government. In February 1986, the Guinness bid was referred by the Office of Fair Trading to the Monopolies and Mergers Commission. The grounds for complaint was that the union of Bell's and Distillers' whiskey brands would give the new group two fifths of the market, well above the proscribed limit of 25 percent. Although Saunders and Seelig were both aware of this possibility, they had hoped that the bid would be cleared without a referral because nine tenths of the whiskey was for export. They were wrong. Most merchant bankers would have backed off from a referred bid, but Seelig was not one to beat retreat, accept defeat, or let millions of pounds in fees slip away. So he convinced Saunders to soldier on, arguing as Saunders later recalled that if he turned back, "Nobody in the City would ever listen to me again. We would never have the credibility to make another major bid. My reputation was at stake, so was the company's, so was Morgan's."[59] Saunders paved the way for clearing the bid by unloading five Bell's brands on his friend, the ever ready entrepreneur, Tiny Rowland.

In early 1986, the battle for Distillers degenerated; all vestiges of civility seemed to disappear as both sides mounted major advertising campaigns. One hard-hitting Argyll advertisement pictured a plate of Guinness products selected from its recent acquisitions, and asked: "After consuming all this, are Guinness in any state to swallow 150 Scotches?" But Guinness was not so hungover as to take such charges lying down and quickly filed suit for damages. Its own campaign was equally low. Guinness publicized the fact that Gulliver's *Who's Who* entry misleadingly suggested he was a graduate of Harvard Business School whereas he had studied there for only a few weeks on an executive education course.

The real battle took place in secret. Because both sides offered to exchange their shares for a Distillers bill that promised to be in the neighborhood of £2 billion, whoever succeeded in increasing demands for its shares was likely to win. This was a great advantage for Guinness, given Morgan Grenfell's financial expertise and moral flexibility.[60] The bank tried to support its client's cause by stockpiling Guinness shares. Although it pushed Stock Exchange regulations to the limit in so doing, no sharp rebuke, much less punishment, was forthcoming. In the meantime, Argyll and its advisers, Samuel Montagu & Co., were up against an illegal share-support operation intended to artificially massage upwards the Guinness share price.

The "masseurs" included some of the most powerful businessmen in London. The dirty dealing seems to have been contemplated from the outset. Anthony Parnes, the freewheeling broker who rounded up the capital used to sabotage Argyll, was, to his own delight, nicknamed "the Animal." Style aside, Parnes brought on board powerful clients, preeminent among them Gerald Ronson, the philanthropic chief of Heron, a billion-pound conglomerate owned by his family. Parnes also recruited Ephraim Margulies, chairman of British Sugar, and Sir Jack Lyons, an industrialist who was a director of Bain & Co.'s London office. Only a few days after the Guinness bid for Distillers began, Parnes went to see Ronson in his Winnington Road mansion in Hampstead. According to Ronson, Parnes had told him that top Guinness management had sanctioned an operation to persuade "friends" to buy its shares. To sweeten the deal, Guinness offered what it had itself obtained from Distillers: an indemnity against loss. Moreover, it promised a £5 million success fee if the bid succeeded. In none of this did Ronson (or his compatriots) find anything suspicious, much less illegal. Or so they said.[61]

The denouement of the bitter contest for Distillers came on April 17, 1986, when S. G. Warburg held an auction for 10.6 million Distillers shares. Argyll began with what seemed an unbeatable advantage. Its cash offer was 30 pence more than its rivals and law prevented Guinness from raising the stakes at this point. In the end, however, Cazenove, joint brokers to Guinness, won with a highly suspicious £7.05 bid. When the Takeover Panel, which was supposed to superintend prospective mergers and acquisitions, tried to ascertain whether or not Cazenove was acting on behalf of Guinness, Morgan Grenfell and its client patently denied any such arrangement.

Nothing could have been further from the truth. Not to be hamstrung by Guinness's inability to raise its cash offer to win the auction, Seelig simply made other arrangements. He asked one of Saunders's closest advisers, Thomas Ward, a Washington lawyer involved in the Distillers bid from first to last, to send Cazenove the needed funds. Ward contacted Dr. Arthur Furer, once Saunders's boss at Nestlé's and now a non-executive director of Guinness. They arranged that a Leu subsidiary, Pipetec AG, would advance £76 million to Cazenove in order to buy the needed 10.6 million shares at £7.05. When Ward contacted David Mayhew, the Cazenove partner in charge of the Guinness bid, to confirm the funds' arrival, a colleague mistakenly told him that the money had not yet come. By the time Mayhew discovered the error, it was too late: Ward had already sent an additional £76 million of Guinness's money, which Cazenove returned the next morning. But none of this was mentioned to the Takeover Panel.

On April 18, 1986, Morgan Grenfell had the pleasure of announcing that Guinness controlled a majority of Distillers shares, for which it paid £2.5 billion plus £110 million in underwriting fees. Having won the day, Morgan Grenfell sat by and watched as Saunders set about breaking various pledges made in the heat of battle. For example, he welched on his promise to make Sir Thomas Risk of the Bank of Scotland the chairman of the merged companies. Only in the coming months did the war's hidden costs came to light, however. At the end of May, Saunders, Ward, and Oliver Roux (the Bain consultant in charge of Guinness's finances) invested £70 million in an Ivan Boesky investment fund in New York. They failed to inform the rest of the Guinness board until weeks later. Such a generous vote of confidence was certainly suspicious, but the real story did not come out until Boesky's arrest. Among much else, he revealed to American authorities that when the Guinness bid for Distillers began, persons representing Guinness asked him to buy large amounts of its stock in order to drive up its market price to make the bid more attractive. For his trouble, Boesky was indemnified against loss and promised a profit and a $100 million investment in one of his funds. It was, therefore, no accident that the Guinness share price rose as the American markets opened.

Ivan Boesky did not go down alone; he grassed on his associates. Caught in the disaster, among many others, was Morgan Grenfell. On December 1, 1986, two inspectors from the Department of Industry visited the firm in search of all files related to dealings in Guinness shares. Seelig denied dealing with Boesky, but this seemed all the more implausible when word of the Guinness investment in Boesky's fund leaked out.

There was more to come. In late December, Morgan Grenfell was directly linked with an illegal repurchase deal of Guinness shares between Seelig and Sir Patrick Spens of Henry Ansbacher. When the Guinness share price dropped as a result of profit taking after swallowing Distillers, Guinness encouraged big-time shareholders to hang on by indemnifying them against loss. This revelation finally spurred Morgan Grenfell to resign as advisers to Guinness, which was about to dismiss them anyway. Roger Seelig was fired and scapegoated. For his part, he claimed that Saunders and Ward had duped him and that they were to blame for the share-support operation. Whatever the truth, Seelig had cause to resent his treatment by Morgan Grenfell, which had profited handsomely from his talents. "You can't take a taxi without getting authority for it in this bank," he declared. "Anyone who thinks I acted on my own must think I'm six feet taller than I am."[62] Both Christopher Reeves and Graham Walsh, the head of corporate finance (and, ironically, a former Takeover Panel official), denied knowledge of Seelig's deals. But if they did not know about what he did—which is hard to believe—they should have done.

Meanwhile, it was in the Thatcher government's interest to act, and to be seen acting, to punish the growing list of offenders implicated in the Guinness Scandal. The fact that Paul Channon, the Secretary of State for Industry and Trade, was himself a member of the Guinness family tied his hands. Even worse, Morgan Grenfell had donated £25,000 to the Conservative Party. But such support did not quell Mrs. Thatcher's resolve that heads would roll at Morgan Grenfell before the scandal tainted her bid for a third consecutive term in office. So Nigel Lawson, the Chancellor, let the Bank of England know that it was time to get rid of Reeves and Walsh, as soon as possible. Faced with the prospect that the Bank would suspend Morgan Grenfell's banking license if they were not forced to resign, Lord Catto, the chairman, offered them a golden parachute lined with £562,000.

But the resignations did not end the scandal. As authorities sought to explain some £25 million in shadowy payments made by Guinness, the trail led to the arrest of Parnes, Ronson, Margulies, and Lyons for their alleged roles in the share-support operation. The fact that all these men were Jewish was well publicized. As it happened, though, the Guinness Scandal was nothing if not ecumenical, involving Jews and Gentiles. Saunders, who was arrested soon after resigning from Guinness, was generally assumed to be Jewish. But this would have surprised those who knew him as a strong supporter of his local church.

For Morgan Grenfell, the Guinness Scandal marked the end of an era of great profit undone by weak ethics. With its reputation severely damaged by its role in the scandal, and its financial condition threatened by losses sustained in the Stock Exchange crash on Black Monday in October 1987, Morgan Grenfell itself became, ironically, a takeover candidate. By the end of 1988, it closed its securities operation. Weakened, if not necessarily chastened, it was finally taken over by Deutsche Bank. In the wake of the scandal, Morgan Grenfell became a symbol of capitalist greed and its dire consequences.

V

DURING THE THATCHER YEARS, THEN, BRITAIN's BUSINESS CULture did become more competitive, profit-oriented, and entrepreneurial. The stories of ICI, Jaguar, and Morgan Grenfell all suggest, however, that changes had already begun to take place before Mrs. Thatcher took office. In this sense, the Prime Minister was the herald of a capitalist revolution already in progress. The recession of the early 1980s accelerated a shake-out that ultimately stimulated the healthy but killed the sick. ICI emerged a stronger company from the fray. In 1993, ICI sold off its biosciences businesses, becoming considerably smaller and more focused as a result. Jaguar's "Fix it or close it" mandate was a necessary shock. But it was the preparation for privatization, rather than the act itself, that brought a once proud company back to life. For that matter, these preparations succeeded partly because of a commitment to worker participation that owed nothing to Mrs. Thatcher or Milton Friedman. If freedom from state control brought Jaguar riches, it also made possible its fall to Ford. The financial boom from which Morgan Grenfell profited so handsomely enshrined a short-term mentality that prized quarterly results at the expense of long-term capital investment, and research and development. There was no cause to mourn the weakening of the old gentlemanly order that excluded those who did not have the "right" background and accent. However, the coming of "Big Bang" did nothing to strengthen a commitment to honesty or fairness.

Were the men implicated in the Guinness Scandal truly "Thatcher's children"? Surely the new entrepreneurial spirit that had taken Morgan Grenfell to the top of the takeover league was also at the bottom of its downfall. But the acquisitiveness of Morgan Grenfell and its brethren was, in fact, far removed from the "Victorian values" of the Prime Minister, who had little taste for the huge salaries paid in the City at the height of the boom. For all Margaret Thatcher's applause for the creation of wealth, she never intended the "enterprise culture" to justify dishonesty, much less criminal behavior.

However, the Thatcher government did little to prepare for the onslaught of greed released by financial deregulation. And it placed more emphasis on high profits than ethical conduct. What took place at Morgan Grenfell was the result of failed leadership by managers driven by financial results and unrestrained by honor. It was also the result of enormous growth untempered by managerial controls that could have compensated for the senior partners' lost intimacy. But if the ethical failures of the wayward bankers lay in themselves rather than their stars, the Guinness Affair exposed the insufficiencies of a system overly reliant on self-regulation. The Stock Exchange and associated regulatory authorities failed to put the brakes on Morgan Grenfell before putting the cuffs on the offenders.

Dubious as some changes in Britain's business culture were, many top managers agreed that real shifts in business values had taken place during the Thatcher years.[63] A "can do, must do" attitude sprang up as firms experienced crises and seized opportunities. The performance of the service sector and small business was particularly heartening. Britain became attractive once again to foreign investors. The number of business start-ups suggested an increasingly entrepreneurial stance.[64]

Yet fundamental problems remained. The rate of commercial failures revealed how difficult it was to prosper in the new competitive environment. Still, Britain had world-class competitors in pharmaceuticals, aerospace, and defense; even British Steel, long a lame duck, staged a remarkable comeback, becoming a highly efficient, productive firm. In general, though, manufacturing remained relatively weak. Investment in new equipment lagged behind in a variety of firms and sectors. This was nothing new. Whatever the problem's provenance, however, the Thatcher government and its commercial allies had not hit upon an adequate solution. Moreover, they failed to remedy a persistent weakness in industrial training and education—a costly mistake in view of the emergence and applications of new technologies during the 1980s.[65]

For Mrs. Thatcher's critics, the bragging of politicians and the aspirations of capitalists were secondary. For those who had no interest in seeing Britain become leaner and meaner, the only honorable attitude to the capitalist revolution was resistance.

CHAPTER

NINE

A Plague on Both
Your Houses

I

SOON AFTER MARGARET THATCHER BECAME SECRETARY OF
State for Education in 1970, she invited Sir John Pope-
Hennessy, director of the Victoria and Albert Museum (V &
A), to have sherry with her.

Their first meeting had taken place at Mansion House.
Erected in 1739–53 as the official residence for the Lord Mayor
of London, it is a Palladian building made of Portland stone
with six giant Corinthian columns. The portico carries a ped-
iment with a relief that would have delighted the Iron Lady
of enterprise: it represents the Dignity and Opulence of the
City, depicting London trampling on Envy and leading in
Plenty.[1]

When the newly appointed Cabinet minister, dressed in
vivid green, was announced during lunch, Sir John took the
opportunity to introduce himself. After he finally persuaded
Mrs. Thatcher that she was indeed "responsible for him," she
looked up and said: "Anyway it's so nice for us to have someone really distinguished to deal with, instead of all those
dreary schoolteachers." This snobbish and improvident re-

mark, made all the worse by her use of the royal "we," was at least half right, for Sir John was indeed distinguished both in social background and in intellectual attainments.

But there was little or nothing in their respective roots that augured any affinity to unite the minister and the mandarin. Born to the establishment in 1913 in a house on Grosvenor Place overlooking the garden of Buckingham Palace, Sir John was the scion of a family well stocked with Army officers, colonial administrators, and the like. His mother was a high-spirited, intellectual woman who had stenciled phrases from Nietzsche on her bedroom wall as a girl, and became a prolific writer and art collector; his father was unusual for an Army man, an admirer of Swinburne's poetry and Renoir's painting, who became a major general. These were people who brought up their son "on the assumption that I would write books. There was a typewriter in the nursery from as far back as I can remember."

When Sir John looked around Mrs. Thatcher's office over sherry, he noticed two empty bookcases lined with dark green silk. Suddenly aware of the reason for his presence, he asked: "What are you going to put in them, Secretary of State?" She replied: "I was hoping for some ceramics."[2] In search of suitable decoration, Mrs. Thatcher went along to the Victoria and Albert, whose roots went back to the Great Exhibition of 1851 when Prince Albert and Sir Henry Cole envisioned a popular educational museum dedicated to design and craft. It was her first visit.

If Mrs. Thatcher had come to celebrate the sources or purposes of art, she kept her mission well hidden from her host. Sir John offered her three china services to choose from for her office, two of which were "very pretty." Instead, she chose a conventional Chelsea service with pastel-colored fruit. As if this was not bad enough, his "heart sank" as they toured some of the galleries. Not one flicker of response did the future Prime Minister display in front of a medieval English masterpiece, the Clare Chasuble. Donatello's work did not move her; Bernini's art did not touch her. It was only when they came to the Conservation Department that "a miracle occurred." What caught Mrs. Thatcher's eye was not "the interesting or progressive parts" of the V & A, but instead the sight of two women sticking pieces of textile together with plastic fixative. Once a research chemist, she delighted in reciting the relevant formulae and chatted with the women, lingering in the room so long that Sir John could hardly get her back to the main entrance.

Sir John's view of Mrs. Thatcher's conduct was nothing if not haughty. Years later in a cutting article in *The New York Review of Books* (and later in his memoirs), he denounced her "quite extraordinary lack of comprehension," which was without parallel "even among the many philistines I have escorted around the museum." If nothing else, however, she did not affect aesthetic concerns she lacked, which is more than many museum visitors could honestly say. And Mrs. Thatcher was decent enough to take a genuine interest in the specialist staff she met—which was more than her host could claim. Virtually "blind" as she may have been to the lure of art, Sir John seemed equally blind to the mysteries of science. Together they were a walking epitome of the rift between C. P. Snow's "two cultures."

Indeed, the Prime Minister decided in 1984 "to equip the museum ... with a board on which no member had a vestigial knowledge of works of art." In search of a director whose willingness to "carry out our policies" would not be hampered by backbone or burdened with vision, the trustees hit upon Mrs. Esteve-Coll in 1987. She quickly proved herself to be, in Sir John's discerning eyes, a "relentless vulgarian," whose preference for "housekeeping" over scholarship threatened to destroy a great museum.[3]

I I

SIR JOHN POPE-HENNESSY'S UNHAPPY ENCOUNTER WITH MRS. Thatcher was typical of the collision between the woman who idealized the "enterprise culture" and those who suffered from its apparent dominance.

During the 1980s, much of the British intelligentsia wanted to contain and even reverse the capitalist revolution. Although the historian can discern a certain ideological coherence in this varied group, it was never a highly organized or cohesive movement. On the face of it, Margaret Thatcher's intellectual opposition seemed to be a counter-culture, and indeed it did attract some avant-garde, or, at least, marginal figures, who rebelled as they felt their career prospects and personal ideals trounced by Mrs. Thatcher's policies. And yet the leading social critics often came from, or belonged to, the powers that be.

The Prime Minister neither garnered nor sought the approval of those who valued sensibility over sense. Indeed, it would be difficult to exaggerate the degree of animosity toward Mrs. Thatcher and her policies in mainstream cultural institutions such as universities, museums, galleries, theaters, publishing houses, and the media. Moreover, she managed to arouse, and did little to douse, hostility to her capitalist revolution in both the Church of England and the higher echelons of the Civil Service. Although she was not universally unpopular, her adversaries were articulate and visible. In 1988, Sir Peter Hall, director of the National Theatre, announced that "well over 90 per cent of the people in the performing arts, education, and the creative world are against her."[4] The critical core of the anti-Thatcherite movement came from the varied group which became known in the 1980s as the "chattering classes." Mrs. Thatcher found "vain intellectuals" insupportable. Vain or not, they returned the compliment, and then some.

Although the 1980s witnessed the rise of many right-wing intellectuals such as Roger Scrutan and John Casey, Mrs. Thatcher's foes were more numerous. Philistinism angered writers and artists who had no respect for a woman who admired Rudyard Kipling and whose favorite reading did not go beyond the thrillers of John le Carré (certainly not a mark of shame) and Frederick Forsythe. The fact that she had given public poetry readings from Francis Palgrave's *Golden Treasury* (hardly a modernist Bible) as a girl in Grantham and had sung in the Balliol-Somerville choir as a student at Oxford was no consolation. Equally unimpressive was the fact that she had placed one of Henry Moore's smallest sculptures in an alcove in the main hallway of Number 10.[5] To be sure, the Prime Minister's prosaic no-nonsense style and her undisguised contempt for anything "airy fairy" was a far cry from the literary achievement of Winston Churchill (decried though it was by Evelyn Waugh), the bookish taste of former publisher Harold Macmillan, and the donnish manner of onetime Oxford economics scholar Harold Wilson. Even her successor, John Major, is a member of the Trollope Society. And there was little reason to believe that intellectuals who extolled complexity, ambiguity, and irony, and, moreover, tended to equate wisdom and sadness, would have any use for the nannylike ministrations of a woman who demanded that everyone simply get on with it.

Mrs. Thatcher's taste and origins provoked uncontained outbreaks of snobbery, social and intellectual alike, on the part of honest doubters threatened by the enterprise culture. Jonathan Miller, trained physician, famed theater director, and acknowledged master of "haute vulgarisation,' considered her "loathsome, repulsive in almost every way." He took particular exception to her "odious suburban gentility and sentimental saccharine patriotism, catering to the worst elements of commuter idiocy." Mrs. Thatcher fared no better at the hands of Mary Warnock. The philosopher who became Mistress of Girton, Cambridge, and a life peer in 1985, indicted both the Prime Minister's person and her policies. Even Mrs. Thatcher's "patronising, elocution voice" was objectionable, ostensibly because it embodied the unabashed upwardly mobile aspirations of the grocer's daughter. Her choice of clothing was likewise disturbing. Lady Warnock could not quite get over the sight of the Prime Minister on television choosing clothes at Marks & Spencer.[6]

"An intellectual hatred is the worst," wrote W. B. Yeats. However strong and aversive the reactions to the Prime Minister, the intelligentsia's antagonism to what she stood for was more than a merely personal loathing. Rather, it was deeply rooted in British cultural traditions. Indeed, the revolt against Thatcher and Thatcherism was, on one level, another battle in an ongoing war against industrial capitalism. This was an ideological struggle that hearkened back to the time when William Wordsworth indicted the factory system for causing economic distress to the working class, destroying the harmonious fabric of the traditional family, and threatening the peaceful beauty of the English landscape.

The intellectual opposition to Mrs. Thatcher had its roots in Victorian England, but much of its power came from the birth of the "new class" in the postwar era. This "new class" was, by and large, far removed from the dull, vulgar realities of material production. Its members had a higher mission: to purvey symbolic knowledge in the name of civilizing Britain. Education, therapy, and planning were among its major activities; universities, communications, social service agencies, and counseling networks were among its major domains.[7] The proliferation of the new knowledge class was closely tied to the advent of the Welfare State, and in particular to the reforms of Clement Attlee's watershed Labour government, which "nationalized" culture along with much else of far more dubious value.[8] In 1948, T. S. Eliot (by his own definition a Tory, an Anglican, a royalist, a classicist, and certainly not a socialist) was good enough to point out that culture "is recognised both as an instrument of policy, and as something socially desirable which it is the business of the State to promote."[9] Even cultural conservatives, not to say outright reactionaries, knew where their scones were buttered.

The profound pride in "British values" that surfaced during the war effort encouraged the Attlee government to invest public money to enrich cultural life and make it accessible to the people. Shortly before Churchill went down to cruel defeat in the general election of 1945, his Coalition government announced the creation of the Arts Council—an independent, chartered body funded by public monies. Its purpose was "to encourage knowledge, understanding and practice of the arts in the broad sense of that term." Government funding made possible the establishment of important cultural institutions such as the Royal Opera House in Covent Garden, which became the national home for ballet and opera, as well as the creation of the National Theatre and the Institute of Contemporary Arts.[10]

But the benefits of nationalizing culture, as it were, went well beyond the question of self-image. In the postwar era, British writers and artists became increasingly dependent upon the state for their livelihoods, as did dons and lecturers at Oxbridge and other universities, all of which were funded by public monies. So Percy Shelley's "unacknowledged legislators of mankind" found material rewards and personal recognition in the world of the Welfare State. And it was, on the whole, Labour rather than Conservative governments that proved the most reliable supporters of the arts and education, rescuing would-be bohemians from obscurity and putting them in full public view on suitably sophisticated programs on BBC2. The intelligentsia's largely adversarial stance toward modern industrial capitalism persisted, but in the socialist age such attitudes accorded reasonably well with dominant political ideologies. So it was possible to have someone else's cake and eat it too.

The antagonism of the postwar "new class" to Mrs. Thatcher's capitalist revolution was an ideological struggle with a hard material edge. She assaulted their interests by insisting that rewards came from economic productivity rather than intellectual or aesthetic achievement. What made the British intelligentsia particularly vulnerable was the fact that a substantial proportion of its number depended for their livelihoods on government payrolls or subsidies.[11]

The fact that the new heroes of Mrs. Thatcher's "enterprise culture" were entrepreneurs and managers, men like computer entrepreneur Alan Sugar who started out by hawking goods in the market stalls of the East End, angered much of the British intelligentsia. Especially those who had seen, or remembered, better times, had to gasp for breath when they learned that their charwoman's (cleaner's) son was making a pile in the City and driving around in a red Porsche. By raising the bottom line to the top of the national agenda, the Prime Minister downgraded, intentionally or not, those who had dedicated themselves to cultural excellence rather than brute productivity. In so doing, she provoked a severe case of what the great American historian Richard Hofstadter described in another context as "status anxiety."[12] The fear of losing prestige, power, and position helps explain the ferocious hostility aroused by the woman who tried to push into the shadows the rulers and the rank-and-file of Oxbridge, the BBC, the National Theatre, the British Museum, the Institute for Contemporary Arts, and the like. Miserably paid writers, artists, and educators whose self-esteem depended on social status and public attention had every reason to resent being ignored or dismissed, much less pilloried.

Asking the heirs of William Shakespeare to become born-again disciples of the Victorian apostle of self-help, Samuel Smiles, was bound to offend. On one occasion Mrs. Thatcher suggested to Hugo Young, a moderate left-winger who was the *Guardian*'s leading political commentator, that he open a small business.[13] This arrogant piece of unwanted advice was unlikely to endear the Prime Minister to an elegant literary stylist who came from an upper-middle-class family and was educated at a public school, Ampleforth, and at Balliol College, where he read law. But Young took her advice, after a fashion, making a good deal of money for himself by writing a best-selling biography of Mrs. Thatcher.

The British intelligentsia was understandably, and defiantly, opposed to the Thatcher government's wanton cuts in spending on education and the arts. Between 1981 and 1985, universities lost 15 percent of their grants. The Prime Minister insisted that the National Theatre, the Royal Shakespeare Company, and the Royal Opera House obtain a greater part of their budgets from subscriptions and gifts from business. She also insisted that museums like the Victoria and Albert charge for admission as did their counterparts in France, Italy, and America. This outraged many, among them Arnold Weinstock, a cultured industrialist who recalled that he would never have been able to go to a museum as a boy if his mother had had to pay for the honor.[14]

What otherwise might have been a relatively quiet cultural split became a very public rupture as the woman responsible for privatizing state industries pulled the plug, as it were, on nationalized culture. Mrs. Thatcher might have coopted her intellectual adversaries by allowing them to go on as they had before. But she could not leave well enough alone.

In *The Downing Street Years*, Mrs. Thatcher tried to counteract her image as a tightwad Philistine. The premise for her arts policy was that "Artistic talent—let alone artistic genius—is unplanned, unpredictable, eccentrically individual. Regimented, subsidized, owned and determined by the state, it withers. Moreover, the 'state' in these cases came to mean the arts lobby." Therefore, she took the position:

> I wanted to see the private sector raising more money and bringing business acumen and efficiency to bear on the administration of cultural institutions. I wanted to encourage private individuals to give by covenant, not the state to take taxes. But I was profoundly conscious of how a country's art collections, museums, libraries, operas and orchestras combine with its architecture and monuments to magnify its international standing.[15]

The capitalist revolution was both a cultural struggle and a class war. Victory entailed vanquishing the allegedly unproductive elements of British society—whether they were trade unionists whose strikes undermined businesses, the long-term unemployed who lived off the dole, or cultivated folk who depended on Arts Council grants for their projects. Faced with cutbacks in funding, the intelligentsia bit the hand that had stopped feeding them. They grasped what often escaped Mrs. Thatcher: that the ability to retain political power and sustain social change are partly matters of legitimation; in other words, the Prime Minister had to prove that her policies were just. Arguing that "there is no alternative" was inadequate and, as a bevy of artists and intellectuals tried to show, it was also untrue.

III

WHEN SIR KEITH JOSEPH BECAME EDUCATION SECRETARY OF the Thatcher government in 1981, he naturally had ample occasion to visit British universities. Admired or dismissed as an intellectual in politics, he was no stranger to the British academic world. A graduate of Magdalen College, Oxford, and a Fellow of All Souls, Joseph had cause to feel at home with the customary round of high talk at high table. The author of tightly argued and suitably austere works of political theory that could never be confused with the political thrillers of his Tory colleague, Jeffrey Archer, he had spent considerable time in the mid-1970s touring campuses in search of converts to the new monetarist dispensation.

British universities might have extended a decent welcome to so cultured an Education Secretary, but they didn't. On one occasion, Joseph's official car was surrounded and nearly overturned by a throng of protesting students. Indeed, his campus visits came to excite so much anger that it was necessary to lay on extra police protection. And then there were some additional precautions. When Sir Keith's successor, Kenneth Baker, once traveled with him in his car, he noticed that his driver kept a large wooden truncheon under the front seat.[16]

While visiting Leicester University in October 1988, Baker and his party found that "militants" (a term that the new right usually applied indiscriminately to their varied opponents, student and worker alike) had laid siege to the building they had entered. Determined to face the protestors, Baker and local MP David Tredinnick, who had been an officer in the Guards, along with two security men, decided to push through the crowd. But the little band of stalwarts failed to part the angry waters with their resolve. Indeed, the students drew blood, hitting the visitors with sticks, breaking Baker's glasses and knocking him to the ground.[17]

But for all the personal and ideological conflicts that rent the mythological ivory tower, in the arts subjects there was still a measure of consensus on the value of the humanistic ethos that emanated from Oxbridge and spread to centers of higher learning throughout Britain. It hearkened back to the

Aristotelian belief that "there is a form of education which should be given to our sons, not because it is necessary, but because it benefits a free man and is noble."[18] In 1963, Noel Annan, Provost of King's, Cambridge, and eminent historian of ideas, echoed the philosophy of education enunciated by his old headmaster, Roxburgh of Stowe. Annan had little doubt about the mission of the university. It was for

> The intellect... the intellect... the intellect. *That's* what universities exist for. Everything else is secondary. Equality of opportunity to come to the university is secondary. The need to mix classes, nationalities, and races together is secondary. The agonies and gaieties of student life are secondary. A university is dead if it cannot in some way communicate to the students the struggle—and the disappointments as well as the triumphs in that struggle to produce out of the chaos of human experience some grain of order won by the intellect.[19]

The period from 1945 to 1975 was the "golden age of the don," in Annan's words. "The stereotype of the absent-minded professor ... transformed into the keen-eyed inventor in a white coat.... The don rose in public esteem: became an indispensable back-room boy in Whitehall: became an adviser to politicians ... began to be seen in London salons. To be a don became an attractive way of life."[20] The number of dons as well the opportunities open to them proliferated, largely thanks to the adoption of the Robbins Report (1963), which fostered an unprecedented expansion in British higher education but did so, according to its critics, at the price of hiring the terminally mediocre as well as the truly excellent. In any case, the early 1960s witnessed the establishment of six new "plate-glass" universities (as the successors of the Victorian and Edwardian "red brick" universities were called). Among the most innovative was Sussex University, where the distinguished historian Asa Briggs tried to escape the territorial constraints of the traditional departmental structure by creating interdisciplinary schools of study.

During the 1960s, a British version of the French *hautes écoles* or the German *technische hochschulen* was also established. The "polytechnics," as the new institutions were called, were established to provide training geared to the technological and managerial needs of British business and industry. Unlike the plate-glass universities such as Sussex, their mission was meant to be fundamentally different from the refined shaping of mind and character. The "polys" soon deviated, however, from this consciously utilitarian course. Far from providing a new and improved vehicle to make Harold Wilson's promised technological revolution a social reality that fostered national economic success, the polys aped Oxbridge. In so doing, they fell under the sway of an old model which had little relevance to the social purpose for which they were created. Instead of setting up new courses on management, the polytechnics took up sociology.

The traditional humanistic ethic and its upholders were attacked from another direction as the new right queried the economic value of classic liberal education. This became all the more explosive an issue as the education budget soared while the national cupboard began to look particularly bare. In 1956, the capital spending program of the British university system cost £3.8 million; eight years later, it was £30 million and rising fast. When supply-side economics ended up supplying too little revenue, the Thatcher government endeavored to cut the budgets of vulnerable domains. Higher education and social welfare seemed to be a more fitting, and exposed, target than the defense of the realm. Although the cuts' extent and effect varied considerably, in some cases they led to the closure of entire departments and the elimination of degree courses.

Borne partly out of fiscal necessity, the Thatcher government's higher education policy soon took on the odor of ideological blood sport. When Margaret Thatcher was Education Secretary she had issued a White Paper arguing against the idea of awarding places in higher education to meet estimates of the country's need for qualified people.[21] The shaping of the mind could not be reduced to economic imperatives alone. By the time she became Prime Minister, though, the lady had turned considerably to the right, and was intent on forcing free market principles down the gullets of Keynesians and other lesser mortals.

Mrs. Thatcher's new hard-line thinking on education was much influenced by Sir Keith Joseph, a man who quoted Alexis de Tocqueville one minute and then decried universities the next for squashing the entrepreneurial spirit. Despite or perhaps because he hailed from a privileged and insulated family background, he extolled barrow boys (who hawked their goods in East End market stalls) for their grit and industry. "God bless them," he passionately said.[22] Joseph's conviction that the humanistic education that he himself had received at the public schools and Oxbridge "ruined people" for business was strengthened by contemporary historical writings. Conservative intellectuals used, and in certain respects, misused, Martin Wiener's *English Culture and the Decline of the Industrial Spirit 1850–1980* and Correlli Barnett's *The Audit of War* to criticize the destructive economic consequences of the intelligentsia's anti-industrial ethic. The good news for intellectuals was that, for once, their public influence was duly recognized; the bad news was that they were viewed as a baneful force which had failed Britain. The imagined "trahison des clercs" provided Joseph with a historical rationalization for a holy war against British universities when he became Education Secretary.

However unfair and wrongheaded the Thatcher government's ideological bias against the universities was, nevertheless it was difficult to deny that the financial condition of the country made some changes necessary. In short, Britain was running a high-cost educational system with relatively low output. Only one in eight eighteen-year-olds went on to higher education (far lower than in any other major industrialized democracy), but spending was proportionally higher in Britain than in any Western European country save the Netherlands.

The Thatcher government tried to make British universities more market-oriented, cost-effective, and demand-driven institutions to bolster the enterprise culture rather than simply drain the public purse. And so the capitalist revolution brought an abrupt and inglorious end to the "golden age of the dons." By far the most dramatic blow was Kenneth Baker's elimination of academic tenure, the virtual guarantee of a job for life. This once sacrosanct prerogative was shunted aside as the special pleading of a protected class. At the same time, Baker injected "market demand" into the rigid, and paltry, academic pay scale by providing higher compensation for those who taught practical subjects like law or science. (This was commonplace practice in the United States, where the most pedestrian accounting professor was usually far better paid than the cleverest literary critic.)

Baker also transformed the financial structure of universities to better suit the values of the market economy. He abolished the formula that protected the high ratio of lecturers to students by hinging any rise in student numbers to a pro rata increase in funding. Instead, he instituted an arrangement that linked expansion to student demand so that universities would have greater incentives to better serve their "customers." Finally, he pushed universities to derive a larger portion of their income from private sources, using the dubious justification that this would protect academic freedom (as if budget cuts were the bulwark of liberty). Rhetoric aside, the bottom line of Baker's reforms was to improve the bottom line.

In all fairness, the Thatcher government managed to squash the golden age of students as well as their teachers. Sir

Keith Joseph eliminated the bargain price of a British university education for foreign students, a practice that was a vestige of the days of Empire. He forced them to pay a higher proportion of the cost of their studies, but tempered the blow by providing additional scholarships for foreign students.

Academics had a different model. They saw themselves as closer akin to the cultured, idealistic civil servant caring for the public good. When it came to the intrinsic worth of knowledge or the ongoing search for truth, the vagaries of the market seemed quite beside the point. Living in an insulated, though hardly luxurious, milieu, most British academics had neither the experience nor the inclination to explain their worth to the nation in merely utilitarian terms. In a word, marketing was vulgar. So when Thatcherite critics asked why their vacations were so long, why their research was so important, and why so many taught so few, the questions seemed contemptible and the answers obvious to those trained in the old humanistic mold. But the failure to provide speedy and compelling replies to such queries damaged the public reputation of the universities.

The budget cuts of the early 1980s focused the minds of scholars who were more at home in the world of ideas than the world of things. When West German President Richard von Weizsacker received an honorary degree at Oxford in the summer of 1988, he took tea at St. John's, which was one of the university's wealthiest colleges. "There's only one thing I wonder," he said to Professor Ralf Dahrendorf. "What *is* going on inside all those brilliant heads?" To which the German-born sociologist replied: "That's very simple. . . . Only one thought. Money."[23]

The position of Oxford dons, however strained, was far preferable to that of unemployed PhDs, especially in the humanities and social sciences, who found that the enterprise culture's alleged rewards for intelligence, energy, and work did not extend to those with nothing of obvious practical use to sell. Sir Keith Joseph's "new-blood" lectureships did provide some opportunities for new PhDs, but in Britain, as in America, they were victims of the academic job crisis.

To be fair, the job crisis had begun in the mid-1970s and was itself the offshoot of widespread expansion in the 1960s which left few openings. Before Thatcher, academic salaries were low even by the modest standards of their American counterparts; in 1977, a new lecturer with a PhD might make as little as £3,500 (c. $5,700). The fortunate few enjoyed the beautiful surroundings of charming Oxbridge architecture, but even so eminent a figure and strong supporter of Mrs. Thatcher as Sir Geoffrey Elton, Regius Professor of History at Cambridge, did not have the help of a secretary. So he typed his correspondence himself.[24]

Protest, adaptation, and exit—these were the leading responses of British academics to the capitalist revolution that endangered their self-image, social status, and economic opportunities. It was the rising expectations of those who had benefited from the golden age of the don and those who felt entitled to its continuation that fueled the opposition to Mrs. Thatcher.

The most telling, and public, protest took place at Oxford, where humanistic and scientific values collided with the new enterprise culture. Close as the beautiful old medieval town of Oxford is to the car factories of neighboring Cowley, the university was traditionally much closer to the world of government than to the world of production. But when it came to the likes of Margaret Thatcher, Oxford had as little time for the one as for the other. The trouble began at the end of 1984, when the Hebdomadal Council, the university's ruling body, announced that it intended to confer an honorary degree on her (the other candidates included the opera singer Sir Geraint Evans, the president of Italy, and a number of eminent academics). Under ordinary circumstances, such an announcement would have been unobjectionable, for Oxford had conferred this distinction on all postwar prime ministers who were its graduates. And Margaret Thatcher, already Honorary Fellow of Somerville College since 1971, was, for better or worse, one of the university's best-known, if not best-loved, alumna. Even though she had not been a distinguished Education Secretary, Mrs. Thatcher had still defended the Open University (the national adult institution). But when it came to the question, "What have you done for us (or to us) lately?" the answer was not encouraging. She seemed like the archangel of academic death.

To be sure, it was the massive budget cuts that took needed funds out of the dons' own well-versed mouths, and those of their students, that galvanized them to stand in the way of pronouncing the Prime Minister honorific. As it happened, though, Oxford itself was fairly well insulated from the cuts both because of its powerful friends on the University Grants Committee (which allocated funds), and because it was richer than its newer offshoots in the first place. But Oxford dons indicted Mrs. Thatcher nonetheless for policies that had done "deep and systematic damage" to education.[25] The critics thought it hypocritical to honor a woman whose policies had undermined higher education so badly and baldly. How could Oxford, in good conscience, reward the head of a government which seemed intent on reducing higher education to job training; and which seemed blind to the value of knowledge for its own sake? "It is craven and abject for Oxford to do this," argued Steven Lukes of Balliol College, a well-known sociologist who had written a study of Emile Durkheim. "Politicians have enough rewards as it is."[26] Others regarded the matter differently. Lord Goodman, the wily and worldly Master of University College, argued that an honorary degree for Mrs. Thatcher should not be a political or partisan issue.

At the end of January 1985, then, more than a thousand Oxford dons, administrators, and M.A.s filed into the Sheldonian

Theatre to vote for or against conferring an honorary Doctor of Civil Laws degree on the Prime Minister. It was an extraordinary turnout for an occasion that usually excited less interest than the election of a Professor of Poetry. The speeches, predictably, went on for two hours and finally were cut short. A particularly impassioned speech came from a shy cardiovascular physiologist who described himself as perhaps the saddest professor ever to take up a chair at Oxford. Professor Denis Noble had received the gold medal of the British Heart Foundation, only to find that his research team had lost their £60,000-a-year budget. "This may be the best chance for any serious academic institution to stop the catastrophe that we face as a scientific and educational nation," he said.[27]

The 738 "no" voters crowded the building's exit well after the 319 "yes" voters had departed. And so Mrs. Thatcher, who had not lost an election since she failed to win a parliamentary seat in Dartford, went down to defeat.

The intellectual opposition had returned fire and wounded their oppressor. But this was at best a Pyrrhic victory, for public humiliation only further antagonized an already formidable adversary. "If the dons don't want to confer the honour, the Prime Minister is the last person to wish to receive it," a spokesman explained.[28]

The affair was an incredible example of political ineptness on the part of a university so long and so closely tied to Whitehall and Westminster. Had Oxford offered Mrs. Thatcher an honorary degree when she first became party leader or Prime Minister, the controversy would never have taken place. As it turned out, the outcome made the dons seem foolish and self-indulgent, at least in certain quarters. Harold Macmillan (Lord Stockton), Chancellor of Oxford, feared that Mrs. Thatcher's drubbing would "rebound on the honour and position of the university."[29] *The Times* called it the culmination of a "nasty campaign which has oscillated between political spite and logic chopping."[30] Business allies such as corporate raider Sir Gordon White, who once suggested endowing a professorship in Common Sense, thought the dons a "miserable bunch."[31]

Even if Oxford could protest the incursion of the capitalist revolution into academia, its lesser brethren like the University of Salford had little choice but to adapt to what they could not change. An unprepossessing institution, Salford's face was as plain as its mission. It was founded to provide practical training to "horny-handed sons of toil" with modest roots but high hopes. A technologically based institution, its core was applied knowledge rather than humanistic learning. Located in the North of England next to Manchester, the rough-hewn lion of the Industrial Revolution, Salford had some title to being a town of almost unrelieved gloom, lacking the delightful Victorian Gothic facades that enlivened the bustling city center of neighboring "Cottonopolis."

In 1981, though, the deprivations of art and the hardships of history were less pressing than the fact that the University Grants Committee had translated the average cut of 17 percent to higher education to a massive, and possibly fatal, 44 percent cut for the University of Salford. It would be very difficult to imagine a more savage indication of where this institution stood in the pecking order, fairly or not: the bottom of the league table.

The man forced to confront this crisis was the new vice-chancellor, John Ashworth. A biologist by training, he was a professor at the University of Essex when he was seconded to the Cabinet Office in the late 1970s as the chief scientist in the Central Policy Review Staff. This group was responsible for putting forth policy changes that were loosely referred to as "Thatcherite"; among them the sell-off of shares in BP which took place under Jim Callaghan's Labour government and the sale of council houses which did not. Neither a member of the Conservative Party nor a supporter of Margaret

Thatcher, in the course of his work in Whitehall Ashworth arrived at what he later called a "pretty standard Friedmanite critique." Education had been captured by the providers—the faculty—and was insufficiently responsible to consumers—students. The University Grants Committee itself was the creature of Oxbridge devotees and badly needed a shake-up. For all of John Ashworth's intellectual acuity, he was mercifully lacking in the pompous manner of the stereotypical mandarin. When he took over as Director of the London School of Economics in 1990, he enrolled in an introductory economics course and went to class in blue jeans and a T-shirt so as to better understand how students saw the institution.[32]

Soon after Ashworth arrived at Salford in the spring of 1981, he found himself "hoist on his own petard." Having advocated certain Friedmanite policies, he landed in the hottest seat in higher education. As Ashworth himself later admitted, his situation had a certain poetic justice. Such ironies aside, however, he had to overcome suspicion from faculty who considered him to be Mrs. Thatcher's hatchet man and, therefore, an ideal local scapegoat. As a result, he had to attack her government very harshly to establish his legitimacy. In fact, Ashworth pretended that he was far more opposed to certain policies than he really was. On one level, though, the cuts were a great advantage to him because only a dramatic shock could have made fundamental change acceptable. And the magnitude of the cuts was such that it was clear that the system would have to change and attitudes would have to alter if Salford was to avoid bankruptcy and extinction.

Unable and unwilling to fight the capitalist revolution head on, Ashworth used certain of its principles to salvage and transform Salford. He began with the assumption that the University Grants Committee had made a fundamental error by encouraging all institutions to imitate Oxford and Cambridge. The country simply couldn't afford to fund so many copies of the ancient universities; the originals would have to suffice. Salford needed to become a British version of the *technische hochschule* or the *grandes écoles*.

A week or so after the cuts were announced, the new vice-chancellor called a meeting for all members of staff. After he greeted the five hundred or so demoralized individuals who sat in the lecture hall, he asked them to shake hands with those on both sides of them. And then he told his audience (echoing the horror stories told to countless premeds among others): "one-third of you won't be employed here in three years." Shocking as this piece of intimidation surely was, its point was not simply to terrify the already frightened. Ashworth's message to the Salford staff was: Your fate is in your own hands. The last thing he wanted, or could afford, in a time of crisis was a confrontation with staff or students both of whose unions initially opposed him but eventually worked with him to good purpose. For all his support for certain Friedmanite principles, Ashworth's turnaround plan for Salford was also shaped by Japanese corporatist management philosophy.

Faced with a massive loss of resources, Ashworth needed an equally large reduction of overhead. The only realistic way to do so was to cut back teaching staff. So he asked faculty to resign on the understanding that if they cooperated, he would do his best to get alternative employment for them. Some described this process as the most manipulative spectacle they had ever witnessed. In any event, Salford had little choice but to turn to industry to provide the funding it needed to survive. The vice-chancellor, therefore, told all those interested in research to go out and get grants. But saying that "we have a bit of capacity and are tremendously bright" wasn't enough. What they had to do was to find out what businesses wanted and then try to provide it. Aggressive marketing was a key to survival; therefore the university took the unprecedented step of setting up a marketing department, CAMPUS (Campaign for the University of Salford). In search of revenue, it also established a business services unit to help correct managerial deficiencies of British business. The novel "customer orientation" extended to students, especially foreign students, who Salford pushed to recruit because they paid much-needed higher fees.[33]

All in all, Ashworth's strategy worked. The collaborative search for outside funding was the key to saving Salford. Government funding went down by 34 percent during the Thatcher decade, but student numbers fell by only 20 percent, thanks to greater productivity. And there were indications that the quality of instruction improved as did the performance of students. The number of first-class degrees trebled and the average degree class rose. It is easy enough to ask whether the new Salford was doing what a university should do. But such questions seemed a luxury in an era of capitalist revolution.

As the enterprise culture threatened academics' values, status, and options, exit often seemed a more desirable strategy than protest or adaptation. The "brain drain" that began among scientists and engineers in the 1950s became a veritable hemorrhage of talent during the Thatcher years as a horde of highly able academics left British universities for more lucrative positions in the United States. Among the many fine historians who emigrated were Simon Schama who went to Harvard, Sir Michael Howard and Paul Kennedy who went to Yale, Harold Perkin who went to Northwestern, and David Cannadine who went to Columbia.

If the intellectual migrants were lionized sometimes in the United States, some Americans resented them for taking away already scarce jobs. There was no great joy in some quarters at the prospect of American universities becoming a retirement home for the British academic classes. Some objected to the fact that certain left-wing migrant scholars bailed out of the enterprise culture in disgust with the eruption of greed, but then turned around to take up far better compensated positions in the fortress of capitalist material- ism. But was there really anything wrong with deserting a sinking ship?

I V

SLIGHTLY TO THE NORTH OF CENTRAL LONDON IN THE VICIN- ity of Regent's Park, NW1, is a neighborhood much favored by affluent writers, producers, and the like. More likely to be found in certain gentrified roads of Camden Town such as Albert Street (or Canonbury Square in Islington, N1) than in the magnificent white stucco Nash terraces around the cir- cumference of Regent's Park, this area has great appeal on both practical and symbolic grounds for the intelligentsia and kindred spirits. Located far enough from London's poshest and wealthiest neighborhoods like Belgravia and Mayfair to avoid the taint of the old or "chi-chi" aristocracy or the sight of *nouveaux riches*, NW1 is equally far removed from nonde- script outer suburbs like Finchley, Margaret Thatcher's longtime parliamentary district. But the area is still close enough to permit easy access to the theaters, galleries, and museums of the West End. Containing enough graceful but suitably worn classical and neoclassical facades to be charm- ing, it also has enough rough patches such as council houses and poor residents to be "mixed" and therefore politically ac- ceptable. So it is unsurprising that NW1 is a popular center for those who enjoy bourgeois styles of life while professing socialist values. This is a phenomenon which might be called contemptuous consumption.

In an article in the *Atlantic Monthly*, written in December 1991, Geoffrey Wheatcroft, a journalist for the right-of-center *Daily Telegraph*, recounted an occasion which underlined the fact that there is perhaps no surer way to stop conversation or engender disbelief at social gatherings in literary London than to say a kind word about Margaret Thatcher; describe her as something more than a monstrous Philistine; or suggest that her "success" was anything more than a mirage. At any rate, a friend of Wheatcroft's gave a dinner party in 1987 when the "Question of Thatcher" came up. Asked for her opinion, the hostess said that "although she could see how tiresome the Prime Minister sometimes was, how bullying and querulous, one still had to admit all the same that she had done something for the country." Not exactly the ringing endorsement one would have hoped for from the faithful at a Tory Party Conference, surely. It was sufficiently positive, though, to offend a "fashionable writer" (defined contemptuously by "having a literary following" but barely known to the large public). Two days later, his friend received an unusual thank-you letter from this man in which he stated that, "in view of what she had said, he could never see her again." Wheatcroft concluded: "She might as well have been explaining that for all his faults, Hitler had great achievements to his credit." A hyperbolic comparison, to be sure, but it nonetheless conveyed the depth of outrage Mrs. Thatcher could, and did, provoke.[34]

But there were, at least, a few members of the British intelligentsia who found the "Thatcher effect" far more pleasing. One of her most distinguished admirers was Philip Larkin, who managed to become Poet Laureate even after reading in some writers' manual that his surname was not fit for a serious character. He delighted in the fact that Mrs. Thatcher told the British home truths that had been forgotten. Her great virtue, he told an interviewer in 1979, "is saying that two and two makes four, which is as popular nowadays as it always has been." Later the same year, he elaborated on another point of accounting: "I adore Mrs. Thatcher. . . . Recognizing that if you haven't got the money for something you can't have it—this is a concept that's vanished for many years." Larkin was no less taken with her appearance. In private meetings she proved to be no mean eyeballer. "I got the blue flash," said the poet. "What a blade of steel."[35]

In May 1980, Larkin met Mrs. Thatcher at a Downing Street reception. Greeting the Poet Laureate, the Prime Minister told him that she liked his wonderful poem about a girl. When this vague reference drew an apparent blank, she said: "You know, Her mind was full of knives." Larkin took the fact that she got the line wrong as a compliment. For it suggested that if it weren't spontaneous, she would have got the line right. As he told Julian Barnes, though, he was a child in such things.[36]

Larkin's friend Kingsley Amis also admired Mrs. Thatcher for more than her free market principles. An "angry young man" in the 1950s when he wrote *Lucky Jim*, his hilarious satire of university life (and the lack thereof), the young radical became a true-blue Tory (following a path similar to that of Wordsworth, Coleridge, and Southey) who saw liberty and equality at odds. From the time Amis first met Mrs. Thatcher at a dinner party at her Chelsea home, it was obvious that she was not one of those terminally frumpy creatures who confused indifference to appearance with high intellect.[37] Amis's verdict was unequivocal: "One of the best looking women I had ever met. . . . This quality is so extreme that, allied to her well-known photogenic quality, it can trap me for split seconds into thinking I am looking at a science-fiction illustration of some time ago showing the beautiful girl who has become President of the Solar Federation in the year 2220."

Amis remained a loyal supporter of his "dream girl" despite some fairly rough treatment at her hands. When, in 1980, he took Mrs. Thatcher a copy of his novel *Russian Hide-and-Seek*, she was singularly unimpressed by its subject, a future Britain under Russian occupation. "Huh, she cried. 'Can't you do any better than that? Get yourself another crystal ball!' " This was the woman who continued to be the recurring female figure in Amis's dreams. But such fantasies did not stop him from disliking her government for anti-intellectual policies that undermined "education as education, definable as the free pursuit of knowledge and truth for their own sake."[38]

The likes of Amis and Larkin were definitely in the minority when it came to Mrs. Thatcher. Their fellow writers were hugely critical of the Prime Minister and her much-vaunted "enterprise culture." The June 20th group, brought together by Harold Pinter and Lady Antonia Fraser in 1988, was one of the few systematic intellectual attempts to organize against Thatcherism. This circle of dissenters met at their very grand home in Holland Park to discuss politics from a left-wing perspective. But their surroundings recalled the Whig aristocracy of Melbourne's day rather than the Socialist Workers' Party of Trotskyite persuasion. However ironic a setting this was to create a new, or revive an old, socialist alternative to Thatcherism, the June 20th group brought together some of England's finest writers and artists, members of an established cultural elite. Among the notable figures involved in it at one time or another were the playwright David Hare; the novelists Margaret Drabble, John Mortimer, Salman Rushdie (before his exile), and Ian McEwan; the feminist theorist Germaine Greer; the political biographer Ben Pimlott; and the architect Richard Rogers. This was a strong group on anyone's scorecard.

Adversaries of capitalist greed that the June 20th group were, some of its members had themselves done rather well in the 1980s. As Margaret Thatcher herself might have said, "And why not?" David Hare's plays enjoyed long runs at the National Theatre. John Mortimer's novels and stories became television serials shown in Britain and the United States. And Richard Roger's high-tech Lloyd's Building symbolized the new image of the City of London. In such success there was no cause for shame; why not reward excellent work? But there was, on one level, a certain tension between the left-of-center political ideology and the relatively comfortable economic position of certain members of the June 20th group. In no sense, though, did this invalidate their social commentaries. The contradiction between class position and political ideology was nothing new in the history of the English left. After all, William Morris, perhaps the greatest of Victorian critics of industrial capitalism, used his inherited income (which came from his father's lucrative speculation in tin) partly to help finance his crusade against exploitation of the proletariat. To be fair, this did not diminish or blunt the socialist vision of *News from Nowhere* or make his lectures to the working class any less passionate or worthwhile.

The coterie apparently derived its obscure, if seemingly pedestrian, name from a group of intellectuals who rose against the Luxembourg government on June 20, 1856. Exiled to Paris, they defiantly drank champagne—a stylish gesture, to be sure. But this colorful allusion did little more than give new meaning to the opprobrious term "champagne socialists," a label the June 20th group could not, and did not, avoid, for all their panache. The group was quickly and mercilessly criticized by Tory ministers like John Moore who wanted to take the "elegant writers from Hampstead" to visit the new owners of council houses who took a very different view of "fairness."[39] The group also came in for what seemed to be endless abuse in the press. It was no surprise that the *Daily Telegraph* derided them as trendy, rich socialists. But even Peter Jenkins, the liberal columnist for the *bienpensant Independent,* had little patience for their project.[40]

In a similar vein, left-of-center intellectuals founded a journal to generate an alternative to the "Victorian values" of the enterprise culture. Unfortunately, they decided to bestow on it the name *Samizdat.* It was surely understandable, on one level, for Mrs. Thatcher's critics to invoke enormously courageous underground writers like Vaclav Havel who risked their own welfare and safety to speak out against the Communist regimes of the Soviet Union and the Eastern bloc. But the implicit analogy between their situations was misleading, to say the very least. The Prime Minister had been foolish to try to stop the publication of Peter Wright's *Spycatcher* and, moreover, to exert undue pressure on the BBC to change its tune when it displeased her. The British intelligentsia's worst enemies, however, were greedy materialism and spending cuts. To be sure, these were lamentable, but hardly the same menace to human dignity as a police state. It was one thing to have Big Brother watching you; quite another to have Big Sister ignoring you.

The corruption of English manners and morals in the 1980s became a prominent theme in the political dramas of David Hare, who is a leading social critic opposed to Thatcherism. A number of his plays were great commercial and critical successes. Among the most popular and effective was *Pravda* (written with Howard Brenton), a play which revealed the failure of the liberal establishment to organize against an egregious South African press lord, played superbly by Anthony Hopkins. When the moment to fight arrived, good could not stand up to evil. "Even if a man believes in nothing," Hare observed, "he will always triumph over the man who cannot decide what he believes."[41]

David Hare himself had arrived at some of his enduring commitments early on. Coming of age in the 1960s, the asthmatic young radical braved the "chilling mists and slate-grey skies" of Cambridge, perhaps the worst climate he could have chosen, to complete his education. He decided on Jesus College so that he could study English Literature with Raymond Williams, the preeminent Marxist critic of his day. While at Cambridge, Hare was convinced that "Britain was transparently in crisis. Its institutions were bankrupt. Its ruling class was anathema. Its traditions were a joke." So it seemed natural for Hare to join in a game that was popular with undergraduates of his year, who whiled away evenings arguing about where a single campaign of bombardment might be directed to best effect: the main candidates for destruction being Buckingham Palace, the Houses of Parliament, or the City of London.[42]

Unlike those who disliked Mrs. Thatcher because of where she came from, Hare disliked her for a far better reason: what she believed in and what she had done to the country. A few days after the Tories had won their third consecutive election victory in 1987, Hare had dinner with some friends of his own age in a Somerset village. The man sitting next to him was a successful novelist whose books were regularly in the running for Britain's most prestigious literary prizes. He happened to ask what Hare did with whatever extra money he earned from his writing. When Hare responded that he put it in the bank, the novelist replied: "Well, your bank manager must *love* you." The novelist, like everyone else he knew, had a portfolio of stocks to which he devoted an hour each morning before sitting down to write. This exchange brought home to Hare "that it was I, not he, who was way out of step with the mood of the times. Only a few years ago a novelist who began his day by scanning the *Financial Times* would have been a figure of universal fun. But now a playwright who was too stupid to know that a crazy boom was going on had become the contemporary figure of mockery." The most remarkable Conservative achievement of the 1980s was to "make any of us whose eyes wander from the main chance feel guilty and foolish for our lack of acumen."[43] And yet did not Hare himself profit from his literary work during this period. Was this immoral also?

In *The Secret Rapture* (1988), Hare dramatized the impact of Thatcherism on certain enlightened middle-class individuals who had led comfortable, decent lives and enjoyed their businesses. The play hinges on the contrast between two sisters and their values. The one, Marion, is a thrusting Tory politician in the Thatcherite mold, a junior minister at the Department of Environment, dedicated to self-help and contemptuous of charity. Marion's only apparent regret is that her political position is such that it prevents her, more or less, from benefiting from the great economic boom of the mideighties. "Unfortunately I've got to help drive the gravy train. I'd rather be clambering on the back and joining in the fun," she tells her sister, the fun in question being making money.[44] Profiteering is far from the mind of her sister, Isobel, a humane and kind-hearted commercial artist. For all her aesthetic dedication to her craft, Isobel is still mindful of her personal obligations and takes care of her irresponsible, alcoholic stepmother after her father's death.

The Secret Rapture delivers a heavy-handed attack on entrepreneurial values. When Marion and her husband Tom, an evangelical businessman, approach Isobel with an offer to infuse much-needed capital into her firm in exchange for ownership, she is reluctant to accept. Marion insists: "Don't be ridiculous. Are you crazy? There's money to be made. Everyone's making it."[45] Isobel finally relents. The expansion, however, does not lead to the bonanza predicted, and Tom quickly reneges on his pledge not to interfere in the business. Determined to protect his investment (while saying a prayer, no doubt), Tom closes the design firm irrespective of the consequences for all those involved, his sister-in-law included. Isobel asks for no quarter for herself, remarking, "I think I have just been *asset-stripped*. Isn't that the term for it? 'Objectively,' as you would say, I have just been trashed and spat out in lumps."[46]

The Secret Rapture is a passionate critique of the greed, materialism, and selfishness that Hare saw overtaking England during the Thatcher years. And yet, was Tom and Marion's greed endemic to capitalism, and the desire to make money, necessarily evil? Had Tom been willing to sustain his support for Isobel's expanding business, the result would have been more jobs, and more secure jobs, for more people—surely not an ignoble result. But Hare stacks the deck against the entrepreneurial ethic as if there's something wrong with trying to make a profit, as if a business can survive without a surplus and commercial mediocrity is a badge of honor.

In the face of such moral corruption, David Hare celebrated "English values," an undefined blend of compassion, caring, and community that would prevail over "Thatcherism," an insidious historical aberration. And yet his paean to humanitarian sensitivity and critique of capitalist greed falls prey to a certain romantic nostalgia for a mythical past.

In Hare's film *Strapless* (1989), starring Blair Brown, Bruno Ganz, and Bridget Fonda, he contrasts the hollowness of business with the humanity of service. Lillian Hempel, an expatriate American doctor working in the National Health Service, does good work curing or comforting the sick, but carefully maintains a strict sense of detachment from her patients, holding both life and death at arm's length. She falls in love with and marries Raymond Forbes, a rootless man with an uncertain past. An archetypal finance capitalist, he is a culture hero of the capitalist revolution, but not for Hare. When Lillian and Raymond meet, she asks what his job is. "Entrepreneur," he replies. "What on earth does that mean?" Lillian responds. "I buy and sell."[47]

Meanwhile, the National Health Service hospital in which Lillian works faces "a period of almost infinite contraction" because of chronic underfunding and budget cuts from the Thatcher government. Contrasted with the bustling, dilapidated, and overcrowded hospital wards in which devoted doctors and nurses strain to take care of their patients is the slick, modernistic emptiness of Raymond's office in the City. Looking out onto St. Paul's Cathedral, the rooms are almost bare, aside from a fax machine, a computer screen, an electric typewriter, and a desk full of cables and telexes—emblems of "paper entrepreneurialism."[48]

But Raymond's glittering affluence proves to be as much a mirage as the Thatcher boom. Financially bankrupt and morally dubious, the entrepreneur has bought but not sold; lived on borrowed money while racking up large gambling debts; and satisfied his consuming passions with a flood of gifts for Lillian. Equally incapable of facing up to the dailiness of an unmystified life with her or paying off his shady creditors, Raymond, a man whose packed overnight bag is always handy, flees the country. It is his bewildered but always responsible new wife who picks up the bill.

As Lillian loses her illusions about Raymond, she finds it in her heart to take up the fight to defend her hospital and patients against the cuts that threaten them. Addressing her fellow staff at a protest meeting, she confesses to sailing to England "for an idea of Englishness which perhaps was ridiculous, but which, incredibly, I have always managed to find."[49] So Lillian finally commits to taking political action in the name of the caring spirit which Hare idealizes as the genius of the English people, their capacity to create networks of support and mutuality. The film ends with a powerful image of a group of women doctors and nurses who put on a fashion show to protest the cuts. Their strapless dresses, designed by Lillian's sister, Amy, symbolize art in the service of humanity. They shouldn't stand up, Amy comments, but they do, and they do so together just as their models stand in common cause to save the hospital and the people it serves.

Two of John Mortimer's novels, *Paradise Postponed* (1985) and *Titmuss Regained* (1990), explore how enterprise culture has contaminated English manners and morals. Like Hare, Mortimer was a member of the June 20th group and indeed had a flat near Hare in Notting Hill in West London, a reasonably trendy, racially mixed, and suitably literary quarter best known for the Portobello flea market and the annual carnival. Even though Mortimer was extremely critical of Thatcher and Thatcherism, his "terrible tendency to like people" softened his views. He went so far as to admit (but also kept in check) a certain sympathy for Norman Tebbit, the free market street fighter, who was what he was, made no bones about it, and didn't much care who knew it. By the same token, Mortimer became quite fond of his own fictional Thatcherite, Leslie Titmuss.[50]

The barrister son of a barrister father, Mortimer was best known at the time as a lawyer for fighting against the censorship of D. H. Lawrence's *Lady Chatterley's Lover*. And he was also the creator of the delightful stories of Rumpole of the Old Bailey, the curmudgeonly hack who hit Shakespearean heights while defending the criminal depths, prowling the local wine bars, and evading as best he could the dictates of his wife Hilda, "she who must be obeyed." Hailing from the professional middle class, Mortimer was reared in a rather genteel milieu in which business was considered slightly disreputable, money unmentionable, and the accumulation of wealth undesirable. A sense of moral superiority was easy to come by for those who could take their material well-being for granted. But such an attitude to economic success was errant nonsense for the working class, who could not afford to condemn what they did not have.

A man of the old rather than the new left, Mortimer belonged to the generation who came of age during World War II, a time when "everyone was on the same side." So he objected to the divisive spirit with which Margaret Thatcher rent the postwar consensus. Present at the birth of the Welfare State, Mortimer was opposed to her attempts to reform it in the name of self-help. Trying to turn England into a more "American" society preoccupied with getting ahead, making money, and so forth offended both his inherited social values and his acquired political commitments. Surely it was bad enough that the Thatcher government had assaulted the universities and neglected the arts. What was far worse, though, was that the main choices in the 1980s were becoming a middle-class success or surviving in a cardboard box, jumping on the bandwagon or falling by the wayside.[51]

So Mortimer remained loyalty to the old-time religion, the socialism of his youth. But he was also aware that this led to certain ironies. He recalled the eightieth birthday party of Barbara Castle, the formidable grande dame of the Labour Party who served in and chronicled Wilson's Cabinet. The guests all got rather drunk and cried while singing "Jerusalem" and "The Red Flag." This scene disgusted his daughter's friend, a Russian poet who asked how they could sing such a filthy Communist song? It was, Mortimer responded, like singing, "Auld Lang Syne."[52]

In Leslie Titmuss, Mortimer has created the only really plausible Thatcherite in contemporary literature. Titmuss hails from modest stock. His father was a clerk who worked all his life in the local brewery and his mother worked in the kitchen of Doughty Strove, MP, a dim Tory squire who believed in capital punishment, corporal punishment, large subsidies for landowners growing sunflower seeds, and an end to diplomatic relations with France. Hardworking and clever, if charmless and unimaginative, Titmuss cuts nettles in other people's gardens to make money—an emblem of his low station and prickly personality. What he lacks in polish, he more than makes up for in determination. After attending the village school, Leslie wins a scholarship to Hartscombe Grammar School, trains as a chartered accountant, and becomes involved in the local Conservative Party—all in the name of getting on. But the old-fashioned, old-line county Tories look down upon Leslie, who rents a dinner jacket and pre-made bow tie to attend the Young Conservatives' dance. Snubbed by his betters at this gala event, some of the more vicious snobs end his evening by hoisting him out of his boat and into the river, "with his arms and legs waving helplessly."[53]

Yet Titmuss eventually triumphs over the old Tory squirearchy and their heirs, thanks to commercial success and marriage to a local magnate's daughter. His clarion call for Thatcherism lauds "the people who know the value of money because they've never had it. . . . The people who've worked hard and don't want to see scroungers rewarded or laziness paying off."[54] This helps him become the Conservative candidate, and then MP, for Hartscombe and South Worsfield. Along the way, he vaults over the scion of an established gentry family. His new Toryism vanquishes the old, just as Mrs. Thatcher dispatched her paternalist rivals.

But Titmuss's gain is England's loss. Mortimer has a certain sympathy for a man who had to overcome county snobbery and working-class deprivations, yet he also depicts his creation as nasty, dishonest, manipulative, and greedy. Eventually Titmuss becomes Secretary of State for Housing, Ecological Affairs and Planning (HEAP), where he aids and abets those who want to concrete over the "green and pleasant land" idealized by Romantic social critics since Wordsworth. In *Titmuss Regained,* Mortimer depicts the destructive incursion of market forces that threaten, and damage, the beauty of rural England and the peace of its small towns. The novel dramatizes the conflict between capitalist profiteering and ecological preservation, between those who want England to be leaner and those who want it to be greener. Once a "small and sleepy riverside town" with brick and flint houses, Hartscombe itself and the Rapstone Valley that surrounds it are under threat. The town no longer has a butcher, an ironmonger, or a fish shop. Instead, local businesses sell life insurance, shoes, electrical appliances, Jacuzzis, gold-tapped bidets, and scented hangers.[55]

David Lodge's *Nice Work* (1989) also captures the tension between the capitalist revolution and its intellectual opponents, but does so more even-handedly than Mortimer's or Hare's work. A writer and critic who grew up in industrial Birmingham and taught for many years at Birmingham University, Lodge was well placed to observe the worlds of production and art. His highly allusive novel, rooted in the condition-of-England fiction of the mid-nineteenth century, uses a thick web of citation to connect Victorian and contemporary conflicts. The action takes place during 1986, which the Thatcher government designated as "Industry Year." A "Shadow Scheme" brings together university lecturer Robyn Penrose with manager Vic Wilcox.

The protagonists figure as polar opposites. An upwardly mobile, relentlessly practical Philistine, Vic comes from a working-class family without airs or graces. Educated at a local grammar school and college of advanced technology, he never acquired the cultural veneer of his social betters. What Vic lacks in genteel manners, though, he more than makes up for in sheer push. "If it wasn't for a bit of aggression, he wouldn't be where he is now."[56] His own hard work propelled the mechanical engineer into the managing directorship of J. Pringle & Sons Casting and General Engineering, and with it a 4.2 Jaguar saloon and large, centrally heated suburban house with constant hot water and four toilets. This is a huge step up from the "back to back" with an outhouse in which his grandparents had lived. Robyn Penrose comes from a "very different social species." Daughter of the professional middle class (her father was a professor of diplomatic history), the counter-culture of the late 1960s and 1970s shaped her commitment to personal liberation, sexual freedom, and the inner life. The aptly named Dr. Penrose becomes a feminist, post-structuralist critic who manages to write a dissertation on the industrial novel without even entering a factory. For all her ability, this victim of the Thatcher government's cuts to universities was only able to find a temporary lectureship.

Initially, Robyn and Vic have little sympathy for each other. If they were, in Carl Jung's symbolic sense, "shadows" of each other, this affinity was obscure to them both. Having come up the hard way, Vic doesn't believe there is a free lunch (even if he couldn't attribute the statement to Milton Friedman). So he has little patience for Robyn's argument that British universities need more money. "Who pays?" and "Can the country afford it?" he asks. Such talk is anathema to Robyn, a trendy left-winger who thinks that education should be about ideas and feelings rather than how machines work. She finds Vic's works "appalling. . . . The noise. The dirt. The mindless repetitive work. The everything." By contrast, her work is "nice work. It's meaningful. It's rewarding. I don't mean in money terms."[57]

Gradually, though, Robyn and Vic come to appreciate each other and their respective worlds. Whereas Elizabeth Gaskell's Margaret Hale and John Thornton eventually marry in *North and South,* their modern counterparts have only a brief affair. But by the end of *Nice Work* they arrive at a rapprochement. Vic becomes a serious reader of literary texts and Robyn appreciates economic realities. The lecturer begins to understand the workings of the market, and the manager comes to see its limitations. So Lodge symbolizes the prospective end of the battle between Britain's intellectual and business cultures.

V

No such common ground seemed to exist between Margaret Thatcher and the Anglican clergy.

Located within a mile of each other in the prosperous Liverpool suburbs of Mossley Hill and Woolton are Archbishop's House and Bishop's Lodge, the respective residences of Derek Warlock, the Roman Catholic archbishop of the city, and David Sheppard, the Anglican bishop. Both lived far from the broken center of Liverpool, well away from the sights and sounds of poverty, but neither avoided them. Instead, the prelates had worked closely together since the mid-1970s when they arrived on the scene in the old port city as unemployment grew and opportunities contracted for young or old alike. That Liverpool had long been in decline was no consolation to anyone.

Neither churchmen is a theological radical, much less a political revolutionary. Yet both share a profound commitment to social action. It was their religious beliefs which led them to a "bias for the poor," in the words of "Bishop David," as local priests call him. A famous former England cricketer who experienced a conversion to Christ while at Cambridge, this gentle, muscular Christian retained his athletic frame long after he first donned a purple tunic. In a hurt city, he was convinced, faith was a healing force. Caring for the soul of the individual cannot mean neglecting the good of the whole. If a group is falling out of the opportunities of God's world, then getting them back in must be a priority. But how could faith assuage the pain of the earthly city if it did not go beyond the confines of church and cathedral?[58]

"At the moment *spiritual* and *political* considerations are not to be found separated in neat and distinct compartments," Sheppard and Warlock wrote in 1989. At a time when self-help was the rock on which Margaret Thatcher built her government, they offered a very different philosophy epitomized by the title of their joint work, *Better Together.* "The deprivation of our neighbour is a matter of concern to our faith. There are faith-issues underlying unemployment, inadequate housing, educational disadvantage, powerlessness and hunger. Can it seriously be contested that despair, loneliness, lack of vision and the crushing of the human spirit are also faith-issues calling for the urgent attention of the Church?"[59]

Such pleas for Christian social action did not please everyone. There were some radical clerics who did not think that these ecumenically minded princes of the church were willing to go far enough. For example, a local priest organized a vigil to protest the closure of the Bird's Eye plant, one of the few large employers left there. Apparently, this did not please Bishop David, who reprimanded him for "ruining everything." Convinced that the closure was already a fait accompli, he had worked secretly behind the scenes for months to strike a deal with the firm. As a result, Bird's Eye pledged to leave funds for community activities. But this was not enough to satisfy the local priest, who would not be swayed from standing in solidarity with those who lost out by economic decisions.[60]

The two churchmen also faced a different brand of critic. At a lunch hosted by a group of businessmen, a man unknown to Derek Warlock told him: "You two bishops have got your values all wrong. . . . I can measure my success by my bank statement. It's quite simple. The bigger the balance, the greater my success." In due time this would enable him to employ more people. "What's wrong with that?" asked the businessman. No believer in the efficacy or morality of trickle-down economics, the archbishop endeavored to explain that there were other values in life, but to no avail. The conversation eventually turned to fly-fishing on the River Itchen, where Warlock himself had been brought up. His neighbor had the temerity to tell him: "The trouble with you is that you're in the wrong business. . . . You should be like me—have more money in the bank and more time for yourself."[61] It was such attitudes that the prelates had to counter in order to help the people of Liverpool.

When the two bishops learned that United Biscuits, one of the last large employers on Merseyside, was about to close its Liverpool plant, they journeyed to London to seek a reprieve from its chairman, Sir Hector Laing. A Scot born to a wealthy business family, Laing was not one to dismiss the claims of faith or the responsibilities of business. Sometimes described as Mrs. Thatcher's favorite businessman, he was a capitalist with a conscience. As chairman of Business in the Community, an organization whose patron was Prince Charles, he worked on the premise that as government stepped back in the 1980s, business had to step forward.

So the prelates had reason to believe that Sir Hector would at least listen to their cause. Sitting in his company flat in a comfortable building in Knightsbridge, they duly explained that closing the United Biscuits plant would only aggravate Merseyside's already horrendous unemployment. Finally, Bishop David asked: "Hector, is there anything we can do to change your mind?" Sir Hector gave a memorable reply: "Yes, there is. Get down on your knees and pray—that people eat more biscuits."[62] Whether the bishops followed suit or customers flocked to the supermarket we do not know, but at all events Laing went ahead with his plan to shut down the works.

This tale of bishops and biscuits is typical of the conflict of values that set the Christian hierarchy against the Thatcher government. The outbreak of hostilities between the Church of England and the Conservative Party seemed to fly in the face of the traditional alliance between two pillars of the establishment.

But the fact that the Anglican Church was not a comfortable bastion in the 1980s for Tories at prayer should not have been altogether surprising. For the ecclesiastical hierarchy had long been dubious about the capitalist spirit. It was indeed slow initially to respond to the advent of industrialism and the social problems that accompanied it. By the mid-nineteenth century, though, at least some clergymen such as the Reverend James Hole, who set up a mission in Leeds, began to address the needs of the alienated poor. When the aristocratic hero of Disraeli's *Sybil*, Charles Egremont, called for an alliance between the nobility and the people to end the rift between the "two nations," he could invoke the church as an ally. In a similar fashion, Thomas Carlyle idealized the ordered world of the medieval monastery in *Past and Present*. And F. D. Maurice used the Gospels to support Christian socialism. In the 1880s and 1890s, the "discovery of poverty" spurred a number of Christian groups—the stalwart Salvation Army among them—to minister to the needs, both material and spiritual, of the poor and wayward in the East End of London.

In fact, the Church of England's decidedly anti-industrial tone never abated. Its leadership, nearly all educated at the top public schools and Oxbridge, found it natural to disapprove of the business world.[63] Clergy of different political stripes joined together in presenting the rush for economic growth as a threat to the integrity of a moral society. The dean of St. Paul's Cathedral, William Ralph Inge, criticized the passion for accumulation in modern life, denouncing "economism" and "consumptionism." R. H. Tawney, the leading light of the Anglican left, shared some of these views. This graduate of Rugby and Oxford hailed from a prominent family that was involved with beer, banking, and engineering during the Industrial Revolution. But when the Tawney company happened to deliver its records to the London School of Economics, the historian displayed not a flicker of interest in their contents. Such attitudes were in keeping with the social gospel preached in the interwar era by William Temple, the archbishop of Canterbury, who saw unemployment as the great social evil and whose popular *Christianity and Social Order* was typical of the church's unease with industrial development.[64]

In view of the clergy's long-standing antagonism to industrial capitalism, the Church of England naturally contributed to the choir of idealistic dissent. More surprising, though, was the intensity of the ecclesiastical reaction against the capitalist revolution, which many tended to see as a direct assault on the poor. It was the bishop of Durham (whose unorthodox theology and sympathy with the miners had already aroused

Mrs. Thatcher's ire) who struck the keynote in an address at Bristol Cathedral in 1986. Horrified that the average salary for one firm of City stockbrokers was £47,000 (plus stock options), Durham asked: "But what about the several millions of our fellow citizens who have no prospects whatever, either immediately, or in a medium-term foreseeable future, of taking part in this type of sufficiently-resourced participation in an ownership democracy?"[65]

The most telling response came at the end of 1985 with a publication by the archbishop of Canterbury's Commission on Urban Priority Areas. Its authors included socially committed members of the church hierarchy such as Bishop David Sheppard and laymen such as Limbert Spencer, the head of Project Full Employ, who provided a first-hand view of inner-city life.[66] Charged by the archbishop, the Reverend Robert Runcie, with examining the state of the city and suggesting what could be done by church and nation to ameliorate the plight of the poor, the report recalled Victorian explorations of the alienation of the laboring and non-laboring poor from the church. *Faith in the City*, as the report was called, displayed little faith in the current policies of church or state. Rather, the report portrayed a clergy largely removed from the struggles of the people of the inner city. Moreover, it suggested a number of ways to allay their suffering, such as the creation of a Church Urban Fund.

What aroused a furor, though, was *Faith in the City*'s indictment of the policies of the Thatcher government. Starting with the principle that the church should remember the poor, as St. Paul insisted, it cited both the Old and New Testaments to support its exhortations against the excessive individualism and unbounded materialism of the capitalist revolution. Researched and written at a time when unemployment was at its height, *Faith in the City* refused to accept the official government line that "nothing could be done" to help the jobless. And its authors were no more willing to accept the fact that the pain of rationalizing industry fell on those least able to absorb it. The communitarian message of the report was unmistakable:

> The creation of wealth must go hand in hand with just distribution. The product must have some intrinsic value, and its production must have due regard to social and ecological consequences. There is a long Christian tradition, reaching back into the Old Testament prophets, and supported by influential schools of economic and political thought, which firmly rejects the amassing of wealth unless it is justly obtained and fairly distributed. If these provisos are not insisted upon, the creation of wealth cannot go unchallenged as a first priority for national policy.[67]

This passage takes for granted the ability of the individual or the nation to create wealth or jobs. It blurred the fact that Jewish and Christian economic ethics were not the same and indeed that there was considerable variation within each faith. And the passage does not explain precisely what "just distribution" actually means. (Is it just that those who do work must support those who refuse to do so?) Yet the report did not take an entirely negative stance toward Thatcher policies. It did, for instance, make some mention of the value of local enterprise and of small business. But this was hardly a dominant theme in a document which the archbishop himself characterized as a Christian critique with political implications.

Shooting or silencing the messenger seemed preferable to listening to the message, as far as the Prime Minister and her allies were concerned. The reaction to *Faith in the City* was broadly similar to certain responses to the bishops' sharp critique of Reagonomics in America. More than willing to allow the Roman Catholic Church into the bedroom to shape public policy and private conduct when it came to matters of birth control and the like, conservatives resisted intervention in the boardroom. Controlling private parts was one thing; regulating private enterprise quite another.

Nothing if not eager to extinguish a political hellfire before it began, Tory MPs denounced *Faith in the City* as "Marxist" (which it certainly was not) and "collectivist" (which was not far from the truth) even before its publication. It was easier to dismiss, or marginalize, the churchmen as "Pink Bishops" than to take their ideas to heart. Mrs. Thatcher herself confessed to reading the report "with the greatest possible interest." But interest does not connote respect, much less admiration. Unwilling to look at, much less attack, the underlying structural causes of social problems, she criticized *Faith in the City* for failing to make recommendations concerning individuals and families.[68]

By far the most controversial response to *Faith in the City* came from the man often referred to as the Prime Minister's favorite clergyman, Sir (later Lord) Immanuel Jakobovits, the Chief Rabbi of the British Empire. Not one to turn away from controversy, the German Jewish émigré from Nazism (who had served as Chief Rabbi of Ireland before a stint at a Fifth Avenue synagogue in New York) was one of the few notable Orthodox Jews to criticize Israeli policy on the West Bank and to call for better treatment for Palestinian refugees. Liberal on foreign policy Sir Immanuel sometimes was, but no such description applied to his domestic social attitudes. Opposed to any force which, in his view, detracted from the family, he was highly critical of both feminism and homosexuality.

Sir Immanuel was also a good soldier of the capitalist revolution. Having criticized the Welfare State as early as 1977 for encouraging a "get something for nothing attitude" at odds with Jewish tradition, the chief rabbi took on the established church in his pamphlet *From Doom to Hope* (1985), a spirited defense of self-help, individual responsibility, and the work ethic. (In a similar vein, his successor, Dr. Jonathan Sacks, legitimized aspects of Mrs. Thatcher's social philosophy by recourse to the Hebrew Bible in a pamphlet the same year entitled *Wealth and Poverty*.) Certain that "cheap labour is better than a free dole," Sir Immanuel argued that government policy should promote work rather than welfare, even though he recognized the importance of the safety net for the unfortunate. Work provided a means to build self-respect and nurture pride, both of which were cornerstones of economic success.

Rather than look to government for aid as the authors of *Faith in the City* recommended, Sir Immanuel offered a very different approach to the people of the inner city. He exhorted ethnic minorities, particularly West Indian blacks, to emulate the example of Jewish immigrants, whose prosperity came from their own efforts, who took care of their own people, and who respected the law. What the chief rabbi failed to address, however, was the degree to which the unique culture and experience of European Jews really could provide a model for those who did not have the benefit of a highly literate tradition and strong families that valued educational achievement and supported economic ambitions. The fact that Sir Immanuel's message was similar, in certain respects, to that preached by Black Muslims, who also called for self-help, did not make it any less inflammatory. More to the point, Sir Immanuel's individualistic creed failed to give sufficient attention to the Jewish emphasis on communal obligation and charitable work. By 1990, though, he was articulating a more moderate position, emphasizing his dissatisfaction with the harmful impact of Thatcher policies on the decline of public services, particularly the threats to the National Health Service.[69]

Within the "Jewish community" and indeed within the far larger category known as "non-Jews," the chief rabbi's response to the bishops caused a major flap. His position was no shock to conservative Jews in areas of Northwest London such as the Prime Minister's own Finchley constituency, which was full of middle-class business and professional families who had worked their way up from modest circumstances and out of the East End. But even those who agreed with the chief rabbi, voted for Margaret Thatcher, and endorsed the enterprise culture feared an anti-Semitic backlash from too close an identification with her policies. Other Jews were embarrassed by Sir Immanuel's refusal to buckle under to the bishops or, at least, to keep duly quiet. Liberal or left-wing Jews, courageous or craven, were particularly eager to dissociate themselves, for obvious reasons, from any link between Jewishness and Thatcherism.

One of the most disturbing salvos came from an enlightened man, Hugo Young, in a *Guardian* column written around the time of the Prime Minister's first official trip to Israel. Mrs. Thatcher, he wrote, "is in some senses an honorary Jew herself." His piece also implied that she was overly influenced by Jewish values and indeed by the state of Israel. He stopped short of urging a return to Christian virtues, but some believed that this was his subtext. In any case, Young's account was misleading. He paid scant attention to Jewish values that had little place in Thatcherism. He had little to say about the importance of charity in Jewish life and tradition. And he ignored the social commitment of Jewish entrepreneurs and businesses, such as the Sieff family of Marks & Spencer.[70]

The piece caused an explosion. On the morning it appeared, Julia Neuberger, a well-known Reform rabbi and broadcaster who happened to be a friend of Young's, received no less than twenty-eight phone calls before 8:00 A.M. from Jewish *Guardian* readers troubled by its implications. Although the rabbi and the journalist had a short-lived row over the piece, her husband, Anthony Neuberger, who teaches at the London Business School, urged him not to be put off by the controversy.[71] For his part, Young, who was apparently both shocked and troubled by the offense he unintentionally gave, offered a far more judicious and balanced view of the matter in his biography of Mrs. Thatcher.[72]

Julia Neuberger, though, agreed with neither the Prime Minister, the chief rabbi, the bishops, nor Hugo Young on the question of the capitalist revolution. Actively involved in a wide range of social work and charitable causes, she was certainly aware of the importance of the issues raised by *Faith in the City*. But she considered its social, economic, and political analysis deeply flawed. The strengths of the report were its success in calling attention to the plight of the poor and its often moving account of the problems they faced. While Neuberger considered the chief rabbi's response "profoundly unhelpful," and indeed irrelevant to the British situation, she totally rejected the bishops' "bias to the poor." It wrongly assumed that the poor were morally superior to the rich. What made this position particularly objectionable was that it often came from parish clergy who decried the fruits of capitalism while living comfortable lives in lovely towns and villages in the South of England.

The bias to the poor had little resonance in Jewish tradition, which had no equivalent to the Franciscan ideal of poverty. Indeed, it found considerable attractions (as well as dangers) in being rich, not the least of which was the ability to use money to do good for the community and to help the needy. A strong but not uncritical advocate of entrepreneurship, Neuberger was impatient with the genteel hypocrisy of those who found inherited wealth more or less acceptable but liked to look down on those who made fortunes by building businesses. Eschewing the extremes of the left and the right, she sought a balance between competition and compassion. Her centrist approach combined her reform Jewish roots with her commitment to the Social Democratic/Liberal Alliance. Encourage a free market but temper its excesses and mitigate its inequities by welfare and cooperation—this was her position.[73]

The Prime Minister herself said little in public about the reactions of the Christian clergy to her policies, if not her person, much as she preferred to ignore Oxford's refusal to confer on her an honorary degree. And yet such hostility must have been painful to Margaret Thatcher, who considered herself to be a good Christian, a faithful member of the Church of England, and an able defender of its faith. For the irony of all the uproar was that the woman whose policies were being attacked was perhaps the most religious of twentieth-century prime ministers. Moreover, her government arguably took a more serious interest in matters religious than any of its predecessors since Gladstone.[74]

Not one to keep silent forever, though, Mrs. Thatcher finally provided a full explanation of the relationship between her religious beliefs and her political convictions. This was the theme of her address to the General Assembly of the Church of Scotland in Edinburgh, in May 1988. Giving almost equal weight to the testimony of the Old and New Testaments, the onetime Methodist found in the Bible a basis for "a view of the universe, a proper attitude to work, and principles to shape economic and social life." In her address, the Prime Minister drew on Holy Scripture to legitimate the values of the enterprise culture. To the surprise of no one, personal responsibility was near the heart of her interpretation of the Christian message. So she purposefully repeated, but wrested out of context, St. Paul's statement to the Thessalonians, "If a man will not work he shall not eat," as if he was a Poor Law Commissioner of the 1830s dispatching the feckless to the almshouse and kicking them for good measure. And she quoted with approval his warning to Timothy that anyone who neglects to provide for his own house (meaning his own family) has disowned the faith and is worse than an infidel.[75]

But was not the quest for wealth Mammon's work? "Thou shalt not covet," the Tenth Commandment, suggested the dangers of making money and owning things. Yet Mrs. Thatcher argued, with some justification, that "it is not the creation of wealth that is wrong but love of money for its own sake." She was also partly right to argue that it was difficult to respond "to the many calls of help . . . unless we had first worked hard and used our talents to create the necessary wealth." It does not follow, however, that "the spiritual dimension comes in deciding what one does with the wealth."[76] Mrs. Thatcher's blinkered approach jumbled means and ends and in so doing begged a crucial question which the Quaker industrialist George Cadbury asked of his fellows: "but how did you come by the money?"

And how could a faithful Christian negotiate the respective obligations of the individual and the state? The Prime Minister endorsed the idea that "the only way we can ensure that no-one is left without sustenance, help or opportunity, is to have laws to provide for health and education, pensions for the elderly, succor for the sick and disabled."[77] In other words, it was not possible to do without the safety net of the Welfare State. Yet Mrs. Thatcher emphasized that "any set of social and economic arrangements which is not founded on the acceptance of individual responsibility will do nothing but harm."[78] Individual action was therefore better than state intervention, just as charity was better than welfare. Such was her Christian defense of the capitalist revolution's morality. But what good did such words do for those in need?

VI

THE HOSTILE REACTIONS TO THE PRIME MINISTER'S ADDRESS were one more sign of the ongoing cultural struggle that rent England during the iron age. Just as Margaret Thatcher damaged the standing of the intelligentsia with the charge that their anti-industrial bias had contributed to the nation's economic decline, they struck back with the charge that the enterprise culture she preached was nothing more than a heartless and vulgar materialism. In the economic world, Mrs. Thatcher succeeded in ending the rule of state industry and curbing the power of the trade unions, turning England, for better or worse, into a meaner and leaner society. In the political world, she sent packing the old-line Tory paternalists who adhered to the postwar consensus, putting in their stead far hungrier individuals with heartier appetites.

In the cultural world, though, Mrs. Thatcher was notably less successful in reversing the tide that threatened her control of the kingdom. Much as Victorian and Edwardian social critics contained, but were unable to destroy, the radical spirit of the Industrial Revolution, dampening the ardor for the practical, the profitable, and the productive, their intellectual heirs stood in the way of Mrs. Thatcher's attempt to revive the enterprise culture. No legislation could undo the "cordon sanitaire," in Martin Wiener's words, which attempted to keep industry at the cultural borders of the world's first industrial nation.[79] Yet the so-called chattering classes resisted the onslaught of Mrs. Thatcher's capitalist revolution in the name of preserving a kinder, gentler Britain as well as guarding their own threatened territory.

Like Matthew Arnold's ignorant armies who clash by night, the advocates and adversaries of the capitalist revolution fought to determine Britain's fate. Both sides were partly right and partly wrong. The intellectual opposition had good reason to protest the excesses of materialism and the want of compassion they saw in the Thatcher years. They were right to argue that education and culture had an intrinsic worth over and above what they fetched in the marketplace and that access to museums and the like should not be confined to those who could afford to pay the price of admission. But they seemed blind to the fact that Britain could not go on forever distributing what it had not produced. And they seemed equally obtuse about the legitimacy of efforts to make money in order to provide the basis for a secure life. For their part, Mrs. Thatcher's allies were right to point out that the country had to make its way in the world and that there was no shame in that. But if "getting on" was not an invidious plot of the wicked against the righteous, there was something ignoble about getting on on the backs of the poor.

With each party convinced of the justice of their cause and the wickedness of their opponents, there was cause to declare a plague on both your houses. For the cultural struggle of the Thatcher years obscured the necessity of arriving at a middle ground that reconciled two visions: on the one hand Britain as a garden and on the other hand Britain as a workshop. This was a tragic schism, for if the workshop faltered, little could be done, in the long run, to help those who were needy and disaffected. And yet if the garden was ruined, what would be left to enjoy?

Whatever the strengths and weaknesses of the intelligentsia, it did not succeed in unseating Mrs. Thatcher. Yet she fell anyway. Why and how is the final question.

CHAPTER

TEN

Things Fall Apart

I

ON MAY 4, 1989, THE TENTH ANNIVERSARY OF MARGARET
Thatcher's ascent to power, a dinner took place at Number 10
for Cabinet ministers and their spouses. "It was a truly
Thatcherite function," Kenneth Baker recalled, "as each of us
paid for ourselves and our wives to enjoy the very English
dinner of salmon, lamb and raspberries. Such self-financing
economics did not, however, blunt the jollity of the occasion." Sir Geoffrey Howe, the Foreign Secretary, called the
long-time leader the greatest peacetime Prime Minister of
the twentieth century.[1] If any of the assembled number had
doubts about her, they kept them well hidden.

Yet there was reason to ask whether Mrs. Thatcher's decade in office had blunted her sense of proportion and perspective. Only recently she had stood on Number 10's steps
and cradled her new grandchild in her arms while announcing: "We have become a grandmother of a grandson." The
Prime Minister's syntax and use of royal language suggested
that her long tenure had obscured her ability to distinguish
between having an heir and holding a crown. Even sentimen-

talists convinced of the divine right of grandparents blinked at such pretensions. Certainly the press, and public, did.

Mrs. Thatcher's tenth anniversary in power would have been an ideal moment to step down. In so doing she would have improved her claim to be one of the most remarkable prime ministers in modern British history. Some of her closest advisers, Denis Thatcher among them, suggested that she retire. But she would not let go. Eighteen months later, she suffered a reversal of her own fortunes. What undid the Iron Lady, and threatened her capitalist revolution, was the result of a series of battles over the economy, Europe, and the poll tax. Ultimately, though, it was her own character and style that detonated these political minefields.

I I

THE CONSERVATIVE PARTY HAD WON THE GENERAL ELECTION of 1987 largely thanks to an economic boom. The mid-1980s were a period of brisk growth. Productivity rose; inflation dropped. Even unemployment fell, albeit slowly. Voters who found more money in their pockets learned to live with aspects of the Thatcher government that they did not much like. A larger house, a fancier car, a better foreign holiday made the Prime Minister's manner and policies more palatable than they might have been otherwise. Critics argued, however, that the "economic miracle" was, in fact, a mirage. Manufacturing output still lagged that before the crash of the early Thatcher years. Affluence was an illusion fueled by a consumer boom that could not last.[2] But the prosperity of the mid-1980s, and its tangible fruits, certainly felt real. The happy majority's standard of living was rising fast. So the sense of economic recovery, well founded or not, helped the Conservatives win a third consecutive election victory.

The hero of the day was Nigel Lawson, the Chancellor.

He had never been popular in his own party. His intellectual ability won him few friends, and his arrogant manner grated. In the wake of the 1987 election, though, Lawson was the man of the moment. If all was not forgiven, it certainly was forgotten. Some talked of the Chancellor as a future Foreign Secretary; others saw in him a future Prime Minister. In his memoirs, he titled one chapter "An Election Won on the Economy." What made his political triumph all the more delicious was that it took place despite "The Effort to Keep Me Out."[3] So Lawson called the largely unsuccessful attempt of the Prime Minister's election team to keep him off television and out of the limelight.

The mixture of economic abundance and electoral success only gave Lawson more cause for confidence and less need for modesty. "The trouble with Nigel is that he's a gambler," said the Prime Minister.[4] It was a common charge—and true—for he liked playing the pools. But he was not the most fortunate of gamblers or investors. He had had to sell his home in Hyde Park Gate when his investments went awry.[5] At any rate, Lawson's victories naturally made him more assured than ever. As one of his associates commented: "The fact of the matter is that he became rather cocky, and this undoubtedly affected the way policy was conducted."[6]

Lawson's gamble was to change the approach to controlling inflation.[7] A leading monetarist in the early years of the Thatcher government, he called off the sentry watch on monetary targets in the run-up to the 1987 election. Instead, he wanted Britain to join the Exchange Rate Mechanism ERM) of the European Monetary System (EMS). But Mrs. Thatcher, ever suspicious of things European, demurred. Not easily put off, the Chancellor fixed on using the exchange rate of sterling as a key to fiscal management. In practice, this meant "shadowing" the Deutschmark. The term had a romantic sound, but a prosaic reality. It meant intervening in the markets to ensure about a three-to-one ratio between the pound and the D-mark. The premise was that gearing the pound to the Deutschmark would help Britain achieve the price stability Germany enjoyed. At any rate, the strategy seemed to work, at least for the moment.

After the 1987 election victory, though, the Chancellor and the Prime Minister fell out. While he denied having his eye set on the top spot, talk of succession disturbed her. "The trouble began," Lawson suggested, "when she discovered that I was widely seen in the Party as the man who had won the 1987 election. For the first time, she started to see me in a completely new light, as a potential rival."[8] Thatcher was not ready to be measured for her political casket. And she was not willing to go along fully with Lawson's economic policy. He wanted to intervene in the market to hold down the escalating pound, but she wanted the invisible hand to decide its level. "There is no way in which one can buck the market," the Prime Minister announced in the Commons. Lawson considered this position naive. More damaging than the argument itself was the harm it did to their personal relations. Mrs. Thatcher believed that the Chancellor had misled her by supposedly not disclosing the fact that he had been shadowing the Deutschmark. "How could I possibly trust him again?" she asked in her memoirs.[9] Was she disingenuous or disillusioned? In any case, the accusation outraged Lawson.[10]

The whiff of dissent between the tenants of Numbers 10 and 11 Downing Street had serious repercussions. It turned the boring technical issues of fiscal policy into juicy news. It also provided fodder for the Labour Party. In May 1989, Labour Leader Neil Knnock asked the Prime Minister at Question Time if she was in full agreement with the Chancellor's economic policy. Mrs. Thatcher was visibly evasive. She complimented Lawson's running of the economy. But she could not, or would not, bring herself to say that she agreed that it was undesirable for the pound to rise any further.[11]

By the autumn of 1989 Lawson had tired of battling on exchange rate policy and the like with the Prime Minister and Alan Walters, the monetarist guru who was her personal economic adviser. In the end, Lawson was forced to choose between submitting to her will and fleeing her dominion. " 'I must prevail' was the phrase that finally broke Nigel Lawson's bond of loyalty and affection," observed Geoffrey Howe, for whom much the same held true.[12] Weary of Walter's criticisms and Thatcher's halfhearted support, the Chancellor went to see the Prime Minister on October 26 to ask her to sack his rival. Only this course of action would steady the financial markets and shore up Lawson's wounded pride. But Mrs. Thatcher rejected his plea. She must have known that the result might be his resignation. Shortly before two o'clock, Lawson returned to the Prime Minister's study on the first floor of Number 10. He handed her his letter of resignation. At first, she refused to take it. Then she slipped the letter in her handbag but said that she did not want to read it. "She begged me not to resign," Lawson later wrote, "heaping extravagant praise and flattery on me." Mrs. Thatcher even mentioned the possibility that one day he might become Governor of the Bank of England. Lawson would not be moved, though.[13] Hours later, John Major, then young, little known, and inexperienced, was named as his successor.

However detrimental Lawson's departure was to the government, the problems that remained went far beyond the question of appearances. An explosion of bank credit and mortgage lending, much of it provoked by the real estate boom, resulted in an overheated economy. Interest rates went up to 14 percent in May 1989 to cool off lending. This move squeezed major players like the Reichmanns, who were then building Canary Wharf. Rocketing interest rates also affected ordinary people. Those who had bought their council homes at bargain rates found it increasingly difficult to pay their mortgages (because in Britain monthly payments are not fixed). In February 1990, mortgage rates reached 15.5 percent.

By then, Britain was in recession. By October, inflation was at 10.9 percent. The economic downturn was a worldwide phenomenon, but it was particularly pronounced in Britain and the United States. Margaret Thatcher had been able to blame the recession of the early 1980s, rightly or wrongly, on her Labour predecessors. This time the buck stopped with her. What made this all the worse politically was that the Prime Minister had staked her claim to power on competent fiscal management and good economic results. If those who lived by the sword died by the sword, those who prevailed in a boom were not likely to survive in a bust.

I I I

CONFLICTS OVER BRITAIN'S PLACE IN EUROPE ALSO ENDAN-gered the fate of the capitalist revolution and its leader.

This had been a bone of contention since the first debates over Britain's prospective entry into the European Economic Community (EEC). When Heath finally succeeded in pushing Britain into the EEC in 1973, much of the Labour Party remained unreconciled. But Mrs. Thatcher was no great resistor of the move. Indeed, she did not show great interest in the matter. First and foremost, she was an Englishwoman of the type gently parodied by Gilbert and Sullivan. Rarely prone to look or go abroad, she was even less likely to approve of what she might have seen there. Her reflexes were traditional rather than chic. In good Victorian fashion, the Prime Minister did not much like the French. Growing up during World War II, she had much more cause to distrust the Germans, whose recent history had shown that they were capable of nearly anything. Her foreign ties, such as they were, extended across the Atlantic rather than the Channel.

Insular Englander that Mrs. Thatcher was by disposition, few could have predicted how central, and indeed disastrous, a role her stance on Europe would be in her undoing. As early as the 1979 campaign, though, she had declared a position she later elaborated. "We believe in a free Europe, not in a standardized Europe. Diminish that variety within the member states, and you impoverish the whole Community."[14] During her first year in office, she put the EEC on notice that she would not simply ante up Britain's unduly large contribution to its budget. Penalized for late entry into Europe, its share of expenses was disproportionate to its income. "I cannot play Sister Bountiful to the Community," she noted in the Winston Churchill Memorial Lecture, "while my own electorate are being asked to forego improvements in the fields of health, education, welfare and the rest."[15] In the event, she did not shrink from insisting on substantial reductions in British contributions. Banging on the table ("handbagging" was the sexist phrase her critics used), the Prime Minister demanded "our money" from the likes of Giscard D'Estaing and Helmut Schmidt. The deal she finally came away with was not as good as she had hoped, but at least it offered a three-year solution to a chronic problem.[16]

What set Mrs. Thatcher seething on Europe? She did not oppose the Single European Act of 1986, which provided for the free movement of capital and labor across Europe by January 1, 1993. But when it came to Jacques Delors's plan for European unity, she showed no such equanimity. A socialist, an intellectual, and a Frenchman to boot, the president of the European Commission did not appeal to her.[17] His multistage proposals culminating in a single European currency and a Social Charter regulating workers' rights (not a vivid notion for her) appealed to the Prime Minister even less. By the summer of 1988, "he had altogether slipped his lead as a *fonctionnaire* and become a fully fledged political spokesman for federalism," she later wrote. So she decided to play dog-catcher and tie up the stray herself.

In a landmark speech before the College of Europe in Bruges, Mrs. Thatcher warned of the dangers centralization posed to the liberty and integrity of individual nations. "We have not successfully rolled back the frontiers of the state in Britain only to see them reimposed at a European level, with a European super-state exercising a new dominance from Brussels." She endorsed "willing and active co-operation between independent sovereign states." What she feared, above all, was a loss of British sovereignty to a European Community controlled by a Franco-German axis. "Europe will be stronger precisely because it has France as France, Spain as Spain, Britain as Britain, each with its own customs, traditions and identity."[18] The Bruges speech did not repudiate the idea of Europe, but it did mark the need for continued boundaries. "Stunned outrage," as Mrs. Thatcher put it, was a fair description of official reactions in Europe.[19]

While the Prime Minister's position on Europe struck a populist chord at home, it also provoked hostile reactions from enthusiasts for Europe inside and outside her own party. In June 1989, the Conservatives took a drubbing from Labour in the European elections. Four years earlier, they had won 45 seats to Labour's 32, but this time the voters reversed the results. Such an electoral setback punctured the confidence of Conservative MPs, who began to fear for their seats if Mrs. Thatcher refused to temper her views. Her suspicious attitude to Europe also put her at cross purposes with the Foreign Secretary, Sir Geoffrey Howe. A dedicated advocate of European unity, he had ushered the Single European Act through Parliament and indeed had done much the same for the legislation that first took Britain into the EEC.

The battle came to a head just before the Madrid Summit. Early on Sunday morning, June 25, the Foreign Secretary and the Chancellor called on the Prime Minister. Their avowed purpose, Howe later wrote, was to end the "semi-public dispute before it caused real damage."[20] Shown into her study, they sat down facing her on the other side of the fireplace. Howe insisted that Mrs. Thatcher step forward at Madrid and specify under what conditions and by what terminal date sterling would enter the ERM. If she refused, they would resign. It was a stunning move. She could ill afford the resignation of her two most powerful ministers. So in Madrid she did their bidding, more or less, while denying that she had done so.

But Mrs. Thatcher bitterly resented "The Ambush Before Madrid," as she later called it. This was hyperbole, at best. For unlike most prospective ambushers, Lawson and Howe had put their intended victim on notice with joint minutes before the act. This did not stop the Prime Minister, however, from seeing their united front as a cabal, or from laying blame. "I knew Geoffrey had put Nigel up to this," she wrote, for he was "now out to make trouble for me if he possibly could." He believed that "he had become indispensable—a dangerous illusion for a politician."[21] If so, it was an illusion she shared about herself.

Mrs. Thatcher wanted to punish the offenders. But Lawson was too powerful to dispatch easily. She respected his nerve even after she had lost faith in his economic judgment and lost patience with his independent attitude. Demoting Howe seemed altogether simpler. In July 1989, therefore, the Prime Minister reshuffled her Cabinet and dismissed the Foreign Secretary. Still, she was not in a position to get rid of him entirely without endangering her own position. As a result, she offered him the leadership of the House of Commons. He accepted on the proviso that she name him Deputy Prime Minister as well. Soon enough, it was clear that this was no great honor. When asked what the post entailed, her Press Secretary, Bernard Ingham, all but said that it meant nothing at all.

So much for allowing Howe to save face.

What made his public whacking even more demeaning was the fact that his altered position meant that the Howes lost both their official residences, Carlton Gardens in London and Chevening in Kent. As a result they were left with no home of their own for the moment—an ironic position given Elspeth Howe's advocacy of the homeless. When Howe first appeared before the House as Leader of the Commons, Conservative backbenchers rose from their seats and warmly applauded him. Mrs. Thatcher should have taken this as a sign that his sacking would come back to haunt her. But then as he announced, "The Business of the House next week will be . . . ," a Labour MP answered: "House hunting." The "Sir Geoffrey Houses" affair, as it came to be known, only exacerbated existing tensions and resentments.[22]

Reshuffling the deck did not solve Mrs. Thatcher's problems with Europe or Europeanists' problem with her. July 13, 1990, proved an unlucky day for Nicholas Ridley, Secretary of State for the Environment and a loyal Thatcherite if ever there was one. In the course of an interview with Dominic Lawson, the Chancellor's son and youthful editor of the *Spectator* like his father before him, the Secretary of State for Industry let fly on the matter of Europe. When it was over, there was no doubt where Ridley stood on the "German problem." "I'm not against giving up sovereignty in principle, but not to this lot," he remarked. "You might just as well give it to Adolf Hitler, frankly." Just in case Ridley's words were not enough, the *Spectator* drove the point home with a spicy image. It pictured a small Ridley running away from a large poster of an equally large Kohl made up to look like Hitler.[23] For a few days, Ridley tried to avoid resigning. First he cried foul and claimed that his remarks had been off the record. Then he apologized. But he had gone so far over the top that he had to walk the plank, even though Mrs. Thatcher wished it were otherwise. Not only did his resignation deprive her of her most reliable Cabinet minister, but many assumed that Ridley had articulated what she felt.

I V

As if Mrs. Thatcher did not have more than enough to handle with matters European and economic, she managed to shoot herself in the foot with the so-called community charge. Dubbed the "poll tax" (since it used electoral registers to identify prospective taxpayers), it was a colossal mistake by any name, the single largest political blunder the Prime Minister made during her tenure.

The quest to reform local government finance began reasonably enough. Nearly everyone agreed that the rates—the current system of property taxation—needed reform. When Mrs Thatcher became Leader of the Opposition in the mid-1970s, she pledged to abolish them. The system was unfair. A widow living on a pension paid as much on her home as four adults who lived next door. A resident of a government-owned council house paid nothing at all. Millions enjoyed representation without taxation: they elected local councils, but paid little if anything toward their expenditures. Those who spent time and money improving their homes found that their investments led to higher rates—a result Mrs. Thatcher found especially reprehensible.[24]

All in all, then, there was cause to look for another method of financing local government. But a second motive came into play and made the prospect of scrapping the rates particularly attractive: the desire to discipline local government. What the Conservatives needed was a means to control and punish "spendthrift" Labour-controlled councils (the worst offenders were in Liverpool and parts of London) who would not stop spending other people's money.

The "community charge" promised, but failed to deliver, a

change for the better. Intricate and unwieldly in practice, its premise was simple: Everyone pays. In other words, if every adult beneficiary of local council spending shared equally in the costs, the result would be "clear accountability."[25] The annual charge's amount would vary, but one prediction held that it would be relatively low, on average £180. Under Kenneth Baker's plan, every adult eighteen or over would pay, but persons with low incomes would receive state assistance. Central government would inform local authorities of their grant for the coming year, so that they could plan accordingly. Every penny they saved would benefit the council and community. But there was a clincher: each additional pound they spent would have to come from their own coffers. The premise was that once the electorate recognized that increased spending led to higher community charges, they would throw the scoundrels out. As it turned out, the scoundrels they blamed were in the Thatcher government.

Many Conservatives had had their hands on planning the community charge, though few freely admitted it after the fact. But Lawson condemned the idea from the start and warned Mrs. Thatcher that it was a huge mistake. "I pointed out to her very early on the many dangers it posed; but without any support from Cabinet colleagues I was unable to persuade her that they were real."[26] Yet she had not simply "bounced" his fellow ministers into accepting it.[27] Nevertheless, there were plenty of warning signals auguring the impending political disaster. In July 1987, a Gallup Poll revealed that public opinion had turned against the poll tax: only 27 percent thought it was fairer than the rates. When the Local Government Finance Bill came to a vote that December, the government majority sank by some 29 votes as Conservative MPs voted against the bill or abstained, as did Michael Heseltine. Despite the protests that accompanied the poll tax's introduction to Scotland (where nearly everything the government did went down badly), Mrs. Thatcher and company went ahead with their plan in England.

Fatally flawed, the poll tax was hard to understand, hard to collect, and hard to pay for. In the event, it proved far more expensive than early predictions had suggested, in some cases to the tune of three or four times higher. It was also strikingly unequal. Consider the positions of Londoners who lived south of the river in Conservative-controlled Wandsworth and north in Labour-controlled Harringay. The former's community charge came to a bargain price of £148 while the latter was saddled with £573. To make matters worse, a nanny who lived in an affluent Highgate household and made £8,000 or so a year was bound to pay as much as her employer who earned far more. The poll tax outraged Robert Horton, a moderate Conservative and chairman of BP (British Petroleum), who had two homes. The gardener who landscaped the chairman's country house had to pay a much higher community charge on his own home than Horton did on his far more expensive Westminster residence. This seemed so unjust that Horton's wife declared herself unable to vote Tory in good conscience.[28] Small wonder, then, that a "can't pay—won't pay" campaign against the poll tax caught on or that Trafalgar Square protests in April 1990 degenerated into a riot.

The poll tax became a symbol of injustice. Although its intentions were not all unreasonable, it dramatized and confirmed the belief that Mrs. Thatcher was uncaring and unfair. If this was the capitalist revolution's end result, how long would the public, to say nothing of her own party, support the Iron Lady of Downing Street?

V

BY THE AUTUMN OF 1990, THEN, THE THATCHER GOVERNMENT was in serious peril. But even if the Prime Minister's fall was in some sense overdetermined, a number of contingencies combined to jettison her from office.

The fiercest push came from Sir Geoffrey Howe. He had swallowed or deflected public abuse for years from Mrs. Thatcher. It is hard to believe that he did so out of loyalty alone. But as his chances of succeeding her faded and her conduct toward him worsened, the payoff for duty and restraint disappeared. She had removed him from a position he relished; deprived him of houses; and shoved him to the political sidelines. The Prime Minister's style, her insistence on dominating the Cabinet and limiting the power of its committees, disturbed him also. All this was reason enough for Howe to strike back. What provoked him beyond toleration, though, was a combination of personal outrage and principled disagreement.

The catalyst was Europe. On October 5, Mrs. Thatcher finally allowed her new Chancellor, John Major, to bring sterling into the ERM, but this did not mean that she had become reconciled to the prospect of European unity. This came to the fore on October 30 when she reported to the House on the results of the Rome Summit. Pressed by Neil Kinnock, she took aim:

> The President of the Commission, Mr. Delors, said at a press conference the other day that he wanted the European Parliament to be the democratic body of the Community. He wanted the Commission to be the Executive and he wanted the Council of Ministers to be the Senate.

Then Mrs. Thatcher fired: "No, No, No." During her outburst, Howe sat beside her and tried to smile, while no doubt
entertaining very different sentiments. For her proclamation
of national sovereignty flouted his vision of Britain playing a
central role in a united Europe.

As if this was not enough to make Howe consider his options, the Prime Minister gave him further cause. At Cabinet
on November 1 she took him to task, "probably too sharply,"
she later admitted.[29] The suggestion that Howe "had fallen
down on his job" was untrue and intolerable. Amazed by her
outburst, Howe thought: "what the hell? This is positively
the last time."[30] On other occasions, he had rearranged his
papers, absorbed the punches, and carried on as befitted a
man who was once awarded "best loser" in a boxing competition he had been compelled to enter.[31] Not this time. Later
that day, Sir Geoffrey resigned. By then, he had served the
Thatcher government for nearly eleven and a half years. In
his resignation letter, he expressed the hope that Britain
would play a more positive role in fostering economic and
monetary union in Europe. Whatever the causes, the last survivor of the 1979 Cabinet was gone. Only Mrs. Thatcher remained; but for how long?

With Kenneth Baker's help, the Prime Minister tried to
make Sir Geoffrey's resignation seem like a question of style
rather than a matter of substance. In fact, it was both. For
Mrs. Thatcher's part, the conflict was highly personal. In
her memoirs, she confessed that she had come to find his
company "almost intolerable" and assumed he felt the
same. She slated Sir Geoffrey for his conduct during his final
year in office: "In the Cabinet he was now a force for ob-
struction, in the Party a focus of resentment, in the country a source of division."[32] Her critics would have said the
same and more about her. Moreover, there was much worse
to come. On November 8, Labour won the Bradford North

and the Bootle by-elections by comfortable margins.

Around 4:20 in the afternoon on Tuesday, November 13, Howe delivered his resignation speech before a fully packed House of Commons. There was nothing outwardly extraordinary in his mien. His clothing was reassuringly restrained: he wore a gray suit, a white shirt, and a gray-blue tie with white spots. At his right side sat Nigel Lawson. On the front bench sat Mrs. Thatcher, with Kenneth Baker on her left and John Major on her right. Before Howe spoke, Mr. Speaker Weatherhill reminded the House of the custom of the day: a resignation statement is heard in silence and without interrogation. For the moment, then, the floor belonged to Howe alone.

He had come to bury Thatcher, not to praise her. The onetime barrister began by making clear that he had not left the government because of style alone. "Indeed, if some of my former colleagues are to be believed, I must be the first Minister in history who has resigned because he was in full agreement with government policy." This led to long, loud bursts of laughter. Then he went on to make plain his differences with Mrs. Thatcher. Her delay of Britain's entry into the ERM had brought about inflation's return. It was, therefore, her stubbornness rather than Mr. Lawson's policy that was to blame for the recession.

When it came to the question of Europe, Howe lambasted the Prime Minister's views on maintaining Britain's national sovereignty at all costs:

I have to say that I find Winston Churchill's perception a good deal more convincing, and more encouraging for the interests of the nation, than the nightmare image sometimes conjured up by my Right Honourable Friend, who seems sometimes to look out upon a continent that is positively teeming with ill-intentioned people, scheming, in other words, to "extinguish democracy," to "disown our national identities" and to lead us "through the back door into a federal Europe." What kind of vision is that . . . ?

The House gasped as he spoke.

For good measure, Howe indicted Mrs. Thatcher not only for her policies but also for an obstructive style of government that undermined leading officials in the name of keeping power for herself. When it came to the vexed question of a European currency, her stridency had made it impossible for the Chancellor and the Governor of the Bank of England to act as "serious participants" in the debate. Picking up on a cricketing metaphor she had used in a recent speech, Howe slammed her with her own bat. "It is rather like sending your opening batsmen to the crease only for them to find, the moment the first balls are bowled, that their bats have been broken before the game by the team captain." This too set the House howling.

Howe ended on a powerful and serious note. "The time," he said, "has come for others to consider their own response to the tragic conflict of loyalties with which I have myself wrestled for perhaps too long." So much for Healey's old jibe that being gored by Howe was like being savaged by a dead sheep. The patient and dutiful servant of the state turned out to be more like a latter-day Samson. He brought down the temple on his tormentor's head, but did not want to destroy the entire order she had built. Unsparing in its clarity and ruthless in its denunciation, Howe's speech was especially devastating because few if any thought him capable of such a forceful performance. What made its effect all the more stunning was that everyone knew him as one of Thatcherism's builders, a monetarist Chancellor, the author of the fabled 1981 budget, and the last man to survive from the original Thatcher government. Afterwards, there was "bemused silence," followed by mounting noise as MPs headed for the exit astonished by what they had witnessed. "A lot of people, semi-traumatised," Tory Minister Alan Clark reported in his diary, "didn't want to talk about it. the atmosphere was light-headed, almost."³³ Moods apart, the damage was done.

What did Howe hope to accomplish or gain by gunning for the Iron Lady? Certainly he had long thought of himself as the Prime Minister's successor—a perception she did not share. More than unbending fealty and lawyerly discretion had kept him in Margaret Thatcher's Cabinet until she finally forced him out in what was her most brutal cut of all. Perhaps Howe secretly hoped that a brilliant resignation speech to the Commons would galvanize Tory colleagues to declare in his favor. Realistically, however, he recognized that whatever his virtues he was not a credible challenger. In Howe's memoirs, *Conflict of Loyalty* (1994), he denied that his resignation speech was an attempt to position himself to replace Mrs. Thatcher—beguiling as such a prospect was. Indeed, Howe ruefully noted that he was "everybody's second choice" or "the ideal compromise candidate" rather than "the man to take everyone to the ramparts."³⁴

Was Howe's intent, therefore, to catapult Michael Heseltine into the leadership or, at least, prod him finally into a challenge? If so, Howe, ever the careful barrister, consciously avoided any commitment that could convict him of conspiracy. Before his resignation speech, he refused to respond one way or the other when Heseltine asked for his support. Such niceties aside, however, Howe surely knew that a no-holds-barred assault on the already weakened Prime Minister could well result in Thatcher's end. By clearing the way for Heseltine, Howe struck back at the woman who he had served so long and who had used him so badly. But more than vengeance inspired him. The prospect of Thatcherism without Thatcher was also tantalizing, all the more so because her political demise might draw deserved attention to the importance of Geoffrey Howe's role in the capitalist revolution.

In any case, Margaret Thatcher should have worn black

rather than dark blue for the occasion. During Howe's performance, she had no choice but to sit on the front benches in full view of the cameras. Somehow or other she managed to keep her "mask of composure" during the onslaught. While her accuser set forth the charges against her, Mrs. Thatcher's thoughts shot forward to how her colleagues were likely to react in the lobbies and thereafter.[35] When Howe's speech was over, she turned to Baker and said: "I didn't think he would do something like that."[36] Shock soon turned into a conviction of betrayal. Whatever conflicts had taken place between them, she later asserted, had been behind closed doors (though they became public knowledge anyway). She had not forgotten the battles they fought together, but "he had not been similarly swayed by those memories. After living through so many difficult times and sharing so many policy successes, he had deliberately set out to bring down a colleague in the brutal and public way."[37] Her outrage was heartfelt, but her perceptions were skewed.

In any case, Howe had all but asked, "Will no one rid us of this woman?" In so doing, he had handed a sword to Michael Heseltine. Sitting in the Commons during the speech, Heseltine had to know that the time to strike had come. Since resigning from the Thatcher government in 1985, he had struggled to keep alive his political ambitions and keep himself out of the wilderness. He had thrown himself into a punishing regime of after-dinner speeches and local visits up and down the country. Just before Howe's resignation, he had written an article exhorting the government to play a greater role in Europe. Then he sent a letter to the chairman of his Henley constituency, regretting Howe's departure and urging partnership in Europe again. But when the Henley Conservative Association expressed support for the government, he backtracked and repeated what he had said many times in recent years: Mrs. Thatcher will lead us into the next election and win it. There is little chance that Heseltine believed this and much less that he thought it desirable. But he had fired up speculation that he was about to challenge Mrs. Thatcher for the leadership. If there was any chance that he would hold back, an alleged "dirty tricks" campaign against him by the Conservative Central Office combined with taunts against him in the press to remove it.

On the morning after Howe's resignation speech, Heseltine and his wife Anne stood outside their Belgravia home as he declared his candidacy for the party leadership. He cited the need for an immediate and fundamental review of the poll tax if he won. And he claimed that he now had a better prospect than Mrs. Thatcher of leading the Conservatives to a fourth electoral victory.

It was not to be. Those Conservative MPs who feared losing their seats or resented Mrs. Thatcher provided Heseltine with the votes needed to wound her. But he did not have adequate support to take her place.

This was the long path that brought about Thatcher's end, and brought the Cabinet to visit the Prime Minister in her room at the Commons on the night of Wednesday evening, November 21, 1990, just after Big Ben struck six o'clock.

V I

IN THE FACE OF BRITAIN'S LONG, RELATIVE DECLINE, A CAPITAList revolution was necessary when Margaret Thatcher came to power in 1979. The back of British socialism had broken, but as of yet no new dispensation had taken its place. Whether shifts such as privitization might have happened anyway is impossible to prove. While the Prime Minister rode the crest of social, economic, and political waves that made a sea-change imaginable, her leadership nonetheless provided a unique surge for this prospective alteration. Without Mrs. Thatcher's clarity of vision, force of will, and strength of purpose, it might have never taken place or it would have been very different. Reaching beyond the guardians of the progressive consensus, she mobilized a counter-establishment to challenge the old truths. She moved beyond the cozy world of the affluent, galvanizing skilled workers to join her quest to restore British prosperity and power.

A woman of conviction, Mrs. Thatcher rightly believed that politics is not simply about the pursuit of money or the exercise of power. It is also a realm of ideas and values in which parties and nations invent and reinvent themselves. Imbued with a profound commitment to political liberty and market economics, her commanding virtues were indispensable to Britain's capitalist revolution. A woman, or a man, who had lacked her sense of self-righteousness, or who felt the need to compromise to be liked or accepted, might have left things as they were. But she did not believe that Britain's long goodbye was inevitable. In a country that had resisted change in the name of compassion and consensus, she stepped forward while others stood back. She acted while others whinnied.

Mrs. Thatcher's story contains certain elements of classical tragedy. For all her intelligence, courage, and perseverance, her character had cardinal weaknesses. The very traits that enabled her to swim against the tide blinded her to the need to win wide support for the changes she sponsored among those left on the beachhead. Consensus was not necessarily gutless evasion. Rocking the boat was unavoidable, but throwing dissenters overboard was not. Her martial nature enabled Mrs. Thatcher to launch an unusually ambitious program for change, but it also provoked a backlash. She frightened the faint-hearted and outraged the tender-hearted. The former deserved short shrift, but the latter merited a closer hearing. Her inability or unwillingness to express public compassion for the dispossessed made her seem colder than she was and made her capitalist revolution more selfish than it had to be. Having pulled herself up to the heights, she did not know how to deal with those who could not escape the depths by their own efforts.

Mrs. Thatcher's tragic flaw was a mixture of intellectual pride and moral arrogance. This dangerous blend led a great protagonist to believe that she alone knew what was good for the country. Controlled and controlling, she could not—or would not—suspend her own point of view. In more ways than one, Mrs. Thatcher was afflicted, sadly, with Dupuytren's Contracture—a temporary contraction of the fingers that affected her right hand. Chris Patten, Secretary of State for the Environment, told Kenneth Baker: "The thing she suffers from is also known as Coachman's Grip." An eighteenth-century term, it described an ailment that gripped those who had clutched the reins too tightly and for too long.[38] Finally, she had to let go.

As in tragic drama, Thatcher's end entailed a stunning and painful fall. But, to all appearances, her reversal of fortunes brought neither a moment of recognition nor a feeling of catharsis. She never seemed to grasp how she had contributed, however unwittingly, to her undoing.

Mrs. Thatcher's capitalist revolution remained incomplete. Ambiguity clouded many of its achievements. Trade union reform was indispensable for restoring economic order. But bringing trade unions under the rule of law did nothing to provide a productive means for worker participation. Privatization lifted the dead hand of the state from nationally owned firms that needed a firm, if friendly, whollop. It proved less appropriate in public utilities that demand careful regulation for the common good. While inflation came down in the mid-1980s, it came back at the Thatcher years' end.

The goals of the capitalist revolution, though, went beyond curing specific ills. Mrs. Thatcher and her allies wanted to reverse decline and revive the nation. Whether they succeeded is a complex and controversial question. As of now, it seems that they stemmed the tide of decline, but never quite found a handle to turn the British economy as thoroughly as they needed to. This was true in part because a decade is only a short time to affect, and sustain, radical change. But Mrs. Thatcher's partial diagnosis of Britain's economic maladies hampered her. She was right to tackle overzealous government intervention, excessive public spending, runaway inflation, trade union power, high taxes, and an uncontrolled money supply. Nevertheless, she did not get to the bottom of a host of other problems that now loom larger, notably the lack of sufficient investment and of a substantial and highly skilled labor force.

The Iron Lady understood that reviving a rusty realm depended on transforming its economic culture. This meant changing broad attitudes to enterprise, profit, and industry in the face of an entrenched anti-industrial ethic (exaggerated though it sometimes is). Such cultural shifts, by definition, are bound to be slow. Nonetheless, the Prime Minister proved more successful in discrediting socialism (with Labour's inadvertent help) than in making Britain a nation of capitalists. The cultural changes that took place during the 1980s were most pronounced in the business world. Firms and industries became meaner and leaner when confronted with sharp competition, high rewards, frequent bankruptcies, and a government averse to bail-outs. The quest to forge a new enterprise culture met with great resistance, however, in the intelligentsia. The genteel biases against profit, growth, and productivity fashioned by figures such as Wordsworth, Arnold, and Forster persisted and indeed impeded the capitalist revolution. It is possible that the polytchnics' recent elevation into universities could eventually create an atmosphere more hospitable to enterprise. Perhaps the students they educate and the inellectuals they train will break down the barriers between culture and business. But for now the old divides remain.

To what extent the capitalist revolution changed broader social attitudes is much harder to gauge. Outraged public reactions to top chief executives' pay showed that the old envy was alive and well. It is still more acceptable in some circles to make a fortune in soccer, entertainment, or the pools than in business or industry. Indeed, the preoccupation with "greed" and "corruption" in the 1980s strengthened negative stereotypes. Mrs. Thatcher's critics argue that the British people rejected or dismissed the rhetoric and reality of the "enterprise culture." Yet they contradict themselves in the next breath by complaining that Britain has become more selfish, greedy, and materialistic than it had been before Thatcher. This amounts to a backhanded admission that the country has indeed changed.

The results of opinion polls, for what they are worth, do not indicate that Mrs. Thatcher succeeded in dramatically changing attitudes to enterprise, profit, industry and the like. A poll conducted in June of 1988 by MORI (Market & Opinion Research International) captured the capitalist revolution's ambiguous results. About 70 percent of the respondents agreed that Britain has become a capitalist society. Private interests and free enterprise are priorities. Increasing efficiency takes precedence over keeping people in work. The individual is encouraged to look after himself. People are allowed to make and keep as much money as they can. The creation of wealth is rewarded more highly than caring for others.[39] These responses suggest that the capitalist revolution had triumphed. But the poll also revealed a more ambiguous reaction to the question of whether such changes are desirable. Certain "socialistic" values—caring, compassion, and service—remained as ideals even while they faded as realities.[40] Whether this has much to do with how people actually feel or behave is another question. The fact that an individual might praise the Welfare State and extol the caring society in a poll may or may not reveal his or her true feelings. Very few of us admit to being mean-spirited, selfish individuals out for ourselves at all costs.

Yet the capitalist revolution ultimately failed to change Britain as quickly or deeply as its proponents hoped it would. Its shortcomings were both material and moral. The majority's standard of living rose during the 1980s. Yet money alone does not legitimate a social order. "Our principal mistake," Geoffrey Howe admitted, "was to give less sympathy and understanding than we should have done to those who faced the upheaval" of economic disruption, the victims of rationalization and unemployment.[41] Margaret Thatcher deserves credit for teaching the British the truth of Hillel's dictum, "If I am not for myself, who will be for me?" Every individual is responsible for trying to provide for himself and his family and to contribute to the common good. However, she did not grasp the second part of the dictum: "But if I am only for myself, what am I?" Too much of what she did came at the expense of those on the bottom. In the end, her dream of creating a "property-owning democracy" or an "enterprise culture" did not sufficiently move the British imagination to ensure lasting cultural change. She dismantled the socialist city on the hill, but did not inspire a rush to suburbia.

A conflict between perceived economic imperatives and engrained cultural values hampered the success of the capitalist revolution. However partial Mrs. Thatcher's dignosis of Britain's economic ills, there is little doubt that large-scale changes were needed to reverse decline and regenerate the nation. The cold shower that she turned on the British people imposed a salutary realism about the facts of the world economy. It was indeed necessary for Britain to raise productivity, increase efficiency, and create wealth. The party was over. But she failed to win more than a grudging acceptance for industrial rationalization, trade union reform, privatization, and so forth. Indeed, such measures collided with the socialistic ideals of postwar Britain. Mrs. Thatcher's unabashed free market ideology flew in the face of the Welfare State's commitment to providing full employment and social security for everyone.

In other words, Mrs. Thatcher's cultural failure was her inability to spur widespread commitment to the capitalist revolution. Admittedly, this was not an easy task. Capitalism is prosaic: it lacks a strong mythic or heroic streak.[42] Given that "fire in the minds of men" has led to death camps rather than Utopia in the twentieth century, this is more a virtue than a vice. Although socialism had not delivered the New Jerusalem promised in 1945, it provided heartening cultural ideals that made sacrifice worthwhile, even obligatory. The Prime Minister was unable to hit upon a moral equivalent that made capitalism seem equally noble. Early in her tenure as Party leader and then as premier, Mrs. Thatcher sometimes tried to connect economic freedom with nationalistic grandeur. But the spirit of Dunkirk did not extend easily to Mammon's altar. The "enterprise culture" she envisioned was, at best, a pale imitation of the "American dream." On the other side of the Atlantic, capitalist mythology had both an idealistic and materialistic side—a perilous ocean voyage to a new land full of prospects providing worthy immigrants the opportunity to go from rags to riches. No such romance informed Mrs. Thatcher's policies or philosophy, despite the fact that the saga of industrial Britain was replete with suitable material.

The upheavals of the 1980s only exacerbated the tension between economic imperatives and cultural values. Had Mrs. Thatcher taken the sting out of her economic policies by providing protection for the displaced and the unfortunate, she might have won genuine support for her plans. It was all well and good for the Prime Minister to provide a ladder (or, at least, talk of a ladder) for those on the bottom, but pulling out the floor from under them sent them hurtling downward rather than upward. Not only did she weaken the moral foundation of the capitalist revolution by favoring the rich over the poor, but also Mrs. Thatcher undermined its legitimacy and appeal by an indifferent or mean-spirited attitude to those who could not help themselves. Presenting economic freedom, entrepreneurial vigor, and self-reliance exclusively in terms of individual self-interest was a mistake. Had she also framed her efforts as a nationalistic crusade that would benefit that commonweal, she might have tapped the wartime spirit of solidarity and unity that her reforms violated. As it was, she went against the grain of a socialistic ethic that was more effective than the economic machine attached to it.

But the manifest inequities that Mrs. Thatcher's government reinforced, the growing divide between rich and poor, and the lot of the homeless caused a backlash against the capitalist revolution and undermined its legitimacy. Even some who benefited from the new regime (and many more who did not) thought it was unfair. So by the time the economy went into recession toward the end of Thatcher's tenure, the capitalist revolution lacked a solid enough moral foundation to sustain it. The specter of economic failure further weakened its support. The diehards were more likely to hock the barricades than to save them.

The capitalist revolution had a profound impact on British politics, for Mrs. Thatcher changed the terms of debate. She largely turned Conservatives away from the postwar consensus and shook them out of their acceptance of the inevitability of socialism. The old-style paternalists remained; not so much of their power. But Michael Heseltine was a powerful symbol of enduring divisions between Margaret Thatcher's Conservative advocates and adversaries. Her fall suggested that she had been unable to sustain support in her party or the public for her capitalist vision. In Thatcher's wake, the Tories remained divided, with Europe still an explosive issue. Yet fifteen years after Mrs. Thatcher's first electoral victory, they remained in power, even if John Major had not proved to be the unwavering Thatcherite she once took him to be. When the next election takes place, the Labour Party led by Tony Blair will be a far different adversary from the one Conservatives vanquished in 1979. This change owes much to Mrs. Thatcher. Her capitalist revolution forced Labour's leaders, Neil Kinnock and then the late John Smith, to purge the militant left, move to the political center, distance the party from the trade unions, dispense with talk of re-nationalization. and guard against tax-and-spend rhetoric. Labour may remain committed to equality, welfare, and community, but it is not the Socialist party that it once was.

Mrs. Thatcher's capitalist revolution was more necessary than glorious. Indeed, it is tempting to conclude that Britain's last successful political revolution took place in 1688 when Parliament declared its sovereignty over the Crown. The country is a more realistic society now than it had been in socialism's heyday, but it is neither kinder nor gentler. Although Britain is somewhat more efficient, this is still not its strong suit. Paying more attention to economic imperatives was unavoidable, but this process whittled away some of the inimitable charm and style that delighted foreigners. Under Mrs. Thatcher's iron rule, Britain became a disenchanted isle, more aware of the need to earn its way in the world, but less able to captivate or inspire it.

Notes

One: Thatcher's End

1. Margaret Thatcher, *The Downing Street Years* (New York: Harper-Collins, 1993), p. 842.
2. *Ibid.*, p. 843.
3. Alan Watkins, *A Conservative Coup: The Fall of Margaret Thatcher,* 2nd edn. (London: Duckworth, 1992), p. 1.
4. See Kenneth Baker's memoirs, *The Turbulent Years* (London: Faber & Faber, 1993), p. 303.
5. *Ibid.*, p. 301.
6. Julian Critchley, *Heseltine: The Unauthorized Biography* (London: Coronet Books, 1988), p. 29.
7. See Michael Heseltine, *Where There's a Will* (London: Hutchinson, 1987).
8. Thatcher, *Downing Street Years,* p. 843.
9. *Ibid.*, p. 844.
10. Watkins, *Conservative Coup,* p. 170.
11. *Ibid.*, pp. 3–4.
12. Thatcher, *Downing Street Years,* p. 844.
13. *Ibid.*, p. 845.
14. *Ibid.*, pp. 846–47.
15. *Ibid.*, p. 851.
16. *Ibid.*

17. Baker, *Turbulent Years,* p. 406.

18. *Ibid.*

19. Thatcher, *Downing Street Years,* p. 852.

20. Baker, *Turbulent Years,* p. 406.

21. *Ibid.*

22. *Ibid.,* p. 407.

23. Thatcher, *Downing Street Years,* p. 855.

24. *Ibid.,* p. 856.

25. Watkins, *Conservative Coup,* p. 25.

26. *Ibid.,* pp. 25–26.

27. Thatcher, *Downing Street Years,* p. 857.

28. *Ibid.,* p. 413.

29. Watkins, *Conservative Coup,* p. 206.

30. Thatcher, *Downing Street Years,* p. 862.

31. Quoted in David Butler and Dennis Kavanagh, *The British General Election of 1979* (London: Macmillan, 1980), p. 167.

32. Quoted in Peter Riddell, *The Thatcher Decade* (Oxford: Basil Blackwell, 1989), p. 7.

33. See Kevin Phillips, *The Politics of Rich and Poor* (New York: Random House, 1990).

34. Interview with Reverend Colin Marsh.

35. For the term "capitalist revolution," see Peter Berger, *The Capitalist Revolution* (New York: Basic Books, 1986). For the early usages of revolution, see Simon Schama, *Citizens* (New York: Knopf, 1989), p. 6.

36. For the American scene, see Phillips, *Politics of Rich and Poor;* Garry Wills, *Reagan's America* (New York: Penguin, 1988); and Lou Cannon, *President Reagan: The Role of a Lifetime* (New York: Touchstone, 1992).

37. See Francis Fukiyama, *The End of History and the Last Man* (New York: The Free Press, 1992).

Two: Queues or Ladders?

1. Thatcher, *Downing Street Years,* p. 23.

2. See Hugo Young, *The Iron Lady* (New York: Noonday Press, 1990), p. 396.

3. On Pim and the Map Room, see Martin Gilbert, *Winston S. Churchill,* Vol. VI, *Their Finest Hour, 1939–1941* (London: Heinemann, 1983), pp. 159–62, 164.

4. Martin Gilbert, *Churchill: A Life* (New York: Henry Holt, 1991), pp. 854–55, and Gilbert, *"Never Despair": Winston Churchill 1945–1965* (London: Heinemann, 1988), pp. 74, 105.

5. George Orwell, *The Lion and the Unicorn* (London: Secker & Warburg, 1962), p. 67.

6. See Correlli Barnett, *The Audit of War* (London: Macmillan, 1987), pp. 11–37.

7. See Jose Harris, *William Beveridge* (Oxford: Clarendon Press, 1977), p. 2.

8. On Wilson and Beveridge, see Ben Pimlott, *Harold Wilson* (London: Collins, 1992), pp. 62, 61–76.

9. *Ibid.*, p. 62.

10. Harris, *Beveridge*, p. 1.

11. William Beveridge, *The Pillars of Security* (New York: Macmillan, 1943), p. 120.

12. Martin Gilbert, *Churchill's Political Philosophy* (Oxford: Oxford University Press, 1981), p. 15.

13. Quoted in Barnett, *Audit of War*, p. 27.

14. Quoted in Gilbert, *"Never Despair,"* p. 13.

15. Quoted in *ibid.*, pp. 32–33.

16. Quoted in *ibid.*, p. 35.

17. See *ibid.*, pp. 105–10.

18. Gilbert, *Churchill*, pp. 855–56.

19. Interview with Pat Kinna, quoted in C-SPAN, "Remembering D-Day," May 31, 1994.

20. Quoted in Gilbert, *"Never Despair,"* p. 643.

21. George Orwell, *The Road to Wigan Pier* (New York: Harcourt, Brace, 1958), pp. 51–107.

22. Jonathan Raban, *Hunting Mister Heartbreak* (London: Collins Harvill, 1990), p. 88.

23. Interview with Lord Hanson.

24. See Asa Briggs, *Marks and Spencer 1884–1984: A Centenary History* (London: Octopus Books, 1984); Charles Dellheim, "The Creation of a Company Culture: Cadburys, 1861–1931," *American Historical Review*, 93 (Spring 1987):11–44.

25. Quoted in Barnett, *Audit of War*, p. 55.

26. Quoted in *ibid.*, p. 5.

27. *Ibid.*, pp. 143–86.

28. Orwell, *The Lion and the Unicorn*, p. 73.

29. See Kenneth Harris, *Attlee* (London: Weidenfeld & Nicolson, 1982), pp. 326–27.

30. Gilbert, *"Never Despair,"* p. 643.

31. Noel Annan, *Our Age: Portrait of a Generation* (London: Weidenfeld & Nicolson, 1990), p. 347.

32. *Ibid.*, p. 407.

33. Alastair Horne, *Harold Macmillan, I: 1894–1956* (New York: Penguin, 1989), pp. 10–11.

34. *Ibid.*, p. 36.

35. *Ibid.*, p. 74.

36. Alastair Horne, *Harold Macmillan, II: 1957–1986* (New York: Penguin, 1991), p. 64.

37. *Ibid.*, p. 65.

38. See Pimlott, *Wilson*, pp. 33–34.

39. *Ibid.*, p. 25.

40. *Ibid.*, p. 276.

41. *Ibid.*, p. 303.

42. Annan, *Our Age*, p. 348.

43. *Ibid.*

44. Interview with Sir Gordon White.

45. Interview with Martin Sorrell.

46. For this anecdote and a full-scale biography, see John Campell, *Edward Heath* (London: Jonathan Cape, 1993), p. 10.

47. See Peter Jenkins, *Mrs. Thatcher's Revolution* (Cambridge: Harvard University Press, 1988), pp. 57–58.

Three: The British Disease

1. For a highly detailed political and economic analysis of the IMF crisis, see Kathleen Burk and Alec Cairncross, *"Goodbye, Great Britain"* (New Haven and London: Yale University Press, 1992). For a useful journalistic account, see Stephen Fay and Hugo Young, "The Day the £ Nearly Died," *Sunday Times,* May 14, 1978. The best primary sources are memoirs: Denis Healey, *The Time of My Life* (New York: W.W. Norton, 1990), pp. 372–440; and James Callaghan, *Time and Chance* (London: Collins, 1987), pp. 419–20, 423, 427–47.

2. See Healey, *Time of My Life*, p. 375.

3. These details come from Harrods' stock in 1979, as reported in Tim Dale, *Harrods, the Store and the Legend* (London: Pan Books, 1983), pp. 146–47.

4. See Anthony Sampson, *The New Anatomy of Britain* (London: Hodder & Stoughton, 1971), p. 620.

5. See Healey, *Time of My Life*, p. 427.

6. *Ibid.*, p. 66.

7. *Ibid.*, pp. 1–46.

8. *Ibid.*, p. 579.

9. Interview with Sir Douglas Wass.

10. On the Treasury and its ethos, see Sampson, *New Anatomy*, pp. 275–85, and Peter Hennessey, *Whitehall* (London: Fontana, 1990), pp. 175–78, 250–52, and 207–09.

11. See Healey, *Time of My Life*, p. 381.

12. See Tony Benn, *Against the Tide: Diaries 1973–76* (London: Hutchinson, 1989), pp. 218–19.

13. See Alfred Browne, *Tony Benn* (London: W. H. Allen, 1983), pp. 190–200.

14. Vermont Royster, "Britain, A Model Study," *Wall Street Journal*, August 20, 1975.

15. Anthony Howard, "Angry Wage Earners, Floundering Politicians," *New York Times Magazine*, December 26, 1976, p. 36.

16. For a few examples of the large literature on the "British disease," see "What Is the British Disease?" *The Times* April 29, 1971; Peter Jenkins, "A Nation on the Skids," *Manchester Guardian Weekly*, October 8, 1978; Isaac Kramnick, ed., *Is Britain Dying? Perspectives on the Current Crisis* (Ithaca, NY: Cornell University Press, 1979); Ralf Dahrendorf, *On Britain* (Chicago: University of Chicago Press, 1982); Bernard D. Nossiter, *Britain: A Future That Works* (Boston: Houghton Mifflin, 1978); R. Emmett Tyrell, ed., *The Future That Doesn't Work: Social Democracy's Failure in Britain* (Garden City, NY: Doubleday, 1977); Tom Nairn, *The Break-up of Britain* (London, Verso, 1981); Samuel Beer, *Britain Against Itself: The Political Contradictions of Collectivism* (New York: W.W. Norton, 1982); Robert Bacon and Walter Eltis, *Britain's Economic Problems: Too Few Producers* (New York: St. Martin's Press, 1976); and *The United Kingdom in 1980: The Hudson Report* (New York: Halstead Press, 1974).

17. See Callaghan, *Time and Chance*, pp. 426–27.

18. Healey, *Time of My Life*, p. 444.

19. Kenneth Morgan, *Labour in Power, 1945–51* (Oxford: Clarendon Press, 1984), p. 12.

20. Healey, *Time of My Life*, p. 340.

21. Callaghan, *Time and Chance*, pp. 168, 174, and 197.

22. *Hansard*, 5th series, vol. 920, November 11, 1976, pp. 640–42.

23. Quoted in Philip Whitehead, *The Writing on the Wall: Britain in the Seventies* (London: Michael Joseph, 1985), p. 197.

Four: Spiritless Capitalism

1. *Evening Standard*, April 15, 1983.

2. *New Statesman*, May 27, 1983, pp. 1–xvi.

3. Interview with Sir Ralf Dahrendorf.

4. Berger, *Capitalist Revolution*, pp. 7–8.

5. Michael Porter, "The Competitive Advantage of Nations," *Harvard Business Review* (March–April 1990), vol. 90, no. 2: 81–82.

6. Martin J. Wiener, *English Culture and the Decline of the Industrial Spirit* (Cambridge, Engl.: Cambridge University Press, 1981), p. 166.

7. See C. Dellheim, "Imagining England: Victorian Views of the North," *Northern History*, vol. 22 (1986):216–30. For a more detailed scholarly view of the relationship between cultural values and economic behavior, see Dellheim, "Notes on Industrialism and Culture in Nineteenth Century Britain," *Notebooks in Cultural Analysis*, 2 (1985):225–47.

8. See Asa Briggs, *Iron Bridge to Crystal Palace* (London: Thames & Hudson, 1979), pp. 7–8. See also F. D. Klingender, *Art and the Industrial Revolution* (London: N. Carrington, 1947).

9. See Asa Briggs, *Victorian People: A Reassessment of Persons and Themes, 1851–1867* (Chicago: University of Chicago Press, 1972), pp. 15–51.

10. See Wiener, *English Culture*, p. 28.

11. Karl Marx to Friedrich Engels, October 13, 1851, in *Karl Marx on America and the Civil War*, ed. Saul K. Padover (New York: McGraw-Hill, 1972), p. 37.

12. See S. D. Chapman, *Jesse Boot of Boots the Chemist* (London: Hodder & Stoughton, 1974).

13. See Aaron Friedberg, *The Weary Titan* (Princeton: Princeton University Press), p. 21.

14. On Chamberlain, see Asa Briggs, *Victorian Cities* (New York: Harper & Row, 1965), pp. 185–240.

15. Charles W. Boyd, ed., *Mr. Chamberlain's Speeches* (New York: Kraus Reprint, 1970), vol. 1:144.

16. *Ibid.,* p. 177.

17. See Friedberg, *Weary Titan,* p. 70.

18. W. J. Reader, *ICI: A History* (London: Oxford University Press, 1970–75), vol. I: 218–19.

19. Alfred Chandler, *Scale and Scope* (Cambridge: Belknap Press, 1990), pp. 239–95, 397–428.

20. See Asa Briggs, "Modern Britain," in Norman F. Cantor, ed., *Perspectives on the European Past* (New York: Macmillan, 1971), 2:185–87.

21. Wiener, *English Culture,* ch. 1.

22. W. L. Burn, *The Age of Equipoise* (New York: W. W. Norton, 1965).

23. On the Duke of Westminster, see Mark Girouard, *The Victorian Country House* (New Haven and London: Yale University Press, 1979), pp. 1–4.

24. Thorstein Veblen, *Imperial Germany and the Industrial Revolution* (New York: Viking, 1954), pp. 141–42, 48–49.

25. See Alfred Marshall, "Memorandum on the Fiscal Policy of International Trade," *Official Papers of Alfred Marshall* (London: Macmillan, 1926), pp. 405–06.

26. Quoted in Wiener, *English Culture,* p. 127.

27. *Ibid.,* p. 142, and D. C. Coleman, *Courtaulds: A Social and Economic History,* 3 vols. (Oxford: Clarendon Press, 1969–80), II: 215–21.

28. William Wordsworth to Charles James Fox, January 14, 1801, in *The Letters of William and Dorothy Wordsworth,* arranged and edited by Ernest de Sélincourt, revised by Chester L. Shaver, 2nd edn. (Oxford: Clarendon Press, 1967), pp. 312–15.

29. William Wordsworth to William Ewart Gladstone, October 15, 1844, in *ibid.,* vol. VII (Oxford: Clarendon Press, 1982), pp. 115–16.

30. Lionel Trilling, *Matthew Arnold* (New York: Columbia University Press, 1949), pp. 15–35.

31. Quoted in *ibid.,* p. 230.

32. Quoted in Briggs, *Victorian People,* p. 143.

33. Quoted in *ibid.,* p. 166. On the Rugby experiment, see Edward Mack and W. H. G. Armytage, *Thomas Hughes* (London: Ernest Benn, 1952), pp. 227–50.

34. See Harold J. Perkin, *The Rise of Professional Society* (London: Routledge & Kegan Paul, 1989).

35. See Wiener, *English Culture*, pp. 41–80.

36. See George Mosse, *The Crisis of German Ideology* (New York: Grosset & Dunlap, 1964); Fritz Stern, *The Failure of Illiberalism* (New York: Knopf, 1972); and Bruce Collins and Keith Robbins, eds., *British Culture and Economic Decline* (London: Weidenfeld & Nicolson, 1990).

37. See Lionel Trilling, *E. M. Forster* (Norfolk, CT: New Directions, 1943), pp. 113–35.

Five: A Different Voice

1. Horne, *Harold Macmillan, Vol. II: 1957–1986*, p. 618.

2. *Ibid.*

3. *Ibid.*, p. 619.

4. Brian Harrison, *Separate Spheres* (New York: Holmes & Meier, 1978).

5. Young, *Iron Lady*, p. x.

6. See Nikolaus Pevsner and John Harris, *Lincolnshire* (Harmondsworth, Middlx: Penguin, 1964), p. 540.

7. Jonathan Raban, *God, Man, and Mrs Thatcher* (London: Chatto & Windus, 1989), p. 25.

8. *New Yorker*, February 10, 1986, p. 75.

9. For Orwell's, Marx's, and Wells's views (as well as a good general discussion), see Arno Mayer, "The Lower Middle Class as an Historical Problem," *Journal of Modern History*, *47* (September 1975):409–36. See also Geoffrey Crossick, ed., *The Lower Middle Class in Britain 1870–1914* (New York: St. Martin's Press, 1977).

10. Jenkins, *Mrs. Thatcher's Revolution*, p. 85.

11. Thatcher, *Downing Street Years*, p. 11.

12. Patrick Cosgrove, *Margaret Thatcher: A Tory and Her Party* (London: Hutchinson, 1978), p. 68.

13. Kenneth Harris, *Thatcher* (London: Weidenfeld & Nicolson, 1988), p. 42.

14. Graham Little, *Strong Leadership* (New York: Oxford University Press, 1988), p. 92.

15. See the valuable collection of interviews in Hugo Young and Anne Sloman, eds., *The Thatcher Phenomenon* (London: BBC Books, 1986), p. 16.

16. Leo Abse, *Margaret, Daughter of Beatrice: A Politician's Psycho-Biography of Margaret Thatcher* (London: Jonathan Cape, 1989), p. 23.

17. Young and Sloman, eds., *Thatcher Phenomenon*, p. 26.

18. Young, *Iron Lady*, pp. 4 and 3–10.

19. Little, *Strong Leadership*, p. 92.

20. See Carol Gilligan, *In a Different Voice* (Cambridge: Harvard University Press, 1982).

21. Quoted in Young and Sloman, eds., *Thatcher Phenomenon*, pp. 25–26.

22. Marina Warner, *Monuments and Maidens: The Allegory of the Female Form* (London: Weidenfeld & Nicolson, 1985), pp. 51–53.

23. *Ibid.*, p. 22.

24. Harris, *Thatcher*, pp. 42–43.

25. Young and Sloman, eds., *Thatcher Phenomenon*, p. 80.

26. See R. J. Olney, *Rural Society and County Government in Nineteenth-Century Lincolnshire* (Lincoln: History of Lincolnshire Committee, 1979), p. 64.

27. Jenkins, *Mrs. Thatcher's Revolution*, p. 83.

28. *Daily Telegraph,* January 10, 1988.

29. Thatcher, *Downing Street Years*, p. 509.

30. *Ibid.*, pp. 509–10.

31. *Ibid.*, p. 509.

32. Geoffrey Alderman, *Modern British Jewry* (Oxford: Clarendon Press, 1992), p. 357.

33. Interview with Rabbi Hugo Gryn.

34. Young and Sloman, eds., *Thatcher Phenomenon*, pp. 13–14.

35. See *ibid.*, p. 17.

36. *Ibid.*

37. See *ibid.*, p. 22.

38. There is some background on Finchley in James McMillan's laudatory *From Finchley to the World* (London: Glendarn, 1989). I also benefited from an interview with Mrs. Thatcher's then Finchley constituency agent, Michael Love.

39. Alderman, *Modern British Jewry*, p. 337.

40. Kingsley Amis, *Memoirs* (London: Hutchinson, 1991), p. 315.

41. Interview with Sir Alfred Sherman.

42. See Robert Blake, *The Conservative Party from Peel to Thatcher* (London: Fontana, 1985), p. 311.

43. Keith Joseph, *Reversing the Trend* (Chichester, W. Sussex: Rose, 1975), p. 4.

44. Interview with Lord Harris.

45. Interview with Sir John Hoskyns.

46. On the Thatcher circle there is some useful material in John Ranelagh, *Thatcher's People* (London: Fontana, 1992).

47. Quoted in Young, *One of Us*, p. 130.

48. See Keith Joseph, "Solving the Union Problem Is the Key to Britain's Recovery," in David Coates and John Hilliard, eds., *The Economic Decline of Modern Britain* (London: Wheatsheaf Books, 1986), p. 104.

49. Quoted in Morrison Halcrow, *Keith Joseph: A Single Mind* (London: Macmillan, 1989), p. 72.

50. See Margaret Thatcher, *Let Our Children Grow Tall: Selected Speeches 1975–77* (London: Centre for Policy Studies, 1977), p. 33.

51. See David Willetts, *Modern Conservatism* (Harmondsworth, Middlx: Penguin, 1992), pp. 79–91.

52. Quoted in Butler and Kavanagh, *The British General Election of 1979*, p. 323.

53. Quoted in *ibid.*, p. 332.

Six: While Britain Awoke

1. Ian Gilmour, *Dancing with Dogma: Britain Under Thatcherism* (London: Simon & Schuster, 1992), p. 17.

2. *Ibid.*, p. 32.

3. The phrase comes from William Keegan, *Mrs. Thatcher's Economic Experiment* (London: Allen Lane, 1984).

4. Nigel Lawson, *The View from No. 11: Memoirs of a Tory Radical* (London: Bantam Press, 1992), pp. 322–23.

5. Geoffrey Howe, *A Conflict of Loyalty* (London: Macmillan, 1994) pp. 5–6.

6. Hennessey, *Whitehall*, p. 324.

7. Nicholas Ridley, *My Style of Government* (London: Hutchinson, 1991), p. 179.

8. Lawson, *View from No. 11*, p. 16.

9. Howe, *A Conflict of Loyalty*, pp. 30–31

10. Philip Magnus, *Gladstone: A Biography* (New York: E. P. Dutton, 1964), p. 145.

11. For the budget speech, see *Hansard*, 5th series, vol. 968, June 12, 1979, pp. 238–64.

12. *Ibid.*, p. 266.

13. *Ibid.*, June 13, 1979, p. 462.

14. Jim Prior, *A Balance of Power* (London: Hamish Hamilton, 1986), p. 119.

15. *Guardian*, June 14, 1979.

16. Lawson, *View from No. 11*, pp. 64–65.

17. *The Times*, February 9, 1984.

18. Lawson, *View from No. 11*, pp. 64–65.

19. See Berger, *Capitalist Revolution*, pp. 195–97.

20. Hennessey, *Whitehall*, p. 631.

21. Ridley, *Style of Government*, pp. 176, 178.

22. Lawson, *View from No. 11*, p. 51.

23. *Observer*, February 25, 1979.

24. Alvaro Vargas Llosa, "The Press Officer," *Granta* (1991), 36, p. 80.

25. Prior, *Balance of Power*, p. 116.

26. Patrick Cosgrove, *Thatcher: The First Term* (London: Bodley Head, 1985), p. 68.

27. Lawson, *View from No. 11*, pp. 3–4.

28. *Ibid.*, p. 250; and interview with Nigel Lawson.

29. Hennessey, *Whitehall*, p. 630.

30. Young and Sloman, eds., *Thatcher Phenomenon*, p. 126.

31. Prior, *Balance of Power*, p. 120.

32. Lawson, *View from No. 11*, p. 44.

33. *Observer*, October 7, 1979.

34. Lawson, *View from No. 11*, p. 45.

35. Keegan, *Mrs. Thatcher's Economic Experiment*, p. 152.

36. *Ibid.*, pp. 152–53.

37. *Ibid.*, p. 80.

38. Christopher Johnson, *The Economy Under Mrs. Thatcher, 1979–1990* (Harmondsworth, Middlx: Penguin, 1991), p. 37.

39. Derek Warlock and David Sheppard, *Better Together: Christian Partnership in a Hurt City* (Harmondsworth, Middlx: Penguin, 1989), pp. 145–46.

40. Lawson, *View from No. 11*, p. 677.

41. *Ibid.*, p. 100.
42. *The Times,* March 30, 1981.
43. Lawson, *View from No. 11,* p. 98.

Seven: A Fine and Private Place

1. *The Times,* July 6, 1981.
2. Hennessey, *Whitehall,* p. 707.
3. *The Times,* July 7, 1981.
4. Hennessey, *Whitehall,* p. 707.
5. *The Times,* July 8, 1981.
6. *Hansard,* 5th series, vol. 981, March 26, 1980, col. 1444.
7. Gilmour, *Dancing with Dogma,* p. 25; speech of March 8, 1980.
8. Prior, *Balance of Power,* p. 139.
9. Howe, *Conflict of Loyalty,* p. 222.
10. Ridley, *Style of Government,* p. 173.
11. Prior, *Balance of Power,* p. 117.
12. Ridley, *Style of Government,* p. 104.
13. Young, *Iron Lady,* pp. 223–46.
14. *Ibid.*, p. 36, and Prior, *Balance of Power,* pp. 139–45.
15. Prior, *Balance of Power,* pp. 13–14.
16. *Ibid.*, p. 154.
17. Thatcher, *Downing Street Years,* p. 104.
18. Norman Tebbit, *Upwardly Mobile* (London: Fontana, 1989), p. 196.
19. *Observer,* February 9, 1979.
20. Prior, *Balance of Power,* p. 158.
21. *Ibid.*
22. Tebbit, *Upwardly Mobile,* p. 230.
23. *Ibid.*, pp. 233–36.
24. Young, *One of Us,* p. 195.
25. Lawson, *View from No. 11,* p. 140.
26. Orwell's 1937 essay, "Down the Mine," is quoted in Martin Adeney and John Lloyd, *The Miners' Strike 1984–5: Loss Without Limit* (London: Routledge & Kegan Paul), p. 9.
27. *Ibid.*, p. 12.
28. Lawson, *View from No. 11,* p. 42.
29. *Ibid.*, pp. 148–49.
30. Ian MacGregor with Rodney Tyler, *The Enemies Within* (London: Collins, 1986), p. 21.

31. *Ibid.*, p. 19.

32. *Ibid.*, pp. 32–33.

33. *Ibid.*, p. 36.

34. *Ibid.*, p. 38.

35. *Ibid.*, p. 94.

36. *Ibid.*, p. 133.

37. Adeney and Lloyd, *Miners' Strike*, p. 24.

38. *Ibid.*, p. 37.

39. Lawson, *View from No. 11*, p. 160.

40. For Mrs. Thatcher's view of the miners' strike, see *Downing Street Years*, pp. 339–78.

41. Lawson, *View from No. 11*, p. 161.

42. *The Times*, September 1, 1982.

43. *The Times*, November 9, 1985.

44. Lawson, *View from No. 11*, p. 202.

45. Quoted in Johnson, *The Economy Under Mrs. Thatcher*, p. 145.

46. Lawson, *View from No. 11*, p. 226.

47. Interview with John Moore.

48. Lawson, *View from No. 11*, p. 203.

49. Interview with Sir John Harvey-Jones.

50. See Gordon Brown, *Where There Is Greed* (Edinburgh: Mainstream, 1989), p. 13. For a good critique of Thatcher policies, see Paul Hirst, *After Thatcher* (London: Collins, 1989).

51. John Rentoul, *The Rich Get Richer* (London: Unwin Paperbacks, 1987).

52. On Graham's work, see *Shocks to the System: Social and Political Issues in Recent British Art from the Arts Council Collection* (London: South Bank Centre, 1991), pp. 23, 45.

53. For a judicious view of economic realities, see Peter Riddell, *The Thatcher Decade* (Oxford: Basil Blackwell, 1989), chs. 2, 3, and 5.

Eight: Leaner and Meaner

1. Quoted in Anthony Sampson, *The Anatomy of Britain* (New York: Harper & Row, 1962), p. 89.

2. Interview with Hugh Parker.

3. D. C. Coleman, "Gentlemen and Players," *Economic History Review*, 2nd series, 26 (February 1973): 92–116.

4. See Caryl Reich, "The Confessions of Siegmund Warburg," *Institutional Investor* (March 1980), pp. 177, 181. On the Warburg family, see Ron Chernow, *The Warburgs* (New York: Random House, 1993).

5. Interview with Richard Giardano.

6. On institutional rigidities and economic decline, see Mancur Olsen, *The Rise and Decline of Nations* (New Haven and London: Yale University Press, 1982).

7. *Sunday Times* (London), July 16, 1972.

8. On ICI's organizational culture, see Andrew Pettigrew, *The Awakening Giant: Continuity and Change in Imperial Chemical Industries* (Oxford: Basil Blackwell, 1985), pp. 69–79, 381–91, 328–34, and 215–33.

9. *Ibid.*, p. 330.

10. *Ibid.*, p. 409.

11. "Sir Maurice Hodgson: The Race for Profits at ICI," *Director* (March 1980), p. 38.

12. *Ibid.*

13. "ICI: Helped and Hurt by North Sea Oil," *The Economist*, March 15, 1980, p. 75.

14. "ICI: The Axeman Cometh," *The Economist*, October 18, 1980, pp. 95–96.

15. Pettigrew, *Awakening Giant*, pp. 376–437.

16. *Ibid.*, p. 273.

17. *Ibid.*, pp. 397–98.

18. Interview with Sir John Harvey-Jones.

19. Pettigrew, *Awakening Giant*, p. 395.

20. *Ibid.*, p. 398.

21. "ICI's Search for a New Imperial Wizard," *The Economist*, October 31, 1981, p. 77.

22. *Ibid.*, p. 78.

23. Sir Harvey-Jones, *Making It Happen* (London: Collins, 1988), p. 139.

24. *Ibid.*, pp. 90–91.

25. Interview with Sir John Harvey-Jones.

26. Interview with Sir Christopher Hogg.

27. *BusinessWeek*, January 24, 1983, p. 42.

28. Interview with Jack Randle.

29. John Underwood, *The Will to Win: John Egan and Jaguar* (London: W.H. Allen, 1989), p. 17.

30. See Michael Edwardes, *Back from the Brink* (London: Pan Books, 1984), p. 48.

31. Interview with William Turner.

32. Interview with Jack Randle.

33. Quoted in Walter Goldsmith and David Clutterbuck, *The Winning Streak* (London: Weidenfeld & Nicolson, 1984), p. 49.

34. Edwardes, *Back from the Brink*, p. 247.

35. *The Times*, February 22, 1978.

36. Edwardes, *Back from the Brink*, p. 55.

37. *Ibid.*, p. 233.

38. *Ibid.*, p. 99.

39. Quoted in Underwood, *Will to Win*, p. 66.

40. *Ibid.*, p. 65.

41. *The Times*, July 13, 1983.

42. Interview with Sir John Egan.

43. Interview with Jack Randle.

44. Interview with Gerry Lawlor.

45. Debra Isaac, "How Jaguar Lost Its Spots," *Management Today* (April 1984), p. 44.

46. Interview with Sir John Egan.

47. *BusinessWeek*, July 23, 1984, p. 83.

48. Interview with David Boole.

49. See "Commentary: Richard Rogers at Lloyd's of London," *Progressive Architecture*, 10 (October 1986), p. 35. I am grateful to Reed Kroloff for his assistance with the above discussion.

50. Quoted in Haynes Johnson, *Sleepwalking Through History* (New York: W. W. Norton, 1991), p. 215.

51. *Ibid.*, pp. 216–17.

52. See especially Margaret Reid, *All Change in the City: The Revolution in Britain's Financial Sector* (Basingstoke, Hants: Macmillan, 1988).

53. On the corporate culture and history of Morgan Grenfell and for a highly detailed account of the Guinness Affair, see Dominic Hobson, *The Pride of Lucifer* (London: Hamish Hamilton, 1990), pp. 190–201. There is also useful material in Nick Kochan and Hugh Pym, *The Guinness Affair* (London: Christopher Helm, 1987); Ivan Fallon and James Strodes, *Takeovers* (London: Hamish Hamilton, 1987); and James Saunders, *Nightmare* (London: Hutchinson, 1989).

54. Hobson, *Pride of Lucifer*, pp. 221–49.

55. *Ibid.*, p. 191.

56. Kochan and Pym, *Guinness Affair*, p. 107.

57. *Ibid.*, p. 95.

58. *Ibid.*, pp. 103–104.

59. Hobson, *Pride of Lucifer*, p. 342.

60. *Ibid.*, p. 349.

61. *Ibid.*, pp. 381–83.

62. *Ibid.*, p. 374.

63. Interviews with Hugh Parker, Sir Adrian Cadbury, Sir Paul Girolami, Richard Giardano, Martin Sorrell, Lord Hanson, Sir Peter Parker, Lord White, Sir Christopher Hogg, Sir John Harvey-Jones, Eugene Anderson, David Sainsbury, Lord Weinstock, Sir Nicholas Goodison, and Ralph Halpern. All of these men claimed that some change had taken place in the business environment, though they did not agree on the extent or the causes of the shifts.

64. For a balanced, well-documented synthesis on the economic realities underlying the enterprise culture, see especially Peter Riddell, *The Thatcher Decade*, ch. 4.

65. For highly critical views of the Thatcher economic record, see Paul Hirst, *After Thatcher*, and Gordon Brown, *Where There Is Greed*.

Nine: A Plague on Both Your Houses

1. Nikolaus Pevsner (revised by Bridget Cherry), *London: The Cities of London and Westminster*, 3rd edn. (Harmondsworth, Middlx: Penguin, 1973), p. 196.

2. John Pope-Hennessy, *Learning to Look* (London: Heinemann, 1991), p. 164.

3. John Pope-Hennessy, "The Fall of a Great Museum," *New York Review of Books*, vol. 36, no. 7. April 27, 1989, pp. 10–12.

4. *Sunday Telegraph*, January 10, 1988.

5. See Thatcher, *Downing Street Years*, p. 24.

6. See Young, *Iron Lady*, ch. 18.

7. On the "new class" debate, see Berger, *Capitalist Revolution*, pp. 60–68.

8. See Janet Minihan, *The Nationalization of Culture: The Development of State Subsidies to the Arts in Great Britain* (New York: New York University Press, 1977), pp. 215–50.

9. T. S. Eliot, *Notes Towards the Definition of Culture* (London: Faber & Faber, 1948), p. 83.

10. See Minihan, *Nationalization of Culture*, pp. 215–50.

11. Berger, *Capitalist Revolution,* p. 69.

12. Richard Hofstadter, *The Age of Reform* (New York: Vintage, 1955).

13. Interview with Hugo Young.

14. Interview with Lord Weinstock.

15. Thatcher, *Downing Street Years,* p. 632.

16. Baker, *Turbulent Years,* p. 232.

17. *Ibid.,* p. 233.

18. Annan, *Our Age,* p. 360.

19. *Ibid.,* pp. 378–79.

20. *Ibid.,* p. 377.

21. *Ibid.,* p. 372.

22. Interview with Sir Keith Joseph.

23. Interview with Sir Ralf Dahrendorf; and Jeremy Paxman, *Friends in High Places* (Harmondsworth, Middlx: Penguin, 1991), p. 173.

24. I owe this information to Norman Cantor.

25. *The Times,* January 25, 1985.

26. *The Times,* December 27, 1984.

27. *The Times,* January 30, 1985.

28. *Times Educational Supplement,* February 1, 1985.

29. *The Times,* February 4, 1985.

30. *The Times,* January 30, 1985.

31. Interview with Sir Gordon White.

32. Interview with John Ashworth.

33. *Ibid.*

34. See Geoffrey Wheatcroft, "That Woman Versus the Chattering Classes," *The Atlantic,* vol. 268, no. 6 (December 1991): 34.

35. Andrew Motion, *Philip Larkin: A Writer's Life* (London: Faber & Faber, 1993), pp. 479, 497.

36. *Ibid.,* p. 497.

37. Interview with Sir Kingsley Amis.

38. Amis, *Memoirs,* pp. 315–19; and interview with Sir Kingsley Amis.

39. Interview with John Moore.

40. Interview with John Mortimer.

41. David Hare, *Writing Left-Handed* (London: Faber & Faber, 1991), p. xiii; and interview with David Hare.

42. *Writing Left-Handed,* pp. 5–7.

43. *Ibid.,* pp. 157–58.

44. David Hare, *The Secret Rapture* (London: Faber & Faber, 1988), p. 39.

45. *Ibid.,* p. 38.

46. *Ibid.*, p. 68.

47. David Hare, *Strapless* (London: Faber & Faber, 1989), p. 22.

48. The term is in Robert Reich, *The Next American Frontier* (New York: Times Books, 1983).

49. Hare, *Strapless,* p. 82.

50. Interview with John Mortimer.

51. *Ibid.*

52. *Ibid.*

53. John Mortimer, *Paradise Postponed* (New York: Viking Penguin, 1986), pp. 110–12.

54. *Ibid.*, p. 248.

55. John Mortimer, *Titmuss Regained* (New York: Viking, 1990), p. 15.

56. David Lodge, *Nice Work* (Harmondsworth, Middlx: Penguin, 1989), p. 5.

57. *Ibid.*, p. 86.

58. Interview with Bishop David Sheppard.

59. Warlock and Sheppard, *Better Together: Christian Partnership in a Hurt City,* p. 291.

60. Interview with Reverend Peter Winn.

61. Warlock and Sheppard, *Better Together,* p. 303.

62. Interview with Sir Hector Laing.

63. Wiener, *English Culture and the Decline of the Industrial Spirit,* p. 116.

64. See *ibid.*, pp. 111–18.

65. David Jenkins, "The Necessities and Limits of the Market," in *God, Politics, and the Future* (London: SCM Press, 1988), pp. 16–17. For Christian Conservative responses, see Martin Allison and David L. Edwards, eds., *Christianity and Conservatism* (London: Hodder & Stoughton, 1990).

66. Interview with Limbert Spencer.

67. *Faith in the City: A Call for Action by Church and Nation* (London: Church House Publishing, 1985), p. 52.

68. See Young, *Iron Lady,* p. 417.

69. Interview with Lord Jakobovits.

70. Hugo Young, "When Mrs. Thatcher Sings of Jerusalem," *Guardian,* May 27, 1986.

71. Interview with Rabbi Julia Neuberger.

72. See Young, *Iron Lady,* ch. 18.

73. Interview with Rabbi Julia Neuberger.

74. David Martin, "The Churches: Pink Bishops and the Iron Lady,"

in Dennis Kavanagh and Anthony Seldon, eds., *The Thatcher Effect* (Oxford: Clarendon Press, 1989), p. 335.

75. See the reprint of Mrs. Thatcher's speech (and an excellent, if hardly friendly, exegesis) in Jonathan Raban's *God, Man and Mrs. Thatcher*, pp. 12, 14.

76. *Ibid.*, p. 13.

77. *Ibid.*, p. 15.

78. *Ibid.*, p. 14.

79. See Wiener, *English Culture*, ch. 1.

Ten: Things Fall Apart

1. Baker, *Turbulent Years*, p. 273.

2. See William Keegan, *Mr. Lawson's Gamble* (London: Hodder & Stoughton, 1989), pp. 202–03.

3. Lawson, *View from No. 11*, pp. 694, 700.

4. Baker, *Turbulent Years*, p. 312.

5. See Watkins, *Conservative Coup*, pp. 98–99.

6. Keegan, *Lawson's Gamble*, p. 201.

7. *Ibid.*, pp. 200–33.

8. Lawson, *View from No. 11*, p. 708.

9. Thatcher, *Downing Street Years*, p. 701.

10. Lawson, *View from No. 11*, pp. 795–77.

11. *Ibid.*, p. 834.

12. Howe, *Conflict of Loyalty*, p. 251.

13. Lawson, *View from No. 11*, pp. 960–63.

14. Thatcher, *Downing Street Years*, p. 60.

15. *Ibid.*, p. 79.

16. See *ibid.*, pp. 62–64, 83–86.

17. Watkins, *Conservative Coup*, p. 117.

18. Thatcher, *Downing Street Years*, pp. 744–45.

19. *Ibid.*, p. 746.

20. Howe, *Conflict of Loyalty*, p. 576.

21. Thatcher, *Downing Street Years*, pp. 711–12.

22. Baker, *Turbulent Years*, p. 285.

23. Watkins, *Conservative Coup*, p. 134.

24. Lawson, *View from No. 11*, p. 568.

25. See Michael Forsyth, *The Case for a Poll Tax* (London: Conservative Political Centre, 1985).

26. Lawson, *View from No. 11*, p. 584.

27. *Ibid.*, p. 561.

28. Interview with Robert Horton.

29. Thatcher, *Downing Street Years*, p. 834, and Baker, *Turbulent Years*, p. 379.

30. Howe, *Conflict of Loyalty*, p. 647.

31. Watkins, *Conservative Coup*, p. 113.

32. Thatcher, *Downing Street Years*, pp. 834 and 832–35.

33. Alan Clark, *Mrs. Thatcher's Minister: Alan Clark's Private Diaries* (New York: Farrar, Straus & Giroux, 1994), p. 347.

34. Howe, *Conflict of Loyalty*, pp. 658–660.

35. Thatcher, *Downing Street Years*, p. 839.

36. Baker, *Turbulent Years*, pp. 385–86.

37. Thatcher, *Downing Street Years*, p. 840.

38. Baker, *Turbulent Years*, p. 257.

39. For the MORI survey, see Ivor Crewe, "Values: The Crusade That Failed," in Kavanagh and Seldon, eds., *The Thatcher Factor*, pp. 241–50.

40. *Ibid.*, pp. 239–51.

41. Howe, *Conflict of Loyalty*, p. 286.

42. See Berger, *Capitalist Revolution*, pp. 194–209.

Bibliographical
Note

What follows is a list of books I found most useful in preparing this book; it does not purport to be a comprehensive bibliography on Thatcher's Britain.

Chapter One

The main sources for the story of Thatcher's end are memoirs: Margaret Thatcher, *The Downing Street Years* (New York: HarperCollins, 1993), and Kenneth Baker, *The Turbulent Years* (London: Faber & Faber, 1992). There is also some useful information in Nigel Lawson's *The View from No. 11* (London: Bantam, 1992). The fullest journalistic account is Alan Watkins, *A Conservative Coup* (London: Duckworth, 1992). On Heseltine, see Julian Critchley, *Michael Heseltine: The Unauthorized Biography* (London: Coronet, 1988)

On the capitalist revolution, see Peter Berger, *The Capitalist Revolution* (New York: Basic Books, 1986). For the American scene during the Reagan years, see especially Kevin Phillips, *The Politics of Rich and Poor* (New York: Random House, 1990); Garry Wills's *Reagan's America* (New York: Penguin, 1988); Haynes Johnson, *Sleepwalking Through History* (New York: W. W. Norton, 1990); and Lou Cannon, *President Reagan: The Role of a Lifetime* (New York: Touchstone, 1992). For a philosophical appraisal of the age of capitalist revolution, see Francis

Fukiyama, *The End of History and the Last Man* (New York: Free Press, 1992).

Chapter Two

On postwar British history there are a number of useful works, including Correlli Barnett, *The Audit of War* (London: Macmillan, 1987); Paul Addison, *The Road to 1945* (London: Jonathan Cape, 1975); Peter Hennessey, *Never Again: Britain, 1945–51* (London: Jonathan Cape, 1992); Anthony Sampson, *Anatomy of Britain* (New York: Harper & Row, 1962) and his *New Anatomy of Britain* (London: Hodder & Stoughton, 1971). See also Kenneth Morgan, *A People's Peace: British History, 1945–1989* (Oxford: Oxford University Press, 1990), and Keith Middlemas, *Power, Competition and the State* (London: Macmillan, 1986), and Noel Annan's delightful *Our Age: Portrait of a Generation* (London: Weidenfeld & Nicolson, 1991).

For the political scene, there are many extremely valuable biographies. See especially Martin Gilbert's one-volume condensation of his multi-volume Churchill biography, *Churchill* (New York: Henry Holt, 1991); Kenneth Harris, *Clement Attlee* (London: Weidenfeld & Nicolson, 1982); Alastair Horne, *Harold Macmillan*, 2 vols. (New York: Viking Penguin, 1989–91); Ben Pimlott, *Harold Wilson* (London: Collins, 1992); and John Campbell, *Edward Heath* (London: Jonathan Cape, 1993).

Chapter Three

On the IMF crisis, see especially Denis Healey, *The Time of My Life* (New York: W. W. Norton, 1990), James Callaghan, *Time and Chance* (London: Collins, 1987), and Kathleen Burk and Alec Cairncross, *"Goodbye, Great Britain": The 1976 IMF Crisis* (New Haven and London: Yale University Press, 1992).

There is a large scholarly literature on the British disease. See Isaac Kramnick, ed., *Is Britain Dying? Perspectives on the Current Crisis* (Ithaca, NY: Cornell University Press, 1979); Ralf Dahrendorf, *On Britain* (Chicago: University of Chicago Press, 1982); Bernard D. Nossiter, *Britain: A Future That Works* (Boston: Houghton Mifflin, 1978); R. Emmett Tyrell, ed., *The Future That Doesn't Work: Social Democracy's Failure in Britain*

(Garden City, NY: Doubleday, 1977); Tom Nairn, *The Break-up of Britain* (London, Verso, 1981); Samuel Beer, *Britain Against Itself: The Political Contradictions of Collectivism* (New York: W. W. Norton, 1982); Robert Bacon and Walter Eltis, *Britain's Economic Problems: Too Few Producers* (New York: St. Martin's Press, 1976); and *The United Kingdom in 1980: The Hudson Report* (New York: Halstead Press, 1974).

Chapter Four

This chapter is based on years of study on British culture, business, and society. My views on economic culture were shaped by Peter Berger, *The Capitalist Revolution* (New York: Basic Book, 1986). And my views on modern British history were molded especially by various historical writings of Asa Briggs, notably his trilogy *Victorian People* (Chicago: University of Chicago Press, 1972), *Victorian Cities* (New York: Harper & Row, 1965), and *Victorian Things* (London: Batsford, 1988). Martin J. Wiener's *English Culture and the Decline of the Industrial Spirit 1850–1980* (Cambridge, England: Cambridge University Press, 1981) is the key work on the relationship between cultural values and economic behavior in modern Britain. Harold Perkin, *The Rise of Professional Society* (London: Routledge & Kegan Paul, 1989), puts a different spin on the Wiener thesis and much else. For a friendly critique of the Wiener thesis, see Charles Dellheim, "Notes on Industrialism and Culture in Nineteenth Century Britain," in *Notebooks on Cultural Analysis*, vol. 2, 1985: 226–47. For a much more skeptical view of cultural interpretations, see W. D. Rubinstein, *Capitalism, Culture, and Decline in Britain 1750–1990* (London: Routledge & Kegan Paul, 1993). Alfred D. Chandler's *Scale and Scope* (Cambridge: Belknap Press, 1990) is an unmatched study of the dynamics of industrial capitalism in Britain, America, and Germany. The best approach to individual figures such as William Wordsworth, Matthew Arnold, and E. M. Forster is through their writings. Both Briggs and Wiener provide extremely valuable analyses of nineteenth-century British cultural history.

Chapter Five

There is already a prodigiously large literature on Thatcher and Thatcherism. The best biography is Hugo Young, *The Iron Lady* (New York: Noonday Press, 1990). Also valuable is a set of interviews extensively quoted and discussed in Hugo Young and Anne Sloman's *The Thatcher Phenomenon* (London: BBC Books, 1986). There is useful material in Geoffrey Smith, *Reagan and Thatcher* (London: Bodley Head, 1990); Graham Little, *Strong Leadership* (New York: Oxford University Press, 1988); Kenneth Harris, *Thatcher* (London: Weidenfeld & Nicolson, 1988); Patrick Cosgrove, *Thatcher: A Tory and Her Party* (London: Hutchinson, 1978); Wendy Webster, *Not a Man to Match Her* (London: The Women's Press, 1990); and Penny Junor, *Margaret Thatcher, Wife, Mother, Politician* (London: Sidgwick & Jackson, 1983). Leo Abse's *Margaret, Daughter of Beatrice: A Politician's Psycho-Biography of Margaret Thatcher* (London: Jonathan Cape, 1989) is long on speculation and short on evidence, but stimulating anyway.

Peter Jenkins, *Mrs. Thatcher's Revolution* (Cambridge: Harvard University Press, 1988), and Peter Riddell, *The Thatcher Decade* (Oxford: Basil Blackwell, 1990), are particularly valuable general accounts. Other worthwhile studies include Peter Riddell, *The Thatcher Government* (Oxford: Basil Blackwell, 1983), Robert Skidelsky, ed., *Thatcherism* (London: Chatto & Windus, 1988), Dennis Kavanagh, *Thatcherism and British Politics: The End of Consensus?* (Oxford: Oxford University Press, 1987), Dennis Kavanagh and Anthony Seldon, *The Thatcher Factor* (Oxford: Clarendon Press, 1989), Stuart Hall and Martin Jacques, eds., *The Politics of Thatcherism* (London: Lawrence & Wishart, 1983), Stuart Hall, *The Hard Road to Renewal* (London: Verso, 1988), and Andrew Gamble, *The Free Economy and the Strong State* (London: Macmillan Education, 1988).

On the Thatcher circle, there is some useful material in John Ranelagh, *Thatcher's People* (London: Fontana, 1992), and Morrison Halcrow, *Keith Joseph: A Single Mind* (London: Macmillan, 1989).

Shirley Letwin's *The Anatomy of Thatcherism* (New Brunswick, NJ: Transaction, 1993) is a strongly partisan account. Both Alan Walters, *Britain's Economic Renaissance* (Oxford: Oxford University Press, 1986), and Brian Griffiths, *The Moral Basis of the Market Economy* (London:

Conservative Political Centre, 1983), offer spirited defenses of Thatcherism. David Willett's *Modern Conservatism* (Harmondsworth, Middlesex: Penguin, 1992) is a lucid study of theory and practice.

Richard Critchfield's *An American Looks at Britain* (New York: Doubleday, 1990) is an entertaining survey of contemporary Britain.

Chapters Six and Seven

David Butler and Dennis Kavanagh, *The British General Election of 1979* (London: Macmillan, 1980), *The British General Election of 1983* (London: Macmillan, 1984) and *The British General Election of 1987* (London: Macmillan, 1988) are the best guides to Thatcher's three electoral victories. Martin Holmes, *The First Thatcher Government 1979–93* (Brighton: Wheatsheaf, 1985), Wiliam Keegan, *Mrs. Thatcher's Economic Experiment* (London: Allen Lane, 1984), Christopher Johnson, *The Economy Under Mrs. Thatcher* (Harmondsworth, Middlesex: Penguin, 1991), and Hugh Stephenson, *Mrs. Thatcher's First Year* (London: Jill Norman, 1980), are all useful on the interplay between politics and economics.

One of the richest sources for understanding the Thatcher government are the memoirs and other assorted works of its members. The most interesting are Nigel Lawson, *The View from No. 11*, Geoffrey Howe, *A Conflict of Loyalty* (London: Macmillan, 1994), and Kenneth Baker, *The Turbulent Years*. Also useful are Nicholas Ridley, *My Style of Government* (London: Hutchinson, 1991), James Prior, *A Balance of Power* (London: Hamish Hamilton, 1986), Ian Gilmour, *Dancing with Dogma* (London: Simon & Schuster, 1992), Norman Tebbit, *Upwardly Mobile* (London: Fontana, 1989), Alan Clark, *Mrs. Thatcher's Minister* (New York: Farrar, Straus & Giroux, 1994), Francis Pym, *The Politics of Consent* (London: Hamish Hamilton 1984), William Whitelaw, *The Whitelaw Memoirs* (London: Aurom, 1989), and Peter Carrington, *Reflect on Things Past* (London: Collins, 1988). Jock Gardyne's *Mrs. Thatcher's First Administration* (London: Macmillan, 1984) provides an inside look at her first years in office.

The best general work on the miners' strike is Martin Adeney and John Lloyd, *The Miners' Strike 1984–5: Loss Without Limit* (London: Routledge & Kegan Paul, 1986). For Ian MacGregor's side of the story, see MacGregor with Rodney Tyler, *The Enemies Within* (London: Collins, 1986). On privatization and popular capitalism, see John Redwood, *Popular Capitalism* (London: Routledge, 1988), and Oliver Letwin, *Privatising the World* (London: Cassell, 1988).

This chapter benefited greatly from interviews with politicians and fellow travelers: Sir Geoffrey Howe, Nigel Lawson, John Moore, Lady Janet Young, Sir John Hoskyns, Lord Ralph Harris, Sir Alfred Sherman, Lord Owen, the late John Smith, Roy Hattersley, and Bryan Gould. Interviews with the following commentators were also extremely valuable: the late Peter Jenkins, Peter Kellner, Hugo Young, Lord Rees-Mogg, Sir Geoffrey Owen, Samuel Brittan, and Craig Whitney.

Chapter Eight

The most valuable source for this chapter was interviews with leading business figures (with a few academics and consultants thrown into the mix): Sir John Egan, Hugh Parker, Sir Adrian Cadbury, David Sainsbury, Richard Giardano, Sir Paul Girolami, Sir Peter Parker, Eugene Anderson, Martin Sorrell, Sir John Harvey-Jones, Lord Hector Laing, Sir Charles Villiers, Lord Rothschild, Lord Hanson, Sir Gordon White, Robert John, David Boole, Sir Arnold Weinstock, Sir Christopher Hogg, Georges Bain, John Stopford, and Sir Nicholas Goodison. On issues of business and social responsibility, Graham Bann, David Grayson, Gerry Wade, Victoria Secretan, Julia Cliveden, and Limbert Spencer were all helpful.

On ICI the standard history is W. J. Reader, *ICI: A History* (London: Oxford University Press, 1970–75), and the best source on its recent organizational culture is Andrew Pettigrew, *The Awakening Giant: Continuity and Change in Imperial Chemical Industries* (Oxford: Basil Blackwell, 1985). The Jaguar story comes largely from my own fieldwork there in November 1984. On the transformation of the City of London, see especially Margaret Reid, *All Change in the City: The Revolution in Britain's Financial Sector* (Basingstoke, Hampshire: Macmillan, 1988). On Morgan Grenfell, the official history is Kathleen Burk, *Morgan Grenfell, 1838–1988* (Oxford: Oxford University Press, 1989). The best account of Morgan Grenfell's recent history and the Guinness Affair is Dominic Hobson, *The Pride of Lucifer* (London: Hamish Hamilton, 1990). See also Nick Kochan and Hugh Pym, *The Guinness Affair* (London: Christopher Helm, 1987), Ivan Fallon and James Strodes, *Takeovers* (London: Hamish Hamilton, 1987), and James Saunders, *Nightmare* (London: Hutchinson, 1989).

Chapter Nine

This chapter was based on two main sources. The first was sets of interviews with Sir Kingsley Amis, Beryl Bainbridge, David Hare, and John Mortimer; Bishop David Sheppard, Reverend Peter Winn, Reverend Colin Marsh, Hilary Russell, Lord Immanuel Jakobovits, Rabbi Julia Neuberger, and Rabbi Hugo Gryn; and John Ashworth, Lord Annan, Norman Stone, Ben Pimlott, Paul Hirst, Sir Ralf Dahrendorf, and Baronness Tessa Blackstone. The second source for this chapter was primary works. These included novels such as John Mortimer's *Paradise Postponed* (New York: Viking, 1986) and *Titmuss Regained* (New York: Viking, 1990); plays such as David Hare's *The Secret Rapture* (London: Faber & Faber, 1988) and *Racing Demon* (London: Faber & Faber, 1990); and David Lodge's *Nice Work* (Harmondsworth, Middlesex: Penguin, 1989). Also useful are films such as David Hare's *Strapless, How to Get A Head in Advertising,* and Mike Leigh's *High Hopes.* Ben Pimlott, ed., *The Alternative* (London: W. H. Allen, 1990), is a collection of essays by anti-Thatcherite intellectuals. Chatto & Windus's series, Counter-Blasts, provided a more extended forum for dissidents. Among the most interesting pamphlets published in the series was Jonathan Raban's *God, Man and Mrs. Thatcher.* For provocative general critiques, see Paul Hirst, *After Thatcher* (London: Collins, 1989), and Gordon Brown, *Where There Is Greed* (Edinburgh: Mainstream, 1989).

For artistic critiques of Thatcherism, see *Shocks to the System: Social and Political Issues in Recent British Art from the Arts Council Collection* (London: South Bank Centre, 1991). A small but interesting exhibition on British photography during the Thatcher years was held in the Museum of Modern Art, New York, during the spring of 1990. See Susan Kismaric, *British Photography During the Thatcher Years* (New York: Abrams, 1990).

For the theological debate, see *Faith in the City: A Call for Action by Church and Nation* (London: Church House Publishing, 1985); Derek Warlock and David Sheppard, *Better Together: Christian Partnership in a Hurt City* (Harmondsworth, Middlesex: Penguin, 1989); David Jenkins,

God, Politics, and the Future (London: SCM Press, 1988); Martin Allison and David L. Edwards, eds., *Christianity and Conservatism* (London: Hodder & Stoughton, 1990); and Immanuel Jakobovits's pamphlet, *From Doom to Hope.*

For popular attitudes, the best source are the various annual reports published by *British Social Attitudes* (Aldershot, Surrey: Gower Publishing, 1984–88), as well as reports by MORI and Gallup.

Chapter Ten

The best primary sources on the final Thatcher government include Thatcher's memoirs *The Downing Street Years,* Baker's *The Turbulent Years,* and Lawson's *The View from No. 11.* William Keegan's *Mr. Lawson's Gamble* (London: Hodder & Stoughton, 1989) provides a critical appraisal of the Chancellor's economic policies, and Watkins's *A Conservative Coup* provides a detailed account of Mrs. Thatcher's fall.

Index